THE EVENING COLONNADE

Other books by Cyril Connolly

The Rock Pool
Enemies of Promise
The Unquiet Grave
The Condemned Playground
The Missing Diplomats
Ideas and Places
Previous Convictions
The Modern Movement
Les Pavillons

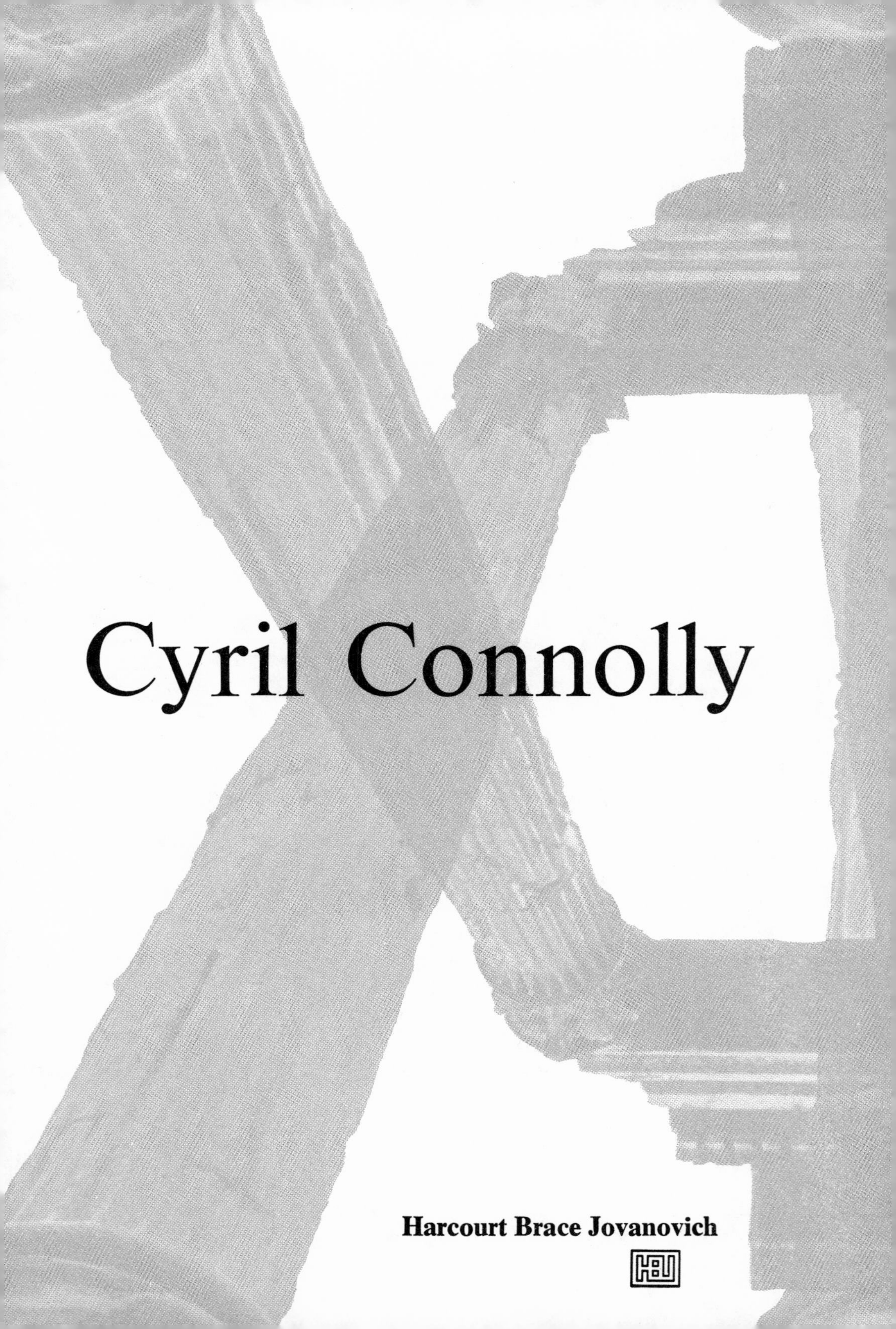

Cyril Connolly

Harcourt Brace Jovanovich

THE EVENING COLONNADE

New York and London

Printed in the United States of America

Library of Congress Cataloging in Publication Data
Connolly, Cyril, 1903–
The evening colonnade.
I. Title.
PR6005.0393E9 809 74-11475
ISBN 0-15-129387-2

First American edition 1975
B C D E

For Deirdre

Contents

INTRODUCTION

SOME WRITERS have no problem: their title descends in tongues of flame, it's just a matter of choosing a book. *Paradise Lost—Vanity Fair —War and Peace—Farewell to Arms—The Waste Land. . . .* My own tend to be somewhat ambivalent—*Enemies of Promise, The Unquiet Grave*—I like them slightly romantic, not too clever or allusive; they should describe the book yet grow on the reader. If a quotation, it should stand on its own nor should it be in French or Latin nor contain words which no one knows how to pronounce like pericope or pangolin.

The search tells me something about myself. Why do I look for a quotation this time and not invent one? Because to cite a favourite author is to repay a debt, to proclaim an allegiance. In this case the title must also cover a collection of essays both critical and autobiographical written mainly over the last ten years.

At first I noticed that every ten years I had produced such a book: *The Condemned Playground, Ideas and Places, Previous Convictions.* There might still be a final collection to come after this one. So my first title was *Penultimatum,* a portmanteau word with a touch of aggression. More thought revealed that I needed a poetic undertone, something which better illustrated my own attitude to life. I consulted the oracles.

First the Romans: Lucretius, Horace, Virgil, Propertius. This really meant Dryden, for his translations from the first three are consistently exciting in themselves. But Propertius is about love, Lucretius about sex and the fear of death, Virgil about farming. I had by now re-read many translations including the whole of the Nonesuch *Latin Portrait,* so well edited by Rostrevor Hamilton. All this had been a wonderful experience, in particular the rediscovery of Lucretius whose towering greatness and protective sympathy for humanity reminded me of Buddha's. No one has written more wisely of love or death or man's destiny than this lyric liberator, author to my mind of one of the loveliest lines in Latin—

. . . umida saxa,
Umida saxa, super viridi stillantia musco

(wet rocks—the wet rocks, over green moss dripping down). Dryden's translation loses too much of the sweep of the hexameter by conversion to the couplet; there is nothing to beat R. C. Trevelyan's *Lucretius* (Cambridge, 1937).

Dryden's translation of Horace—III 29 (Tyrrhena regum) allows room for the original and is the greatest translation of an Ode in English—and he thought so too. "One Ode which infinitely pleased me in the reading I have attempted to translate in Pindaric verse and I have taken some pains to make it my masterpiece in English." It is so well known that I turned instead to Pope's "Imitations of Horace":

'Learn to live well, or fairly make your will;
You've play'd, and loved and eat, and drunk your fill:
Walk sober off; before a sprightlier age
Comes tittering on, and shoves you from the stage.'

(No title there, I hope.) But we are getting warm: writers of special significance for sexagenarians hungry for both sound and sense are Donne, Dryden, Pope, Johnson, Montaigne, Proust, Wordsworth, Yeats and Eliot. Meanwhile I turned to Eastern poets: I had long relished a phrase of Hafiz, "this House of Two Doors," for the world of birth and death.

From out this Hostel of Two Doors the signal calls us away
Alike if low be the roof-tree or lofty dome upswing
We conquer only through anguish the resting-place of delight.

(Leaf's translation.) But one can't use "Hostel," while "House of Two Doors" is lacking in emphasis.

My next choice was Indian, a poem by Basavanna translated for the *Penguin Book of Indian Verse* by A. K. Ramanujan. It was written in A.D. 1168.

Does it matter how long
A rock soaks in the water
Will it ever grow soft?

Does it matter how long
I've spent in worship
When the heart is fickle?

Futile as a ghost
I stand guard over hidden gold
O Lord of the meeting rivers.

"Futile as a ghost I stand guard over hidden gold" . . . not a bad definition of a critic and my title "The Meeting Rivers" suggested the two strains in my make-up, the passion for nature and the love of art, in whose confluence lay my originality as a writer. But "The Meeting Rivers" is rather flat and the vowel sounds lack resonance: it could be a volume of political memoirs not the watersmeet where Basavanna awaited his lord Siva.

Forward to the moderns. After I saw a glow-worm on the lawn, Wordsworth's magical description started me on "The Prelude" (the greatest poem of the nineteenth century)—but one can hardly call a book of literary essays "The Voiceless Worm."

The child
Of summer, lingering, shining by itself
The voiceless worm on the unfrequented hills . . .

But I did run to ground a much more appropriate couplet:

Such pleasant office have we long pursued
Incumbent on the surface of past time . . .

"The surface of past time"! A private summons, a tap on the shoulder—but too evocative, and Proustian, too backward-looking, and retarded by all those s's.

I went on to Eliot and came up with "Time and the Bell."

Time and the bell have buried the day
The black cloud carries the sun away . . .

But it reminded one friend of boxing, another of the names of American magazines.

Then followed an obsession with the word "critic." "After all, that's what you are."

Condition critical
Critic on the Shelf
Critically well.

Critic on the bias, on the hop, on the run, on the slide, in the sun, in the shade, in the galleys.

I am *nothing if not critical* (Iago). I turned to Pope's "Essay on

Criticism," written when he was a very young man seeking "the Poet's bays and Critic's ivy."

> *Such once were Critics;* such the happy few
> Athens and Rome in better ages knew
>
> But you who seek to give and merit fame
> and justly bear a *critic's noble name*

"The generous Critic," "the constant Critic" . . . It came to me that I didn't want to be called a critic. What about Epicurus? A fig for Epicurus—a carp for Epicurus?

> The Downright Epicure placed heaven in sense
> And scorned pretence
>
> —Vaughan

"The Downright Epicure"—but that's not me either. I'm daedal and deathdivining. Death lurks round every corner and colours my every thought. What a decimation since I last published—Eliot, Forster, Maugham, Stravinsky, Hemingway, Cummings, Wilson, Waugh, Huxley, Edith and Osbert Sitwell, Maurice Bowra, Elizabeth Bowen.

> Quick eyes gone under earth's lid
> Quorum tellus amplectitur ossa

Interviewer (Richard Kershaw): "What would you really like to do? Would you like to see the rest of your life in terms of the library and reflections on the past? What would you like to spend your time doing?"

"I should like to see a great many more elephants in the wild. I have a deep devotion to them, I can't have enough. I agree with Donne

> Natures great master-peace: an Elephant
> The onely harmlesse great thing. . . ."

Love of nature, love of books:

> In wholesome separation the two natures
> The one that feels, the other that observes.

Perhaps the separation is not so wholesome as Wordsworth imagined. I experienced it in my childhood, my mother's passion for birds and landscape spending itself against my father's chilling accuracy. A soldier and conchologist, whose voice I hear whenever I clear my throat. One parent endowed me with imagination and feeling, the other with analytical intelligence and memory, yet the combination but served to perpetuate their own incompatibility and all but froze me in a permanent block. Nevertheless, a little water still manages to well up—*umida saxa*—from between the stones. Meanwhile what of the title? There is another side to Pope, Scarlatti of the English rococo, the impeccable musician. Early in the 1930s I had copied out his lines on Lady Mary Wortley Montagu

> 'What are the gay parterre, the chequer'd shade
> The morning bower, the ev'ning colonnade
> But soft recesses of uneasy minds
> To sigh unheard in, to the passing winds?'

The Evening Colonnade. Is not my work compact of columns, in this case all that's left standing from some five hundred of them?

And a painting came to mind which had hung before the war in Peter Watson's collection in the Rue du Bac . . . "Chirico's early work [I wrote in 1952] presents a closed world of the imagination, already perfect and passing away, a dream of urban apprehension, a haunted inner city of squares and statues, of freight trains and grief-stricken colonnades in the last second before the explosion."

Acknowledgements

"Oxford in Our Twenties" first appeared in *Harpers & Queen,* "Humane Killer" in the *London Magazine,* "Art Nouveau" in *Art News* (New York) and the *London Magazine,* "Little Magazines" in *Art and Literature* (Paris), the first of the pieces on George Orwell in the *New York Times,* and "Memories of Gide" in *Adam.* Permission to reprint two letters from Orwell is from Mrs. Sonia Orwell. The introduction to the "Modern Movement" exhibition at the University of Texas was printed for the first time in the British edition of this book. All the remaining contents are from the *Sunday Times* and I am grateful to the editor for permission to reprint and particularly to Mr. Leonard Russell and Mr. J. W. Lambert for their unfailing encouragement and to the chief librarian Mr. F. E. Brazier for his painstaking research into the files. Mr. Godfrey Smith as editor of the Colour Magazine commissioned "Destination Atlantis," hitherto unpublished and consequently uncut. Quite a different acknowledgement must be to Mr. A. W. Rossabi who has assisted as editor with David Bruce & Watson not only by procuring a vast mass of material but by going through it with me. One of the penalties of writing so much and for so long is a feeling of impotent repugnance when confronted by reams of newsprint and tattered galleys. His zeal and patience rekindled my own and we were thus able to agree on the structure as well as the contents. I only hope his judgement will be rewarded.

1

Dew on the Garlic Leaf

"How swiftly it dries
The dew on the garlic leaf . . ."

170 Chinese Poems
trans. by Arthur Waley

THE TWENTIES

In 1920 I was a schoolboy; in 1930 I got married. The decade was the most formative of my life. It broke in half about 1926; the years from the General Strike to the slump of 1929 were not as insouciant as the period of

> Après la guerre
> There'll be a good time everywhere

which started in 1918. It was a period of great hardship and inequalities for people all over the world, for the Central Powers it meant suffering and inflation

> Jerusalem, Athens, Alexandria
> Falling towers . . .

What we mean by the Twenties is a climate of dandyism and artistic creation which came to a head in 1922, year of *The Waste Land, Ulysses,* Valéry's *Charmes,* Rilke's elegies, *Jacob's Room* and *The Forsyte Saga.* Proust was at his zenith, Bloomsbury boomed, Huxley and the Sitwells scintillated; Lawrence was still respectable. Hardy, Conrad, Moore were all alive. France was cheap to live in, and demobilised fugitives from Prohibition or the family business reinforced Montparnasse. The Diaghilev ballet flourished. Paris went expatriate.

It is inevitable to confuse the delights of being young with the place and time we were young in. We discovered the Balkans and Spain, the South of France in summer, the Marquesas, Bali, Surrealism, Stravinsky, Freud. My Oxford generation were all highly successful social climbers, they never quite recovered from this preliminary boost. They had no political awareness (I am speaking of the writers): Acton liked the Prince of Wales, Waugh the Lygons, Betjeman Irish peers. How different to the political thrusters of the Thirties do these delicate aesthetes seem.

Clothes were an intoxication. Waisted suits by Lesley and Roberts, white waistcoats from Hawes & Curtis with only a narrow white strap at the back, monogrammed silk shirts arriving in cardboard boxes, top hats, opera hats, Oxford bags. Credit seemed unlimited, fathers had no idea what they were in for. Food and wine came into their own. Lobster Newburg, foie gras sandwiches, Yquem daily crossed the Quad. Hired cars used to carry one's guests out to Thame where John Fothergill presided, initiations in London followed, by Monsieur Abel of the Ivy or Boulestin in Leicester Square or, best of all, Stulik at the Eiffel Tower where one saw Nancy Cunard, Napier Alington, Augustus John. The Café Royal was still intimate; night-clubs intoxicating, particularly the Bat, the Embassy, the Café de Paris.

After twenty-two years of male society our celibate lives were then invaded by women, by hostesses who descended unpredictably from their thrones and came to tea, by debutantes, all diminutives and large hats, by intellectual girls with short hair who swore, by meltingly inaccessible married women, by sisters and mothers of school friends, or visiting Americans, or the Blackbirds, inviolate at many a bottle party, or the clergymen's daughters, for five pounds a time at Mrs. Fitz's.

None of this cost very much, even a trip to Paris with visits to Foyot or Montagné, or the Ballet, or the Boeuf sur le Toit. The note of frivolity ran through clothes, picture-books—through the publications of the Nonesuch Press, the Gides and Valérys at Zwemmers, or the Sunday performances of the Film Society.

People were determined to enjoy themselves at last and also to put the Humpty Dumpty of the pre-war social structure back. The "freedom" of the Intellectuals, the Aesthetes, the Pleasure-lovers of the Twenties was the privilege of the few, who constituted a secret society, like homosexuals. They were buttressed by private incomes, by innumerable servants, by the admiration of the masses which they took for granted. They wanted to keep the security and opulence of 1913 with the avant-garde ideas and sexual emancipation of 1923.

There was also an over-all feeling of hopefulness, domestic and international. The particular bitterness and pessimism of the Gumbrils and Prufrocks was not borne out by the host of happy entertainers, from Firbank, Van Vechten and Cocteau to Arlen and Coward.

Besides, the world was small. There were few Americans. All London was contained in one telephone book. The literary worlds met: Gide was Bloomsbury, the genial Stulik at the Eiffel Tower had his private rooms decorated by Wyndham Lewis. There was no thumbs down jury of unfrocked Leavisites to stifle our modest exhibitionism. No rumble of a distant drum.

(1969)

OXFORD IN OUR TWENTIES

I WAS at Oxford from 1922 to 1925. The real changeover had already taken place when the war veterans had returned in 1918. We were heirs to the earlier generations of the Sitwells, Aldous Huxley, Leslie Hartley, Cyril Radcliffe, described in Maurice Bowra's autobiography. As a young don, Maurice was to figure just as prominently among the undergraduates of my own day. We were also the last, or almost the last, of the womanless Oxford. Men who liked women were apt to get "sent down." A romantic interest in our own sex, not necessarily carried as far as physical experiments, was the intellectual fashion.

It was also a period of great social awareness, when to be accepted by the upper class, then in possession of money and authority and even glamour, was a natural ambition. Just as the following generation was to try to join the working classes and became Communists to get away from their parents, we tried to escape from middle-class homes by rising above them. This explains such meteorites as John Betjeman and Evelyn Waugh. I suppose my generation will be judged for some time to come by Evelyn's diaries (all vomit and Debrett) rather than by his own autobiography or Sir Maurice Bowra's. At first he was quiet and studious, then he joined a kind of bibulous bohemian underworld which centred round the Hypocrites' Club (at first mostly Balliol) but then ascending, through Robert Byron and John Sutro, into the upper-class aesthetes' world of Harold Acton, Hugh Lygon, Bryan Guinness and Michael Rosse. Waugh's talent was as an artist; his was a very strong personality, but we had no idea what line it would take.

Among the Balliol Hypocrites was Richard Pares, future historian and fellow of All Souls, a Winchester scholar of captivating charm, with the look of a Rossetti angel with a touch of Mick Jagger. He was the first new friend I made at Balliol and as we were in the same college we could see a lot of each other. I never knew until Evelyn told me many years later that he was keen on him and had felt great jealousy about me, nor that A. L. Rowse, then an undergraduate, had also fallen victim to his charm and desperation.

I came up to Oxford from College at Eton with a small group of scholars and for most of my time there I was hardly to see anyone else. This group included (Sir) Roger Mynors (Balliol), now the Professor of Latin; Robert (Bobbie) Longden (Trinity), who became headmaster of Wellington and was killed in an air-raid; Kenneth (Lord) Clark (Winchester), a close friend of Bobbie's; Maurice Bowra, who shaped our personalities; and "Sligger" Urquhart, the Dean of Balliol and most civilised member of its Common Room, who took us on Reading Parties. To these we added two or three more Balliol friends, Piers Synott, a scholarly Anglo-Irish landowner, and the enchanting Patrick Balfour, now Lord Kinross. Peter Quennell was also a great friend and in my last year Henry Yorke (the novelist Henry Green) joined the group, and Anthony Powell.

News of Bobbie, Roger, Sligger, Maurice, and K. (Kenneth Clark) features in all my letters with enthusiastic regularity. We were intellectuals (except for Sligger) with a passion for literature, travel and the visual arts. K. was already a formidable connoisseur but we also liked him because of his gramophone and his motor car in which he took us sight-seeing. Maurice introduced us to Yeats, Proust, Eliot and the art of conversation. On the whole this group was relatively unworldly and I remember being rather taken aback when Kenneth Clark announced that "Sibyl Colefax is really a very nice woman." I think that I, however, was the first to insist on visiting the Mediterranean in summer and to found "the Cicada Club" (five members) for this purpose. I also propounded the superiority of archaic Greek art over the classical, which was then considered a heresy.

There were many other sets at Oxford, as there always have been. One was called "the Kindergarten" and consisted of decorative and well-born aesthetes rather older than us, who frequented Lady Ottoline at Garsington and went about in a large group. They tended to speak in a hurried breathless way—the accent can still be heard in the broadcasts of David Cecil. They consisted of "Puffin" Asquith, David Cecil, Edward Sackville-West, Lord Hambleden and his brother, Eardley Knollys, Bob Gathorne-Hardy, Kyrle Leng and Lord Sudley, brother of the present Earl of Arran. They were replaced by a very different group of aesthetes, far more aggressive and unconventional, which revolved round Harold Acton, Robert Byron and Brian Howard, Alfred Duggan, Mark Ogilvie-Grant, with its attendant groups of peers for reassurance and protection: Lords Rosse, Stavordale, Weymouth and a sympathetic don, Roy Harrod. Another group of "house hearties" was rather more Bullingdon and wore tweed caps: Lord Jessel, Sir Alex Douglas-Home, Cosmo Crawley, and two Americans, Ben Kittredge and Bob Coe. The aesthetes gave the parties. Politics were at their lowest ebb. There were innumerable other societies: foreign noblemen at Balliol, Graham Greene who was of us but not with us, rugger men, rowing men, Union men, brilliant Wykehamists like Sylvester Gates, John Sparrow and Jack MacDougal, outposts of Bloomsbury like Philip Ritchie and Roger Senhouse, "college" men who took all their meals in hall, gourmets who drove out every evening to John Fothergill's at Thame. (Balliol was famous for lobster Newburg.) Dandies went in for the palest "Oxford bags" and turtle-neck sweaters, fur coats or immaculate tails. Lesley and Roberts were the aesthetes' tailor, Adamson for hearties, with Halls of Oxford for silk ties and long credit. Germers was the hairdresser for those of us who couldn't trust ourselves with a razor. The only exercise we took was running up bills.

I haven't described what people looked like; the young can be very decorative and I'm always taken aback by the beauty of these English ephebes in groups of someone's Oxford or Cambridge "twenty-firster." Kenneth Clark was a polished hawk-god in obsidian, Bobby Longden an intellectual Antinous, Archie Lucas an Adonis, as were Nat Alexander and Ian Campbell-Gray, both fencers; Sligger's rooms would fill up every evening with such memorable profiles.

But all this passed me by: I could never shake off my three-year day-dream; snatches of poetry, Greek verses which I wrote freely, Proustian egotism, neurotic dependence on Bobbie and Maurice, the less exacting companionship of genial Patrick and moody Piers.

Here is a typical letter of my last year. It is not what people want or even expect Oxford to be like. But it is authentic.

May 1925
I am not quite at the suicidal stage. Running away is all I was contemplating, disappearing when I get a weekend off before Schools, vanishing on the Orient Express probably . . . Piers finds life "an aggressive vacuum," Maurice odit et amat. Sligger "can't understand what all these young men find to grumble about," K. has had a letter from his father saying "The new budget makes things easier, 6d off up to £30,000 and 1/- after," to celebrate which he has asked Roger and me to tea a week in advance. I really am miserable.

I had Tony Powell, Henry Yorke and Bobbie to breakfast, Eastwood to lunch, Penderel Moon to tea and Bobbie is coming to dinner.

I went to a concert alone on Sunday night and heard the *Mother Goose* suite [Ravel]. The first "Belle au bois dormant," I found incredibly moving with its picture of the rainy leafy troubled woods and the tragedy known only to a few birds of the still house among them:

"Beneath these laden boughs the
  gardener sighs
Dreaming in emptiness
  forgotten beauty lies."

I haunt the Oxford Canal where the squat tower of the castle looks more like Provence than anything, furnaces and railway engines . . . old houses, flowering chestnut and lilac hang over the dirty water and music comes from ancient inns

"I heard someone in the yellow
  crane house
Playing on the sweet bamboo
  flute
The tune of the 'Falling Plum
  Flowers'
It was May in the waterside
  city." [Li Po]

I canoed with Peter Quennell who writes the best poetry in Oxford.

My last letters were written from the Examination Halls.

The examinations are pretty crashing. I know very little history and haven't read half the prepared books, it is a death struggle between style, intelligence and plausibility and a stern board of examiners who have only a remorseless desire to see if people know their stuff. My ignorance is colossal. It is like a cat playing with a mouse—just as I feel secure and playful a great paw knocks me over with Constitutional History from 1307. "Fear and the pit and the snare are upon thee. O inhabitant of the earth."

(1973)

HUMANE KILLER

This fragment—designs for a Persona—was written in the mid-Thirties shortly before *Enemies of Promise* and *The Rock Pool,* as an attempt to achieve greater anonymity. The name is an anagram. C.C.

Lincoln Croyle was an American with an English mother, "a jennet" as he phrased it, "instead of the commoner mule." He was educated in England and lived at first with his parents in London and Dorset. He travelled a great deal, was married in Philadelphia and settled in Paris and the South of France. He was a familiar figure on the Left Bank and I remember meeting him in the little back room at Sylvia Beach's—a stocky, dark, compact-looking American with a pleasant smile and a cultured, rather plaintive voice, like one of Henry James's old-young men, but with a vein of Middle Western savagery. We knew he wrote, but he did not show his work, though he was supposed to have had some poems under another name in *transition*. He was neither poor nor rich and did not seem to make or require friends. We gathered he had been married but knew nothing of the circumstances, nor of the mental illness to which he refers in his journal. His suicide in Florida two years ago caused little comment, being obscured by those of Harry Crosby and Hart Crane. A few weeks after his death Miss Sylvia Beach received a package from the State Department enclosing his papers and the following message:

Dear Sylvia,
If "anything should happen to me" and I have now lived 33 years, which my Redeemer considered long enough, I wonder if you would mind taking charge of this—perhaps one of your clever young men might edit it—if so give him carte blanche—if not, I hope it may come in useful to wrap around other books, as I have seen you do with so many odd sheets. All I request is that, if it be published, nothing is said about me—no foreword you understand. I would rather play my flute in the dark. Anything about my family and myself is either in the journal

or not of any importance. Good-bye. Consider me as lost—even by the Lost Generation—withdrawn at candidate's request.

L. C.

I have nowhere altered his manuscript, which Miss Beach has entrusted to me and seems to have a certain "period" interest, but I have had to suppress one or two names and omit some passages of an impersonal nature.

Cyril Connolly

TO BURN while Rome fiddles. That is my ideal.

I could write so many books, instead I fritter everything away into articles. The idea behind this is to gather up the occasional cravings for dignity and quiet which beset a journalist. I want it to be something so unfashionable, so intellectually dowdy that you would fancy yourself transported to the schoolroom in a country house in Ireland. The children have all grown up and only one unmarriageable daughter sits in the ink-stained armchair drivelling into a torn exercise book.

The way I live everything is silting up. My mind is active, but I can't think any more. I can't read books by dead authors. I can't read books that I don't have to review. I prefer the Evening Standard.

The arteries are silting up too.

Nicotine and gin.

All the same most English people are subnormal when they don't drink. They need drink in this city as the first source of civility; till you've had a drink you can't take any interest in anyone.

I do not see any point in a book unless it be subversive. I used to admire the explosive kind like that book of Gide's which ends "now you have finished, throw this away and go out." But now I prefer a subversive book, like those rings people wear to keep off rheumatism; they may be of some use, who knows? That is the way I want you to wear this book.

Places. Just now there is nowhere I want to be. Only London. There is no happiness outside the telephone book. Living for beauty. "Such a beautiful little place, we were sorry we ever had to leave it." How that dates! Only a painter can travel now with a good conscience, for he doesn't only live for beauty, he lives off it. But it is a dream we journalists have, that last milk-blue ripple of the wave as it dies on the mollified sand.

Time is the humane killer. Time knows how to circumvent the gland and rob of all its terror the posture of love.

She acted the governess in the cherry orchard. There was something sloppy, German, inconsequent and self-possessed about her. And common, too! The only person on the stage not to talk with a Kensington accent.

Sloane Street, Knightsbridge, Bromptonia—they are the enemy. "Anything, of course; with a Cadogan in it is all right."

But she bounced about the stage and didn't overact. A beautiful frowsy blonde, "fresh, round, pouting lips, and a jut with her bum that would stir an anchorite!"

When you get to know anybody they bring a dirty old pack of cards out of their pocket and begin to show you the queens and knaves, to tell you what are trumps, and make you play some game with it. We all carry round our tattered envelope of picture cards. There is the old home that is not really a house so much as a little place, and the ancestor who refused a title, "then Daddy would have been Sir William" and there is the literary schoolmaster who lent us the Golden Journey to Samarcand, and the don who had such an influence on us at Oxford, and the obscure great man of our generation who was terrific as an undergraduate and nobody quite knows yet what he is going to do in London. And the woman of forty who is so intelligent and understanding, and a few friends whom we pass on to each other with their myths and sagas. Tawdry court cards with which we snap and shuffle and trump and revoke.

The married packs are the worst; the married friends of one's married friends—and the penalties are double.

Nobody says anything nice about you except people who are getting to know you. Old friends only say the things they can never say to one's face, and there are more of these each time we meet. One must be terribly fond of somebody to want to see them.

There are some writers who are so sacred, that their names must be kept secret, and others who are my natural enemies and wish all their lousy affectations on me.

To write for oneself? A book is the place to be alone. Or for others? To make them say No! No! in the middle of a sentence, or yawn and scratch themselves?

Or for glory: The Future: The Infallible Worm?

December the eleventh. The first carol! What horror, what barbarities lie ahead!

When Hark, the Herald Angels sing!
Duck, it is the only thing.
When the first Noel sounds your way
Saint Suicide will have a day.

Men of Letters, ere we part
Tell me why you never fart?
"Never fart? My dear Miss Blight,
I do not need to fart, I write."

Wives of great men all remind us
We can leave our wives at home
Go to places they can't find us
Frig and fuck till kingdom come.

Not a large poetic output for a whole year spent abroad. But living for beauty doesn't make one very poetical, one would rather read a Fortnum's catalogue.

More talk of Christmas. More horror. Philip Heseltine (Peter Warlock) committed suicide on Christmas Day. The stench of these capitalist feasts! Cigars and port and crackers and paper caps—drunks in dinner jackets reeling down the restaurant stairs to the gala. In the counties, in stone manors on the Cotswolds, the fat-armed young women will say: "Don't pay any attention to him—quite mad I assure you—positively loopy." And their brothers, with small moustaches, will add "I suppose they let you out just for Christmas."

Half an oaf is better than no bed.

There are days in London when the air is so putrid that to get ill we have simply to go out. Raw, pneumonic, pusgut air. Everybody quarrels at parties and the streets resound with the bells of fire-engines. Time to think of Tenerife and Tobago.

The Party Trap. It may be YOU they want to meet, but it's THEY they want to talk about.

No one can make one hate oneself like an admirer—de lire la secrète horreur du dévouement dans les yeux. . . .

Every admirer is a potential enemy.

Nine houses out of ten in London should have, as in the days of the plague, a cross painted on the door.

There is a certain dignity in "dating," but you must do it quietly.

He's a regular tea-for-two, a yo-yo.

I am a man of the Twenties, my pleasures, my interests, my diseases were all acquired then, and my medicine chest. Food, drink, trains, books, bed. Many beaches, many bottles, many bars.

When the Twenties become as famous as the Nineties, what will be the Pilgrimages, the most potent stimuli, les attractions?

Montparnasse. The Ile Saint-Louis, Saint-Tropez, Cannes, Villefranche, Toulon (Venice and Capri are earlier); the London of the old Café Royal, the Eiffel Tower and the Ivy, Charlotte Street, Glebe Place . . . Taos, New Mexico.

Figures: Joyce, Hemingway, Proust, Aragon, Gide, Crevel, Pascin, Firbank, Woolf, Heseltine, Huxley, Eliot. I can't be bothered to think of them. And how many of them will survive!

My work is a paperchase in which clues for the reader get thinner and thinner. Here are a few. Can you recognize any of them?

> Favourite writer: He of Aldermaston.
> Favourite painter: He of Valenciennes.
> Place of Education: Red brick, with huge stale elms, an old school saturated in pagan splendour, effete with all the alluvial vices.
> Place of Atonement: A thin quadrangle faced with neo-gothic hutches, where everything tastes of tepid anchovy toast and guilt mounts up at compound interest.
> Plans for the Future: There, I'm afraid, I must be less explicit. I remember once motoring down the valley of the Brandywine, so English except for the little clapboard farms advertising chicken dinners, and being struck by the incongruity of meeting an ill-dressed coloured family, carrying enormous bundles on their heads and looking very inappropriate in such charming Wiltshire surroundings, but that is always the case in America, just when things seem more homelike, there is a correspondingly violent interruption, and so, gliding smoothly away on this false trail, I will leave you, like the liar I am.*

The horror of the human couple—how can we wipe that away? Do you know those American dinners which I used to go to in my old life? —Mr. and Mrs. Lincoln Croyle, I want you to meet Mr. and Mrs. Clapp, Mr. and Mrs. Brawn, Mr. and Mrs. Conger. How do you do Mrs. Conger, pleased to meet you Mrs. Clapp. Mrs. Croyle will you sit next to Mr. Brawn, Mr. Conger will you sit between Mrs. Clapp and Me—and will you sit here Mr. Croyle? We know we all came here quarrelling in our taxis and we will all go away drunk. By the end of cocktails all we want to do is smoke and fight, not eat and drink; by the end of dinner we make a little polite love, dragging our ball and chain about with us,

* Answers: 1 Congreve, 2 Watteau, 3 Eton, 4 Balliol.

then another quarrel on the way home and perhaps a scrap in the bathroom. Mr. and Mrs. Lincoln Croyle. The nakedness of it all! Mr. and Mrs.—tin cans tied to dogs' tails. My wife. My husband. WE.

> When Miss Right shall come along
> Exit Mrs. Never Wrong.

Hyannis, Hyannisport, Sewickley, Syasconset—

Names of places that become names of experiences, names of one's youth, names of oneself—and then recede, names of obscure pains and ailments, names that recall a dull ache, names of places.

Rue Servandoni, Rue de Vaugirard. Rue Delambre. Once I walked down them on angel's pads. Now when I remember it all comes back, yet when I walk down them, I feel nothing. Paris is only for those who are still in love with themselves. They think they love Paris, but when they return there they return to their own personality—a place where books, wine and hotel bedrooms were cheap, where they could act, and find other actors. Now it's expensive and there are no Americans left and I'm too old for romance and think I'm lucky if I've kept a little more hair than my fellows, and Paris seems a very ordinary city. How can we have ever managed to be happy among such disagreeable people as the French? Only by not knowing the language. When you can understand what people say you can't go on living with them. The way to see Paris now is to lie in bed and read about it.

I remember there used to be a bar called the Bateau Ivre, in the Place de l'Odéon—very neat, very expensive and modern with portholes, a narrow winding staircase with a rope banister, and upstairs a tiny triangular dancing floor. There was a coloured pianist called Henry Crowder. I remember sitting there one night with Pierre Batchef, star of the Chien Andalou. But above all I remember it in the great frost—that was early in 1929. It was so cold that crossing from the Rue de Vaugirard we wondered if we would be frozen before we got there. That cold was historic! One felt like the Israelites when they got over the Red Sea and saw it closing up. And in the Bateau Ivre we had hot grogs and heard the cold getting worse outside. And there was another bar a little way down called the Trois et As—I'm going on dragging these names in till I find one that will interest you—and the Restaurant de la Petite Chaise, where the food was half French and half American and they had that 1923 Clos Vougeot. —All gone now, and Montagné's and Voisin's and Madame Genot's and the old Boeuf and the Passage de l'Opéra. That cold spell frostbit the 1920s; the oranges and the eucalypti died on the Riviera and since then it's never had another winter season. What were you doing then? Were you old enough to remember that cold?

The Past is like a dun waiting on our doorstep. We hand him twenty-four hours at the end of every day. A little something on account. But he is insatiable—reminding one at inappropriate moments of things we had hoped forgotten. Remember this when you remember—however pleasantly it starts, it will end in tears. "An old love pinches like a crab," and there is one getting ready to pinch at the end of every day.

Words we may not use, words of terror like Jahweh or Melquarth. No-one. Neoplasm. Terminal. Death is an abstraction, dying the reality.

The small hours—every night they look for me and tonight, shall I escape them?

There is something that has to be written. Everybody has something in them that has to be written. I suppose in my case it is about Paris. But it can wait. Lincoln Croyle, more wick than oil.

My four homes. Four places I have never fitted into: London. The Country. Paris. The USA.

I have a reputation for being malicious, indiscreet and sadistic, and yet I am full of affection, geniality and sweetness. When I go out and get drunk I grow even more affectionate, and genial and sweet and even more and more, and even more and more, and then I don't remember very much—but when I wake up full of sweet thoughts in the morning, I know I have been malicious, indiscreet and sadistic. (I am indiscreet so as to add to my self-importance, malicious because I do not think people like me enough, sadistic because I play up to the masochist in me that way.)

And why don't they like me? Because I'm too intelligent—and the social value of intelligence is about equal to a very large hump. Dans le monde, un homme de génie vaut un bien beau bossu.

It's the whispering and giggling and the little flat bêtises that get me down. Then, too, I can't conceal boredom, can't leave anybody without doing it rudely or join them without seeming impertinent. And I can't bear not being asked to anything. I shan't like it; I won't fit in; but for God's sake ask me.

A day in late August, cowled in black summer mist counterfeiting autumn. Rock-bottom. Kraepelin's Manic-Depressive Insanity and Paranoia . . . "depressive stupor," a man with a black moustache, like a trusty Hungarian Jaeger, looks out at one from his blankets with a terror which is instantly communicated. "Involutionary melancholia," ideas of sin usually play the largest part. "Paranoid melancholia," the mood is gloomy, despondent, despairing, with delusions of persecution. "Delirious melancholia," characterised by profound, visionary clouding of conscience.

He reached his seat just as the curtain was going up; it was the ballet called Cotillon which, although it had been danced before, had managed never to become an old favourite. Croyle leant forward and leaned his arms on the balustrade.

The dancers appeared; Berard's familiar decor, the screens, the gentlemen in black tail-coats and knee-breeches; the Mistress of Ceremonies—Riabouchinska? Rostova?—went her round, looking into the girls' hands. Chabrier's waltz, a desultory tune, made a deep impression on him, as if he were watching the heavy splodge of raindrops on a pane in summer, the wind blowing them sideways, the sea churning beyond the green cornfield, the arrival of a long-awaited letter, then the raindrops splodging again. Now the Palmist seemed to read in one hand a particular fate, something terrible is going to happen to that one, Toumanova? Baronova? The daughter of the house; she totters back on her points. The party is spoiled. The waltz flows smoothly on.

Croyle looked down on the stalls below. Let's see if there's one face. He considered the first four rows. Vacant enthusiasm, programme-squinting, clumsy tongues mopping up in hollow teeth, masks of serene nothingness, an aroma of port and orchids; if he could find just one creature aware of the music, aware of her fate. Yes, there she was—in the fifth row—a small head of yellow hair, level brow, rather sharp nose when seen from above and on the face the look he was seeking, an expression—yes—of horror. It was *her* hand.

(1937–73)

FAREWELL TO PROVENCE

"A MAN has only one virginity to lose and there his heart will ever be," quoted Hemingway to Berenson, adding that "he was an old Veneto boy."

It made me wonder where, topographically speaking, I had lost mine. I suppose it was when still a schoolboy the first time I went to Avignon on my own. "There is the first time we go abroad," I wrote in *Enemies of Promise,* "and the first time we go to Provence. For me they almost coincided, and it would be hard to express what I felt that evening, in the garden above the Papal Palace. The frogs croaked, the silver Rhône flowed underneath, the Mediterranean spring was advancing.

"I have been back so many times to that palace, to Hiély's restaurant with its plate-glass windows, to the Greek theatre at Arles, the hills of Les Baux, the ruins of Saint Rémy, to the Rhône with its eddies and islands, and the cypress hedges where the cicadas charge the batteries of summer, that I can no longer remember what they looked like for the first time. I only know that they are sacred places."

Cicadas prefer pine trees. I doubt if they are found in cypress hedges. No juice. And that was many years ago. But the Blue Guide still calls the view from the terrace above the palace the finest in the Midi.

I had another look last summer, nearly half a century later. Fifty years multiplied by the volume of water passing under the Pont d'Avignon at any given second—how many oceans would that have filled since 1922?

And yet it's all there. One cicada, no frogs. The windswept little garden on the Rocher des Doms with its evergreen oaks and magnolias, the river underneath, the Tower of Philippe Le Bel beyond, the city with its tiled roofs, the soaring façade of the fortress palace, the plate-glass windows of Hiély where we had had a table for two overlooking the square; the broad main street with its plane-trees and cafés leading to the station. Hiély, although unchanged, is now closed. The name has been merged with Lucullus, a little further down, which has maintained a steady two stars in the Michelin rating.

The whole region is a Michelin summit. There is a three-star restaurant at Les Baux (the Baumanière which also has five knives and forks in red for good taste and great luxury); at Noves M. Lalleman's Auberge has lost its third star but kept its lobster quenelles and quail flambé. Right across the river from Avignon the Ermitage at Les Angles also has two stars, maintaining the same level as Lucullus, though nothing like the luxury of Noves or Les Baux.

The trouble with these gastronomic high-spots is that a good meal may easily amount to £10 a head and leave one incapable of doing anything active for the rest of the day. Luckily there are many one-star restaurants which are both interesting and much less expensive. There is the garden of the Prieuré Hotel at Villeneuve, very British, where tennis rallies punctuate the service, with air-conditioning in the bedrooms; there is my favourite, the Auberge de France, next door to the Papal Palace, with a specialty I couldn't keep away from, a very creamy kind of scrambled egg with the local black truffles chopped up in it, called a *brouillade aux truffes* and served in an earthenware pot.

In spite of all its stars this part of the Rhône Valley is not particularly favoured with fish or game. *Brandade de morue* replaces the fish soup of the coast. Apart from the lamb of the Alpilles, cooked in mountain herbs, truffles, crayfish in season, *pâté de grives,* inland Provence depends more on the cook than the ingredients.

It is, however, the country of the Cavaillon melon, known generally as Charentais. The musky globes sprawl over the sunburnt fields like discarded footballs. A whole one is served to each customer, iced with the top taken off. This melon alone is the making of every meal through the long long summer. The flesh is aromatic, the darker the better. It should never be too ripe and should have plenty of weight, like a croquet ball.

Other fruits of Provence are the muscat grapes and the little yellow fig. It is farther along the coast that one finds the green almond or such substantial soups as *bourride* or *pistou* of which basil is the dominating flavour. For an excellent description of *bouillabaisse* with its essential *rouille* see Roy Campbell (*Light on a Dark Horse*). The best wines are local: Gigondas, Tavel, Cornas, Châteauneuf du Pape.

Where should one stay? There is only one choice for me: the Hotel d'Europe in Avignon which belongs to the type of eighteenth-century palace with courtyard and fountain and enormous plane-tree which is found only among old coaching inns. It is both romantic and comfortable—romantic because it is the scene of Moore's *Lovers of Orelay* and also of Lord Berners's lesser-known tale, *Percy Wallingford:* "What attracted me to the place," he writes, "was not the charm of the town itself so much as the memory of a certain room in the Hotel d'Europe. It had the appearance of being left untouched since the days of Louis Philippe. I was a great reader of Balzac and it was a perfect setting for a Balzac novel."

Such rooms survived till after the war. There used to be a Monticelli hanging in the hall but all has been modernised now. Nevertheless it remains the only hotel in the region with a touch of magic.

The Musée Calvet has some good pictures though it is not as interesting as the Musée Fabre at Montpellier or Granet at Aix. The Papal Palace is a monument to the iconoclastic soldiery who mutilated it in the Revolution. Nothing remains inside but a few decorative traces of Renaissance gaiety and some splendid rooms, particularly the great audience chamber and the Pope's enormous chapel.

The lives and times of the Popes and anti-Popes of Avignon are mysterious; although in the fourteenth century they made Avignon the center of the world. Though they loved Avignon and enriched it and were loth to return to Rome, one knows little about how they filled their day. O for some good memoirs or even a good history. One, in particular, the Aragonese Pedro de Luna, has always appealed to me since I first saw his sea-girt home in Peniscola.

Roman Provence is best seen from a centre like Avignon or Arles to which one can return in the evening sure of a cool room or a good meal. The Jules César is a beautiful hotel in an old convent but rather close to the main thoroughfare down which the Aix-bound traffic flows. I am drawn back always to the little square where the Nord Pinus retains its century-old decor, disputing with the Forum for pride of place. Both hotels have kept their old-fashioned lettering.

Arles is a hot town and once one has seen the theatre and the pagan cemetery of the Alyscamps, the arena and the church of Saint Trophime one wants to be out of it. Luckily it is near Les Baux where the Baumanière has a fine swimming-pool in a lovely garden, surrounded by the crags of the Val d'Enfer. It is also near the Camargue and it is in Arles that one can get a permit for the closed part of the Réserve Zoologique, the first national park, I believe, in France. The "little" Rhône here forms a delta with a string of lagoons, now beginning to be invaded by crops and rice-fields. The wildest area, near the sea, affords protection to many rare birds and a few invisible beavers.

It is particularly hot in summer, with the worst horse-flies I have ever encountered. Apart from the bulls and the cowboys the great attraction is the flocks of flamingo. These still visit but have ceased to breed, whether because of some diet deficiency or interference by tourists or air traffic is not known, but the outlook is unhopeful. One may see blue rollers, ibis, bee-eaters, little bustards and uncommon insects and reptiles, i.e., the freshwater turtle. Typical hotels round Les Saintes Maries: the Boumain, the Résidence with bungalows, and the Amphore.

Other places in range of Arles are Daudet's village of Fontvielle, with its mill, the Abbey of Montmajeur and, north of Les Baux, the ruins of Glanum, on the way to Saint Rémy. The "Antiques," as they are called, are outstanding and consist of two structures, the mausoleum and the municipal arch.

The mausoleum is one of the loveliest and best-preserved of Roman remains. It is a cenotaph dating from the time of Augustus, of which only the pine-cone on the summit is missing. The arch is of the same period and shows Greek influence.

What is so invigorating about the Roman remains of Provence is their early date. They have nothing to do with the decadence or the massive clumsiness of the later Empire. The arenas of Arles are among the earliest of the Roman world (46 B.C.), the theatre is of the first century, the Arch of Orange dates from Julius Caesar. The theatre there is one of the finest of antiquity, the arenas of Nîmes, its Maison Carrée and the Pont du Gard are all Augustan.

We know them so well that it is difficult to see them clearly. The "Antiques" still captivate by their unexpected situation on the garrigue, the Pont du Gard has remained unspoiled after two thousand years of being gaped at; its colours, its position, its harmony with the landscape, its impression of gigantic strength and sureness of purpose, its civic grandeur commemorate the splendour of the Augustan age, even as the delicate temple of the Maison Carrée reveals its aspirations to Hellenic grace and elegance.

It is familiarity alone which deadens the impact on us of constructions like the wall of the Theatre of Orange, which Louis XIV called *La plus belle muraille du royaume* (300 ft x 120 ft). In order to appreciate the Roman contribution, one must visit some of the lesser remains in Provence where the element of surprise is still lurking and where the buildings are caught off guard. Such are the four Corinthian columns of Riez and its temple or baptistery, the ruins of the temple of Vernègues, near Lambesc in the grounds of the château (surely the most desirable of the whole region), or the Pont Julien near Apt or the Pont Flavien near Miramas, or the municipal arches of Carpentras and Cavaillon.

The Jardin de la Fontaine at Nîmes has the best of both worlds—a phallus-shaped basin from Roman times set in the formal gardens and stoneware of the rococo. The baptistry at Aix has eight Roman columns. At Venasque, in the Vaucluse, the Merovingian baptistery of the sixth century has been held to be a temple of Venus, giving the place its name. Vaison is enormously worth a visit, for here the Roman remains of houses are unimpeded by the medieval town. (The remotest Provençal town is Nyons, already complete with olives, cicadas and cypresses though far up the valley of the Aygues.)

Provence begins at the gap of Donzère just south of Montélimar. Otherwise its frontiers are vague for it is generally held to include Nîmes to the west with Aigues Mortes and Lunel and even Montpellier, while to the east it runs beyond Aix as far as Draguignan and Fréjus.

For me it includes the Maures but not the Esterel and its influence is felt as far north as Castellane and Sisteron. This roughly corresponds to the northern limit of the olive which needs sun but can stand up to ten degrees of frost, of the cypress, the cistus and the oleander. It is the land of summer drought. As the country shades off into Languedoc, into the departments of Gard and Hérault, so the writers and painters with whom it is associated come to a stop.

I doubt if any well-known artist lives west of Lawrence Durrell at Sommières. He has found an unspoiled town in an unspoiled valley, no mean feat in a part of the world where tourism vies with the atomic industry. He enjoys sun and water but also wind. In winter the mistral cuts the whole Midi down to size.

The patriarch of these western marches is Jean Hugo at Lunel, great-grandson of the poet. He lives in the old family house with its "muscat" vineyard, painting his exquisite devotional lyrics to God and nature.

Otherwise, we have to recross the Rhône to find the remaining artist-colonies. Some are grouped round Maussane or Ménerbes, Bonnieux or Lourmarin. One of my happiest memories is of a birthday spent in their manor farm near Lambesc with my friends the painters Anne and Rodrigo Moynihan. Both gave me drawings and a magnificent *langouste,* the coral pounded up in the mayonnaise, with home-grown melons and muscats. After a siesta and a swim we went a tour of Roman remains to end up with a sumptuous dinner at Noves.

Aix-en-Provence is a true capital. Like Avignon it has a festival, like Montpellier a university; its beautiful squares and streets are well known, less well known are the exquisite "pavillons" which surround it. For those who like perfect combinations of stone and water in a perfect light, the hotels of the Cours Mirabeau and the Quartier Mazarin must give way to the exquisite Pavillon de L'enfant on the Route des Pinchinats or to the Villas de Tournon and de la Gaude, farther up the valley. Only Montpellier can rival such wealth of eighteenth-century houses. Aix numbers eighty within the city.

There remain the Renaissance façade of La Tour-d'Aigues and the three Romanesque abbeys of Sénanque, Silvacane and Thoronet, the Romanesque of Saint Gilles, the synagogue at Carpentras. For landscape there is the Fountain of Vaucluse, a spectacular natural site, as is the plateau above it, one of those scented uplands like the mountains of Lure, or Ventoux or the high plateau of Valensole given over to the drone of bees and the visual ecstasy (for the tourist) of the lavender fields in bloom. For the tree-lover there is nothing to equal the northern forest of the Sainte Baume.

I would stay for preference at the Thermes Sextius in the town of Aix or at the Riviera, with its garden, on the road to Marseille. I once bicycled all night from Sanary to Aix. Then nothing would do but the flesh-pots of the Roy René.

One wonders why the title "Farewell to Provence" came to mind. Why am I not off there now by the crack new Mistral Express? One can't go on for ever returning to places, besides I think Provence has suffered irretrievable damage. The atomic industrial centre of Marcoule, ablaze night and day, can't be wished away nor the vast developments on the Durance, once so unspoiled, nor the *aménagements* of the Rhône itself to make it navigable, nor the oil refineries of Berre, nor the 238,000 colonists from Algeria settled around Marseille and Aix, nor the new motorways.

One can't wish them away and neither can one wish back the lost treasures: the Vieux Port of Marseille or the Quai de Cronstadt at Toulon, Piazzetta of the Twenties and Thirties, with the intellectual galaxy of the Grand Café de la Rade:

Nous avons mangé de la cade
Du pissalat et des radis
Allons au Café de la Rade
Déguster un vermouth-cassis
Nous verrons des peintres célèbres
Derain, Friesz et Segonzac. . . .

and Cocteau, Gide, Valéry, Lawrence and Huxley.

(1971)

BERENSON

A DELIGHTFUL foreword by Sir Kenneth Clark sets the tone for this book,* the most intimate portrait of Berenson ever likely to be published; it leaves scope for only one other—an account of his youth up to the First War. As old people fossilize into public monuments they are beset by biographers and the resulting picture is top-heavy. What we need now is an account of the Berensons in all their vigour, the elopement with Mary (then Mrs. Costelloe), the work on the "Italian painters" series, the founding of the fortune, the rebuilding of I Tatti, the conquest of Paris, Italy, New York. "B.B. at twenty-five was already exactly what he now is, mystical and scientific as regards pictures, interested in origins and development and influences, anti-democratic, anti-philanthropic, believeing in culture above all else" (Mary Berenson to Miss Mariano). It is this demonic young man, the friend of Wilde and Montesquiou, whom one would like to know better.

Nicky Mariano, "half Neapolitan, half Baltic baron," came to live with her father in Florence and by 1914 was in the web of the Berenson circle. Mrs. Berenson liked her enormously and wanted her to marry her protégé Geoffrey Scott, the *homme fatal* of the region, gloomy, frustrated and self-obsessed, for whom she had conceived an unrequited passion which Nicky seemed destined to inherit. The war separated them and when Nicky and her family returned from Russia and she was offered the post of librarian to Berenson, Scott had been snapped up by Lady Sybil Cutting of the Villa Medici, who was later to wed Percy Lubbock. Scott's feelings for Miss Mariano were less apprehensive than for Mrs. Berenson and he was clearly loth to let her go, but meanwhile *le roi soleil* had appeared, fresh from his Paris triumphs.

* *Forty Years with Berenson,* by Nicky Mariano (New York, 1966).

While working at the end of the small library I heard a light step and saw B.B.'s slender elegant figure walking towards me. I was too flustered to say much, noticed his beautiful eyes and his charming smile, heard him utter a few words of appreciation of what I was trying to do and then he was gone.

This was the beginning of the devotion of a lifetime, a relationship which was accepted by Mrs. Berenson, whose own friendship with Nicky never faltered and which also permitted him to continue his sentimental forays among ladies of fashion and even to acquire at the end some new daughter-figures. In this sense the book is almost a moral tale. Here is a man who lived to be ninety-three and earned respect and affection from all those who surrounded him. He had glaring faults—suspiciousness was the worst—but he lived for an humanistic ideal which was shared by his household, and his reputation will never be exposed to the buffeting meted out to Maugham, that other nonagenarian up the French coast.

I once said that longevity was the revenge of talent upon genius. But Berenson was a genius, too. Not as a writer: his style was too fulsome. Nor as a creative artist—but as a kind of tactile computer, a combination of judgement, flair, knowledge and aesthetic perception which had never before been met with and which was fed the appropriate sense-data all his life. I remember him telling me how on his first visit to the Prado he emerged with a clear image of every picture in his mind which was never to forsake him. So perhaps does an eagle memorise a whole mountainside on its first flight. Such a gift is as liable to commercial exploitation as clairvoyance, and there is no doubt that at times he steered a devious course. Miss Mariano makes it very clear, however, that though he lived in luxury he never revelled in it, that his private life was relatively spartan—as when travelling in remote places or in his summer retreat at Vallombrosa. His appetites were small—except for admiration. She compares his attitude to money with Mary's.

The one thing that money can really buy for us is leisure of mind and the liberty to indulge in wholly disinterested pursuits.

His chief indulgence was in his library, which was always at the disposal of guests and students.

More than once I have heard him say that he had missed his real profession by not becoming a second-hand bookseller.

As Sir Kenneth Clark points out, in this happy book we have at last a portrait of Mrs. Berenson (who hardly comes to life in her brother Logan Pearsall Smith's autobiography). She was herself a writer, and her last letter to Miss Mariano, Sir Kenneth describes as "surely one of the most generous and moving tributes ever written by one woman to another." This account from her of a dinner in New York reveals her worldly and spacious puritanism. (Her family were Quakers.)

We attended a millionaire dinner-party the other night. The table literally groaned under orchids, caviar, turtle soup, and golden plate. Twenty-two gross old people sat around it guzzling champagne and all sorts of wine (in spite of prohibition), the women all over fifty, all fat and all except myself nearly naked and hung with ropes of pearls and diamonds. After dinner opera singers came in and yelled horrible music. B.B. nearly fainted away.

His own comment on the New York trip was also typical. When asked whether he was enjoying himself his answer was "I don't know. I just spin."

How will a book like this strike those who never knew Berenson? It is not a book for those without nostalgia, nostalgia not just for the vanished world of European society but also for the feelings of intimacy when life is lived at high pressure by sensitive, fastidious and kindly people. I Tatti could be dreadfully dull when the blank-faced incense-swinging hordes ascended for morning prayer; but it was full of valuable moments when they were gone.

I am sorry Miss Mariano does not give us more examples of B.B.'s vituperation; as when, for instance, he would turn to me with a beaming smile and ask me if I did not agree with him that Eliot was but a thin and squeaking Matthew Arnold. Oddly enough the only surrender to the modish cattiness of today occurs in the one reference to myself and my first wife. It occurs in her admirable chapter on Edith Wharton at Hyères.

Nicky to Mary. December 19, 1930.

Norton is going to take me to the Connollys tomorrow and on Sunday the Huxleys are coming to dinner here. Edith has had both couples here lately and liked Cyril but not as much as Huxley. She says that Cyril's wife is an awful lump but her descriptions of people are not to be trusted especially if they are young and conceivably intimidated by her not always reassuring manner.

"An awful lump"! Who would know if I do not speak up, that she was a beautiful Baltimore girl of nineteen—or with what trepidation we all approached this luncheon party of which I am now the sole survivor? It consisted of Aldous and Maria Huxley, Jean and Cyril Connolly, our hostess and the painter, Robert Norton, a charming dilettante and great friend of Mrs. Wharton. Logan Pearsall Smith had arranged the introduction, and the Huxleys, with whom we were on terms of profound ambivalence, drove us over in their three-seater Bugatti. Jean and Maria

Huxley were highly suspicious of each other and Aldous was quite unaware that my deep admiration for him—which was responsible for us settling in Sanary—had curdled.

We entered the dining-room like two opposing tennis teams before an already biased umpire. (Aldous was an undisputed lunch champion.) The food was delicious. What eggs! But the conversation, except for some rallies from Aldous, hung fire. Unfortunately it turned on differences between Americans and Europeans—Jean mentioned that Americans had a different way of holding their fork, shifting it to the the right hand. This was received by her hostess with blank incomprehension—and allowed by the Huxleys to go to the net. Forty-love. Bravely plunging, like Scott Fitzgerald on a similar occasion, Jean went on to say that many Americans addressed each other as "Mr." on envelopes, not as "Esq." like the English. "None that I know," exclaimed Mrs. Wharton and awarded game to the Huxleys.

Our consolation was that Robert Norton did take to us, and invited us to his other hide-out, Madame de Béhague's. I wrote an account of the meeting to Logan (of which Jean drew a caricature too faded to reproduce). Logan replied: "I feel that you somehow mismanaged that scene at Mrs. Wharton's. From what you say it is plain that she was *terrified* of you all—thought that you regarded her as an old has-been and that she put on, as she does to protect herself, her mask of wealth and worldliness. You ought to have made her drop it, which she would have done at a touch of understanding. With a word or two the delightful creature that she is would have emerged from her carapace and embraced you all. Plainly I ought to have been there."

And a few days later Nicky herself wrote:

B.B. is very sorry to have missed you altogether, he wanted particularly to have a long talk with you and hopes that you will both be in Italy before long and look us up at Settignano. I hope you had a nice time at Cannes. Best messages to both of you from Mrs Wharton, B.B. and Norton. Mrs Wharton will send you word as soon as she is better. Love to Jean and yourself from Nicky.

We had passed the test after all.

(1966)

VENICE: 1

I KNOW of no city which exercises such attraction and repulsion on me as Venice. The repulsion is based on a profound dislike of the régime, of the thousand-year-old police state which was governed by fear, anonymity and informers and which looted Byzantium, bled the Greek world and disgraced so many of its great men.

The sumptuous worldliness of so much of its art, the poverty of its literature (how can there be literature, suggests Mr. Rowdon,* when religion and politics are taboo), the narrow philistinism of its rulers who let Goldoni, Baretti, Vivaldi all slip away and Tiepolo die in misery; such envy of native pre-eminence reminds one of nineteenth-century Dublin or Chicago.

This resentment against Venice (which one doesn't feel against Rome, Florence or Munich) has a physical counterpart in my dislike of the Piazza. Those pigeons! Strutting banality, flying sewers, with the photographers and exhibitionists who surround them; the hordes of Nordic tourists, many lying bibulous on the stones, the undistinguished façades, the bad music. Perhaps it serves as an outlet for everyone who would clog up the circulation if they preferred to be anywhere else.

> St Mark's Place is all covered over in a morning with chicken coops, which stink one to death as nobody, I believe, thinks of changing their baskets, and all about the ducal palace is made so very offensive by the resort of human creatures for every purpose most unworthy of so charming a place, that all enjoyment of its beauties is rendered difficult to a person of any delicacy,

wrote Mrs. Thrale (1739–1821) while Beckford wrote of St. Mark's "the vile stench which exhales from every recess and corner of the edifice and which all the incense of the altars cannot subdue."

* *The Fall of Venice,* by Maurice Rowdon (London, 1970).

So much for the drawbacks; now that the whole archipelago is threatened one clings to the advantages; the twin virtues of its light and air, the light which makes every building and vista change colour hourly and daily, the air which, when not foggy or parched by the sirocco, has the particular maritime freshness that both charms and stimulates, air which removes hang-overs, as the tide removes rubbish, as the sea wipes out the trivialities, so that, stumbling out of the bars, the tourists find the steamers waiting to transport them to the ocean or Torcello, Chioggia or Corfu.

Mr. Rowdon is fortunate, because after reading his enthralling essays one can still return to Venice and see so much that has survived the "Fall." The people are the same, the houses are the same, their water life is the same, the fêtes, the food and drink, the palaces and the museums which preserve some of their contents. What "fell" was political autonomy, independence, the governing class; but by the eighteenth century the city-state was already given over to pleasure, the world's number one tourist attraction.

> The Republic fell for the same reason that the *ancien régime* fell everywhere in Europe: no allowance was made in her government for the existence of the middle classes . . . they were the missing link in the city's crisis . . . whereas in France there was an energetic politically-minded middle class to take over government, in Venice the nobles were all the government there was. They were the Republic and so the Republic fell.

They were, incidentally, more frightened of an internal revolution, a "commune," than of Napoleon. When he presented his ultimatum not a shot was fired. He was twenty-eight years old, ignorant and Spartan; those elaborate façades by the waters meant nothing to him, not for him the nuance of husband, wife and cicisbeo, of Guardi's shimmering Pompeian paintings, Tiepolo's observation, Goldoni's irony, the six months' masquerade. He found the Arsenal shipless, took over some Ionian harbours, and sold the whole country to Austria. It was the Austrian yoke which gave the Venetian aristocracy, or some of it, the chance to redeem itself.

Venice fell but is still standing. So it is with us and there are some interesting parallels between swinging London and the city of the Doges in decline. "They're changing guard at Buckingham Palace" but what about the legions on the Wall?

> Corfu was defended on paper by one company of Venetians and two of Albanians, but the whole force consisted of a couple of Venetian officers who drew pay for the whole lot. Names on payrolls remained perpetual, irrespective of death . . . (In the great arsenal) most of the workmen only turned up for pay day . . . about seventy thousand faggots had disappeared

annually in this way . . . The ordinary Venetian almost certainly never realised the real state of affairs in his prolonged day-dream. "They" would see to it all.

When the French arrived the only firing was a salute to the "Serenissima" from the Croatian mercenaries who were leaving. The people stood outside the noble houses screaming *"Assassini di San Marco."* Renier swept the streets with artillery. On October 17, 1797, the Treaty of Campo Formio sold Venice to Austria, the Byzantine horses of St. Mark's looted from the Hippodrome of Constantinople six centuries earlier were removed to Paris; on January 17, 1798, the Austrian garrison took over.

Presumably the caste system held; the reign of pleasure continued; the masquerade was on. Soon Byron would arrive to give it a fillip, Chateaubriand, Browning, Ruskin, Wagner, Proust. Apart from its visual pleasures beloved of writers and artists, Venice had seen some of the most exquisite entertainments of our time from the Princesse de Polignac's concerts to the Beistegui Ball. The years before and after the 1914 War were a high-water mark of dissipation, in the Venetian sense, for its dissipation was controlled by its healthy climate and consisted largely of making love and music, taking coffee and liberties (behind a mask), gambling and picnicking on the mainland.

The opulence of gondolas and their decoration were very strictly regulated, so were the amount of jewels one could display or courses one might serve; there was even a law against snobbery. You could get six months for boasting about your forebears and be secretly drowned if the offence was repeated. Flirtation was really the be-all and end-all of existence, enriched by the particularly charming and voluptuous quality of Venetian womanhood. They provided the life-enhancement which the Council of Ten and the Inquisition were always threatening to take away. On the other hand the Ten made life easy for the workers:

> On holidays Venice stopped work by law and there were plenty of holidays. And everyone went to church—another reason for the well-being. Nobody thought that life ended with death—an idea more depressant of vigour and serenity than any known to the mind . . . Even Casanova believed in God and prayed all his life.

Then there was music. Today one hears some of the worst music from the Piazza and the gondolas; in the eighteenth century the quality was exceptionally high and the cult was ubiquitous. Mr. Rowdon writes of Monteverdi, Corelli, Galuppi and Vivaldi with knowledge and affection. There were operas, concerts, serenades and church music to choose from. "Classical" and "pop" were one. Then, as now, the only way to know Venice was to live there, to savour the artisanat, to buy happiness by the shilling on the vaporetto. Alas the temperatures are not inviting—32, 41, 43, today 37. Go there when it reaches 60 before the tourists and pigeons.

POSTSCRIPT:

This piece brought an immediate telegram from Ezra Pound's Venice household: "Cheers for you. Ezra delighted. Italian papers please take note." They did and the *Gazetino di Venezia* published an article on April 14. "The guano continues to corrode the stones of Venice. The great bell of San Giovanni Crisostamo collapsed recently through its pivot being corroded with guano. The pigeons are a threat to many buildings and their multiplication is now a danger to health as well. Mixed with rain their excrement becomes an acid which eats away stones and statues. They must either be heavily cropped, which would raise an outcry, deported to other cities with better natural resources, or given the pill (such as exists in Switzerland) which would prove expensive."

(1970)

VENICE: 2

"To take a boat in a pleasant evening, and with music to row upon the waters . . . or in a Gundilo through the Grand Canale in Venice, to see those goodly palaces, must needs refresh and give content, to a melancholy, dull spirit" wrote Burton, and this remedy for melancholy holds good today, nearly four hundred years later. Except for one proviso. Who pays? To enter a gundilo, read the tariff, continue haggling, and get no change out of five thousand lire and perhaps to have to listen to "O Sole Mio" as well is worse for the spleen than taking a taxi from London Airport used to be.

In some moods I have felt like compiling an anti-Venice, the arrival with a choice of taking a launch or crowding on the vaporetto, perhaps missing several, the round of the hotels all sold out to package tours, the sensation of thousand-lire notes running through one's fingers, the first sight of the Piazza, bands blaring, pigeons staling, hippies sleeping on the flags, then being finally conveyed to a hotel which one can't afford—twenty thousand lire a night plus taxes—the smart English couple in the launch to the Lido talking about the party of the year this very night at Cipriani's, the awesome entry into Harry's Bar.

Now the whole place is "at risk" to use the new cliché, and the gondoliers, who have destroyed their livelihood through overcharging, are becoming as picturesquely obsolete as the hansom cabs outside the New York Plaza. "Ultimately," said the controller of public transport and communications, "the story of the gondola will end in failure because the gondola is linked with the future of Venice and Venice is dying."

One cannot read Mr. Holme's enjoyable book* without thinking of the terrifying TV programme on Venice which gave a picture of the deadly process that is destroying Venice and the chaotic indecision

* *Gondola, Gondolier,* by Timothy Holme (London, 1971).

about saving it. "Marghera pours in death," writes Mr. Holme, "and life flows out with the Venetians." For those who missed the film I should explain that Marghera is the industrial zone on the mainland, the creation of Count Volpi, which is now the eighth largest port on the Mediterranean and a maze of oil refineries. Enormous tankers draw up and special canals have to be cut for them which alter the levels of the lagoon, while floods submerge the Piazza through defects in the sea wall; the city itself is slowly sinking, damp rots the foundations, emigration is constant, pollution everywhere. Soon not a fish, not an eel, not a snail, not a worm will be left and barely the ghost of a scampo.

The municipality of Marghera thwarts all the drastic remedies put forward by the city council of Venice, itself divided, and only the scientists are left tackling the problem which they are powerless to remedy. Venice has dropped in population by 50,000 in ten years, the mainland industrial centres increased by 100,000.

Venice took shape as a violent evasive action against barbarian pressure from the mainland, its early culture was Byzantine, the situation turned it into a great naval power with a rich trade with the East. Intelligent dictatorship controlled its fortunes, squeezed between the Turks and the new Atlantic powers. Napoleon handed it to Austria, Italy rescued it.

Nothing of its original purpose survives today, it's all tourists and tankers, and even the fishing industry is now threatened. Meanwhile it remains a freak city, the only one in Europe to have remained basically unchanged for five hundred years; besides the unchanged eighteenth-century décor there is the unique water life which makes a profound appeal to every castaway from the amniotic fluid.

As Europe's most glamorous playground, and greatest testimony, with Florence, Rome, Vienna, Paris, to its own cultural heritage and so to the world's, it is unthinkable that it should be allowed to perish; it is worth a thousand Abu Simbels. The best parts of Bath or Salzburg or Nancy are but villages beside it, the effects of light alone are an earthly paradise.

So what is to be done?

Sun-girt City, thou hast been
Ocean's child, and then his queen;
Now is come a darker day
And thou soon must be his prey . . .
Sepulchres, where human forms
To the corpse of greatness cling
murdered and now mouldering . . .
—Shelley

The rot may have set in in 1881 with the "awful vaporetto" (Henry James) which sealed the fate of the gondolas, whose slow decline began with the abolition of the "felze," the coach-like compartment which permitted comfortable privacy and love-making. What the vaporetti could not accomplish the motor launches did, and now the Rio Nuovo is closed to gondolas whose main task is to ferry people across the *traghetto*.

Rapacious and slightly dishonest though many gondoliers are, they are still expert boatmen forced to depend on too short a season and to maintain their beautiful, specialised craft against ever-increasing wear and tear from the buffeting of backwash, steamers, launches, Shelley's "polluting multitude" and winter exposure through the high cost of garaging.

Mr. Holme, thank heaven, likes gondoliers much more than I do and has made an entertaining book out of them, sticking closely to his subject, which includes such gondoladdicts as Henry James, Mark Twain, Casanova, Hemingway and Corvo. But how can he have missed John Addington Symonds, prototype of all those who have given their hearts to the blue-breeched fraternity (Swinburne's adjective), or the description of the feast of the Redentore in L. P. Hartley's *Eustace and Hilda* trilogy, or any mention of Diaghilev, or the Princesse de Polignac in the heyday of Venetian life or the last owners of private gondolas, like Arturo Lopez or M. de Beistegui.

The Rio di Verona is the hardest for a gondolier to negotiate, and used for driving tests. The all-time champion of the regatta race is still active, the gondolier Albino dei Rossi at the ferry by the Gritti. There are three times as many launches as gondolas (450), the oldest gondoliers become "ganzers" who help us in and out over the water-steps; only two boat-builders remain in action, one at the Square of San Trovaso celebrated by Pound. The minimum fare is four thousand lire plus tip. They are the despair of travel agents who cater for tourists whose average stay is sixteen hours. "The large majority of Venetians would not dream of setting foot in their boats."

Maybe the gondolas won't disappear, but the gondola builder will. It's ten skills in one and that takes a lot of learning. But in the end you've got the greatest satisfaction in the world—turning unshaped wood into a gondola.

Mr. Holme concludes with a wonderful sentence of Henry James which he calls "the quintessence of Venice."

A narrow canal in the heart of the city—a patch of green water and a surface of pink wall. The gondola moves slowly; it gives a great smooth swerve, passes under a bridge, and the gondolier's cry, carried over the quiet water, makes a kind of splash in the stillness.

(1971)

WAGON-LIT

IF HAPPINESS, according to Freud, lies in the fulfilment of childhood wishes, one of mine must have been to become the conductor of a *Wagon-Lit*. I have always known the names and composition of the various European *trains de luxe* from the palmy days of the Orient Express and the poems of Larbaud's Barnabooth to their present sorry condition so well described by M. Paul Morand. But there are still people who enjoy travel for travel's sake, who want only to go and come back, and for them there still exists an indispensable mine of information. There used to be schoolmasters and dons who knew Bradshaw by heart, gourmets who knew all the starred restaurants in the guide Michelin. I commend a humbler aid. Cook's Continental Timetable.

It comes in modest guise priced ten and six; it appears monthly but is surprisingly hard to find and hardest of all on railway book-stalls; and it opens with Stop Press, a page of latest information: "Monte Carlo station will be closed from December 13 . . ." "The London-Paris service via Newhaven-Dieppe will operate through the present winter instead of being suspended as in previous years" (cheers); "The Bland line service between Gibraltar and Tangier will be suspended from November 3 to January 8 during alterations to the m.v. Mons Calpe (see Table 1413)." (Let's hope they don't spoil her.) Then follow the index, distances between stations, visa regulations and age limits for children's fares.

For an Albanian visa one must apply to the Albanian Legation in Paris. For the United Arab Republic "visas are seldom granted to persons of Jewish faith. Authors and journalists have to apply in person." Then come the Averages of Temperature, my favourite reading. One should always carry at the back of one's mind the names of all the nearest places with a high January temperature—let us say sixty degrees—Alexandria, Bahrein, Beirut, Biskra, Cairo, Casablanca, Jeddah and Khartoum (both seventy-five degrees), Madeira, Marrakesh, Las Palmas, Luxor, Malaga and Alicante, while Gibraltar and Tangier just scrape by. And the coolest places in summer? Reykjavik and Tromsö.

Now for the crack trains. These are of three kinds: the old and famous international expresses, the new trans-Europe diesels, and the car-sleepers. The car-sleepers are a new departure, more useful than glamorous, I feel, and I have not heard enthusiasm expressed for the meals, if any, on such trains, but their routes show foresight and originality. By taking the car-ferry and then the car-sleepers Boulogne-Milan and Milan-Brindisi and then the car-ferry to Greece one should be able to get nearly all the way to Athens *without getting into one's car!* Wonderful—and think of the saving in petrol.

When we turn to the *trains de luxe* the picture is less happy. The *"luxe"* is too often confined to a single sleeping-car shunted about amid hordes of milling passengers. It is of course a matter of temperament. Some poetic natures sleep better for the thought of all the cramped neighbours on either side "without their advantages," others like to be accompanied by snoring millionaires from end to end. Three *trains de luxe* carry first-class only, the Talgo, the Rheingold, and the Sud Express (French section); only these compare with certain crack trains in Italy, like the Settebello, and Germany or with our own Pullman expresses.

The Sud Express is a delicious experience. [Alas no longer.] It leaves at a quarter to two, giving one a long morning in Paris, serves an excellent lunch, has two comfortable Pullmans and the first stop is Bordeaux. The Spanish train has some of the new air-conditioned sleepers. I have had so many happy journeys on the Sud Express, especially when it used to leave from the Quai d'Orsay, that it remains my favourite train. One does not experience the South so brutally as on the Blue Train or the Rome Express, but it is more subtle from the moment when the first names in "ac" appear, followed by the tunnel under Angoulème and the crossing of the great rivers, the Dordogne at Libourne and the Garonne at Bordeaux to the Adour at Bayonne and the view of the Pyrenees. Bordeaux now boasts several sky-scrapers and the Chapon Fin is shorn of its glories, but it is still a city worth arriving at, undisturbed in its dignified eighteenth-century core and with the same green-gold light as Venice.

I have never been on the Rheingold; it must be the most luxurious international express, with a "vista-dome" car from Dortmund to Basle, and, I suspect, very good food. To enjoy it one must take the night-boat from Harwich, a deterrent in winter. My plan, around May or June, is to do this and rush up the Rhine by the Rheingold (its twin the Rhein Arrow goes off to Munich), returning from Basle by boat. Here the choice is very difficult. British, Dutch, German and Swiss lines are all in competition.

The trans-Europe expresses are a different matter. They belong to our time as much as a Mini-Cooper. "Fast day services by luxury diesel or electric train between important European cities . . . Prior reservation is obligatory." There are only a dozen of these trains and the seating is more like that of an aeroplane. There is no room for heavy luggage, the trains whizz along knocking hours off the ordinary runs; some of them have good food, others tend to add more and more carriages and become commonplace. Top marks to the Gottardo (Milan-Zurich with stops at Lugano and Como)—the maître d'hôtel wears a frock-coat and, with waitresses, serves elaborate à la carte meals—and to the Arbalète (Zurich-Paris) which connects with Paris-London in summer. They run also from Paris-Milan and Marseille-Milan with a new one from Geneva to Marseille, and are comparable only to such trains as the Mistral (Paris-Nice). Milan, in fact, is the capital for the train-lover.

One of the beauties of this Cook's guide is that it enables one to arrange elaborate combinations of train and boat, making use of the steamship time-tables for North Sea and Mediterranean. The day train to Paris, the business man's sleeper train to Marseille, a day in the Vieux Port and the boat to Majorca (very comfortable) in the afternoon—this was the fruit of these consultations when the Barcelona route was very crowded. Some of the lesser-known trains have the true vintage sleepers, full of beautifully polished wood rather than the modern metal hutches.

The pleasure of a *Wagon-Lit* is in its womb-like protection from the rest of the world, and also in the sensation of deference and luxury. One must be grateful to the ineradicable feelings of childhood insecurity which have made one a snob about travel as about so much else. When one bids good night to the man in brown, reads in bed by the blue veilleuse, hangs an imaginary watch in the watch-pocket and goes to sleep lulled by the wheels and the distant incantation—Frasne, Vallorbe or the lugubrious "Mulhouse"—one is SAFE AT LAST.

J'ai senti pour la première fois toute la douceur de vivre
Dans une cabine du Nord Express . . .

—Larbaud

If we have a well-developed sense of flight, it is a good thing to know what sleepers we can get on most easily. There is always the night-ferry at nine p.m., but I much prefer the two-thirty from Victoria which links at Calais with two sleepers, the Arlberg Express (Calais-Vienna) or the Direct-Orient via Paris, Lausanne, Milan. This is the more preferable. The Rome Express links with the earlier Golden Arrow—still the pleasantest way of leaving England.

Are there any hotels which compensate for the pain of being ejected from one's sleeper? They manifestly have to be even more luxurious. I would recommend the Beau Rivage at Lausanne-Ouchy (leaving the capsule of the Calais-Orient Express sleeper at seven in the morning) or, in high summer, Suvretta House, St. Moritz, via one of the several night expresses converging at Coire. It has some round rooms like the Schweitzerhof in Zurich and a round room—I can't think why—helps to break the fall.

Bon Voyage.

(1965)

LEPTIS MAGNA

THE PUBLISHERS are to be congratulated on this handsome book* which is too good—i.e., too specialised—for the coffee-table. If only it had come out some weeks earlier when I could have read it a few days before visiting Leptis instead of a month after. The desire to see Leptis had grown since reading the chapter in Berenson's *The Passionate Sightseer*. Although there are some fine photographs in *Roman Africa in Colour* (Thames and Hudson) the text is somewhat cursory. In fact, the bibliography of Leptis is astonishingly short and much of it confined to articles in learned journals.

Now at last we have a good team: introduction by the Professor of Archaeology at the University of Rome, Ranuccio Bandinelli, descriptive texts by the late Ernesto Caffarelli, Superintendent of Antiquities in Tripolitania, and Giacomo Caputo (who worked on the reconstruction of the theatre), and 230 excellent photographs by Fabrizio Clerici, who is also an architect. The result is not just a book for those who wonder what Leptis is like but indispensable for those who are determined to go there. And all passionate sightseers ought to go there, for Leptis is one of the wonders of the world.

It is a place of magical evocative beauty, a wilderness of golden columns in a large, lonely landscape by an indigo sea which breaks over the ruined Roman lighthouse and the mosaic pavements—a wilderness which archaeologists are restoring to order, removing sand, planting shrubberies to bind the dunes, uncovering statues, columns, streets, whole buildings from the great capital which around the year A.D. 200 the Emperor Septimus Severus created out of his home town.

* *The Buried City. Excavation at Leptis Magna,* by Giacomo Caputo and Ernesto Caffarelli (London, 1966).

Septimus was one of the army-chosen Emperors, who succeeded to the throne of the Antonines and gave the Empire another twenty years of good government. He was from Africa, but not African, and died at York in 211, being succeeded by his son Caracalla, who murdered his brother and father-in-law but carried on the splendid building programme. The lighthouse depicted in the arch of Severus at Rome may be an allusion to that of Leptis, whose quays and temples came down to the water like the Piazzetta in Venice. To Severus belongs the triumphal arch, "one of the most important monuments in Roman sculpture," and the superb Basilica (completed by Caracalla and converted into a Christian church by Justinian) with its pink columns and exquisitely carved pilasters with the exploits of the two patron gods, Hercules and Dionysus, in panels, like carved ivory.

How can one give an idea of this wonderful place? It is enormous. There are clumps of ruins as far as the eye can see, and the ruins are very solid, with shops and staircases and unfamiliar forms; the round colonnaded pavilions of the Market, the little domes of the Hunting Baths, "authentic examples of the connection between Arabic architecture (marabouts, mosques and baths) and Roman architecture through the catalyst of the Byzantine experience"—and between the ruins, miles of aromatic undergrowth.

And solitude! No guides, no tourists, no coaches, no barbed wire —one starts off down the triumphal avenue and becomes the only possessor of the limestone city, until groups of workmen bob up behind a temple wall. For work is still going on and the "new excavations" are in progress. They include the Circus, Amphitheatre and the so-called "Rotunda of Justinian" near the old Forum, "a last architectural masterpiece" before the sands finally covered the city.

> When Leptis Magna is completely restored with colonnades set up again and the forum cleared, it will be a most exceptional sight, and the work of scholars will be made much easier. The streets in general have retained their ancient impressiveness . . .

Who knows what statues, mosaics, palaces remain to be discovered? Or what unexpected architectural embellishments? For, unlike so many Roman remains in Africa, there is nothing provincial about Leptis. Many of the masons were Greek; after Carthage the city was the largest in all Africa, marble was commoner than brick, the avant-garde ideas of the third century were tried out here.

> Sculpture became pictorial and shapes were accentuated by deeply cut lines to suggest shadows, thus emphasising the contrast between light and dark . . . For the first time in the history of art a taste for colour prevailed over

a taste for plastic or linear shapes (A.D. 180–190). Here was a complex world that sought a tormented form of expression, for it was a tormented world, a society widely different from the far-off classical and Hellenistic life . . .

So rich a city, of course, imported columns and statues and perhaps capitals already carved. Fortunately Leptis was not submitted to much traffic in the opposite direction. Louis XIV took the most. Some of its columns were used for the altars of Rouen Cathedral and St. Germain des Près, and a British Consul, Captain Smith, despatched columns and inscriptions to London around 1836 which are now at Windsor Castle. (Some of these columns grace the shores of Virginia Water.) Have they been collated with the inscriptions *in situ?* The poetry of the scene is well described by Professor Bandinelli (admirably served by the translator—Mr. David Ridgway).

The wind buffets the jetty, with its ruins stretching along the promontory to the lighthouse, and the line of great lonely capitals lying mysteriously along the sea's edge. There is a freshness as one wanders in the shadows among the gigantic blocks of the lighthouse, moving first on flights of steps and then from one great stone to another, while in the cave-like depths below, the sea thunders and breaks in flying spray.

I have not even mentioned the two conventional masterpieces of the city—the Hadrianic Baths, among the largest in the Roman world, with their swimming-pools and lavatories and their copies of Greek statues, and the Theatre, which dates from Augustus, itself worth the journey if nothing else existed.*

Leptis has an equable climate all the year round, the heat being tempered by sea breezes. It is seventy-five miles from Tripoli, which lies

* Sabratha one should see before Leptis. It is just that much less extraordinary. On the Baths is the motto "Enjoy your dip"; in the museum is the admirably displayed peacock mosaic from Justinian's church (praised by Procopius), finer than any single object at Leptis, while the theatre there has been daringly and successfully restored or rather re-erected by the Italians (1930–37) and by now the Temple of Isis mentioned by Apuleius in *The Golden Ass* is arising again by the sea. Sabratha lacked an imperial patron like the Emperor Severus at Leptis but the smaller city witnessed an extraordinary scene: the trial of Apuleius for witchcraft in A.D. 157 of which he was accused by his wife's family who wanted to recover her dowry. He was acquitted and his defence or Apologia survives.

The gem remains the Theatre at Leptis. Here one can sit high up looking out to sea till the carapace of urban anxiety cracks to admit the carefree happiness of the pagan world. "Hours and days, and months and years go by; the past returns no more, and what is to be we cannot know; but whatever the time gives us in which to live, we should therefore be content." Cicero.

on a main air route. It should be made just as easy to get there as to Gibraltar or Djerba and we could then all benefit by a week of winter sun and a liberating visit to this Pompeii of the future.

(1966)

THE FLAWED DIAMOND

My motive for flying to South Africa was strictly personal—to visit my mother. I had always been unwilling to go there before for political reasons, as I imagined I would find myself plunged into an atmosphere of injustice and tyranny. South Africa is indeed one of the most political countries in the world; everyone is obsessed with politics which means for them the rights and wrongs of Apartheid, and as freedom of speech is unrestricted one hears so much about the Topic that one comes almost to dread it. Injustice and tyranny do exist, but they are incessantly debated and one soon feels rather a hypocrite to have arrived with such prejudged conclusions.

Ten years ago John Gunther summed up on South Africa: "Is it a police State? Not quite, not yet," and one can still say this today, though things are worse, not better. (Gunther assumed, for example, that the fear of leaving the Commonwealth was an important moderating factor.) The police state, which means government by the Special Branch through the harsh laws made for their convenience, exists and continues to encroach on the areas of freedom. But a free press, a parliamentary Opposition, an impartial judiciary and active Anglican, Methodist and Roman Catholic churches also continue to oppose it, backed up by many sections of the public, especially teachers, lawyers, students and many professional and business men.

The government, unfortunately, is well aware of this and is constantly devising new action. Press censorship is on its way in and the reporting of subversive activities is becoming more and more hedged about by regulations. An indiscreet cable may land one in gaol. A new distribution of seats has made it harder, if not impossible, for the Opposition parties to win an election. The harshest laws, such as the Ninety Days Clause, are applied independently of the judiciary, and some of the ablest defence lawyers who are not South African citizens are being forbidden to practise.

The government is waging two wars at once, one against Communism and all those who seek to free the eleven million Africans from the moral implications and political restrictions of Apartheid, the other against the British and the settlers of British origin (about forty-five per cent of the white population) who were once all-powerful.

Both these wars are undeclared, and the second would be hotly denied, but the fact remains that non-Afrikaners have less and less chance of entering the government or of reaching a high position in the armed forces or of controlling communications or of dictating policy.

I was constantly reminded of the Anglo-Irish minority in Ireland, with Dr. Verwoerd as De Valera. This refighting of the Boer War comes into the open at election time, but the process of renaming streets with Afrikaner names, the increasing predominance of the Afrikaner language, the playing-down of British achievements, the educational rivalry, and the electoral jockeying for position all point in this direction. "Poor whites" mostly of non-British descent receive many favours and their vote can be depended on.

(The referendum on the Republic, October 1960, showed 850,458 for and 775,878 against. The majority would now be larger.)

A considerable element of British stock accepts this situation and even votes Nationalist: they approve of the government—"This country needs a strong government: it has got one"—in the same way as the Ascendancy made the best of De Valera, partly out of expediency, partly out of patriotism. They share the mixture of contempt with affection for the Africans and willingly accept Apartheid, although they lack the guilty sexual feelings of the Afrikaner. This attitude, reinforced by the influx from East Africa and the Rhodesias and even by the new settlers from Britain, greatly weakens the Opposition forces who derive more strength from the liberal Jewish business and professional men of Capetown and Johannesburg than from the descendants of Pym and Hampden.

All boycotts, of course, unite the governors with the governed; since leaving the Commonwealth the Republic has made it harder for the British-born to keep two passports and shuttle between their two countries; eventually, like the Afrikaners, they will have nowhere else to go, and they are paying for many an unconscious snub inflicted in the heyday of their superiority.

And what are these Afrikaners like? Certainly not like De Valera. They are Africa's Orangemen; logical, courageous, efficient, members of a narrow religious community, the Dutch Reformed Church, with a strong Old Testament-cum-Calvinist outlook, intensely patriotic, convinced that they are right, many of them members of a hard-core secret society, the Bruderbond, which is pledged to eliminate all rival power groups, and above all, convinced that the land belongs to them, that the empty "heartlands" of the High Veld discovered by their ancestors the Voortrekkers, and the lower plateaus of the Karoos, are theirs inalienably. Many of them consider Dr. Verwoerd a dangerous visionary. They are also warm-hearted and sensitive, with a biting, rather pawky, sense of humour and the open good manners of a traditionally hospitable country.

I liked all those I met very much; they are less materialistic than some of the British, and their bilingualism makes them seem more continental. They are open to reason and argument up to a point though convinced on moral or religious grounds that planned segregation is best for the natives as well as themselves. Paternalism reigns supreme.

At present South Africa is enjoying a boom and the visitor who arrives full of righteous indignation is deafened by the clatter of bulldozers and falling masonry as more and more sky-scrapers go up. Everything breathes expansion and prosperity, encouraged by restriction on the export of capital and the urge to be independent of any future boycott. They consequently view our coming election with passionate interest.

"You suffer from a psychological fallacy," an apologist told me. "You think that because you wouldn't like Apartheid yourself the Africans suffer in the same way. They don't. They all want to make money; the man wants a bicycle and the wife a sewing machine and they know this is one of the only places where they can earn them. They are perfectly prepared to accept our conditions if they can get our wages, which is why a million more have entered the country to work here over the last four years. Our problem is how to control the enormous rush to the towns, and deal with this huge urban African population who have severed their tribal connections and include typical gangster elements. What would America be like if the blacks were in relation to the whites of four to one?" (1960 census: total 16 million. Whites 3,088,000; Coloured, 1,500,000; Asiatic 500,000; Bantu, 11 million.)

South Africa is indeed a country where the African can make enough money in a few years to retire to his tribal homeland, if he has one, and doubtless many are prepared to sacrifice political freedom for economic security. But those who struggle to reach the educated fringe, who wish to enter the professions or own property, or become skilled craftsmen, come up against Apartheid. They seek a name and are given a number. "It is practically impossible," a leading industrialist told me, "for an

African, however well-intentioned, not at some time or other to have to go to prison."

The over-all situation is fundamentally tragic because there is no apparent solution. The energetic white minority, with the aid of the cheap black labour force, have built up South Africa into one of the most prosperous countries in the world, economically and strategically viable, yet the atmosphere is one of increasing tension and mistrust.

The Africans have still retained their good-nature, and by no means yet regard the white man as their enemy, but their very numbers generate the anxiety which leads to repressive measures against them and so diminishes this goodwill until the whites have indeed cause for fear.

A multi-racial society here must mean a society in which the whites are politically dominated by the blacks and can no longer settle them in reserves which are never large enough or dole out minimum wages. The whites would have to give up the industry and agriculture, everything their ancestors had conquered over the last three hundred years by endurance, foresight, sheer hard work and bloody battles, and many would rather die fighting. For this reason partition is sometimes mentioned as a desperate measure, that is, the division of the country into two or three completely separate nations, the whites keeping their ancestral heartlands from the Cape to Pretoria, the Cape Coloureds throwing in their lot with them, and the Bantu taking over most of the low-lying East Coast from the Transkei to Zululand, leaving our Durban. This again reserves all the meat on the bone for the whites and would lead to more strife. The Republic as it stands is a geographical entity.

The liberal solution would be to abolish Apartheid and then immediately set about building a multi-racial community in which the assets of still-existing goodwill could be unfrozen, even though large material sacrifices would have to be made. The increasing technical delicacy of so much skilled work performed by Africans in an expanding industry may lead in any case to a gradual break-down of Apartheid. Meanwhile the present strong-arm policy is morally wrong and scientifically false because it is based on imaginary assumptions of racial superiority and so is bound to fail. "Not while we are in power to enforce it," reply the Nationalists. "Once we give in about anything the whole battle is lost—and don't forget it is a battle for mutual respect. We don't want another Zanzibar!"

And the speaker will proceed to enumerate some of the many health and education services enacted for the Bantu, the housing schemes in the new townships, the progress to self-government in the Transkei. He will do, in fact, everything for the native except shake hands with him.

"That leads to miscegenation," as one minister explained. (I heard of only one person who refused to shake hands with me, though there may have been many—a prominent Afrikaner poet who told his prospective hostess that no good purpose would be served by his meeting someone to whom he was completely opposed politically.) "Communist," "liberalist," "Leftist," "libertine," "intellectual," "sentimentalist" are common terms of denunciation, and from time to time new lists of Communists are published—many of them students who have attended a few political rallies—after which their friends drop away and employment becomes difficult.

As in a bad public school a whole series of gruesome penalties is imposed on the politically suspect; beginning with an official warning, raids by the Special Branch, banishment to remote localities (Luthuli), confinement to certain areas, house arrest, curfews, bans by which they cannot publish or be quoted or foregather with more than one person at a time or go to their place of work; or they must give up their passport (Alan Paton) or find their mail withheld and telephone tapped. Worst of all is the intolerable Ninety Days Clause, by which the police can arrest clandestinely and keep suspects in solitary confinement unable to communicate with the outside world for one or several periods of ninety days while they question them. There is evidence that some of the few hundred detainees (though no white ones) have been given electric shock tortures as practised in Algeria, and the solitary Progressive party M.P. (corresponding to our Liberal Party), Mrs. Suzman, made a gallant and lonely protest in Parliament last February against what she called Gestapo methods, while doctors have corroborated her evidence and been supported by the Press. The Bloemfontein sentence on three policemen for murdering a suspected petty thief has just brought this into the open.

"You did exactly the same in war-time: look at 18b or your treatment of spies and IRA gunmen or your interrogation of captured airmen."

"Then you are at war?"

"At war with Communism, yes—we are actually fighting the Cold War; you talk it. Our gold and diamonds, our copper and uranium are coveted by all the Iron Curtain nations and they smuggle in trained saboteurs to stir up trouble. Our job is to anticipate them."

The Year Book, 1964, says: "Marriage between European and non-European is illegal and sex-relations between European and non-European is an offence involving imprisonment. For a comprehensive understanding of this policy the Promotion of Bantu Self-Government Act should be consulted." This leads to a new set of troubles for some who have not consulted it and also gives scope to informers and *agents provocateurs,* since differences of colour are not always as apparent as the Act implies. The Act, indeed, reveals the sexual ambivalence behind Apartheid: prominent Afrikaners were among the first victims.

There is a small but persistent exodus of intellectuals, liberalists, sentimentalists and libertines who have fled to escape imprisonment and who swell the ranks of political exiles. They often become extremely homesick. For there is plenty to be homesick about: it would not be a tragic country if it were not also a beautiful country, a flawed diamond.

When one arrives by air, the morning after shedding the grey cerements of the English winter, we travel for hours over the wilderness of Southern Angola and Bechuanaland, a cracked and parched desert covered by wormy meanders of dried watercourses. Suddenly there is green grass, and a forest of sky-scrapers rises into the air; a great city, the only great city in Africa except Cairo, thrusting forward towards the northern emptiness with its large bustling airport, its fleet of parked cars, its keen air, its incandescent summer light on the bright gaudy flowers and widow-birds hovering in the long grass, their tails like floating pieces of crêpe—Johannesburg.

My first Africans in shabby European clothes, with agreeable southern accents, were smiling and laughing; the drive into the town led past many delicious gardens bright with oleander and bougainvillaea, by little Indian houses like cricket pavilions, even a game of cricket on an oak-shaded lawn, then into the large wide streets of the city, often compared to Dallas, with the hotel in a street lined with young plane trees—like Aix or Salon.

It was on my way back to the airport in the evening that my African driver pointed out what looked like a field of smouldering petrol cans in a fold of the earth, actually a native Bidonville cooking its evening meal. It is a thousand miles from Johannesburg to Capetown, and it was a bumpy flight. I wished I had taken the luxurious Blue Train. When I arrived the terrible south-easter was blowing, a cross between the mistral and an English Atlantic gale. My first glimpse of Capetown was an eddy of torn newspapers on the corner of Adderley Street.

The most important single fact about Capetown is that it is habitable. It is a beautiful city (it could be much more beautiful); it is surrounded by the whitest of beaches, ornamented with charming suburbs, bisected by a superb mountain. Though on the same latitude as Rabat, it contrives to be far more subtropical; strange flowers and trees bloom in abundance, the unique silver-tree, the proteas and lilies, the dapper yet languorous frangipani, while the ubiquitous Norfolk Island pine and Canary palm proclaim that this is a completely Mediterranean climate with winter rainfall and no frost.

It is a climate that seems divinely intended to counterpoint our own. The shortest day is in June, the longest in December; the bad months, July and August, are those when we are least likely to go there; the long autumns and warm springs (Rabat-fashion) are a botanical delight. The sea provides soles, crawfish and kingclip meunière, the drier wines are very drinkable and there is a good mineral water, fruit of all kinds is abundant (muscats sixpence a pound), and tea is served about five times a day.

Below the Mount Nelson Hotel with its palm-fringed swimming-pool (one must go to Lourenço Marques to find another) are the public gardens, some of the best of their kind (more tea, please), and the dignified public buildings—Government House, museums, law courts, Houses of Parliament. Then comes the "down-town" region of banks and shops and theatres and offices flanked on one side by the old Malay quarter and on the other by the Soho-like "Sixth District."

At the bottom is the harbour, too artificial to be intimate, and the "tallest building in South Africa," while Table Mountain frames the city from behind, permitting the old residential quarters to creep up its wooded slopes. There are many historical monuments and a chain of eighteenth-century Dutch houses either just outside or in more unspoilt small towns like Stellenbosch, Somerset West and Paarl.

One is drawn irresistibly to the Cape Peninsula. On the Atlantic side runs a corniche road which, passing through Sea Point and Clifton, gradually takes to the mountain, past a series of dazzling white beaches and a rather severe Mediterranean landscape (this is the colder aspect), where huge breakers foam over the sands, and aloes and heaths and umbrella-pines abound. On the east side the sea is ten degrees warmer and the mountain curves in to enclose the pine-woods of Tokai, the vineyards of Constantia, and the marvellous botanical garden of Kirstenbosch.

Both roads unite before the long tip of the peninsula: the Cape of Good Hope wild-life sanctuary. This was my first introduction to the world of the animals which was later to play such a large part in my visit, and like many of these kingdoms it was guarded by baboons who appear before one's car like the suspicious customs officers of some newly liberated state.

These proved the only wild life we were to see, but the landscape made up; ashy blue moorland with green drifts and brown tips of rushes fading to distant peaks and the sea breaking far below among boulders and cormorants. The director, Ernest Middlemiss, took me back to his other sanctuary, a small reed-fringed lake, Rondevlei, fenced off from African townships on the Cape Flats and still the home of a hundred flamingoes, a hundred pelicans, and many more herons. I liked this man who could write: "For five years a cobra has occupied the territory in front of my house and has grown considerably from about twenty-four inches when it was first seen."

I soon found I had at least four obsessions: elephants, snakes, sharks and bilharzia. This last disease I had come across in Egypt (where it is found even in mummies), but it is spreading now over the whole of Africa, the liver fluke being carried by snails and some animals as well as by natives, so that it is now unsafe to bathe in any stream flowing eastwards into the Indian Ocean. Fifteen seconds' immersion is enough for the parasite to penetrate the skin.

I never saw a snake outside captivity but became a repository for harrowing snake stories. The Cape possesses some of the most venomous in the world, the Cape cobra, the puff adder, the spitting cobra and the boomslang or tree snake—"a quiet trusting snake which will pass within inches of one" according to Mr. Middlemiss—while the sluggish puff adder is easily trodden on and turns aggressive in the mating season.

I have said that the light in South Africa is particularly beautiful. It replaces architecture and produces greens and blues and far horizons so bright and luminous as to seem incredible, that liberate the accumulated well-being of remembered summers.

My next visit was to George, famous for its climate; it took me to some of the most enchanting scenery in the world. The Outeniqua Mountains, five thousand feet high, covered with green scrub on their seaward side, descend to a broad plateau where everything from apples to avocados flourish. The pine forests and granite peaks behind look like Aviemore or Pitlochry transfigured in the marvellous light, but a few hundred feet below the Indian Ocean breaks on vast beaches beside a chain of subtropical lagoons. George is like Tenterden rebuilt after a fire. There is an expression, "the Outeniqua rust," for the gradual failure of will which is said to oppress those confined by the rainy, mountain-shielded landscape of George, or the beaches of Wilderness and the inland sea of Knysna; certainly the outer world does indeed grow painfully remote, as if, listening to the metallic *ku-kooroo* of the Cape doves or the night trains hooting like lost souls, one is trussed and gagged in a gangster's cupboard. Homesickness for England is worst, I am told, in April, when the leaves are falling. Yet, in fact, the area is thriving, with a strong British influence, an Anglican cathedral and bishop, lawyers and doctors, an excellent golf course, Marbella-like beach-houses and (unworried by the urban tensions) a warm-hearted retired British colony (bridge, sailing, riding, bowls, bird-watching, amateur theatricals).

Along the coast is a chain of indigenous forests now sadly reduced but still containing some of the tallest trees in Africa, millennial yellow-wood and fragrant stinkwood—a unique evergreen landscape now the domain of a once formidable herd of elephant.

The Elephants of Knysna! How to explain their hold on my imagination? That these, reputed to be the largest of their kind, thirteen or fourteen feet high at the shoulder, should exist so near to the rose-gardens and club-houses in a vegetation not unlike the wet side of Tangier . . . And then the contradictory stories of their numbers, which shrank as one got closer to them, and the sadness of all things doomed to extinction—of the Lacandones or the Australian aborigines or the mediatised princes of the Almanach de Gotha. "Said to consist of two herds, one of five, one of three and a rogue. There is a calf, and the cow killed a coloured boy who got between them a few months ago." Mrs. D. saw one "as big as a pantechnicon."

"One night they hauled all the fishing boats up the bank." "A forester once heard them trumpeting all night and saw them going round and round a dead calf which they covered with branches." "They ate a thousand pounds worth of apples on a fruit farm last week." In 1883 the "whole area is infested with elephants. One spends all one's time up a tree or else running to find one." Now probably not more than eight after the massacre by Major Pretorius in 1920. They include two very old bulls, one of which lost a tusk when overturning a Massey-Harris tractor. Last birth, 1956.

Finally, I was introduced to Mr. Hjalmar Thesen, of the timber firm of Knysna, who had actually seen three and taken their picture within the last year. "Only his trunk moved from time to time, and the only sound was the deep sighing of his breath," he writes. "I took one last photograph as his ears began the outward spread of warning, then the screaming peal of trumpeting seemed to shake the forest and I ran as I have seldom run before."

Mr. Thesen thinks there are only seven; four bulls (two very old), two cows, and a half-grown calf. "No new calves whatever they tell you," added a forester. "The herd is doomed to extinction unless new blood is added."

The Thesens' head forester, Mr. Roelovse, drove me into the woods and we started to walk in the thickest part of the evergreen Deepwalls forest, with its brown pools and shafts of sunlight between the 150-foot-high trunks, the whole forest ringing like a flicked bowl from the invisible chorus of wild bees and the occasional notes of an oriole or fly-catcher. He showed me a bank of dry earth rubbed clean by an elephant taking a skin-bath and two big trees, one scarred by the elephant's mud up to fourteen feet, both felled to provide a few mouthfuls of mistletoe (a great delicacy). "They are fantastically strong," he said, "but this one must have worked here all night. What a way to earn one's living."

Another happy dedicated man. "You will never find a forester with ulcers!"

I also saw their huge crater-like hoof-marks and their circular droppings.

"That one is sick."

"I don't see how anyone chased by an elephant ever manages to climb these trees."

"Fear lends you wings, Mr. Connolly; it is coming down that is difficult."

I was much taken with a page of the Johannesburg *Sunday Times* which seemed typical of South Africa. At the top was an article on some newly named Communists, with their pictures—one was a pretty young art student—while below was a large photograph of an elephant looking somewhat raffish, with a caption to explain that it was tipsy on the fruit of the marula tree and had knocked a railway worker, also drunk on marula beer, off his bicycle which it had then destroyed. Severity to the subversive, indulgence for the alcoholic—the old story.

The elephants gulp down the fallen fruit which ferments in their stomachs and provides a built-in cocktail cabinet for several weeks: this fact was corroborated by Mr. P. Van der Merwe, liaison officer in Pretoria for the parks and also editor of *Koedoe* (Kudu), the journal for scientific research in the national parks which became my favourite reading.

To Mr. Van der Merwe I made my usual plea for the free-roaming Knysna elephants, the nearest to the South Pole. "Yes, they are very important," he said. "True, there are only eight, but the cows are in good condition—though the bulls are not too good."

The herd is safe for forty years, he claimed, and in ten to fifteen it would be possible to import new blood and fence them in, perhaps in the new reserve to be made in the Tsisikama Forest. Fencing is essential; it keeps out poachers and satisfies the farmers, who think game spreads foot-and-mouth disease. Human beings come first—only they know enough to regulate the ecology, to decide when predators are doing too much damage or when the large animals like elephants and hippos are destroying their own habitat.

More important even than fencing, he went on, is research, especially into breeding habits, food chains and diseases. Here the biggest advance is the pumping of drugs and tranquillisers into large animals by darts—which enables them to be transplanted to suitable localities (e.g., hippos to Addo)—and the revival of game-farming or of stocking game on farms, by which something of the old Africa is coming back into being.

Now I was ready to leave for the Kruger Park with Grant Purvis as my guide, an old acquaintance in the Consular Service who was taking a few days' holiday.

We drove out of Johannesburg in the early morning, past the skyscrapers and golden mine-dumps, over the dull ranching country of the High Veld—Salisbury Plain in a heat-wave—then through the coalfields; and suddenly over the edge of the plateau into the dramatic Schoemanscloof, a long valley with limestone cliffs on either side and woods blazing in a forest fire and the usual incandescent light on cypresses and orange orchards, the first exotic trees and creepers. We lunched at White River and reached the next escarpment a few miles later. Beneath us the Low Veld lay extended like an infinite New Forest, the trees spread widely with grass in between and occasional rocky knolls streaking out to the blue haze of the Lebombo Hills, the frontier of Mozambique.

As far as we could see stretched the Kruger Park or the adjoining game farms, and soon we were signing in at the Numbi Gate. The park is more than seven thousand square miles, larger than Wales or Palestine: it runs north and south from the Limpopo (inside the tropics) for some three hundred miles, crossing several large rivers and enclosing many different zones of vegetation. It contains about a dozen rest camps and a network of roads. The tourist is not allowed to leave his car or exceed twenty-five miles an hour or be out at night, though he can sit in his car as long as he likes and visit several hippo pools on foot. A system of fines extends to all infringements of these rules, which are devised for the tourist's safety. It is also forbidden to feed animals, as it may start quarrels; lately hyenas and ground hornbills have taken to begging.

The game, protected now for forty years, accepts the car with amiable indifference. A game fence round three sides of the park prevents poachers getting in or animals being enticed to the neighbouring game farms. Tourists spent £187,000 in the park in 1963, much of which was ploughed back in maintenance, research, the provision of more waterholes and food-plants, roads, camps, staff and other improvements, besides keeping at bay the farmers and land-hungry.

The reward is one of the wonders of the world—something quite unlike anywhere else, for so many smaller national parks are now fighting a losing battle.

There are more than 400 kinds of birds in the park and 1,400 trees and plants—and it is forbidden to pluck a single flower. The car-system gives the fauna complete privacy when away from the roads, while three-quarters of the park is closed to the public in summer.

Round the first corner we came on impala, the gazelle-like antelope which can jump thirty feet and which provides the general meal-ticket; next, blue wildebeest, baboons and kudu. Then a siesta in our rondavels at Pretoriuskop, the coolest camp in the park.

At sunset we went for another drive and saw only two jackals, but a strange pungent cloying smell and a pile of small pear-shaped fruit on the red earth proclaimed the marula tree. I tasted some and found them refreshing, with a flavour of their own, a little like kvass; later on we found marula jelly served with ancient mutton at dinner. (Meals in the park are so dull that I wonder if the chef is an ungulate.) The lights are turned out at half-past ten and I lay awake with a new phobia—a mamba in my lavatory.

The next morning we set off early for Skukuza, capital of the park, meeting our first zebra and giraffe. To quote Julian Huxley:

> To see large animals going about their own natural business in their own natural way, assured and unafraid, is one of the most exciting and moving experiences in the world, comparable with the sight of a noble building or the hearing of a great symphony or Mass.

There is more to it than that; a reconciliation, perhaps, with this estranged archetypal world of our childhood that everywhere else has been destroyed, a sense of harmony and reparation, a feeling that everything in the animals' Eden is wisely ordered for their good, that the most hideous crocodile is protected, even cherished, and that this is one of the few places in the world where nothing is going to be allowed to go wrong.

I had a long talk that day with the chief warden and nature conservator, a bronzed young Zeus, Mr. Brynhardt. Only research and tourists, he said, can keep a park going. If there weren't enough tourists there wouldn't be enough revenue to protect the animals from poachers or farmers, and industrialists who demand the land. I asked him what his three wishes for the Kruger would be. First, he said, the removal of the unfenced railway which runs through the south-west corner of the park and serves the new phosphate mine at Phalaborwa. The trains have increased to six a day and will eventually rise to thirty-five, dividing the park into two. Nine buffalo, two giraffe, three zebra, twenty-one animals in all, had been killed on the line in a month. Secondly, he would like the western frontiers extended to take in the old game lands. Third wish—to see the tourists observe the speed limit.

His best news is that white rhinoceros are being reintroduced into their old haunts in the park at the rate of two a week (up to thirty-four); eventually the black rhino will be added and the park will be complete as far as the larger and rarer mammals are concerned. Elephant and hippo may one day have to be thinned out as they are reaching saturation (1,750 elephant at present). Only the delicate roan and oribi antelopes are not increasing.

"And the Knysna elephants?" "They are too few to be saved and, besides, the farmers don't like them. They are doomed because nobody *sees* them."

I asked Mr. Brynhardt in what respect, if any, he felt the Kruger to be superior to all other parks. "In the harmony achieved between tourist, animal and ranger," he replied, "and in the combination of comfort and discipline in the camps." And one might add, in Mr. Pienaar, the resident biologist, and his laboratory.

Mr. Brynhardt was worried about the threat to the Etosha Pan. This lies in the north of South-West Africa, a truly vast area amounting to 37,000 square miles, the largest game reserve in the world and forming a reservoir for most of the game of the Western Rhodesias and Southern Angola in time of drought. The Pan is the only water for these vast herds in summer, and the area is made so large to ensure their protection on their journey.

Under the new Odendaal scheme for South-West Africa the South African government is to turn four-fifths of this land over to 200,000 protein-hungry Ovambos. Some 3,500 elephants will have to be killed and innumerable eland, and the reserve confined to the Pan itself which the game, however, will never be allowed to reach. This is surely a case for the World Wild Life Fund, an animal Abu Simbel.

I was loath to leave the Kruger, and even now I am haunted by the sights and sounds of this earthly paradise; the anticipation of a new face round every corner; the red roads mottled by elephant-pats; the sudden fragrance of the marula fruit and the sounds of the birds; a liquid *dik dik dik* followed by a coarse chuckle (? the grey Lourie), and another, a single melodious note with an ominous Siegfried-like expectancy, the liquid elixir of summer.

The next lap took us over the coastal plain to Lourenço Marques. Bicycles and sewing machines are left behind, for the Shangana wear native costume and carry loads on their heads; merry gipsies quite unlike the sullen robots of Johannesburg.

It is a beautiful town, and the Portuguese have made an enormous effort to overcome the climate and raise a modern capital. The scarlet blossoms of the flamboyants adorn every street, the coconut palms lean along the coast road; there are coral islands and avant-garde architecture, cafés with grilled prawns and *vinho verde* and in the evening nostalgic *fados*. The sea is blue, not muddy, as at Durban. The museum contains a variety of stuffed animals in realistic scenes of carnage, their hides plastered with predators, as if to say, "You've seen the Kruger: this is what goes on when you aren't around; a bloody, inefficient and meaningless slaughter-house."

Next afternoon we turned back across the baking plains, past groves of fever-trees, delicate thorns with pale yellow bark and even paler green leaves that seemed like an hallucination. Late in the day we reached the mountains of Swaziland where, across the frontier of Stegi, flew the Union Jack. This enclave of old England, with its paramount chief, feudal warriors, democratic constitution, village inns and good conversation, its sugar, avocado and pineapple plantations and its one-street mountain capital, is like a subtropical Andorra, even down to a hot mineral spring and projected spa and casino. There is no colour bar. I liked everything about it except the man-made forest, a vast metallic conifer desert, and the heat. In winter it must be paradise.

Swaziland with its industries, asbestos, agriculture and water has everything, including a good climate, but is subjected to a cold war from the Union. The British idea is that it should become a show window for a multi-racial society on South Africa's doorstep, no easy matter on a grant of a million and a quarter pounds a year.

The new democratic constitution is to be heralded by a general election in June, while the Republic tempts the chiefs with an eventual Bantustan, a feudal society with all white settlers removed. Our own problem is how to obtain more land for the rapidly increasing native population. To find oneself in a country still governed by the British seemed almost indecent.

Rather than face the fire-balls and sheet-lightning that alarmed me on the long night journey out I decided to fly home by day. Once more across the wilderness, with not a building in sight till Leopoldville and then again utter solitude until Lake Chad—a vast shallow sea of kidney-shaped sand-banks—and then sunset over the Sahara, the sand plaited into long manes by the wind or pitted with bunkers like a miniature golf course.

Hours later, out of the dark, the first crescent-shaped lights of Mediterranean sea-fronts. Then Rome. There is nothing in all Africa like hot chocolate and rolls in the Caffé Greco, or the pink façades by the Spanish Steps or the Piazza Navona.

What one misses most in Africa are interesting towns, country walks, safe swims, imaginative cooking, book-shops, news-stands and somewhere to go in the evening. But a Polish expatriate told me that after two or at most three trips to Europe the homesickness for South Africa grows stronger than the pull in the opposite direction; the sun and emptiness, the brown landscape flecked with patches of livid green that one sees from the air, become indispensable, the tidiness and perfection of Europe seem overcrowded and overdone. Perhaps Africa is like bilharzia: after you have had it twice, you can't take the treatment any more.

How will it end? Miracle or massacre? We are all involved in South Africa and must desire the same results as if we lived there; we must support the policy least likely to lead to civil war, bearing in mind that no government, however strong, could withstand eleven million Africans properly led and organised with world opinion behind them. Such an eventuality is at least ten years away according to some, five years according to others, or it may prove only two. Somehow the wisdom and devotion that protect the Kruger must be extended into the whole Republic, but this can only be done by a change of heart among the Afrikaners themselves, since they control the destinies of all three races.

(1964)

ON SAFARI

THE only way to reach Uganda is to fly. BOAC, BUA (Gatwick) and East African Airways issue interchangeable tickets. A delay of eight hours in Rome Airport resulted in East African Airways flying me there by day. The air has its beauty-spots and one of these, familiar to travellers to Africa, is the huge panorama of Lipari, the cone of Etna and the Straits of Messina as one crosses the instep of Calabria with the Ionian Sea ahead and the forests of the Sila underneath.

After that the wilderness—one does not see another house for two thousand miles. First comes the yellow Libyan desert gradually more and more corrugated by wind-patterns. Then the sand darkens to rock and grows veined like a leaf; dried watercourses snake their way and finally the ribbon of the White Nile is crossed and we reach a country of what seem waterlogged golf courses; a cluster of buildings at Juba, then the lakes appear, surrounded by vast cloud-bergs, against the mountains of the Congo. Lake Albert is surely one of the most beautiful sights in the world, waters of pale steely blue with greenish-yellow bog-islands and dark patches of jungle. Lake Victoria, immense; about the size of Scotland, inviting as the Gulf of Saint Tropez. The humpy green golf courses grow clearer, the bunkers become little hills with farms and huts; the greens, patches of maize and banana.

Entebbe—where the customs confiscate my button-hole. A drive through the botanical gardens plunges one straight into the mystery of Uganda: green lawns and official residences, now surrounded by barbed wire for the first time since the British left, minicabs full of picnicking Indians, stands of untouched jungle (*Tarzan* was filmed here) with tall flowering trees festooned with orchids and lianas, monkeys, parrots, sunbirds, birds such as one has never imagined, a miserable little zoo, and everywhere the rotten fish tang from the huge lake, the poor man's

Maggiore, inviolate through bilharzia. Crucial sadness of tropical evenings!

Uganda is a republic which has freed itself not only from the British but from its hereditary tribal rulers, not just the Kabaka but all five of them. Their palaces are commandeered or frown with troops; the thatched royal graves are neglected. Where are they now who only a year ago were crowned with such pomp and served by courtiers crawling on their stomachs? The Omugabe of Angkole, the Omukama of Bunyoro, the Omukama of Toro and the Kyabazinga of Busoga? They have mostly been moved, I am informed, to cheap hotels.

Uganda is the most pro-British of the three East African republics; the inhabitants are progressive and friendly but it is wise to give the army a wide berth. This is the "short rains" season: torrential downpours, grey skies and suddenly the sun shines all the more brightly on the invariable red earth and banana plantations or the papyrus swamps gleaming beside the road.

At fifty miles an hour by the car's open window it is always cool, an ideal progress; red road, red earth, banana, papyrus, stands of ironwood and a mountain on the horizon.

Only the tribes change, the laughing subjects of the Omugabe give way to the laughing subjects of the Omukama until we climb through a superb montane forest (Kamezi) and look down from the pass on the green plains of the Western Rift studded with tiny thorn-trees, the blue of Lake Edward, the volcanoes of the Congo.

The Queen Elizabeth National Park extends to one side of Lake Edward, the Parc Albert in the Congo to the other.

All Western Uganda suffers from the closing of the Congo border; there the dramatic scenery of the volcanoes, the Parc Albert, Lake Kivu and the Ituri Forest all belong to the same tourist nexus as Uganda's Kabale—Queen Elizabeth-Fort Portal route. The Uganda-Kivu area once reopened, the Congo luxury hotels de-bedbugged, the gorillas preserved, the frontier humanised, could provide some of the most beautiful scenery in the world within a few flying hours of London.

At Mbeya, headquarters of the Queen Elizabeth Park, the slow-flowing Kazinga Channel is navigable by small launches which enable one to get extremely close to the game on the banks as the early-morning mist rises. I went with Mr. Din, the scientfic adviser. In any park one meets the same crowd and it is difficult to realise that not only the animals but most of the birds simply won't be there once we have left the park boundary. The best argument in favour of the parks is that practically no wild life exists outside them.

Meanwhile, there is a rush of impressions. The bank unwinds like a film: buffalo, intractable, cunning, strong, cattle's revenge on man, looking more dangerous even than they are; elephant, in the distance like pieces in some elaborate war-game, infallibly exciting by their size, eleven feet high, weighing up to five tons, come always as a surprise. Their front legs are surprisingly long, their ears flap like canvas on a dinghy, they move in complete silence at seven and a half miles an hour walking, fifteen when in a hurry. Their droppings are like enormous *vol-au-vents.*

Like many wild animals they "demonstrate" rather than attack. Danger signals; the trunk rolled up or held out rigid, the tusks raised, parallel with the ground, "or it may first swing its head up sideways and eye you with one eye, always a very dangerous sign." Passionate, perfectly co-ordinated colossus, thy kingdom come!

The Kazinga Channel is the stronghold of the hippo, so numerous here that they have destroyed their own habitat and had to be cropped. (Hippo meat is immensely rich in protein; it is cut up and sold to butchers on the spot.)

Hippos, with their huge piggy faces and terrier ears, are the pyknic's dream of supreme sensual fulfilment. They look like prosperous African churchmen, Harlem revivalists stepping into their limousines. Most of their activities take place under water but one can hear them eating at night, browsing and chopping with the monotonous efficiency of a motor mower; their call, usually represented as a repeated long and three or four short grunts, *hosh-haw-haw-haw-haw,* is mysteriously comforting.

When the launch got too close to a large family the bull would retaliate by taking a vicious chop at the behind of a smaller rival who squealed with pain but could not get away fast enough. In spite of their jovial and benign appearance they fight savagely and as a herd submerges one glimpses bottoms covered with weals like clients pulled in from a house of flagellation. The floor of Lake George (which lies mostly in the park) is entirely lined with their droppings and contains more fish for its size than anywhere in the world. Grass into guano. This is surely a good reason for protecting them.

My favourite creature of the channel was the monitor lizard, a clockwork gangster five feet long with the air of a primitive dragon. It swims like a science-fiction monster and runs with its tail in the air. Its favourite food is crocodile eggs.

What makes this Eden so enchanting is the grouping on sandy spits or favoured beaches of different forms of life in mutual tolerance.

Alongside the hippos were a pair of these huge lizards, groups of pelican, Egyptian geese, white-necked cormorants, two buffalo, one elephant, storks in heraldic stance with their wings held out to dry in the sun, a fish-eagle on its nest, great white heron and goliath heron (enormous, immobile), and pied and pygmy kingfishers weaving among them. The cry of the fish-eagle, like the hippo's, is one long and three short blasts but attaining a pitch of musical desolation.

By now we are at Lake Edward, an alkaline shimmer with the Congo mountains lowering in the distance. The launch returns by the other bank where all the same performers await us. A fishing village on this bank rather spoils it. We say good-bye to Mr. Din and the chief warden, Mr. Odur, who wants more and more tourists so that he can open a "Treetops" in the south for watching lion and chimpanzee.

On the long drive northward to the Murchison Falls Park the great event is Ruwenzori. "The largest and most important group of snow mountains in Africa" (Margherita, 16,763 feet). As with Kilimanjaro and Mount Kenya I never saw the whole mountain, even from the air. The only town between the two parks is Fort Portal, capital of Toro, in a tea-planting district and deliciously cool.

Where there is tea there is health though the close-shaved privet-like shrub is somewhat monotonous, redeemed here by pink or white frangipani—surely the most beautiful of all small trees. Fort Portal has two hotels, the Mountains of the Moon, set among official residences with a large garden and many Siamese cats, and the luxurious Tea-hotel, under Belgian management.

I drove by a narrow one-way mountain road round the flank of Ruwenzori to visit the low-lying Bwamba Forest which joins up with the Ituri and stretches for hundreds of miles into the Congo. The Semliki River is the frontier and the tsetse fly and the yellow fever mosquito preserve it completely. The Mongiro Springs of bubbling sulphur steam among the tropical vegetation. The sun comes out; there are monkeys, orchids, lianas and a pygmy village: stunted women with breasts like bagpipes, tourist-crazed children trying to sell tufts of monkey fur.

All this area could be incorporated into another national park which would make Fort Portal a major tourist attraction and link up the two other parks. First should come the whole of the Ruwenzori Forest Reserve from a height of about nine thousand feet upwards—this would be chiefly flora—bamboo and the giant lobelias and groundsel, but include elephant and buffalo. The scheme is supported by the director of conservation for Uganda, Dr. Katete. But there is also the Bwamba forest with four hundred species of birds and some animals, especially monkeys, found elsewhere only in the Congo, then the Toro and Semliki game reserves at the south end of Lake Albert.

The forests of Western Uganda are under increasing exploitation and will soon be in as much danger as the animals. They also constitute the main reserve of such beautiful birds as turacos, parrots, hornbills, sunbirds and of colobus monkeys, tree pangolins, galagos, giant forest squirrel, golden monkey and golden cat. The gorillas of Kigezi sanctuary, incidentally, have been practically exterminated by a huge black leopard which has now been shot.

The Murchison Falls Park is everything that a national park should be; it is solid and compact, as big as an English county; it has a central feature, the Nile with the Murchison Falls which form a national park by themselves, and it includes huge bogs round the junction of the Albert and Victorian Nile, wide savannahs with miles of golden grasses, a forest (the Rabongo), now in decay and some distant hills. Of its 1,500 square miles much is inaccessible and with the adjoining Acholi Elephant Sanctuary which is almost as big, it forms an imposing reserve for the largest herds of this destructive animal.

The Nile here includes as well the largest remaining crocodile population and there are also a few white rhino transplanted from their shrunken habitat on the West Bank.

Here again the classic excursion is by launch up the seven miles of river to the falls, so popular that boats seating a hundred will soon be in service. Unlike the Kazinga Channel the Nile is fast-flowing. At the delicious Chobe Lodge at the west exit from the park it thunders over the rapids and cools the air with spray. This is a new and comfortable hotel with an English manager, ideal for fishermen and honeymoons. Nile perch here come to over 200 lbs. and tigerfish provide the fighting.

The drawback of all national parks is that one can never set foot outside the lodges; fishermen seem exempt and the crocodiles have so far spared them. To take the trip up the Nile is like wandering through an ancient Egyptian fresco. Once the whole river was like this but without the elephant and buffalo.

As we ascend, the crocodiles get larger and larger: some lie like fossils in slits in the earth just above the water-line, others jampacked on sand-spits, their mouths full of yellow leather held rigidly open. The snaps of the jaws or the whisk into the water of these impregnable ancients is sudden and alarming, revealing their permanent ferocity. Their only enemies are monitor lizards who eat their eggs (so do baboons) and pythons. Crocodiles are much poached to make handbags and it would be most profitable to farm them, especially near a meat-packing factory where there is plenty of offal. Some of the biggest may be two hundred years old.

On a sand-spit near the falls, clearly an exclusive club, I noticed several families of hippo, one roaring, one asleep, one lifting up the tail of his neighbour to bury his snout in her genitals. It was still thus engaged when we came back. There were also baby hippo like small suitcases, ten water-buck, tern flying around two saddleback storks and a Hadada ibis and the inevitable goliath herons and young fish-eagles with their baggy white trousers. Below the falls the Nile becomes a broad lake with a fringe of forest, the air is heavy with the roar of the falls; fish leap, the goliath heron flaps his way across, the fish-eagle screeches; the scene is utterly primitive and savage.

On my arrival the day before I presented a letter to Roger Wheater, the chief warden, and he soon arrived to take me for an evening drive in his Land-Rover. He belongs to a race of vanishing Englishmen, natural but unobtrusive leaders, who decided after the last war that they wanted a larger life and made their way into the game parks via the African Police. Now he is one of the few British expatriates left in a position of such authority. He took me down a track to the Namsika Cliffs and we left the Land-Rover pointing towards them and walked to the edge.

Below us a troop of baboon chittered, the leader barking angrily from his post as sentinel. The bluff overlooked the Namsika River, usually dry, but now flooded with the inevitable hippo exploring it, while beyond the grassland stretched out to the park's distant frontiers. The cliffs fell away round us on all three sides.

"This is where I come when it all gets too much for me at the lodge." He pointed out some blackish-brown magpie-looking birds in a tree—"piacpiac—always mean that elephant or buffalo are near." "Are they on duty now or do they knock off at night?" "No, they're roosting."

All the same I had a premonition—though what is one premonition to the guilty? "It is getting dark. Shall we go back?" As we start to walk to the car an enormous bull elephant appears, soundlessly, over the brow, about thirty feet in front. There is a pause. "Oh dear," said Wheater, "I think you'd better get back to the car." I walk towards it, with the elephant on its other side—with downcast eyes, my hands folded, like a boy bringing up the offertory bag in chapel. Slowly, I climb in and Wheater does the same. We are facing the wrong way and he dare not start the engine. The elephant acts. His huge foot kicks away some red earth. His trunk descends and inhales it. Then sprays it all over his back.

We are safe; it's his bath night. Repeating the process he moves away and we turn the car to drive past him. On the way back we pass within nine feet of two more elephant on the track and the warden explains his tactics. "With elephant one must take the initiative. Don't hesitate. If you stop and wait as one is told to you may be there all day." "What if you get stuck?" "That's too bad—you must know the pot-holes. Elephant have to face round before they can charge. That gives you time to get past and by then it's too late."

Back in his bungalow I enjoyed my whisky. I asked him if it were a usual occurrence to be out on foot when an elephant appeared. "No, it's the first time it's ever happened to me." I savoured this only for a moment. "Something like this always turns up with writers," he reflected. "There was Paul Jennings and the buffalo." I once wrote that there is no visa for elephant-lovers, those who love them must expect the same treatment as those who don't. But since this incident I have felt a braver man, for my host repeated the story and admitted he was scared himself. "If he had charged there was nothing I could do but throw my field-glasses at him."

The next day I spent one of the most interesting afternoons of my life. Going round a park with its warden is like going round a museum with the curator, only in a Land-Rover. We left the track after passing some exquisite button quail, the smallest of running birds, and a European kestrel which interested him far more, and made for the "Superlative Lake," a stagnant wallow full of elephant and buffalo, where he saw, with great excitement, a brown-chested wattled plover. The buffalo scattered before us, an elephant turned sideways and trumpeted but I knew no fear. We climbed over a Salisbury Plain of thorn thickets and waving golden grasses with elephant dotted about to what looked like a small barn: a white rhino and her calf. Perhaps because they are not yet sure of their territorial rights or because they are naturally gentle, one can approach within a few feet and we repeated the process twice more over the grassy downlands, once with a large bull.

We then descended to the Buligi marshes along the Nile where it flows into Lake Albert and out again. The elephants seemed blacker, stuck about the green like draughtsmen. There were crested cranes, a Verreaux eagle-owl on its nest, Abyssinian hornbills, Jackson's bustard, frogs croaking.

Black thunder-clouds were illuminated by the sunset over the Congo mountains and suddenly—what I had scarcely hoped to see—profiled against the sheen of the Nile, solitary, unmoving, a huge, blue-grey bird with bill like a trowel, the shoe-bill or whale-headed stork from the papyrus swamps, living almost entirely on lung-fish, a bird that makes all others look vulgar.

As we turn back we pass a Martial eagle and a young leopard and do the last few miles in the dark among the nightjars. Suddenly our lights reveal an African's eyes popping out of his head with fear. In front are two more elephants he is trying to pass. We stop, switch off our lights, the elephants move on; they are on the way to raid the garbage dump. In the dark they loom like houses in the black-out.

These garbage dumps are a feature of the park lodges as they are flood-lit at night and various animals come to explore them. I am reminded of the night-clubs of my youth when one used to ask impatiently, *"A quelle heure vont passer les attractions?"* And be told, *"A minuit, monsieur."* Here the cabaret is voiceless, but some of the Acholi gardeners make music on drums and xylophones—a wistful Nilotic melody that blends with the hippos munching and the "how could you" wail of the fish-eagle. One leaves every park with regret, but the Murchison with despair; our heart embedded in the Pleistocene.

Until the Congo and the Southern Sudan are reopened and steamers ply on the lakes and the Nile, Uganda remains somewhat of a cul-de-sac. Kenya is more sophisticated and still maintains a background of white settlers, international communications, a booming capital and coast-line. It is altogether browner and barer than Uganda, and seems like Spain after Portugal.

In fact, anyone who loves the Spanish *meseta* will love Kenya with its rolling plateaux and cloudscapes, its deserts and red gullies. Nairobi is astonishingly like up-town Madrid but more Californian and might be subtitled "Jacaranda City."

The height, about the same as Davos or Saint Moritz, plays strange tricks. It suddenly becomes impossible to walk another step or carry a parcel. Rage about some trifle sweeps over one and as suddenly departs. It is best to be speechless with rage, then one doesn't have to apologise.

There are Chinese and Italian restaurants with a little tasteless sea-food. The best meal is breakfast with fresh pineapple and pawpaw which never appear at any other meal. Lunch consists mostly of the "cold table" which covers a multitude of tins.

A visitor's room is his cage where he can retire about nine o'clock if lucky enough to scrounge anything to read. The nights are cool and sleep comes easily. It is good to get back to Nairobi to find letters and newspapers and someone to talk to, and good also to get out of it.

There is so much to see outside. The Masai Steppe, the Aberdare Forest, the White Highlands, the Rift, the Ngong Hills, immortalised by Karen Blixen in *Out of Africa.*

I spent a day among the white settlers in the Nakuru area—Nakuru, postmark of so many old letters from cousins and aunts growing roses while "Jim" went out to shoot the mamba, lioness, Nandi bear, or whatever it is that's mucking up the drive.

Many farms are now split up but the cattle ranches remain; there is still the Molo-Hunt and two polo teams. I lunched off Molo cutlets and "White Highland Cheeses" with an elder statesman who has a fine garden and well-built house and who makes films of underwater life on the coast. We sat and watched them in bamboo chairs from the Brighton Pavilion. He told me that everyone has left by now who is not "well-adjusted."

All the same, he did not see much of a future for the settlers. "They need us, but they don't want us." In fact the country, magic to the tourist, is tragic to the settlers. Nowhere have their English virtues staked out better claims to a homeland and the disappointment is bitter despite the friendship of the new masters. I stayed the night at Rongai in a granite mansion built by one of the founding fathers. My hostess is "well-adjusted" and has many African friends; in fact she seems wanted as well as needed; the staircase is lined with prints of ancestors; we dine by a log fire and listen to the news about devaluation from London. Hyraxes thump on the roof; my room is on a long balcony; all night it pours with rain.

By sunrise the weather was perfect. So was the breakfast. Back at Nakuru I joined John Williams, the great authority on African birds, and we set off after lunch for twenty-four frantic hours of spotting. Driving over the soda-mud-flats of Lake Nakuru to the rose blur of the flamingo flocks from which comes a continuous drowsy croaking, I was happy to be in a park again. The flamingo are grouped like Monet's water-lilies in a pastel continuum, the pelicans and spoonbills are more mobile; the pelicans swim in a flotilla and all plunge their bills into the water simultaneously—by what signal? The spoonbills rake from side to side as though they were scything.

In the late afternoon we reach Lake Naivasha and drive round to Hell's Gate. This is a gorge a mile or two away from the lake which suddenly turns into a primitive piece of old Africa—savage and barren. The track winds under volcanic cliffs where we watch two lammergeyers seeing off an intrusive pair of Verreaux eagles. An extraordinary combat follows in which the great vultures wheel and plane among the formidable eagles, swooping until they have retreated. Some ostriches prance across the grass, and, round a corner, a trim herd of barrel-bottomed zebra. This is a privately owned game reserve—a true luxury. We return to Safarilands, a new hotel by the lake, and sleep in tents which are very comfortable.

Next morning we toured the lake by launch in the early sunshine.

There is always a reason for not swimming or walking in Africa. At Hell's Gate it was puff-adders, here it is leeches. The launch threads a maze of blue water-lilies and papyrus swamp which changes colour through green to brown and encloses herons of all sizes, the inevitable fish-eagles, delicate jacanas or lily trotters, pelicans and pygmy geese.

When the trip ended we had seen 128 different birds since we met at Nakuru. Guinea fowl, with their enamelled polka dots, provide the only link with home.

I dined with some zoologists from the Tsavo Project—a research into the park's ecology financed by the Ford Foundation through the Kenya government and now suffering the embarrassment of delegated authority. The leader is Dick Laws, the atmosphere pure Cambridge with a touch of Huxley novel. Several have made Polar journeys and they discuss the venom in Polar bear's liver, but the talk, as always, comes back to elephant.

Elephant, claims Laws, are far more like human beings than the primates are, by reason of their similar life span and their advanced social patterns; the herds are matriarchal. Faced with greater and greater concentration in the parks and fewer outlets as man encroaches, they seem to be practising some form of birth control. The Murchison females have their first calf some four years later than formerly and with a longer interval between subsequent births. The parks are no substitute for the vast territories over which these most adaptable animals once roamed and the destruction of the trees by them which causes so much damage may proceed from a sense of frustration.

The hippos, he told us, exude a secretion which protects them from the sun and he has tried it as a sun-tan oil. This secretion may account for the extraordinary lack of infection in the terrible wounds which they inflict, despite the "soup" in which they live. He suggested to the BMA that it should be tested as an antibiotic, but nothing more was done.

In the Mzima pool at Tsavo the water is so clear that the hippos can be watched as they run along the bottom with the local carp pulling and twisting the accretions off their skin. Tsavo Park is enormous and includes many closed areas and an excellent lodge with animal "attractions" at Kilaguni.

I drove down by Land-Rover and stopped the night there and lunched next day with the "Project" in the east division of the park. The view here is over the endless blue low-veld, towards the sea. A group of orphaned animals, rhinoceroses of various sizes, two young elephants, and a buffalo keep each other uneasy company like defectors in Moscow. At two years buffaloes become dangerous; the rhinos are still docile, the cow elephant is eight years old and full of maternal tenderness for the bull, who is five. They spend much time with their trunks tucked in each other's mouth.

At Mombasa we reach the true Africa of the Victorian illustrations. The sands are blinding white, a reef protects the beaches, groves of coconut incline along the shore with clumps of banana, mango and baobabs with their skeleton staff of leaves. The Giriama and other tribes are glistening black and wear nothing above the waist, the huts are round and thatched, there are many Indians and many African Moslems in long robes and fezzes. The town has charm and smells like Morocco.

The heat and humidity I found unendurable and I spent hours imprisoned in my air-conditioned room. This four-day spell on the coast was a tactical error as it did not give me the time to visit Tanzania. In the tropics I become the shadow of myself and can never get enough limes. I should have done better to have flown to Arusha, Lake Manyara, the Crater and Serengeti.

Tanzania is now making every effort to attract tourists under the new minister of tourism, aided by the parks director, John Owen. President Nyerere is the most fauna-minded of heads of state. The parks are receiving all the help they want, the Serengeti in particular and vast new reserves like Ruaha are opening in the south, Zanzibar once more welcomes tourists and the Lake Manyara Hotel (near Arusha) is spoken of as one of the best of all lodges, overlooking the park but not in it. One can even go for walks there.

For days I have been obsessed with the wish to launch a campaign for an aquarium in Mombasa; it seems the ideal way to promote the study of its unrivalled reef life and the countless tropical fish and it would give the tourist a rewarding hour and tie the coast up with the parks upcountry. There is nothing of the kind nearer than Durban which lacks the tropical waters. The Florida Club on the old harbour would provide the ideal site. Marine reserves, like the one up north at Turtle Bay, would help preserve the dugong, the turtle (now in real danger) and the over-collected shells and corals.

Back in Nairobi I gave a farewell cocktail party in my suite with two waiters in attendance, to which by various mischances only three people came. It was a strange sensation. One has a special kind of masochist gear which one engages on such occasions and what would have been social agony in youth is no more than a dull prickle in late middle age. The waiters' contempt was the worst. Finally one of them blurted out, as I worked through the stuffed eggs, "But where are the people?" "Don't ask me," I snapped. He handed me a stiff whisky-and-tonic.

Dinner at Muthaiga Club, with its chintz and dinner-jackets like old days at Hurlingham or the Reina Cristina at Algeciras and a ferocious argument breaks out about the ethics of conservation. One of the Tsavo iconoclasts maintains that only species which are of use to man scientifically are worth preserving: no moral or aesthetic values enter in. Moralists are simply humbugs trying to deny that they are animals. "To hell with the whooping crane."

Myself, young Leakey the anthropologist and a charming travel tycoon, Tony Irwin (the host) protest violently. I should have replied, "To hell, sir, with Elsa."

But there is a grain of truth for we all know that the parks survive only because we have convinced the governments concerned that they will bring in tourists. And do the tourists spread as much wealth as if the Murchison Nile were given over to cotton? And how many more lodges and hotels are needed before the parks really pay? When the first cuckoo reaches Europe the whole tourist trade dries up.

I had one more day with the animals when I flew in a Piper Comanche to Nyeri and Treetops, Nanyuki and the Mount Kenya Safari Club and Samburu, a small park with elephant on the runway, cut off at present by road owing to bandits. It has a small but delightfully run lodge with a swimming pool. Treetops is now hoary with tradition but the cabaret is a true water-hole, not just a garbage bin—and you may see the rare and beautiful bongo and the giant forest-hog.

The parent hotel, the Outspan at Nyeri, seemed to me one of the very few where one could spend a week, in lovely country with some charming double rooms (try 12a) and real mayonnaise with the cold table. Treetops is controlled from it. The Mount Kenya Safari Club supplies canned music at lunch; the lamps are modelled as gun-butts, the private sitting-rooms are fitted with real bar-stools, they cost about $60 a night with the view up the green ravines of Mount Kenya thrown in. Just the place to play Russian roulette with a rich uncle.

On my last day I visited the Nairobi Museum and the adjoining snake farm (a most cheerful place). The museum desperately needs money and has the makings of a first-class centre: there are tableaux of East African animals (John Williams shot the gorilla for the collection on his honeymoon), including an okapi, bongo, many small animals as well as birds and birdskins, also a dugong and many fascinating fishes and insects, including an essay on fruit-flies, and the "Nairobi eye," a small inquisitive fly which squirts a blistering poison.

Yet the roof leaks. Could not the Gulbenkian Foundation which has already restored the old Portuguese Fort at Mombasa, so ably looked after by James Kirkham, intervene for this museum and perhaps provide an aquarium too?

The little Nairobi National Park near the airport was my last outing. Here I saw lions for the first time crouching, or rather, dawdling, beside their kill, a wildebeest watched over by a secretary-bird. And mincing ostriches with long eyelashes, and giraffe, symbols of graceful vegetarian bliss. If I have written so much about wild life it is because the animals and the parks are like museums and churches to the traveller in Italy: a day without them is a day wasted, and the further one gets from their innocent world of co-operation and wonder the more ordinary life becomes—a dull matter of politics, greed and business like everywhere else.

The parks have enormous problems; they are an artificial concept devised when the populations were much smaller. They depend on the goodwill of their African rulers and the support of the new generation who are now schoolchildren. They are constantly under fire from the land-hungry. By spending our money to go and see them we help the animals themselves.

The time to go is now, or at any time within the next two years, preferably not alone, and in an off-season like the autumn when the short rains contribute so much coolness and beauty. I would say that Kenya, Uganda and Tanzania are, unquestionably, the most worth-while countries in the sterling area and it is worth laying out from £500 to £1,000, fares included, for at least one visit.

(1967)

TANZANIAN SKETCH-BOOK

When I visited Uganda and Kenya last November I had to omit Tanzania so when Swissair offered a place in the proving flight of their new Nairobi-Dar-Johannesburg service I jumped at the chance. We left Zurich at midnight (tickets include London to Zurich at no extra cost) and after a perfect flight, the early-morning sunlight found me once again over Lake Rudolf, looking down on the little scimitar of beach that had been my last sight of Kenya when leaving Nairobi last December and which now seemed like home. Even Mount Kenya grudgingly thrust its tooth-shaped summit through the cloud.

It is May 3 and everyone has prophesied difficulties from the heavy rains—roads out of order, parks closed. But the sun is shining at the airport; Denis Lakin of United Touring who last year flew me to Tree-tops and Samburu, is there to meet me, and I have time for a bath at the New Stanley before lunching at Muthaiga which looks more than ever like the chintzy Ranelagh or Hurlingham of my youth. Sir Ferdinand (Cavendish-Bentinck) is gloomy about the world. His Bata shoes factory in Tanzania has just been taken over. "We drop half a million"—he leaves to ring up the parent company in Canada. Back to the airport and a hot bumpy trip to Arusha in a DC3. Arrival in a new country for the first time. Geoffrey Mason-Smith (United Touring again) introduces me to my Land-Rover and Babu, my driver. At the New Arusha Hotel my windows look out on the garden and pool and I experience an ecstasy, the first of many.

Mount Meru towering skywards over the green wilderness; the staggering quality of the light, the half-familiar tropical trees, frangipani, red cannas with purple leaves and the welcome siesta, which one takes without guilt, like a prescription. Later on new friends, the Philip Threshers, Canadians in the National Parks Financial Administration, take me to dinner with Dr. Chopra in a lovely house in the foot-hills by a small lake. The Land-Rover plunges blindly through the moonlight vegetation (a short cut), the night sizzles with insect charmers, the height bestows vitality. A tame bush-baby catches a large green mantis and eats it like asparagus.

Now begins one of the happiest weeks of my life, based on prolonged visual intoxication owing much to the intrinsic beauties of Northern Tanzania, and much to the thoughtful planning of the United Touring Co. and the park directors. It began early on Saturday morning with a drive to Moshi and a stroll round the market where the Chagga women (famed for their beauty) are sitting among their piles of black pineapples, pawpaws, golden passion fruit and green bananas whose fragrance is cut by the other staple commodity: dried fish. This was followed by a visit to the College of African Wild Life Management on the hill above which is run by a dedicated ex-brigadier from the Royal Marine Commandos (Tony Mence) who might have been lecturing at the Staff College.

The College, unique of its kind, he told me, trains future game wardens, rangers, and all who wish to learn about the administration of parks in African countries. (He had already heard of my intended visit in a pub in Pangbourne.) The College is financed by a variety of institutions which include the Ford and Rockefeller foundations, the Frankfort Zoo. The students come mainly from three East African countries with a tendency for Tanzanians to predominate. They go through a rigorous field-drill for a third of the period to learn how near they can approach to the various predators; what they may shoot and when; modern control of diet and disease; how to deal with poachers. Six of the staff are ex-wardens, four more are scientists. As I pass a classroom a lecturer with a strong European accent is explaining: "The giraffe is poached for its tail to make fly-visks."

I lunched with Pat Hemingway, an ex-hunter who is now one of the instructors with much of his father's earthy directness and his mother's charm. We discussed Ernest Hemingway's accident "after which he was never the same again." The first, very skilful pilot hit a disused telegraph wire and landed brilliantly on a sand-spit in the Nile just above the Murchison Falls, among the crocodiles and elephant. The plane sent to retrieve him was overloaded (Hemingway knew this) because the new pilot was too much in awe of the VIP's to tell them he couldn't take all their luggage.

We discussed procedure for various animals. If attacked by a lion thrust your arm down his throat. This takes some practice. A charging rhinoceros is unpredictable; it has a tiny brain—step aside! An elephant cannot turn quickly, does not see very well. Never run away, run sideways. A buffalo can turn in its own length like a polo-pony, very dangerous if it charges at all, but the least likely of them to attack. A hippo can chop a man in two if he gets between it and its water. A shot giraffe dies very slowly, going through the motions of running.

We discuss the conservation problem: the College is turning out young wardens whose character and abilities are superior to the jobs they are likely to be offered: they are not always welcomed by the staffs already in possession. Most Africans are not yet animal-lovers and want quick returns. Much is hoped from the next generation. (The parks are being shown to the children.) Poachers are not always to blame. "My definition of a poacher is the man to whom the land belonged before." And always the worst threat is agricultural development as a result of over-population. "The Pill is the major conservation tool. We must first set our own house in order!" But this government has already done far more for conservation than the British. The relevant words from the Arusha Declaration are framed in the director's office.

The brigadier drives me to the airport. I look lovingly at the coffee plantations and the gaily coloured Chagga women as if for the last time. "The coward dies many deaths," it's the source of his strength. Philip Thresher is waiting by his little Cessna which refuses to start. "Have you ever flown one of these things before," he shouts, when we are airborne. I want to reply, "No, have you?"

My confidence seeps back as we climb through the sunshine with only the mountains in cloud; in the distance to the south is the newest national park to be opened, the Tarangiré, now mostly under water, and an hour after leaving we are over Lake Manyara and see a herd of buffalo and white egrets in the trees—the first game—and decide to go on to the Ngorongoro Crater, into which we descend to fly around inside the towering green walls of the Caldera with their rim of forest. We pick out the flamingo colony on the little lake beside which stand two rhino; the first elephants in the forest, groups of wildebeest, before returning to Lake Manyara's precipitous air strip where we land at the second attempt.

Lake Manyara: one of the delights of the world. The hotel is perched on a cliff below which the forest (a national park) stretches down to the lake, misty blue and mountain-fringed like Lake Maggiore from Ascona. There is a large garden and a swimming-pool and one can walk about freely and peer down at the animals below. The magic African hour between half-past five and half-past six we spend in the Land-Rover, standing on our seats and looking out through the open roof, an ideal method for game-watching. The park is tiny (123 square miles) but densely populated. The forest is full of wild figs, mahogany, yellow-backed acacia and bottle-trunked baobabs. In one acacia nine lions are asleep spread-eagled on the branches, bloated with food, blinking, tails hanging. One large snoring female with distended stomach stales noisily, the urine cascading downwards. *"La femme, c'est le contraire du dandy."* There are white pelicans on the lake and elephant everywhere and the *hoosh-haw* of hippo can be heard. *Nota Voluptas!* We are so close to a family of elephants that we can smell them, an acrid pungent odour similar to the wild sage (ocimum) along the lake roads in Uganda, but heavier and more feral.

We dine with the chief warden, Mr. Jonathan Muhanga. This park is one of President Nyerere's favourite haunts, it contains about twenty hippo, sixteen rhino, fifty lion, four to five hundred elephant, thirty to forty giraffe and a few leopard, its specialties are white pelican, flamingoes and yellow-billed stork; the warden would like to see a circular tarmac road there and to introduce some colobus monkeys. There is little poaching in this shop-window of a park in its setting of idyllic beauty. At night I hear a lion's roar, elephants scream, leopards cough, hyenas howl like someone being raped who suddenly decides to make the best of it. I wake in ecstasy to what seems the sound of two distant drums beaten on alternate notes; two long, three short beats answering each other. Philip Thresher says these are ground hornbills.

Sunday morning and farewell to Philip Thresher who carries all the economic problems of the parks in his head as he flies back to Arusha while I continue in my Land-Rover with my sagacious Chagga, Babu. The land journey to the Ngorongoro Crater is hot and seems interminable—at last we reach the cloudy Crater forest, so unexpected and mysterious, the mountain air, and the green Pyrenean turf of the Caldera walls (twelve miles across) seen from the cairn to the memory of Grzimek's son, "who gave all he possessed, including his life, for the animals." The lodge here seems truly alpine yet four elephants are grazing beside it, their ears flapping like punkahs, their behinds wrinkled and reassuring, "the half reasoner with the hand" as Burton called them.

Leaving the forest we get our first view of the Serengeti, a haze of blue lawn and then a descent through foot-hills of yellow marigolds past groups of giraffe with their creamy suède scrotums and long eyelashes beset with flies. We drive round a small lake crowded with storks and reach the rolling grassland of the outer Serengeti and the first huge concentrations of wildebeest and zebra, Grant's and Thomson's gazelle, patrolled by hyenas with faces like sex-tormented scoutmasters. We drive up to a family of cheetah lying in the grass and see a fish-eagle, white-fronted on its tree-stump.

How can one convey the power of the Serengeti? It is an immense, limitless lawn under a marquee of sky; the grasses ripen at different seasons and force the herds sometimes to the boundaries (where they are poached), sometimes to the centre. This is the origin of the vast migration, now in full swing. The light is dazzling, the air delectable: *kopjes* rise out of the grass at far intervals, some wooded; the magic of the unraped American prairie here blends with the other magic of the animals as they existed before man. There is a lightening of the spirit, a sense of atonement, of being able to compound at last for the endless cycle of vanity and greed to which they have been subjected. Nature's world of beauty and justice, without cruelty or compassion. Descriptions are useless because they must fall back on catalogues; photographs fare little better. I print: "There is nothing the matter with Northern Tanzania" on my notebook and leave it at that.

In the afternoon heat we reach Seronera and I am given a rest house to myself where I plunge into sleep. Adorable siestas—nature's unexpected bonus for those of advancing years; the afternoon alibi.

I am the guest of the director, Sandy Field, and we dine together. He is an ex-provincial governor, an astringent Wykehamical civil servant who is excellent company. He could be head of a Cambridge college or an unflappable chief secretary in an Edwardian comedy; he prefers people to animals (an amiable eccentricity) and seems a shade too Stendhalian for the brute creation who form the bulk of his satrapy. His second in command and scientific director is Dr. Roger Lamprey who is almost too large to be true—a handsome giant whose bell-like voice would steal any picture from Gary Cooper or boom through an Aldous Huxley novel: he is a Cambridge biologist and complete man of action combined. He is to fly me over the game migration tomorrow, if Everest or F6 can spare him. Perhaps he is not a giant, his size a figment of my imagination. Statistics are lacking. We have a very good dinner and an animated discussion on Enoch Powell.

Night in the Serengeti! The lights go out around ten-thirty and I am alone in my rest house. Hyenas, I am told, are undergoing a formidable transformation, it is they who now kill for the lion, not the other way round; they carried off a child in the Crater, killed a woman in the Kruger. Hyenas could be outside right now. The pack gathers whimpering and snarling till it plucks up the courage to disembowel the victim. A noise between a belch and a cough. Was that a hyena? Something is munching outside; chewing up boards. The coughing gets nearer. A rhino has a tiny brain—step aside—but a buffalo . . .

There is a sound of some monster defecating from the roof, a clatter of descending cow-pats. The rhinoceros spreads his dung by whisking his tail; the elephant has no such delicacy. I turn up my spirit lamp and carry a large stone to my bed. More bangs on the roof, more coughs, more stomach rumbles. Never was sunrise so welcome. Over our breakfast of scrambled eggs, I make guarded inquiries. Explanation. The coughing, sneezing and champing: Topi antelope (a robust gregarious creature)—noises on roof: hyrax or genet. The hyrax occupy the nearby shrubbery, the defecation was produced by a flapping of wings in some roof-nests. I am not altogether satisfied. Every trace has been removed!

With a marzine and an air-sickness bag I climb into Dr. Lamprey's Piper Super Cub. We soar off the grass and over the sunny plains, first the long grass, then the short turf where the game is concentrated. The herds plunge away from our shadow. The Plains occupy about four thousand square miles, as far as the line of blue mountains on the Kenya frontier: as big as Devonshire or is it Wales? Far below I spot a ratel, fiercest of all small mammals (it will even attack cars) in solitary splendour. More ecstasy: what a Sunday morning. Wotan's music triumphant on my brain. *Jour de ma vie!*

We fly over Baron Van Lawick who is photographing a litter of (much maligned) wild dog, then land to greet an elderly Canadian biologist by his Land-Rover. But though he left Seronera yesterday afternoon he hasn't turned up and his colleague is now anxiously awaiting him. We land again among the wild dog to tell the Baron to keep a look-out.

Dr. Lamprey is sliding imperceptibly into the heroic role. "He may have got stuck in a hole," and we fly back along his presumed route. He is finally located by the Naabi Gate and we land once again, this time on the road as the ground is too boggy. Sitting behind the peerless doctor, I am reassured by his broad back, which seems made in one *monocoque* casting with his machine. The biologist, Tony de Moos, is unshaven, grey-bearded, rather disconcerted by his adventure. He has lost his way, his Land-Rover got stuck, he has spent the night in a cave which he had walled up "so's not to get chopped by hyena," and then walked on to the lodge. With all his Arctic experience he should have stayed in his car. We take off from the road, land once more to tell his colleague where to find him and return to Seronera "before they start looking for *us*."

Then we set out again on a Land-Rover picnic with the director and George Schaller (formerly a gorilla man—now, lion). We drive up to a superbly maned lion crouched on an isolated rock. "What a magnificent beast!" "Yes," answers Schaller. "It is one of mine, and if you look close you will see a small disc in its ear which I put in about eighteen months ago." He knows three hundred lions by sight. We lunch admirably by a rocky outcrop and see a large cobra cross the track—my first wild snake. The Plains here are studded with these rocks, each with one magnificent tree.

The talk, as in many a lonely outpost where strong silent ex-empire builders are wont to congregate, is of the Snowdons with, in this company, the lions of Longleat as a second. I bring up my King Charles's Head—the Erroll murder case. The director's favourite recreation is shooting elephant and he takes his holiday in parts of Africa where this is still permitted. I can think of nothing but learning to fly and acquiring a Piper Cub of my own. Conditions here are so ideal, unless one gets lost in bad weather, that one forgets the clouds and hazards of England, the controls of restricted areas.

Later on we drive round the site for Dr. Lamprey's new scientists' village which will make Seronera the Oakridge of the animal-observation world. Ecology of wild animals is still in its infancy. We have only recently learnt of the limits to aggression in predators as expounded by Lorenz or how hippos act under water. Laboratories are going up; there will be a library and new museum with quarters for visiting biologists. The present one-room museum has some gigantic stick-insects (Palothus) which are studded with imitation acacia thorns.

It is sad the next morning to leave this ultra-sophisticated village. Yet I find my solitary journeys with Babu in the Land-Rover wholly enjoyable. Cruising at fifty there is always a breeze and we soon rejoin the animal corps de ballet: the cavorting wildebeest, Grant's gazelle that never drinks, the zebras with beautifully polished flying buttocks. In these migrations the huge herds march eight abreast, solemnly, with dream-like precision. There are so many wildebeest, zebra, gazelles that the first emaciated Masai cattle outside the park seem like a rarity. We pass depraved hyenas wallowing in the mud, buffaloes whose horny foreheads look like Edwardian aunts in shabby hats, exquisite bat-eared foxes, huge Kori bustards, prancing ostrich. By the Olduvai River another illumination: the river with reeds and feathery acacias, scrub along the banks, tawny mountains beyond, its sand-pits broken by little rapids and, a hundred yards up-stream, two rhino, leathery and primaeval, one standing in the water, one lying down, three tick-birds on each: essence of Africa: sun, wind: the doves interminably calling.

As we climb back into the Crater foot-hills we watch the Col opening out above, the mountains on either side with clouds moored like barrage balloons. We leave the Plains and enter acacia woodland where the giraffes are back again, then the woods end and the sea of marigold begins, papering the whole mountain, and, against the golden drift, zebras in their precise black and white, no two alike, each an unsigned Op art masterpiece, the whole vision like a child's painting.

The montane forest is in the cloud and the trees are hung with moss. At the lodge I meet the glamorous conservator of the Crater reserve, a Masai, the only one in high office, Mr. Olé Saibull, and we discuss the reserve's problems. A rivulet trickles down the forest road. I drink from it and vow to return. A sign-post, occupied by baboons, reads:—MBULUMBULU. There is time for a short rest at the Lake Manyara Hotel, then down again to the ground-water forest. We pick up a uniformed guide and, erect in the Land-Rover, I drive into the park like Hitler entering an occupied city. An old buffalo (a heap of old sacks with a couple of logs on top) in its wallow, an evening of indescribable beauty; a rainbow over the lake, the sun slanting on sulphurous tree-trunks—a duet of forest kingfishers, then a leopard on a bough. It is crunching a bone, then licks its paws and washes flank and leg, its tail hanging down, a deeply disturbing creature, its coat so much richer than a lion's (the difference between walnut and deal), the head smaller, the expression less fatuous and self-indulgent. We are in luck and soon find another, as well as some lions in a tree and groups of roosting hornbill. Every animal I came to see has now appeared as if by magic, except a pangolin.

Next morning we reach Arusha after driving through long stretches of flooded road, picking our way past marooned lorries—Arusha with its scarlet cannas and Nandi flame-trees, bamboos, banana, cassia, coffee . . . a tropical Washington. Mrs. Thresher accompanies us for the rest of the day to the last of the parks, the Arusha National Park, on the forested slopes of Mount Meru. The overlord here is Desmond Vesey-Fitzgerald who labelled the largest trees at Lake Manyara and is an all-round naturalist and administrator. The Crater itself is about four square miles of greensward like an English park surrounded by forested hills with huge trees in the glades where wart-hogs gambol. Above us the lemur-like colobus monkeys in their long black-and-white coats are leaping and shrieking, the branches strain and bend beneath them. Visitors are not allowed down into the Crater but these upper woods round "Rhino Crest" are accessible and this is the first place where I have wanted to sit and watch all day. We hear the liquid notes of the tropical bru bru, a bird seldom seen. The park is compact and rises to twelve or thirteen thousand feet to include the top crater; the forests are full of mahogany, loliondo, wild fig and olive, there are moorlands and high grassland and small lakes with hippo.

The core of this Eden is the idyllic Lake Elkekhoitoto, recently a private farm. We looked across the water to three rhino, with two babies, five giraffe, a bush-buck and a stag party of male water-buck along its grassy verges. Elephant and their trails are everywhere, we see them scattered over the scrub like camouflaged pill-boxes and I am shown the alpine ledge where the Baron von Blumenthal, while selecting his prospective victims, was killed this winter. He had "neglected procedure" a white hunter told me, by letting his gun-bearer carry his gun when among dangerous game, by approaching too close (for which he could be prosecuted if it had not been on his own concession). An angry cow had charged from the forest fringe; the gun-bearer ran to one thicket, the sixty-four-year-old Baron stumbled to another. The gun-bearer fired and missed. The elephant caught the Baron: a tusk entered each side. He was a mighty hunter nicknamed Baron M'boko (Baron Buffalo). His last words were "Give me my spectacles . . ."

A dinner party of white hunters given by Geoffrey Mason-Smith concluded the day. The food endeared me to the New Arusha Hotel more than ever, we ate our way through five courses. The hunters were an impressive group who now represent a threatened occupation. Some have moved on to Botswana where organised safaris are still possible, others will manage lodges in the parks, others crop game for the government. Part-naturalist, part-predator, part-psychologist, they kill the things they love for the entertainment of people they don't, with courage and skill, while the snows of Kilimanjaro are melting around them. I flew over between its twin summits the next day; the snowy cones can usually be seen only from the air and by the afternoon I was enjoying the flesh-pots of the New Stanley Hotel in Nairobi, one of the best in Africa.

Northern Tanzania is complete in itself; it is one of the most beautiful countries in the world, the climate is excellent, the people delightful, the animals unique. Ideally there should be one huge animal empire here which would include the Serengeti, the Ngorongoro Crater reserves, the game regions contiguous to both and some of the other craters together with Lake Evasi. With its variety of plains, lakes and mountains all under one administration it could become the largest protected area in the world, a sanctuary financed by all the institutions with an interest in it, both American and European.

President Nyerere is the most enlightened and wild-life conscious of all African rulers; he appreciates both the aesthetic and scientific arguments. I was delighted by a story that when informed how much the scenery of the Serengeti mattered to us he replied: "When I was in Scotland I was always being told how beautiful the weather was, the moorlands, the heather; I could not agree, but I decided it meant something to you which I would never understand—it is the same with the Serengeti."

Assuming this sanctuary is the ideal we all cherish, how can it be realised? There are serious obstacles. One is the Masai. As their cattle multiply through prevention of diseases they use up more water, as their numbers increase their votes are lobbied for; the agricultural development of their reserves becomes more logical. In order that the parks should pay their way there must be more tourists, which entails better communications and a longer tourist season but also more interference with nature. Northern Tanzania is at present the poor relation which receives the spill-over from Nairobi. There are no air-fields at Moshi or Arusha which can take even "Friendship" jets and the large international airport which is projected between the two might lose money, especially without more hotels. And building hotels requires capital and confidence.

Outside Moshi is the training camp for African guerillas, largely staffed by Chinese, which forms the antithesis to Brigadier Mence and his friendly College of African Wild Life Management. The Serengeti is constantly threatened, not only by poachers but by politicians; strips are eroded from it, game lands to the east dangerously over-cropped, the Crater demoted and maize encouraged where the buffalo roamed. The ideal of an animal kingdom in perpetuity which would stretch from the Masai reserve in Kenya to Seronera, from Seronera to include all the craters and Lake Evasi is still feasible. But will it ever come true? It all seems so far away from the social realism of Dar and the demands of an emerging nation.

Tanzania has two faces. The national parks are administered from Arusha by a dynamic Englishman, John Owen; the Ministry of Tourism is lively and forward-looking; more hotels are under way, two in the Serengeti, another on the Crater lip. Arusha is having a boom. But from Dar comes a spate of anti-Western propaganda. Someone whom the newspapers call "African man" is posed on both feet ready to deliver a last kick at the relics of colonialism; the press is muzzled and Chinese influence is apparent. The animal kingdom has one powerful friend, President Nyerere, who alone has both the power and the vision to preserve it. The Speaker, Adam Sapi, chief of the Wahehe, is another ally. A crisis is approaching as the Commission on Masai Development begins to make recommendations for increased mountain cultivation with regional commissioners to back them up. Proposed extensions to the Serengeti corridor and the Lemai area are mysteriously pigeonholed, the Game Department ruthlessly crops the Eastern Plains.

Once again the best way we can help is to go there. The tourist will find the Africans of Tanzania even friendlier than in Kenya, the scenery even more beautiful, the climate as healthy. Having been there both in the long and short rains I would recommend the off-seasons. Why wait till after Christmas when every bed is booked?

I owe much of my enjoyment of East Africa to cicerones like Denis Lakin and Geoffrey Mason-Smith of UTC or satraps of the parks like Roger Wheater of the Murchison or Philip Thresher and the lords of the Serengeti or to new friends in Nairobi like Jack Block, but even without them I shall keep coming back. When I first flew to Jacaranda City my one idea was to confirm my booking home; when I left Nairobi last May it was with the name of a house-agent on my lips. I like to ask government servants where they would most like to retire—"I don't think I would be happy in England" one replied. "I need sophistication—that means Nairobi. And I want a typical African view—that means Karen." It sent me back to the first sentence of Karen Blixen's masterpiece from which the suburb takes its name. "I had a farm in Africa at the foot of the Ngong hills . . . a landscape that had not its like in all the world . . ."

Nairobi, a less interesting city than Kampala, Dar or Mombasa, is nevertheless a true capital. I grew to like it more and more. When I remember the open-air café round the thorn-tree of the New Stanley or the aviary in the courtyard of the Norfolk or the book-shops, camera shops and safari emporiums or the little pet shop with its bush-babies, I am suffused with longing. The New Stanley by any standards is a glorious hotel. I also found three good restaurants in Nairobi; one Italian, one Chinese and one (Alan Bobbe's Bistro) where I had fresh prawn mayonnaise (from the coast) and a lime sorbet which in dehydrated moments I shall never forget. "How long are you spending in Nairobi?" Billy Collins asked me. "About a week." "That's too short." "Why?" "Because there are so many nice people." And so many nice animals. The snake-farm, or the "orphanage" at the Nairobi National Park, a tiny zoo in a grove of blue-green eucalyptus with troops drilling nearby on the red earth to English bugle-calls and a military band. Caracals, porcupines, genets, wild dog and the famous cigarette-smoking chimpanzee, Sebastian, presented by Geoffrey Mason-Smith because after breakfast it always took *The Times* with it to the lavatory. He was given to Mason-Smith in the Congo with the warning "Him pissee plenty in the night, mister." Best of all is the Nairobi Park itself with its plains for lion and cheetah, its gorges where I saw a crocodile basking in the sun, its giraffe glades and hippo pools. It has everything but elephant, bongo and monitor lizard.

One can only reach these countries by air. We must make the best of it. I have had good flights with Swissair, BOAC and East African Airways. Coming back at midnight by Swissair the preparations are almost a ritual. Hanging up our coats, taking off our shoes, bidding good night over the last snacks and drinks, then the captain's trilingual welcome and the take-off into the cool night with the Southern Cross looming brighter as the lights are dimmed and the landscape snaps back into emptiness. Next stop Zurich.

(1968)

DESTINATION ATLANTIS

IT ALL began with Buddha and a reading of Mr. Saddhatissa's *Buddha's Way and Buddhist Ethics* (Allen & Unwin), leading to a renewed infatuation with this melancholy liberator from craving and illusion who was not afraid to grow old. I imagined myself enraptured with some Buddhist country, meditating among his images, relishing the fruits of two thousand five hundred years of conservation. But which? Tibet and Angkor were out, as was Burma for the moment, Siam was too hot, Nepal and Bhutan too cold, besides I dreaded these immensely long journeys. I found the perfect compromise: Ceylon.

CONNOLEY
ON CEYLON

The anagrams were favourable.

But a misfortune occurred with which arm-chair travellers are familiar. I read myself right through Ceylon; I learned so much about its sights and antiquities, its animals and inhabitants, its mountains and beaches, its landscape and leeches, its rather inadequate hotels and precarious political set-up that I felt the journey (outside the mangosteen season) might prove an anticlimax.

Why not try nearer home? Equate the rage to travel with the materials to hand? A maximum return fare of £200, a flying time of five or six hours, a country open to tourism but not yet destroyed by tourists; sunshine, scenery, animals, good food. Tunis, Cyprus, Libya, Egypt, Morocco measured up but I already knew them all. Then I remembered lunching at the Foreign Office to meet the President of Senegal, Leopold Senghor, a poet, an intellectual educated in Paris, a friend of the Surrealist genius from Martinique, Aimé Césaire, a statesman who had coined the word "Négritude" for the essential quality of the African soul.

There was only one book I possessed: Geoffrey Gorer's *Africa Dances* (Faber, 1935) describing a tour he made with the Senegalese dancer Feral Benga before the last war. Benga had opened a night-club in Paris; I had been there and been overwhelmed by the power of his dancing and the magic of his drum-rhythms. Gorer had much to say about Senegal and Dakar, the sea-girt capital on the cliffs of the Cap Vert. Its winter temperature (hot days, cool nights) seemed ideal. By now I had to go somewhere quickly. I could not read myself in and out of Senegal, there was no time and no literature. A national park, at Niokola-Koba, contained almost the only herd of one of Africa's rarest animals, Lord Derby's eland, and also the nearest wild elephants to Gray's Inn Road. Gorer praised the beauty of the ruling tribe, the Wolof, tall, narrow-waisted, round-headed Mahometans, with their hereditary musicians and family jesters, the "Griots," their sophistication and good cooking: "I have always maintained that a varied cuisine with its resulting appreciation of subtle flavours is one of the certain signs of a refined civilisation." Gorer also mentioned two delicious native fruits, the corassol and the darkassou, and the local oysters and fishes. There were several routes, by France or Spain, Las Palmas or Casablanca, one could combine them, even stop off in Mauretania. There was one snag. Every hotel was full till the middle of March, the palatial N'Gor with its private beach, owned by Air France and said to be designed by Corbusier, the Croix de Sud, the best hotel in the town, and two or three others. No appeal had any effect and telegrams went unanswered. One could either wait in London or try to take it by storm. I decided on approach from Las Palmas for I recalled the joy of touching down there one winter evening on my way to South Africa, and the balmy air of this last outpost of Europe with its Spanish crowds before the interminable night-flight over the Congo. The first day I would go no farther.

As a child of five I remember putting in at Tenerife on a troop-ship bound for the Cape, the barren Anaga mountains above the harbour, caves in the rock, a white chamber-pot on a black ledge. Disgusting! Later the Islands became an obsession with me. ". . . Where falls not hail nor rain nor any snow . . ." They ought to be quite perfect; tropical fruits and flowers, never too hot or too cold, no diseases. Spanish baroque palaces and churches, one of the most beautiful mountains in the world, mentioned by John Donne and described by André Breton. All through the Thirties I had charted the reasons for living there (after the war I became director of an imaginary company—Atlantis Hotels), home of the legendary Guanches, of "Tinerfe the Great, Emperor of Tenerife"—of perpetual autumn

L'orange en même jour y mûrit et boutonne,
Et durant tous les mois on peut voir en ces lieux
Le printemps et l'été confondus en l'automne . . .
—Saint Amant, 1594–1661

One morning in late February, leaving London blacked out in a power-cut, I flew there via Paris. At Orly a zealous clerk at one of the Air France check points removed too much of my ticket, an error (unperceived) that was to cost me dear. The evening set in over Bilbao (seatbelts all the way) and it was night when we landed with a terrible bump at Las Palmas. Leaving the plane one seemed to hit a tornado, my hat blew away in the dark, torrential rain was falling. An amiable young Canarian drove me in a taxi in which the wipers weren't working, the wind-screen was obliterated, head-lights of other cars surged up blinding us through the rain. At last the street lights and the Hotel Santa Catalina with its flood-lit dragon-trees—not a room to be had—not a room in the whole of Las Palmas said the manager who rang a hotel in the mountains—full also. The driver came to my rescue: we drove from one concrete monstrosity to another, each more hideous than the last, down narrow streets where parked cars billowed up and down in the tornado. Utter despair, fatigue's dreaded complication stalked.

The driver was by now tackling smaller and smaller buildings, some of them unfinished. Finally he succeeded at the Semiramis, a small set of "studio apartments" like a hotel in Montparnasse, or in the Soho strip-tease area. A dark red divan-room with patterned wall-paper looked out on a blank wall where neon lights shone and signs were banging. An excellent restaurant, said the proprietor, was nearby, though to cross the street was an effort. One was blown into a brasserie where groups of middle-aged Swedes were doing a Scandinavian boomps-a-daisy. The menu was nothing but outsize steaks in bad Spanish. Torremolinos again. The clown who keeps the table in a roar, the women who drag their partners in comic protest to the floor. Sweden. The country which has taken over these islands and made them an appendage of its eternal night, with a daily jumbo jet service direct from Stockholm. (Twenty-six million tourists visited the island in 1971.) It was better in my room overlooking the air-shaft. "A very depressing beginning," I wrote, "to a fiasco."

Morning—huge waves, mountains capped with low-lying snow, the 200-km-an-hour gale levelling banana plantations where hailstones were seen for the first time, a wave-strewn promenade of concrete hotels curving like a set of Cyclops' dentures. I must be too old to travel—I like only scenery, food, art, architecture; I've never asked anyone what their wages are nor studied trade statistics. I know these islands are prosperous. Bananas, potatoes, tomatoes and tourists, a boom in land. Hills, snow, grey clouds, shafts of sun, sand, sky-scrapers and a few palms and aloes. Bournemouth in a gale. Luckily the bad weather causes cancellations. A room at the Santa Catalina falls my way with a balcony overlooking the tops of the Canary palms and the white buildings of the model village in the park.

Las Palmas consists of two cities, Montparnasse on Sea (Puerto de la Luz) joined to the main town by a long and tatty High Street. It is a good place to get out of; even the group of old buildings, the cathedral, the house of Columbus, the ancient patrician quarter lack dignity and charm. But escaping from it is not difficult, in a Mercedes taxi with a patriotic chauffeur. Only one day more, not counting an afternoon wrestling with Air France about my defective ticket. (No problem; the missing vouchers, Las Palmas to Dakar and back, will be sent here on the next plane.) Air France find a room in Dakar, at the Hotel Vichy. By now I had contracted diarrhoea, I suspect from the first meal out, a cold collation served between Paris and Las Palmas. This condition was to stay with me off and on all the trip, causing me increasing weakness and failure of will-power. Some days I couldn't pass a lavatory without rushing in, like a drunk when the bars first open.

We speed along the coast to Puerto de las Nieves, past walled banana plantations, coffee growing among them, spring flowers, the mountain of Guia shaped like a miniature peak of Tenerife, Galdar with its memories of the Guanches whose caves in the black cliff loom above the green banana fields, the blue sea beyond. The driver buys me the local cheese. Agaete is the mildest place on the island, famous for tropical fruit, an attractive white village with a big church, still unspoiled as Almuñecar used to be. If one was forced to live here this would do. The Puerto de las Nieves is a typical little sea-swept Mevagissey with two restaurants swamped by Swedish coach trips. The wildest coast on the island lies beyond. From a guide-book: "Puerto de las Nieves 'solitary and far away' cried the sad poet Alonso Quesada. Today, with distances shortening, Puerto de las Nieves will be able to keep its loneliness and distance as a 'spiritual memory.' "

On the way back the hill road runs up from Arucas, a large banana town, to Teror, the place with most character. The church is baroque, white flanked with brown, as in Andalusia, with a courtyard of Norfolk Island pines, a street of old houses with balconies. The mountain road to the Parador climbs through oranges and almond blossom to the Pass where the fresh snow is still lying. The Cruz de Tejeda is a sternly alpine building five thousand feet high, with a terrace and friendly waitresses serving stew, a wonderful view down to the arid southern coast and the lighthouse and oasis of Mas Palomas. It is beloved by the British, with their homely red faces and khaki shorts, small exclusive family groups so different from the Scandinavian aphis-swarms. The mountains, about six thousand feet high, are enticing, the air invites walking. A little more will-power and one would stay up here for the evening. On the way down I stop at Santa Brigida, capital of the once famous "Monte" where the British merchants retired from the heat. The hotel has come down in the world but some of the villas have a Mediterranean charm on an island where there are singularly few attractive small houses and gardens—nothing but concrete boxes for peasants and tourist sky-scrapers.

Sore throat—diarrhoea—ticket trouble—once more to the airport where nothing has arrived from Orly and where a temporary ticket is issued till the other is sent on to Dakar. The evening flight there takes about two hours, then the lights of the coastal boulevards appear as a lozenge of diamonds on the edge of the dark Atlantic. The customs are rather grim, a taxi drives me furiously over the parched African plain, passing through Independence Square—"centre of animation"—now apparently deserted, though it is only ten-thirty. The hotel is all-black, no concierge's desk, only a solemn figure in a white burnous who conducts me to a hideous room overlooking a courtyard. It is pleasantly cool. "Terrible nightmares. Gross anxiety, not to be borne."

Three days of my holiday gone with little joy in them. "Where only man is vile." And am I not a man?

More cafard next morning redeemed by excellent breakfast. "The condemned man made an excellent breakfast."

It is always a man, for women, with few exceptions, don't get the satisfaction from a good breakfast which a man derives in the most adverse circumstances. Even when it is served in a nest of writs or his wife rings up from another man's bed it remains an absolute satisfaction. In Dakar it's just continental with a Parisian edge to the coffee and croissants, served by a gigantic Wolof.

"The King Wolof can put ten thousand horsemen and one hundred thousand footmen in the field" (A.D. 1505). The Wolofs are the cream of Africa like the Watutsi and the Wahéhé. They are vastly tall and thin, almost one-dimensional, extremely black, and like the people of Benin and Ashanti, ruled an empire before the white man came. They are doubly sophisticated having their own culture, with their "griots" as bards and jesters and a French veneering through two centuries of occupation. They are Mahometans and not as warlike as the Bambara of the hinterland who provided the "Senegalese" garrisons all over France. The men wear long blue robes, the women green and gold cotton dresses of spectacular brightness which can only be carried off in the blazing sunshine. They are always laughing and chew long sticks to keep their teeth white. Their hair is elaborately striated under their foulard head-dresses. The city is typically French provincial. There are no smells, not even the *bouquet d'Afrique* which greets one elsewhere.

There is much to be said for Dakar, its winter climate is delectable. Almost surrounded by sea, its boulevards skirt the low bluffs of the Cap Vert with their consulates and government offices. The President's palace has true distinction, the better streets are like Rabat but an increasing tattiness announces the native quarter, an enormous shanty town (the Medina) soon to be rebuilt(?). The harbour is approached by avenues of huge trees. There is a zoo, a native craftsman's village, a university and a botanical garden. The "great mosque" with its court-yards and fountains, its carpets from President Bourguiba of Tunisia, its lamps and cedar pulpit from King Hassan of Morocco is green and harmonious. For three months of summer (called *L'Hivernage*) the climate is wet and humid, business is at a standstill—in winter the days sparkle with sunlight which gets rather too hot for walking in the after-noon. After dark the trade-winds blow the heat away and the small hours are cool indeed; some nights the town is covered by sea-mist. I spend sessions with Air France, for my tickets haven't come yet or in the inhospitable "tourist office" or in the many book-shops, well supplied with French literature though almost nothing has been written on Senegal. If the prices were not so high and Senegal could devalue the African franc (now equal to two French ones), which makes the *Sunday Times* cost eleven shillings, it would be a tourist paradise. But then the Swedes would get there and take it over as they have already annexed Bathurst and the Gambia.

The restaurants of Dakar are expensive but good, marred by canned music. The best of them, the Croix de Sud, played a particularly melan-choly song on "repeat"—if "Tristes Tropiques" had a tune, this would be it. Here I sampled the *corassol,* a cruder version of the custard-apple, in fact a sour-sop which though somewhat insipid has a unique bitter-sweet flavour, excellent as a kind of creamy custard over the local strawberries. In Jamaica it is served as a milk shake. A gigantic *cigale de mer,* a kind of clawless decapitated *langouste* from the rocky islets off the Cape, cost a small fortune. All over the world the *langouste,* crawfish or rock lobster is on its way out. Even the prolific Mauretanian banks are overfished and efforts to protect them by stringent regulations as to size and breeding season are hard to enforce. The Canary Island fisher-men are among the worst offenders. Blame the twenty-six million tourists, blame oneself, who cares only for clear soups and sea-food.

Meat and all vegetables except asparagus tempt me less than shrimp or scallop, lobster or crab, above all Dublin Bay prawns. I eat, I pay, I groan with remorse like an alcoholic waking among the empties. Paint me as a primitive Patagonian against a slag heap of claws and shells and round my neck hang a card INSECURE.

Mangoes are not quite ripe but the little red-fleshed melons, the *"charentais de Sénégal,"* are delicious, so are the blood oranges, strawberries, pawpaws. The restaurant of my hotel turns out to be both cheap and good, providing salty oysters from the Cape and its excellent soles, with waiters trained in the French tradition. The Hotel Vichy grows on one, its tall black white-robed staff, its mango tree, the cool night wind, the stuffy salon, the peculiar clientele who have but one thing in common, that they have all missed a connection at the airport. One becomes totally dependent on the local paper which I read in a café/tea-room over a mixture of fresh lemon and orange juice. The café is frequented by Firbankian young members of Dakar's jet (black) set in beautifully tailored suits with their elegant girl friends. The paper absorbs me:

Temperatures. Dakar, January through April, maximum 25, minimum 17, no rainfall. (London between 9 and 2.) But inland a maximum for the same period of 45. There, as in the Deccan, life is only bearable just before dawn.

African newspapers are full of macabre humour. I read of Sekhou Touré of Guinea removing all whites from the travel agencies and staffing them with trustworthy blacks:

"La securité vaut mieux que les divises."

A leading article fascinated me: it described the rounding-up of beggars and vagabonds to make the city safer for tourists in language of appalling facetiousness, especially about lepers and imbeciles. *"Trois cent interpellations en 4 heures. Nombreux sont ceux qui dans notre pays sortent de chez eux sans aucune pièce d'identité, s'exposant ainsi à des ennuis. Il est arrivé plus d'une fois que des gens parfaitement honorables séjournent quelques heures au 'violon' . . ."*

The old punishment of the "imbeciles" was to take them out to the open country and dump them. They usually found their way back. Now the active leper is picked up and taken to the leper village *"où il peut travailler au milieu de ses pairs et ne plus sentir sur lui le regard quelque peu condescendant des 'bien portants'."*

The true prostitutes of Dakar are the taxi-drivers who accost one from their machines all down the street. Outside the hotels they swarm like horse-flies. One lowers one's head and charges through them with a *"non, non, non."* The inevitable drive is to the Palace Hotel at N'Gor with its sickle beach and its blue umbrellas—it has charm and dignity but is generally taken over by package tours. The hotel with its bungalows is owned by Air France and open all the year. The airport is a couple of miles across the Bled which grows more fertile as Dakar is reached, mangoes, tamarinds, bougainvillaea, an occasional flamboyant and the baobabs which are the leafless emblem of Senegal, an elephant of a tree especially when browsing in groups. Otherwise the vegetation is all burnt up and not especially tropical. And no mosquitoes.

Dakar is completed by the island of Goree where the Dutch installed themselves in 1617, calling it after an isle in Zeeland. France obtained it in 1677 and held it for a century with British interruptions. Eventually it remained French and was governed at one time by the gallant poet, the Chevalier de Boufflers. Slaves, gold, yellow fever, tourists . . . the Portuguese, French, British . . . the usual African cycle. The island-village is now the only place (except Saint Louis in the arid north) to breathe an air of the past as a packing centre for the slaves who were disembarked into similar buildings in Port Royal and Kingston. It is a sinister yet welcoming place and the ferry across the bay has a holiday feeling—enormous baobabs, dusty mangoes, a sea-breeze, quiet streets with old houses where Brazza died and the Chevalier courted his *"signares,"* in particular Anne Pepin. The Creole ladies gathered sand from his last footprints to ensure his return.

There is an Hostellerie de Boufflers on Goree and a pleasant open-air restaurant in the former governor's buildings (Le Relais de l'Espadon); a development scheme is under way. The police station is in the old Portuguese church of 1482. There is also a museum, but the most emotive building is the old Slave House of 1776–78; the entry gives on to a small courtyard and a double outside staircase leads up at the far end to the first floor balcony. Underneath on the ground floor a passage leads to the slave cellars where they were penned till the moment of departure. The cells could be observed from spy holes above and a water-gate straight on to the sea was reputedly used to get rid of the dead. The airy rooms on the floor above with their breezy sea-views were reserved for the slave-captains and the merchants and overseers—a rococo monument to human misery and three hundred years of oppression (to 1848) compared to Hitler's thirty, all due to the West's insatiable craving for sugar.

One might well stay on Goree at the Relais which is also the centre for big game fishing; a certain reticence is observed about sharks but marlin and many other fighting fish are available and some records have been set. Otherwise there seem nothing but children and mango-trees and the *va-et-vient* of the ferry decanting dusky belles in their striped foulards on the sandy shore. Slaves and yellow fever are left behind (some sixty medical staff were all wiped out at one go), "development to follow." One pines for the ices and book-shops of Dakar, even the daily session at Air France awaiting the usual telegram about my tickets, now on their way to Las Palmas. In the tourist bureau a plump black lady is asleep on a sofa; her colleague suggests her place is behind her *guichet*—she demurs—he gives in *"mais quand-même"* . . . It is a joy to discover an active tourist agency, "Sénégal Tourisme," in the Maginot building, run by a dynamic Canadian. He knows the form. Three weeks ago the only hotel in the national park at Simenti was burnt to the ground in a bush fire. It will not be reopened till next winter. During the *Hivernage* the park is closed anyhow; it is run by the University and the animals are given a breather. The nearest town is Tambacounda (100 km). There are seventy kinds of animal including lion, hippo, elephant, and Lord Derby's eland and three hundred species of birds. Visitors have risen from one thousand to five thousand in 1969–70. Three hundred miles from Dakar it is best reached by air. It could be combined with a trip to the lovely highlands of the Fouta Djalon or the two primitive tribes to the south of the park, the Bassaris and the Coniaguis with their traditional costume of a penis sheath woven from the *rônier* palm, and a scrap of cloth on the behind. Their rites are as elaborate as their costume is simple. They live in movable huts which they carry round with them on a three-year cycle. The young men are initiated by a *danse du coq,* the girls are not allowed to marry till they have had a child.

Tribes of Senegal: the pastoral Peulh, the Serere, the Malinke, the Toucouleurs. In compensation I took a car early the next morning, or rather a Volkswagen station wagon with a Mandingo driver from Gambia, a fellow-countryman at last, intensely patriotic. After Rufisque we enter the bush, scattered baobabs grow thicker together, clustered over the parched countryside, mango plantations line the villages, the *rônier* palm appears, the sun is like a copper oven; vultures, long-horned cattle, goats, ant-heaps, a troupe of monkeys, red earth, acacia thorn. Africa, where the innumerable aimless dirt roads peter out in the latent aggression of the climate.

M'Bour, capital of the Sereres, peanuts and oysters, then an oasis, Joal, where the coconut palms at last seem really happy. A large house on the shore was the birthplace of President Senghor whose father was a prosperous ground-nut merchant. There is no plaque and no indication except in his own poetry. (*Signares=Señoras*)

Joal:

Je me rappelle
Je me rappelle les signares à l'ombre verts des Verandas
Les signares aux yeux surréels comme un clair de lune
sur la grève

Farther down the coast is Fadiouth with its island, object of our excursion. The island is surrounded by mangrove swamps where the famous oysters cluster, everything seems built on or out of heaps of shell. The village is approached by a long wooden foot-bridge or else by dug-out. It is Catholic and hordes of black pigs root around among the rubbish or duggle in the water, the streets made of crushed cockle-shell are narrow paths between the concrete shacks. Women crouch selling small piles of fruit, smelly fish, black tripe; the men play cards under a grotesque bust of Saint Joseph. More tourists arrive, mostly German, to run the gauntlet before being punted over to the cemetery on another mound of shells and returning through the mangroves in the brilliant morning light.

On the way back we make a detour through the bush to a gastronomic oasis on the estuary of the Somane, the hotel-restaurant of the seahorse (Hippocampe), a breezy spot with many chalets by a lovely beach and winding estuary for a lunch of small grilled *langoustes* in peppery butter followed by a local chicken-and-rice dish and banana fritters. Then the hordes of Germans catch up.

This would be a good place to stay wherever it was, and the French proprietors' cooking makes it nicer. One forgets the brousse and is back in Atlantic Africa, at Mogador or Oualidia. Blue breakers on white sand, crackling weeds under foot, egrets in the shallows, sea-food siestas and the trade-wind blowing sophorifically like the endless canned music.

One last excursion remains; the Casamance, a river province in the extreme south on the edge of the rain-forest. It can be reached by a weekly boat, the Cap Skirring, a converted cargo, which stays there a couple of days then brings one back, or by road through Bathurst where the Swedes have taken all the rooms, or there and back quickly, by Air Senegal.

The capital, Ziguinchor, has the only decent hotel, the Aubert (forty rooms air-conditioned), and gave Senegal its best-known novelist, Ousmane Sembene (b. 1925), whose family were fishermen. He took part in the allied invasion of Italy, then worked as a docker in Marseille. After an injury to his spine he returned to Senegal where "so much remains to do and to write."

The Casamance is the most beautiful part of Senegal, the old Africa of equatorial forest, tom-toms in the night, witch-doctors, fetishists, a balmy sweet-smelling atmosphere, peculiar huts, giant *fromagers* (silk-cotton trees), monkeys, pythons. The night is unbelievably soft, the mosquitoes fierce. Ziguinchor is linked with remoter villages with watery names. Oussouye, with its priest-king; Karabane, linked by dug-out through the mangroves with Elinkine. The beach of Karabane curves beside the curving coconuts. Near Oussouye is the small national park of Lower Casamance with its buffaloes and hippo. In the forest are the scattered huts of the Floups, the most fetishist of the local tribes (Diolos, Mandingues, Mandjacks), whose queen lives in the forest near Oussouye.

The beauty-spot of the future is Cap Skirring itself where the sea is warm enough for bathing all the year round and where there is a small aerodrome and a restaurant (specialty—grilled oysters). Luckily the beaches of Cap Skirring are not too accessible in the rainy season, the dunes are unspoiled—but for how long? Between the Scandinavians of Gambia and the freedom fighters of Portuguese Guinea the Casamance's river paradise, home of the gentle Diolos, the mysterious Floups with their elaborate dances and circumcision ceremonies, is an enclave worth all the trouble of getting there and back, the deep south of Senegal (which is already south enough) . . . *"où les touristes amateurs d'exotisme trouveront le depaysement le plus complet."*

One can fly from the Cape to Ziguinchor with its daily flight to Dakar, hence to Paris and London, or the Casamance can be reached by the flight from Gatwick to Bathurst and then by road. My last journey was to the Dakar airport in the early morning, past N'Gor with its beach hotel and its island to the elegant international airport, not yet overcrowded. I wish I had seen the University and had time to meet some of the Senegalese intelligentsia—but then I would have missed my afternoons in Air France till I came up with a brilliant suggestion, to issue me with a new ticket rather than wait for the missing fragment still shuttling between Paris, Las Palmas, Dakar and back. I left Dakar with sadness, regret for the Wolof with their lemur-like faces and immaculate robes, the laughing women, the strawberries, the baobabs, as the Cap Vert and its islands disappeared and we saw no more land till the delicate feathery summit of the Peak of Tenerife came into view above its sea of cloud. Then down into the clouds, the military hangars, the Scandinavian mêlée of Las Palmas, where a couple of telegrams restore my identity, and on by local plane to Tenerife.

The Hotel Taoro forms part of what was once the old British nexus of Puerto Orotova with its church and club and library. Its huge garden and park are a memento of those spacious days. It is now a link in the chain of Spanish luxury hotels which include some of the best known in the Peninsula. Spaniards do not understand luxury which they equate with formality and ponderous decoration, meals are elaborate and time-consuming, they lack French elegance or Swiss cordiality and only the chambermaids, often elderly peasant women, seem natural. The Taoro, however, is extremely comfortable as well as cosmopolitan. A young German manager breaks down the guest-list for me. Season December to May—60 per cent British, 30 per cent German, 10 per cent Scandinavian, 10 per cent Spanish. Hardly any Americans. A hill-side swimming-pool with chairs round it, gardens with roses and peacocks, spring sunshine, banana fields underneath.

A walk down through them to Puerto de la Cruz in the evening. But what is going on here? Profound gloom. Another Torremolinos. Swedes everywhere, kraut-frumps, corny little bars, rows of hideous sky-scrapers, each clumsier than the last, the chilly Atlantic breaking incongruously at their feet. Spain. A country that has sold its soul for cement and petrol and can only be saved by a series of earthquakes. Oh, for more taste, less greed! Is there any Spain left? Perhaps only in Estremadura. Night now and the frantic search for a restaurant. These big hotels serve only ornate and heavy meals from the preserved cherry on the slice of honeydew to the tinned pineapple in the fruit salad. To order à la carte is to invite disaster, "what do you expect if you eat à la carte" as the waiter said to me when forced to admit the veal was cooked in rancid butter. One pays more for the same dishes and waits an extra half an hour. And in the local restaurants, canned music. I don't know which is worse—sentimental souped-up demi-jazz, "take-off" music or blaring and clanging juke-box style. The mood is soon conditioned to the tinned fish soup and tepid ubiquitous *merluza*. One has only a limited number of dinners left, and only a few years to enjoy them. So bring on the bilge water-melon, tinned ham, botulised beans, goaty white wine while the candles gutter in the Valdepeñas bottles.

Moment of utter desperation. The only pleasure left is sending my laundry.

On the following cloudy morning I walk to the British Club and inspect the clock golf lawn, the bowling-green, all very well kept, the British behinds bent over the croquet. The library is closed as usual and its once mint collection of Henry James and other Victorian three-deckers has been dispersed as far as Capetown. Now for the English church and rectory, solid, gloomy, both in granite. The church was begun in 1890 and consecrated by the Bishop of Sierra Leone in 1893. It is now attached to the Bishopric of Gibraltar. After a bad ten years from 1940, the church, rectory, club and library (with its ten thousand volumes) are thriving again, though there will never be a permanent British enclave. I couldn't find the Protestant cemetery. "Peter Spence Reid 'Don Pedro' 1830–1916 took services (British vice-consul), Thomas Gifford Nash 1850–1921 chaplain 87–95." I am a great reader of tablets, even in All Saints, Orotava.

At the end of the war I ran a series of articles in *Horizon* on possible retreats to which a writer could emigrate. Ian Fleming wrote his first article on Jamaica and I asked an old Liberal M.P., Athelstan Rendall, to do Tenerife. "Some thirty or forty English families have made their homes at Orotava," he wrote. "The Hotel has quite a fair billiard table. A particularly nice section of the English middle-class fills these hotels regularly." Samler Brown's guide to the Islands, first published in the Twenties, gives an indication of this vanished society and its relationship with the Spanish landed proprietors. He noted that it was very seldom that a British resident "got his feet under their mahogany." Then as now, the great excitement was the ascension of the Peak with a view of dawn from the summit for the thoroughgoing. Now there is a funicular.

The road mounts through Orotava, now built over, then up through the hills, chestnut woods, Canary pines, the Montaña Verde which clothes the whole north side of the mountain with giant heath, pines and evergreens, "the laurisilve." We climb for some miles through it below the cloud, 1,000, 1,200, 1,400 metres high and then at 2,000 metres we switch on our head-lights and enter the cloud itself, which envelops the pine-trees with mist. In the Alps one would expect this weather to last all day but here it is like an image of death and resurrection. Suddenly the mist is illuminated, we reach total sunshine with patches of snow on the black lava and the Peak glittering above us, the snowy-breasted pearl; the stunted pines continue, gradually giving way to broom not yet in flower. At 2,000 metres the road from La Laguna joins us and the endless hairpin bends straighten. We are now in the Cañadas, the luminous world above the cloud with flat pockets of snow-strewn lava among tawny boulders, the broom forming little islands on this lunar desert, already marred by an alpine "bar-garage." The highest slopes of the mountain are frequented only by one small grey bird, fringilla Teydea, and one flower, Viola cheiranthifolia. The new *téléférique* to the summit starts near this building and will accommodate many hundred tourists a day (eight hundred already for off-peak September).

Far stranger and more romantic is a range of jagged yellow-ochre peaks opposite the summit across the valley: totally barren, with many pinnacles, the Montaña de Guajara towers over the Parador (rendered uninhabitable by coaches) and the little desert of the Llano de Ucanca, a sandy expanse peppered with moonrocks. We are now in the

National Park of the Cañadas and despite the massive Parador surrounded by buses like a dead rat covered with maggots, there is an indescribable exhilaration. Blazing sun, the orange aiguilles against the blue sky, the good air, the clumps of retama, the snow and sand, the cloud canopy far below us inspire a feeling of being born again into a rarefied world of spirit.

> Search well another world; who studies this
> travels in clouds, seeks manna where none is.

Crossing the central range the road descends to Vilaflor in its forest of giant pines; figs, almonds, organ-cacti, prickly pears appear and small vivid fields of new potatoes, with a view of the long coast and the headland of El Medano. We join the autostrada at Granadilla and so to Los Cristianos, once the warmest and remotest place in the whole island now shattered by krauts and concrete, Swedes and cement like everywhere else. Stage camels wander round the little harbour. But for lunch there are genuine *langoustes* and *langoustines* in the delicious piquante sauce of the island, the *mojo,* made of pimento, garlic and red pepper.

Returning round the coast it is cactus land with clumps of euphorbia, almond blossom, bare grey figs, yellow flowers, and African gorges with a glimpse of the superb basalt cliffs of the awesome Punta de Teno. Playa de Santiago and Los Gigantes are remote beaches now being developed. This must be the wildest coast on the island. Back in the cloud at Puerto de Erjos, and down to the banana fields of Garachico, Icod and its marvellous dragon-tree, now the largest in the islands, and so back to the sky-scrapers of Puerto de la Cruz. The dragon-tree lives up to its name. Its red sap, dried, was sold in the past as "dragon's blood," Roman ladies used it in beauty preparations. The tree grows slowly to a vast size and is almost indestructible, the branches are like limbs of giant tortoise or tail of conger, the sword-like leaves sprout in primitive tufts at the top. *Dracaena draco!* Dante mentions a tree which spurted blood. In the middle ages it was considered a cure for leprosy. On some inaccessible cliffs in the north they form clumps. The one at Orotava (fifty feet round) is gone, the two remaining giants are at Icod and in the garden of the seminary of rainy La Laguna.

On leaving the Hotel Taoro where I had solved the problem of the excruciating *dîners en ville* by a tray in my bedroom I developed an affection for the young managers in their morning coats and the portly concierges. Two afternoons a week the library was open, the Reverend Lonsdale has the key. O for some civilised company here, as in the eighteenth-century salons of La Laguna like that of the Marques de Villanueva from whence proceeded the general *History of the Canaries* by José de Viera y Clavijo, still the best book on the island.

I stop my taxi at the Orotava botanical garden, one of the six best I know. There are town gardens like Montpellier, Bordeaux, La Rochelle, Padua and tropical gardens like Kitchener's Island (Aswan), Hope and Castletown (Jamaica) or Entebbe, but Puerto Orotava's is like a small closed Wallace Collection, being formed in the eighteenth century (1788) for Charles III by the aforesaid Marques de Villanueva del Prado. He paid all expenses himself for forty years. It is now a close-packed arboretum of tropical trees, red-blossomed spathodea, the sour-sop, papaya, rose-apple, mamey, sapote and star-apple but no mango-steen (garcinia). I found the wine palm of Chile, the pride of Brazil, the flame-tree and the peepul and the beautiful royal palm. Here grows the splendid Ombu of the Argentine pampas, jack-fruit and bread-fruit, sausage tree and flamboyant in an enclosure which is now much too small. At the same time constant deforestation proceeds on the islands, the stands of Canary pine are felled, the indigenous evergreen forest sadly depleted. Lunch at Gambrinus, a proper restaurant at last, in Santa Cruz. The capital is the finest city in the islands though inclined to be airless and smelly, the mountains coming too close. It is San Francisco to Las Palmas' Los Angeles, with its leafy boulevards, good shops, a tropical square with a band-stand (San Miguel). Then back by plane to Las Palmas and a pleasant fish dinner at Juan Perez on the Canteras beach. Perhaps the Scandinavian hippies of Nite Town are preferable to the elderly British couples of Orotava? Perish the thought.

One more excursion remained—to Mas Palomas in the extreme south of Grand Canary. I went there fifteen years ago with Stephen Spender and our fairy godmother, Hansi Lambert. It was then a savage oasis of wind-blown palms and white sand with no building but a guingette and the lighthouse and the tents of a film company. A photograph of it as it was then is hung in the lounge of Gandar airport. And now? A monstrous new city (Playa del Inglés)—a Miami of empty apartment houses, rapidly filling up with supermarkets. "You get browner in a day at Mas Palomas than in a week in Las Palmas," said my driver. The oasis and its landlocked creek are now incorporated in the Oasis Hotel, a mammoth brown coprolith set among beautiful gardens; large pool, cold buffet, everyone in beach clothes; one might be in Ocho Rios or Nassau. High praise, for this is easily the nearest place to Gatwick with totally reliable winter sunshine. One can leave England at noon and be in bathing trunks by tea-time, at far less expense than on the Caribbean. Another huge dining-room with "gold lobster" on the menu. Fearful depression. *L'angoisse des tables d'hôte,* remembrance of time wasted in similar clinics of the rich, seeking reassurance from sommeliers. The remedy is in the twisted palms themselves, the roses and the pools with frogs croaking. Then back to the airport past the palace of the Conde de la Vega Grande, the tycoon of the island, and the evening plane to Lanzarote, beside a peasant woman praying. A sunny flight over Fuerteventura (the ugly sister waiting for her concrete ball-dress) and down to the little airport.

Lanzarote: already too well-known with direct flights now being laid on, the rainless treeless volcanic island that once was shunned, now ripe for "urbanisation" and monkeyfication, if the plumbing can ever catch up with the planning. Playa de los Maricones. The beach with the beautiful name!

Meanwhile Arrecife, the village capital of Lanzarote, now boasts a luxury hotel with a French clientèle and the usual impeccable Spanish taciturnity, the torture of the table d'hôte more ingenious than ever but a good bar and a discothèque on the fifteenth floor. The view as the sun sets over the remote lunar landscape and the tidal harbour is infinitely restful. There is something about volcanoes that invites one to dance on them.

The town promenade by the shore is paved in what looks like porphyry in contrast to the white houses; everything is young, young trees, young couples. The air is balmy yet electric, the Californian atmosphere of the other islands missing. This is the desert, and, as in the desert, dawn and sunset form the two principal events.

The roads of the island have been macadamised and driving along them is a pleasure: black lava over the green island with its air of Achill and the west of Ireland or Galicia. There are many small flowers, yellow and violet, cacti, figs, occasional palms, rolling downs on a black tablecloth. Tomatoes form the main crop. At La Geria are the vineyards, each vine scooped out in a small stone circle with a black centre which protects them from the wind, while the dew feeds them. I try half a bottle, it is very cheap, very dry, tawny, rather heavy, half-way between a Château Chalon and a Montilla. Warmly recommended. Yaiza is the local capital with many camels and prosperous houses, including an American's converted windmill. There is a far-west feeling. Now appears the waste of lava, a brown sea of fossilised *mierda* from which rise some small mountains. Alongside one of them, the Montaña de Fuego, a row of camels, each bearing a tourist, climbs biblically. The smell is unpleasant. No wonder the Roman cavalry bolted from them. We stop at the Islote de Hilario, a circular restaurant where vent-holes send out gusts of boiling water and larger orifices cook tins of meat and carcases. There is a peculiar pleasure in watching the guide submit a bucket of water to the subterranean Vulcan. A brief pause for inspection and a spout of condensed steam is ejected like a giant's fart. "He doesn't like us," I explain. The light is very beautiful and the whole petrified sea of island and mountain is so completely desolate and uninhabitable that the authorities have permitted themselves the indulgence of creating a national park. We cross to the salt-pans of Jalubio and the Golfo, a small green lake fifty feet deep fed from the sea with ochre cliffs behind. Huge Atlantic breakers foam in the north wind through caves and blow-holes in the craggy lava. Bathing forbidden. This is the end of the line for my journey and I start lunch off with an omelette at the airport before being borne over the intermediate islands to the next course, a Wiener schnitzel at Las Palmas. By a fluke the same driver who drove me through the storm and the room shortage on my arrival was there to take me back for a look at the cathedral and the old palaces of Las Palmas and a final tea at the Santa Catalina where I touch the rough bark of the dragon-tree in the compulsive knowledge—no need to wish—that I shall come back, like the quarter of a million Scandinavians who visited the islands this winter.

I planned my return by the Iberian jumbo jet which has a daily flight from Madrid to Las Palmas at Spanish—not intercontinental—prices. The difference between the first and tourist is only ten dollars and includes great head-room, vast arm-chairs, absence of children, and a sumptuous Spanish dinner; take-off and landings are unexpectedly abrupt, the flight the smoothest ever. The only drawback is the time it takes so many passengers to board; we might be a religious procession. The Madrid customs open everything; one forgets that the whole Canary archipelago is one duty-free shop: wines, whisky, Havana cigars, cameras, watches, binoculars, tape recorders, radios, Paris scarves, Scotch pull-overs, American newspapers, hands of bananas, sticks of pawpaw . . . everything and everyone is suspect. I notice that I have difficulty in hearing what people say to me. . . .

The Fenix belongs to the chain of Spanish luxury hotels which includes the best in Tenerife and Grand Canary, Seville, Cordoba, the Escorial, etc., but with the difference that it is staffed by Madrileños with their almost Parisian urbanity. And what room service! Despite the intense cold after the sun of Senegal and "the Isles of fragrance diffusing languor in the panting gales" it is bliss to be back in the capital where the Calpe book-shop is worth a dozen duty-free radio sets. I purchase the Destino guide to Tenerife by Alfred Darias in that admirable series and the two volumes of Cela's *Diccionario Secreto* on Spanish double meanings, on the strength of a review in *The Times Literary Supplement*. Speak we nothing but bawdy, even when asking the way to the station?

In Madrid I meet old friends and we prepare for a round of gourmandising. They provide new pills for the diarrhoea that has been my incessant companion, forcing the abandonment of many a project. In the momentary lull we revisit the Jockey, still the most glamorous and possibly the best restaurant in Madrid. Also the dearest. Dominguin the great bull-fighter is at the next table. He is handsome, lean, with very small wrists and hands, beautifully dressed and looks like an intellectual film-star, wears a toupee (my friend whispers), and is with a very pretty girl. He is now forty-five, getting slow, has to go on fighting for tax reasons and was booed in Tenerife with cries of *"Viejo."* We wonder how much he remembers of Hemingway's *Dangerous Summer* when the old artificer tried to involve him in paranoiac rivalry with his brother-in-law, Ordoñez.

One place I always return to in Madrid is La Zambra, the government night-club for the exhibition of uncontaminated flamenco. The first half of the programme is dancing, the second singing (*cante hondo*) and it is that which lures me back to the sickly Sangria or the powdery whisky. The singers are usually elderly and include a marvellous guitarist. Tonight they are three. Rafael Romero (*malagueñas*) large, young, soft-voiced: Miguel Vargas, typical gipsy, lean-faced, harsh-voiced, and Juanito Barea who sings that old song of a doom-fraught woman, the Petenera, a ballad which has always haunted me and which the Niña de los Peines has magnificently recorded. It may be of Jewish origin. "Who ever named you Petenera did not name you properly. He should have called you the Perdition of Men" (tr. Gerald Brenan). His voice is golden, infinitely sad and from another world, the world of Chacón and the Cojo de Malaga, of great singers true of voice in a Spain long vanished like the Granada of the Twenties where I first met the Sitwells with Dick Wyndham and where Manuel de Falla and Lorca staged their festival in the garden of the Generalife.

Next morning my infirmity was back and a new symptom—fearful giddiness on rising; the mind reels, the room spins round. It quickly passes but returns with any sudden movement. An attempted coup d'état from the liver, I surmise. I have to put off lunching at the Embassy but manage to totter round the Prado. How my taste has deteriorated! Bosch no longer enthrals me except for his table of the Seven Deadly Sins with Death in the middle. The wild fantasies of the Garden of Delights seem like comic strips, too many little niggly incidents, no depth. I prefer Patinir, his river Styx, or the marvellous Alpine landscape at the back of Dürer's self-portrait. The early Goyas seem rather flimsy in texture; great satisfaction from the later, especially the Francis Bacon dog—but somehow he's not my man. The usual guides and gaping crowds round the Velasquez with the portrait of the King in the mirror. Only the Fra Angelico really moves me as always, especially the garden. Such is the effect of a touch of nausea which continues in waves till I take my seat in the plane. Eleven planes in a fortnight.

As soon as I got home I saw my doctor. Diagnosis: otitis media, an infection of the middle ear from the bug which caused the other trouble aggravated by too much flying. Temperature 101. Treatment: nose-drops, ear-drops, antibiotics. I clear a wide-open space for my collection of travel brochures, hotel advertisements, air and sea time-tables, post-cards of Lanzarote, guide-books to Tenerife, the English church, the botanical garden, the wonders of the Prado, the *cante hondo* (supplied by La Zambra) the poems of President Senghor, descriptions of the Casamance, of the Ile de Goree, Lord Derby's eland, bananas and baobabs, even "The Prelude." . . .

"and Negro Ladies in white muslin gowns"

And so to bed with my medicine, another holiday over, to start reading Donne again.

'Upon the Islands fortunate we fall
(Not faynte Canaries but Ambrosial.)'

(1972)

2

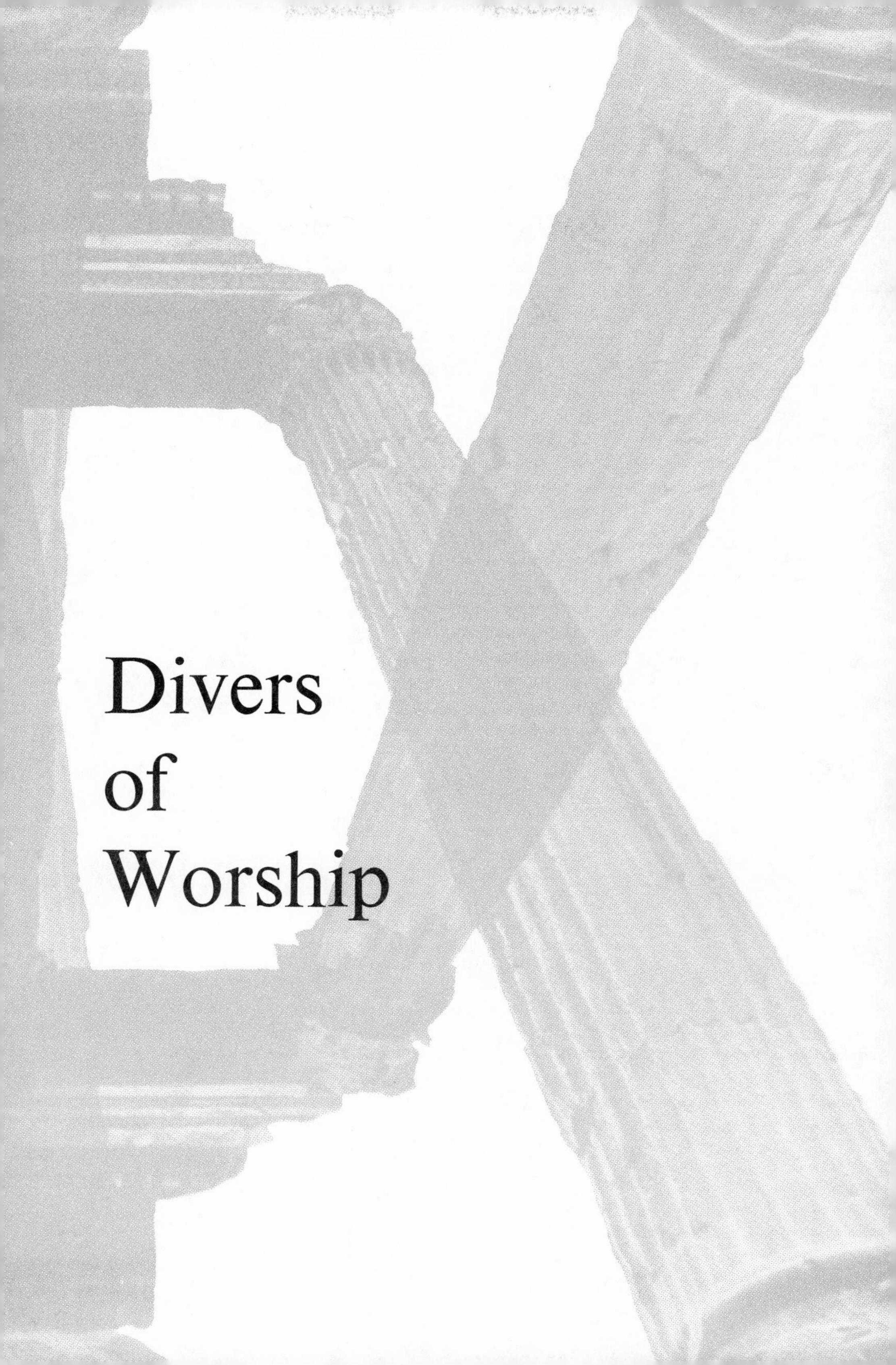

Divers of Worship

LA FONTAINE

EVERY few years I try to gate-crash a charmed society: with their plumed hats and tasselled canes, their embroidered coats and perfect manners, loitering in some formal garden. Lightly they carry their three hundred and fifty years—great Corneille, sombre Racine, honest Molière, Bossuet and Fénelon, La Bruyère and La Rochefoucauld, Madame de Sévigné, Boileau, Madame de Lafayette. The laughter vaporises as I steal up to them: *"Mais qui est ce malotru?"*

There is a whisking of periwigs, an alignment of cold shoulders, a maxim raps out like a ball on a pin-table, followed by the tinkle of alexandrines: *"Retirons-nous"* (is it Racine speaking?) *"dans nos appartements."* Of that Elysian company only one softens the retreat by a broad wink and the gesture of raising a bottle to his mouth: it is the ever-human La Fontaine, butterfly of Parnassus and least pretentious of men.

His is no easy life to write. Little happened to him, and of what happened little is known. His one misfortune was not to please the monarch and thus to spend a lifetime in the disfavour of one who was all-powerful and omnipresent. On the other hand, as Lytton Strachey has pointed out, his whole career is a tribute to the system of patronage and to the great ministers and fine ladies who made of him a household pet, anticipating his wants and encouraging the best vein in his work while turning a blind eye to his feckless promiscuity.

Were he alive today a little reviewing, a talk on the Third Programme or a brush with a documentary unit would be all his *oeuvre,* except a row of empties and the unpaid bills of rival psychoanalysts. For Jean de la Fontaine was certainly abnormal. He had a total horror of responsibility: marriage, paternity, making a home, looking after his small estate or administering a few acres of forest were all beyond him, and sleep, day-dreaming, poetry, wine and flirtation alone within his powers:

Car je n'ai pas vécu, j'ai servi deux tyrans.
Un vain bruit et amour ont partagé mes ans.

His long life was a permanent reverie with which he was always trying to catch up. "No one ever had a better claim to be regarded as an Original and as the first of his species," wrote his contemporary Perrault:

> Not only did he invent the kind of poetry to which he applied himself, but he carried it to its final perfection . . . He never said anything but what he thought, and never did anything but what he wanted to do. He joined with this a natural humility . . .

The *Tales* reveal La Fontaine as the last practitioner of sixteenth-century French literature, with its Renaissance ease and salacity. The *Fables,* however, though redolent of *la vieille France,* became more and more a form of his own and are among the few indispensable books; wise, true, alive, witty, incomparably condensed and seeming-artless. Affection for animals is the honey of misanthropy, and La Fontaine is not, as Eluard suggested, on the side of the strong, he simply knows how much damage they do:

La fourmi n'est point prêteuse
C'est là son moindre défault.

By the fourteenth line of the first fable we are already struck by the exquisite *griffe* which is to remain with us for another eleven volumes, the grasshopper's candid vision.

In her easy, clear and deceptively simple account of his life and work* Mrs. Sutherland takes us modestly and thoughtfully through the fables; they are, of course, not for the young, but, as Sainte-Beuve pointed out, for those who are forty and over. My one complaint about this delightful book is that its author is inclined to shy away from the fabulist's amours, which were highly practical. Was he not the lover of Madame Colletet, rather than in love with her? Should not the whole of Ninon de Lenclos's stinging epigram be quoted, or some of his jokes to Saint Evrémond?

(1953)

* *La Fontaine: The Man and his Work,* by Monica Sutherland (London, 1953).

SWIFT

THIS is a very attractive book.* It is short, concise, written with keen and lively feeling and does credit to Mr. Dennis's talents as much as to his great subject. He has taken a walk round his own mind and settled for objective lucidity, he has circumnavigated Freud and decided to ignore him, he dismisses elaborate theories about Swift's parentage as unimportant—it is Swift's ideas that interest him.

This explanation (that Swift was the son of Sir William Temple or of Sir William Temple's father, Sir John) . . . is unimportant because, as has been seen, Swift passed his whole life in the belief that he was the legitimate son of Jonathan (who died seven months before he was born) and the legitimate grandson of Thomas. His views on politics and religion grew up in the light of this belief; his ambition was rooted in it . . . if he was, in truth, illegitimate, the fact escaped his attention.

As no bibliography is appended one is left uncertain whether in fact Mr. Dennis has read Mr. Denis Johnston's fascinating *In Search of Swift* (Macmillan, 1959) which puts forward the Sir John Temple theory:

Sir John Temple the elder could physically, geographically and in common sense have been Jonathan Swift's father. And while it can never be proved that he was, there is a colossal mass of inconsistencies, of lies and of unbelievable behaviour on the part of at least half a dozen people in Swift's orbit, that cannot be accounted for if he was not.

Yet Mr. Johnston is not so convincing about Swift's knowledge of his birth, and the probability seems closer to Mr. Dennis's statement. Swift's cult of his grandfather, the Reverend Thomas Swift of Goodrich, who was ruined by his militant devotion to Charles I, is not explicable if he

* *Jonathan Swift,* by Nigel Dennis (New York, 1964).

knew he was no relation, while his hostile indifference to later members of the Swift family can have several explanations. Both agree on Swift's madness "being in fact Ménière's syndrome" (first postulated by Dr. Bucknill in 1822 and confirmed by Dr. F. G. Wilson in 1939). This was complicated by senility, for Swift died in 1745, aged seventy-seven.

Where I am indebted to Mr. Dennis is for his interpretation of Swift's mind and principles, all that lay behind his belief in religion and authority, his royalism, his contempt and pity for his fellow-men, his hatred of dissenters and unyielding orthodoxy. He draws a brilliant comparison between him and Defoe, between *Gulliver's Travels* and *Robinson Crusoe*—"the primary text-book of Capitalism." "When we hold each man's masterpiece in our hands we hold the halves of one apple—the apple of discord that, in its wholeness, represents the England of the early eighteenth century." Defoe, of course, is a reasonable materialist, a Whig ancestor of the modern liberal business man. Swift would find it impossible to fit into the world today except possibly as an extremely reactionary headmaster of a small Anglican Borstal:

> The Life we live today descends in a direct line from his doughty opposite . . . To love and admire Swift is a whimsical act for he has no body of followers in his opinions.

On the other hand he is a greater influence on writers than Defoe; one is aware of his influence in Orwell, Waugh, Joyce, Yeats and many French writers—and also on Mr. Dennis himself. The Dantesque grandeur, the forbidding personality of Swift, his tragic life, are always of permanent interest, even while High Toryism and Anglican intolerance languish. His life was tragic through frustrated ambition: "All my endeavours, from a boy, to distinguish myself, were only for want of a great title and fortune, that I might be used like a Lord by those who have an opinion of my parts—whether right or wrong, it is no great matter." And of course he achieved it, and was used like a lord, and stood at the centre of affairs and loved every moment, like a political prelate, not a great writer.

How different from Congreve and Pope, artists who accepted as truth that a writer who does not willingly choose the contemplative life is bound to be unhappy—and probably write badly as well. *Gulliver's Travels* was wrung out of Swift by exile and disappointment, for he was banished to Ireland by the fall of the Tories and was indeed lucky to have in Ormonde a friend who could appoint him to the Deanery, since the Queen had always set her face against him.

For a Tory who could not please Queen Anne, who could not crack the philistinism of the first Georges, exile was perhaps better than the immediate pin-pricks of the ante-rooms. Mr. Dennis notes how empty the success of the Drapier letters and the affection of his adopted people were for this banished Voltaire, who pined only for the power and influence he had forfeited, and lived in a world of *huis clos*—"Dignity and Station, or great riches are in some sort necessary to old Men, in order to keep the younger at a Distance who are otherwise too apt to insult them upon the score of their Age."

And yet how persuasive is the sombre eloquence of reactionary genius; we feel it in Johnson, in much of Shakespeare, in Baudelaire, a call to order and a sense of sin:

> Who that sees a little paltry mortal, drowning, and dreaming, and driveling to a multitude, can think it agreeable to common good sense, that either Heaven or Hell should be put to the trouble of influence or inspection, upon what he is about?

Mr. Dennis thinks Swift's great gift was prescience "in that the changes he opposed so ineffectively have all come to pass, usually in the way he foretold they would." Yet death, disease, war and bereavement continue however our society tries to mask them and we are chilled yet also contented to come on some painful truism tolling through that sonorous prose:

> God, in his wisdom, hath been pleased to load our declining years with many sufferings, with diseases, and decays of nature, with the death of many friends, and the ingratitude of more . . . with a want of relish for all worldly enjoyments, with a general dislike of persons and things, and though all these are very natural effects of increasing years, yet they were intended by the author of our being to ween us gradually from our fondness for life, the nearer we approach towards the end of it.

(1965)

POPE: 1

MR. QUENNELL* takes Pope up to his fortieth birthday, when the first *Dunciad* appeared (May 1728). I believe he contemplated a second volume but decided that the trees were too thick for the wood. To put it brutally, one might say that Pope, considering his fantastic gifts, is a disappointment, and that once he had finished his Homer and *Dunciad* his major work was done.

His later years were given over to illness ("that long disease, my life"), shadow-boxing with nonentities, cooking his reputation, and were redeemed only by the *Essay on Man,* the *Satires* and *Epistles,* which do, however, contain his most finished work. Between 1731 and 1735 he published his *Moral Essays,* and to the same period belongs the *Essay on Man.*

His friends Atterbury and Gay died in 1732 and in 1733 he lost his mother.

So, as a lover of Pope and an admirer of Mr. Quennell I express my regret that he did not carry on a little and I hope that the next edition may be extended so that we can take Pope up to the age of forty-five and hear what his biographer has to say about "The Characters of Women" and the winding-up of the "Lady Mary" polemic, the Addison story, the truth about "Atossa" and the Duchess of Marlborough's bribes, and the epistles which affirm his friendship for Burlington, Arbuthnot, Bathurst and others, all of whom figure so largely in these pages.

No one could do it better than Mr. Quennell, whose *Caroline of England* (1939), so unwarrantably neglected (it is dedicated to me),

* *Alexander Pope: the Education of a Genius 1688–1728,* by Peter Quennell (New York, 1968).

contains an admirable chapter on Pope. This must have been written thirty years ago and it is interesting to compare the quotations which pleased him then with those which he selects now. From *Caroline of England* I derive the impression that Mr. Quennell considers *The Rape of the Lock* and the *Epistle to Dr. Arbuthnot* (especially the "Sporus" passage) the twin peaks of Pope's genius.

Pope is disappointing because, with his marvellous technique and imagination (an imagination which could soar outside the limitations of contemporary sensibility), his choice of subjects are not those best suited to employ his gifts—at least by present-day standards. Are we right or wrong? Of Dryden (another disappointing poet, despite the "hommage" to him), Pope told Spence that he had to write too much to get money. Pope solved this problem by translating Homer. "Dryden cleared every way about twelve hundred pounds on his Virgil and had sixpence each line for his Fables . . . His Virgil was one of the first books that had anything of a subscription" (Spence's *Anecdotes*).

Pope himself cleared about £8,000 from his Homers, enough to keep him for the rest of his life and so attain the freedom and independence hitherto denied to those poets who were not aristocrats or churchmen. Only Bolingbroke remarked that translation was unworthy of Pope, for to his contemporaries the presentation of Homer in eighteenth-century costume seemed well worth his labours. *The Dunciad,* which Mr. Quennell compares to *Bouvard and Pécuchet,* is even more questionable. Nothing dates like hate, and in literature a little of it goes a very long way.

But Pope wrote no *Madame Bovary.* And so we are left, once more, with *The Rape* and the *Moral Essays,* the most Horatian work in English. *The Rape of the Lock* may be called the only rococo masterpiece in English, somehow evoking the decorative triumphs of that other unique dwarf, Cuvilliès. (Mr. Quennell advises anyone who is writing about Pope to measure off his height, four feet six, upon a door before embarking on further criticism.)

One cannot read Mr. Quennell's Life without being reminded of the early Proust. Like Proust, Pope was an infant prodigy, a mother's boy of astonishing sensibility, a master of imitation and parody, a lover of nature who was soon to become the pet of the fashionable world. Like Proust he was to grow into a moralist and then a cynic, to be devoted to his friends and yet to see through them, and to struggle with increasing ill-health. But, unlike Proust, he lacked the Grail-like image of the work of art or the gospel of salvation through art.

He read prodigiously from childhood, wrote and painted, and the illness (Pott's disease) which affected his spine was at first more of an encouragement than a handicap. It was not until Dennis and others had begun to attack him that he learnt to hate and that revenge became an obsession.

Mr. Quennell's method is to proceed chronologically and not hesitate to block in the other characters as they emerge. These make fascinating character-studies. The result is a crowded page presided over by a sympathetic but rather weary impresario who hints delicately that he has seen it all before. Although aware of Pope's deviousness, even cunning, Mr. Quennell retains a belief in his basic morality.

> Pope had always a deep regard for goodness, and he believed, with Boileau, that both a writer's intelligence and the qualities of his heart had an important influence upon his style.

Mr. Quennell also seizes on another key point. "To follow poetry as one ought, one must forget father and mother, and cleave to it alone," was Pope's maxim, but in fact the poetry he wrote appealed completely to the age in which he lived and depended on pleasing his affluent audience.

> In the Romantic view every poet is at heart a born rebel and Pope's intellect was perfectly attuned to the existing social system . . . The poet's attitude toward his audience—friendly, easy, sympathetic—had an important effect upon his literary style. Pope addresses his poems to the *whole* man—not only a man in his desperate, rapturous, elegiac moments, but to the more prosaic aspects of his personality, to his worldly wisdom, his sense of humour, his social tastes and intellectual leanings. Another result of this happy relation was his splendid self-confidence—"the first requisite," decided Johnson, "to great undertakings . . ."

And there follows one of the most understanding accounts of *The Dunciad* I have read:

> Chaos is eternal: Order temporal. Human intelligence is a transitory gleam. It is the poet who rounds off *The Dunciad* in a gigantic burst of lamentation.

(1968)

POPE: 2

I AM inclined to consider *The Dunciad* as the most disappointing of great poems, and, since I love Pope, I am therefore all the more grateful to Mr. Williams* for restoring a grandeur of intention to this dazzling, uneven, supremely competent and yet petty work. He quotes Oliver Elton as saying that *The Dunciad* is more seriously flawed than any other poem that Pope wrote and that "in criticising it we had best be silent about his art and instead of talking of 'its poetic intensity extraordinarily rich in beauty, oddness and surprise' (Leavis), we must talk of its 'tone of furious indiscriminate hatred, the half-crazed misanthropy of the whole poem.' (Gilbert Highet)."

Nothing palls like hatred, no subject more boring than bores. There is always some envy in moral indignation, yet an added difficulty with *The Dunciad* is the peculiar focus of Pope's mind. I suppose no great poet has had such a microscopic lens, such a wrong-end-of-the-telescope attitude to humanity. He often takes an insect view, and some tenth-rate scribbler, some poor glutinous hack, looms up out of the murk as a giant of Grub Street, to be demolished by segments as a sand-wasp bisects a caterpillar. Yet it is precisely this insect-eye that observes what is strange and small so as to produce effects of exquisite beauty, and *The Dunciad* is full of lines of marvellous poetry suggesting the waspy quinces and cankered pears in some perfect yet morbid Dutch still life:

> So spins the silk-worm small its slender store
> And labours till it clouds itself all o'er . . .
> Then thick as locusts black'ning all the ground
> A tribe with weeds and shells fantastic crown'd
> Each with some wondrous gift approach'd the pow'r
> A nest, a toad, a fungus or a flow'r

* *Pope's Dunciad: A Study of Its Meaning,* by Aubrey Williams (Baton Rouge, 1955).

In the poem are two or three of the most exquisite couplets ever written, including Pope's own favourite:

> Lo! where Maeotis sleeps, and hardly flows
> The freezing Tanais through a waste of snows . . .

and

> To isles of fragrance, lily-silver'd vales,
> Diffusing languor in the panting gales.

Such gems are no accident, but part of the deliberate policy of the author. In Mr. Williams's words, "The alternately chaste or mellifluous or grand qualities of Pope's language enable him to keep his own hands clean no matter how much dung is tossed about . . . to keep his *poem* uncontaminated by its 'dull' subject matter."

But is it so dull? Pope himself hinted at some secret meaning. "The author," he said, "in this work had indeed a *deep intent:* there were in it *Mysteries* which he durst not fully reveal"; and even if Mr. Williams has not succeeded in revealing them he has been able to prove that *The Dunciad* is not a mere carbuncle of spite and revenge, but a brilliantly planned attack on the pedantry, rhetoric, and confusion of values which were really the death agonies of the Augustan Age and the classical style.

Pope envisaged England as on the verge of a cultural break-down: "at the heart of the struggle is the concern with the means, use, ends, limits of human knowledge . . ." The "Dunce" was a real menace. "As Pope uses the word, it suggests not stupidity or ignorance, but a perverse misapplication of intelligence, learning without wisdom, the precise opposite of all that is implied by the term 'humanist' . . . Dunces and duncely writings were not, to Pope, matters of little or merely personal import. Such 'words,' such 'art,' inevitably for him, referred to states of mind and soul and to the state of the social order as a whole."

> See Christians, Jews, one heavy Sabbath keep,
> And all the Western world believe and sleep.

Mr. Williams's short book suffers from the desiccating influence of American thesis-writing and some of the points he makes are unimportant, but he does bring out many of Pope's felicities and he explains the structure and very important London geography of the poem. Why does a line like

> And Douglas lend his soft, obstetric hand

so please one? Or the famous quatrain which illustrates the time of day (eleven o'clock) possess such magical overtones beyond its realism—?

This labour past, by Bridewell all descend
(As morning-pray'r and flagellation end)
To where Fleet-ditch with disemboguing streams
Rolls the large tribute of dead dogs to Thames.

Pope comments

> It is between eleven and twelve in the morning that the criminals are whipp'd in Bridewell. This is to mark punctually the Time of the day. The poem, we may remember, commenc'd in the evening of the Lord Mayor's Day . . .

Such close planning and meticulous invention is matched by the magical vowel sounds, the musical variety, the breaks and pauses and strange silences of his magnificent versification.

In vain, in vain—the all-composing hour
Resistless falls: The Muse obeys the Pow'r.

(1955)

VOLTAIRE: 1

This is Miss Mitford's most ambitious flight.* A witty, worldly, life-loving lady, she has flung herself into the task of delineating the wittiest, worldliest and most life-loving of us all, the very symbol and archetype of humanism. This is not, however, the official Voltaire whose bust was installed in every *mairie*. When she ends her tale he still has twenty-nine years to run, years of glorious exile injustice-collecting during which he no longer belonged to France but to the world. She thus avoids being swamped by her own documentation and also confines herself to the Voltaire who still moves within the feminine orbit where a clever woman who is also a novelist is at no disadvantage.

But Miss Mitford is a historian as well, and this is a better book than her *Madame de Pompadour* because it exhibits greater unity, more scholarship and less bias; in particular she has evolved a technique for regurgitating packages of old letters in palatable form which any historian might envy. There is even new material, for Miss Mitford has had help from Mr. Theodore Besterman, editor of Voltaire's correspondence, which will include the unpublished letters from Voltaire to Madame Denis.

These letters are very important indeed: they prove that Voltaire became the lover of his niece in 1744, five years before the death of Madame du Châtelet to whom, in 1741, he had explained that he was too old to make love.

This fact is significant to all students of the sex-war and I, for one, have felt humiliated by Voltaire's abdication, at the age of forty-six, and by what seemed his rather abject acceptance of the new lover, the Marquis de Saint Lambert who caused Madame de Châtelet's fatal

* *Voltaire in Love,* by Nancy Mitford (Hartford, 1957).

pregnancy. She was then wearing a ring which concealed a miniature of her lover (one legend says that it had replaced that of Voltaire). "I replaced Richelieu. Saint Lambert has driven me out. It is the natural order of things, one nail knocks out another, and so it is in this world." But while making jealous scenes with her he was writing to Madame Denis, "I spend my life in cogitating how I can spend the rest of my life with you."

Miss Mitford wisely refrains from passing moral judgements except to tell us that "an affair with a niece is not regarded as incestuous in a Latin country," but she might well have added a brief analysis of the rules of the game as played at Versailles, for they are so different from our own. With us monogamy, fidelity and honesty are the watchwords, we attempt to be faithful to one person, and when we fail we tell them, or they tell us, and we try again with somebody else. But, among the life-lovers, dignity is more important than sincerity and pleasure than either. Everyone is entitled to as much love as he or she requires or can assimilate; accretions of new lovers, whole collections are formed round the man or woman most capable of maintaining them. A beautiful and clever woman retains her husband and perhaps three lovers (who each represent a decade of her life) in grateful bondage. Large houses, agreeable conversation and good cooks are balm to wounded vanity. Less human suffering is caused if promiscuity is permitted and the continuity of human relationships also preserved (they might argue) than by the discarding prevalent in a more idealistic society.

Even so, one might call Madame du Châtelet promiscuous by the standards of the time, for this enlightened and handsome blue-stocking constantly separated her sexual need from her jealous and devouring passion for the first genius of Europe. And Frederick the Great's feeling for Voltaire was also devouring and jealous, though passion played no part in it. He hated Madame du Châtelet and was determined to wrest Voltaire from her; he was prepared to betray Voltaire to the French government to make it impossible for him to return to France—even as Voltaire was willing to pretend to be expelled from France in order to win the confidence of Frederick, and then betray him.

I think Miss Mitford is rather unfair to Frederick and inclined to dislike him as she dislikes the Cardinal de Bernis. Her flaws as a historian are a tendency to neurotic heartlessness—"the current rather excessive punishment for Sodomy was burning at the stake"—an occasional descent into schoolboy language ("stunning," "beastly," etc.), an exaggerated regard for birth and money. But these are tendencies, not faults, and in no way prevent her *Voltaire in Love* from being a most exhaustive, witty and absorbing account of one of the great love stories of the world, singularly fertile in benefits for others. Madame du Châtelet was a serious scientist and her way of possessing Voltaire was to keep him in the country, engaged in study for those formative years which transformed him from fashionable poet and courtier into the philosopher whose thought moulded and transcended his country.

Voltaire was not what we mean by an intellectual. He was a man of action as well as a poet; a financier, a planner and organiser, a courtier, lover, spy, intriguer. It was the seriousness of Madame du Châtelet which fixed his gifts in the right proportion. Miss Mitford understands him and does not try to explain him. "He enjoyed a battle. He liked all forms of human relationship and in some way his enemies were more necessary to him than his friends." Her own comments are also invigorating. "Of all the sorrows which assail our loved ones, the easiest to bear is an attack on them in print."

I have never loved Voltaire overmuch: his mind has no shade—but one must honour him as nature's triumph, as a model of what intelligence can accomplish, and it is wiser to describe him in these earlier years as a lover than to recount the plots of his many plays and pamphlets.

Despite his maxim *"qui plume a, guerre a,"* he was also a man who loved to surround himself with beautiful things; a picture-collector, decorator, garden-planner, amateur of china and silver and author of the phrase *"le superflu, chose très nécessaire,"* and Miss Mitford brings out this atmosphere of astonishing luxury. She does her best with Madame du Châtelet who yet remains faintly ridiculous and forbidding, perhaps because her letters are dull and inclined to self-pity, perhaps because we are not given a specimen of her scientific writing and have to take her talents for granted.

M. du Châtelet is more sympathetic and so are Voltaire's many friends, especially Richelieu and the Englishman Fawkener, Voltaire's host at Wandsworth to whom he continually imparts his happiness and passion. "Yet I am afraid you want two provisions or ingredients to make that nauseous draught of life go down, I mean books and friends . . . Health and places I have not. As to fortune I enjoy a very competent one, and I have a friend besides." It is interesting that he should quote Rochester.

The first threat to this ideal love came from Frederick, a Ludwig seeking a Wagner; but the real danger was Madame Denis in Paris and afterwards the attractions of the King of Poland's little court at Lunéville. Both being such healthy royalty snobs the lovers deserted their château at Cirey to go and stay there when in difficulties with both Versailles and Potsdam; and there lurked the young lover whose embraces (when she was forty-four) were to cause Madame du Châtelet's death. *"Ah! mon ami!"* cried Voltaire, *"C'est vous qui me l'avez tuée."*

The child died too. Saint Lambert became the lover of Madame d'Houdetot and Voltaire set up house with Madame Denis: "The friendship between us, the mutual confidence, the delights of the heart, the enchantment of the soul, these things do not perish and can never be destroyed. I shall love you until I die."

(1957)

VOLTAIRE: 2

MR. BESTERMAN is the great Voltairean who is now bringing out the superlative edition of Voltaire's correspondence. He allowed Nancy Mitford to make use of these unpublished letters* in her book on Voltaire, and this one is dedicated to her. The friendship of scholars can be as generous as their rage.

When I reviewed Miss Mitford I mentioned the importance of this discovery which establishes Madame Denis and not Madame du Châtelet as the love of Voltaire's life, since he spent the last thirty years of his existence with her, for he began his affair on the death of her husband in 1744 and while he was still living with Madame du Châtelet who had not yet become fatally involved with her new lover. The conception of Voltaire as the *amant-cocu,* only slightly less ridiculous than the complaisant husband, must now be radically revised. All parties were, however, extremely civilised people among whom such labels had little meaning. Life was to be lived and they were together to live it. The basis of existence for Voltaire and Madame du Châtelet was intellectual, the husband was generally absent, the lover not unique; while for the greedy Madame Denis her celebrated uncle proved an inexhaustible meal-ticket.

"It is impossible to doubt that Voltaire loved his niece sincerely, tenderly, passionately, and even blindly," writes Mr. Besterman. "He was always true to this love, even after Mme Denis had been guilty of grave offences against her uncle; the evidence for his constancy is in my hands. As for her, did she ever love Voltaire? Scepticism is indicated . . ."

* *Voltaire's Love-Letters to His Niece,* edited and translated by Theodore Besterman (London, 1953).

We must balance, in fact, against their thirty years of cohabitation, her avarice, the fact that she preferred her other lovers, that she refused to follow him to Prussia and sold all his manuscripts on his death. At the time of her own husband's death Voltaire was fifty and Madame Denis thirty-two, making her exactly illustrate the genial man-made adage that a wife should be half her husband's age plus seven. But what a bad fifty he was, even as he was a bad sixty, seventy or eighty!

And what dull love-letters from this prince of letter-writers! I think they are among the worst I have ever read. Many were in glib Italian, most of them are no longer than a postcard, usually explaining that he has been too busy to see her or too ill to make love. (Indigestion!) Everything depends on how much genuine ardour resides in his oft-repeated wish to spend the rest of his life with her—"I should like to live at your feet and to die in your arms."

One might argue that he was a very busy man, deep, at the time of these letters, in the main channel of the world, confederate with kings and princes—so was Swift while writing his *Journal to Stella.* Or that secrecy enjoined banality. But occasionally a phrase of unabashed lubricity gives the truth away. The fault, for fault it is, lies in the great man's conception of love as an extension of friendship on the one hand and a mere mechanism for the release of tension on the other. Humanist love—theatre-tickets, literary advice, well-chosen supper-parties, agreeable intercourse, the "closed car at four"—this was the celebrated *douceur de vivre* and there was no inkling of the splendour or the torment, the glory of the senses, the affliction of the will, the glimpses of eternity, the refining fire which consumed Mademoiselle de Lespinasse or even the deliberately worldly and desperately unromantic Madame du Deffand, shaken by the demon of her unrequited passion for Walpole which thudded behind her curtain of blindness.

We are having a little supper-dinner on Tuesday between five and six o'clock in the evening, with your sister, the Abbé du Resnel and Marmontel and Sister Jeanne. Don't fail me, my dear. ["Sister Jeanne" meant that passages from Voltaire's *La Pucelle* would be read] . . . At half-past five on Wednesday, my dear. Don't fail me. The party is for you.

Occasionally there is a genuine and beautiful letter. Here is the best:

You are the unique end of all my aims and I flatter myself that I shall soon be happier. You are my consolation, and I have no other desire than to make you happy during my life and after my death. I will always love you tenderly until the day on which the law of nature separates what nature and love united. Let us love each other until then. A thousand kisses.

The maxims of humanism are best applied to other passions:

Art is infinite, its rewards an empty dream; only the labour is real. Yet let us not lose heart. Let us work, my dear. The pleasure of working consoles for all, but it does not console me for being so far from you . . . Try to organise your life, my dear, so as to be happy. Consider that there is nothing else for us to do in this world, that the past is nothing and that our sole concern is to live peacefully today and tomorrow. All else is illusion . . . The pleasures of the senses pass and flee in the twinkling of an eye, but the affection that binds us, the mutual confidence, the pleasures of the heart, the sensual love of the soul, are not destroyed and do not perish thus. I will love you until death.

. . . You will find there in my bedroom the four tickets for *Armide*.

Theatre tickets—that is perhaps the clue. In humanist love there is neither ecstasy nor despair—above all—no action. We select a partner with whom to enjoy the spectacle of life, a couple of stalls till death us do part as we exchange criticism, comment and reminiscences. Play follows play, some amusing, some tragic, actors come and go, but the two stalls remain filled night after night by the same eager, expectant, and slowly crumbling couple. And if one of them is Voltaire his true existence is taking place in the functioning of his ever-celibate mind.

Mr. Besterman's notes are brief yet admirable, and he is to be congratulated on this great literary discovery. Madame Denis even contemplated marrying her uncle—who was, however, averse to the publicity.

(1958)

SADE

IT WAS the author of this book* who won the confidence of the first broadminded descendant of Sade, the late Marquis, and was empowered to explore a wealth of correspondence and unpublished manuscripts in the family mansion. Up to the time of the German occupation, there was even a miniature which was the only authenticated portrait of Sade. The letters have been admirably edited by M. Lély in three volumes, and, with other new material, have contributed to this, I hope, irrefutable biography.

In the last fifty years Sade, once known only to a few choice spirits, has taken his place beside Voltaire and Rousseau as the third great destructive force of the French eighteenth century; the patron saint of the Surrealists and M. Maurice Heine; and an obsession for many other modern poets and psychologists.

Little known in this country, his writings have not yet kindled the greed of a publisher nor attained the ubiquity of a paper-back; and, when they do, they will come as a revelation for they are among the most disturbing books in the world; yet also, in my view, among the dullest—as one might expect from a madman.

Was Sade mad? It was on these grounds that his lifelong enemy, his mother-in-law, Madame de Montreuil, had him imprisoned for eleven years by a royal *lettre-de-cachet;* and there are signs that this harsh imprisonment further warped his reason and developed a cerebral obsession with sex where, hitherto, there had been only an irrepressible lechery. Prison made a writer, a most lucid and persuasive writer, out of

* *The Marquis de Sade,* by Gilbert Lély. Translated by Alec Brown (New York, 1962).

a man who had hitherto been merely suspected of holding subversive opinions and who had been convicted of holding orgies with prostitutes.

His real crime, in the eyes of his mother-in-law, was to have made a public tour of Italy with his wife's married sister and thus dragged the family name into disrepute. Prison remained the only place where he could be prevented from further disgrace and extravagance—her family had the money. The two sisters had accepted the situation and his wife was utterly devoted for as long as he would let her be; she endured the horror of seeing the family name slowly adopted into the French language through her husband's methodical debaucheries, yet she neither betrayed nor forsook him.

I think he was a manic-depressive who, under duress, went mad: there is a glitter, a sheen of indefatigable egotism about his work, a compulsive sexual obsession, a passion for detail which one associates only with the insane, even down to his persecution mania and terrifying logic. Society recognised in him a dangerous enemy.

Not that Sade was a cruel man; he was against the death penalty and, though he glorified murder in the name of lust, he never in his own acts went beyond flagellation. As a prisoner he was the supreme nuisance; his scenes, complaints, escapes and voluminous correspondence must have made him the *bête noire* of every governor. In fact, during his prison years, he was in a state of cerebral satyriasis, driven inexorably to a fantastic eruption of wishful sexual and subversive thinking. His lost works alone are more than most men's whole output.

The most important to survive (which he believed lost) was the *Cent Vingt Jours de Sodome,* written from prison in his tiny writing on rolls of toilet-paper. Despite an introduction of the most sombre brilliance, it soon becomes an obsessional catalogue of his favourite perversions and lacks the scientific detachment claimed for it by those disciples who see it as an anticipation of the great work of Krafft-Ebing.

His published novels, *Justine, Juliette,* etc., cry out for abridgement, for he had all the long-winded artificiality of the French eighteenth-century story-teller and no gift for narrative or the creation of character, only for philosophical dissertation. His strongly developed masochism enabled him to obtain as much pleasure from his characters' misfortunes as from those who inflicted them, and whose behaviour appears at times to shock him. *Justine or The Misfortunes of Virtue* seems to have been considered the most deleterious by a civilisation determined to believe that virtue, in this life, is rewarded.

Sade's morality was simple: God was ludicrous, so was "Nature," the God set up by the philosophers, which, if it willed at all, willed only man's destruction. The true God was in our own heart and resided in the deep happiness we feel when we are doing exactly what we want: and what we want is, he thought, to gratify lust, avarice, cruelty and ambition at the expense of others. Human beings are divided by temperament and opportunity into predators and victims; predators recognise and respect one another. Even if they sometimes, in play, enjoy pretending to be victims, they rule the world and apportion it into zones of lust. When they are too old to enjoy, they can still look on and vent their rage. There are no ties between human beings, beyond a temporary sympathy between those who happen to be enjoying the same vice. The rest is humbug.

One can see the attraction of such a philosophy as a liberating force, especially among full-blooded adolescents growing up in a world of cant. It might easily take root in the schoolroom or the prefect's study, even in the officers' mess, and it encourages hypocrisy as a means of gaining one's end. But one can also, I hope, see the deadly dullness of any system of life which makes the gratification of sexual appetite the major goal.

M. Lély struggles manfully against the overwhelming monotony of his subject (thirty years of whose life were spent in prison), but his adoption of the annalistic method in the interests of greater accuracy is monotonous in itself. This is by far the most detailed account of this spiritual *grand mutilé* to have been written or likely to be written. It also quotes fully from his correspondence, and from other authorities on the subject like M. Heine: and it has been well translated by Mr. Brown who, despite occasional fluffing of difficult sentences and many printer's errors, has recaptured the huge irony, the manic obstinacy, and microscopic observation of the original. It is, however, not so much a book for the lover of eighteenth-century personality as for those who have read some bad books about Sade and are now ready, with some effort from themselves, for a good one.

(1961)

BOSWELL

ANOTHER volume* of the Boswell diaries is always exciting. I grabbed it on the strength of the blurb: "The long London journal of 1778 is now printed for the first time; it is the last major journal of Boswell's known to have survived that has not previously been published."

Much of it, however, he used in his *Life of Johnson* so we are given an original source but by no means original material, except for the scenes where Johnson was not present. The London diary has been thoroughly annotated by Dr. Inge Probstein. The other journals in this volume are Scottish (including the interview with Hume), except for the visit of Boswell and Johnson to Ashbourne in Derbyshire, here much fuller than in the *Life*.

Boswell "in extremis" refers to his fluctuating state at the time: his melancholy, the alcoholism against which he vainly struggled and the growing conviction, apparent to both the reader and himself, that he is not going to make a success of his career at the Bar. Luckily the *Life* was to bestow on him the immortality which eluded his more successful contemporaries, Scottish peers surrounding Lord Bute, legal luminaries and Edinburgh divines.

Silly, snobbish, lecherous, tipsy, given to high-flown sentiments and more than a little of a humbug, Boswell is redeemed by a generosity of mind, a concentration on topics that will always appeal (like death, ghosts and human frailty), and a naïvety that endeared him to the great minds he cultivated. He needed Johnson as ivy needs the oak, he preened himself in that unflattering mirror, he extracted material from their visits to the Club such as the Goncourts took from Flaubert at the Magny dinners, but without their malice.

No two figures in literature have gained so much in stature during this

* *Boswell in Extremis 1776–1778,* edited by Charles McC. Weiss and Frederick A. Pottle (New York, 1970).

century as Boswell and Horace Walpole. The flood of new material, the devotion of their editors have enlarged their personalities which had only their grasp of the topical in common. Walpole was not impressed by Johnson, his political enemy and an uncouth, blown-up provincial bully in the eyes of the fastidious aesthete who was a far more successful snob than Boswell could ever hope to be.

Despite his eye for character, his ear for dialogue, his good memory, Boswell lacked the visual sense. He gives us no impression of what London in the high eighteenth century looked like, how it smelt or tasted. Tea and "chocolade" were favourite beverages; also coffee, claret and pints of port. Lord Pembroke lends Boswell his "chariot": the Thrales have a coach, Johnson a "black" (Negro servant); Mrs. Rudd keeps a brothel; "36" is an old mistress Boswell visits. Besides hangovers, he suffers intermittently from gonorrhoea about which his friends tease him; he is constantly "feeling" and occasionally "tailing" (Johnson's word) servants and girl friends. "Sposa read my journal and was justly displeased with my fondling of maids at inns"—after which he writes "felt" in Greek letters.

But there is a sad lack of sense-perceptions and even the worked-up conversation, the quintets and sextets at the Club have the air of being orchestrated by Boswell from a very scrappy score. Johnson is always in character, Langton always a butt, Garrick faintly ridiculous, Gibbon makes very little impression. Boswell is happiest with father-figures like Paoli or Scottish cronies of his father's from whom he can expect a loan or preferment. In the crude reporting of the Journal the Boswell-Johnson symbiosis seems occasionally caricatured, as if everyone were conniving at the future *Life*. They seem to know their conversation is being bugged for posterity.

Yet the greatness of Johnson is indestructible; it comes out not in his repartee and his rudeness but in his lucidity, the natural force of mental horse-power. That he was kind and compassionate as well lends a glow to his many appearances.

We are all envious naturally. But by checking envy, we get the better of it, as we are all thieves naturally. A child always tries to get at what it wants the nearest way. By instruction and good habit this is cured, till a man has not even an inclination to seize on what is another's, has no struggle with himself about it.

A man who is asked by a writer what he thinks of his work is put to the torture, and is not obliged to speak truth . . .

The insolence of riches will creep out.

He (Dr. Percy) said Johnson at once probed the human heart, where the sore was. He said the conversation of Johnson was so strong and clear, like an antique statue, every vein and muscle distinct and bold.

Nevertheless, this book is Boswell's—including the crushing retorts made against himself and the occasion when, drunk, he gate-crashes a grand supper-party of Topham Beauclerk's and gets brutally snubbed.

> Beauclerks. A company of ladies and gentlemen of their own class. A table for supper. Was Awkward. He said "Who's that?" Somebody said, "Mr. Boswell." I went round and shook hands. He said, "How did you get in at this time of night?" No sooner had I taken my chair than he said, "WHEN do you go to Scotland?"

When he visits an old down-at-heel pornographer like Cleland (author of *Fanny Hill*) it's his turn to crow.

> Called on Cleland. Found him in an old house in the Savoy, just by the waterside. A coarse, ugly, old woman for his servant. His room filled with books in confusion and dust. He was drinking tea and eating biscuits. I joined him. He had a rough cap like Rousseau and his eyes were black and piercing. He was very polite to me and made me better pleased with myself than with him. For I did not find in him that solid and clear thinking to which Dr. Johnson has accustomed me.

Even the learned Dr. Probstein, who traces so many classical allusions falls down on this one.

> Away and met 36, vastly smug. I said, "What harm in your situation?" 36 said, "To be sure. Or in yours provided it does not weaken affection at home." (What a slut! To be thus merely corporeal!) Twice. Good Dutch landlord. Refreshed.

The note reads "Obscure. Perhaps a compliment to '36' on her hospitality."

"36" we learn, was Mrs. Love, the actress, an old flame of Boswell's now nearing sixty. The allusion must be to his gonorrhoea (and hers?) which did indeed "scare and chill Mrs. Boswell" (Introduction). Here we find Boswell summed up. "He differed from most men in his extraordinary avidity for sensation. In spite of the greed with which he devours experiences, he always felt that the best part was escaping him." The editors even suggest that the uncompromising views of Hume ("it was a most unreasonable fancy that we should exist for ever . . .") in his last interview released some spring in Boswell, causing him to make love whenever in the dying philosopher's vicinity.

> Called at Mr. David Hume's, wishing to converse with him while I was elevated with liquor, but was told he was very ill. I then ranged awhile in the Old Town after strumpets.

(1971)

THE DANDY: 1

WHAT is a dandy? "One who pays an exaggerated attention to dress," answers the dictionary. "And who thereby expresses his contempt," one might continue, "for all that is not external: morals, intellect, feeling." According to Baudelaire dandyism is "heroism in decay"; it is rather a gesture of defiance, a flower of vanity, courage and stupidity, but a delightful flower which has a particular appeal for self-conscious artists. With the passing of youth, the dandy's calculated insensibility, his grace and insolence reveal an undertone of melancholia. Love, art, religion and philosophy are closed worlds; to the fortunate remains the club, to the rest banishment. While still at Eton Brummell became a Beau. From the age of twenty-two to thirty-eight he reigned in metallic splendour; but the next twenty-four years were passed in exile. Calais. Calais. Caen . . . and he died penniless and insane.

What Brummell was to Byron, D'Orsay became for Disraeli; a friend, a temptation and a warning. But as dandy the Frenchman falls far short of his predecessor whose turn-out was as discreet as his sallies were insufferable and whose gloves fitted so as to reveal the contour of the nail. For one thing D'Orsay was an aristocrat while the true dandy should appear from nowhere; he should come, be seen and conquer. For another he was an all-round sportsman and athlete while the dandy is essentially urban; and finally he was an artist. A bad artist, be it said, but the germ was there and led him (another black mark) to frequent the society of writers. Introduced to Victor Hugo, Brummell could only rise to "Splendid work, sir!" but D'Orsay actually dined with the fellow and was intimate with Landor, Dickens, Thackeray.

Byron remarked that dandies as a rule detested men of letters. In fact D'Orsay was too kind and intelligent to be a dandy at all, he was merely a *grand seigneur* born out of his time, a penniless prince who was convinced that the world owed him a standard of living worthy of his forebears. The only mark of the true dandy was his debts: £120,000 of them. These are evidence of a lurking ferocity. Brummell would have respected this splendid sum even as he would have disliked the sky-blue outfits with gold chains strapping the trouser to the instep which revealed the soul of his imitator.

Mr. Connely's book* gives an enormously full account of D'Orsay, particularly as the companion of Lady Blessington. He provides a well-documented panorama of social life from the *flamboyante* of the Regency down to the solid decorum of Victoria. His is an industrious rather than a great biography because these are neither great nor even very interesting people. Blessington was an absentee Irish peer with thirty-five thousand pounds a year, a weakness for drink and theatricals and a talent for interior decorating, his wife a tarnished and rebellious beauty with an insatiable greed for position and celebrity. They adopted their Antinous for life and Blessington wedded him to his daughter of sixteen by a former union and then bequeathed his fortune to her. The marriage was never consummated and she was aided by her mother's relatives in gradually withdrawing her income from the clutches of her husband and stepmother. Hence the debts.

Though a wonderful companion to her son-in-law, Lady Blessington was, according to Greville, "ignorant, vulgar and commonplace," a shallow but spirited blue-stocking, a lion-huntress harassed by financial expedients. Her debonair and florid giant (no mean interior decorator either), though hospitable and talented, seems strangely vapid.

Misers and dandies are closely connected. The slave of Mammon loves to ant it over fashion's fool. When a dun finally penetrated Gore House with a writ and D'Orsay fled, like Brummell before him, Lord Hertford, then amassing the Wallace Collection, was one of the first to arrive at the sale. The proceeds seemed enough to permit the two devoted rattles to reopen a new salon in Paris and continue to have their cake and be eaten. But death put an end to the routine. Lady Blessington went first, and though twelve years younger, D'Orsay followed her in two years to the gracious mausoleum he had designed for them.

(1952)

* *Count D'Orsay: The Dandy of Dandies,* by Willard Connely (London, 1952).

THE DANDY: 2

ANOTHER book* about dandies to swell the literature on Brummell and D'Orsay, Baudelaire and Wilde. The same quotations, the same illustrations, the delving into Captains Jesse and Gronow, Barbey, Boulenger, Willard Connely and Mario Praz. It seems only yesterday I reviewed a life of D'Orsay, that caponised Brummell. Such was my preliminary grumble. But Ellen Moers (Vassar, Radcliffe and Columbia University, Ph.D., aged thirty-two) proceeded to dispel my doubts.

She has found a subject that had to be treated, seen a shape left unfinished in the quarries of the nineteenth century and proceeded to hack it out. She has brought French and English dandyism into perspective and related the physical assertion of the Regency Buck to the intellectual stance of the Left Bank poet. This needed doing, but what Miss Moers has also perceived is the nature of the literary conflict between Regency dandyism and Victorian gentility as typified by the attacks on Bulwer Lytton, and how both Dickens and Thackeray were secretly unsettled by it.

Driven underground by the earlier attacks of *Fraser's Magazine,* of Thackeray and Carlyle (which caused Lytton to bowdlerise his novel *Pelham*) dandyism reappears as a symptom of the reaction to the Victorian age in Whistler, Wilde and Beerbohm. *"Eternelle supériorité du dandy!"* as Baudelaire wrote.

What is a dandy? Carlyle was right. Essentially he is "a clothes-wearing man," and therefore dandyism is prevalent at the age when clothes matter most, shall we say from fifteen to thirty-five. But the whole attitude is one of defiance, either of the staid bill-footing father or

* *The Dandy,* by Ellen Moers (New York, 1960).

of conventional morality and bourgeois values. It is antisocial, although it attempts to lead society rather than ignore it. "The dandy does not preserve his integrity by living in retirement, but goes purposefully among the romantics, pedants, athletes, bailiffs and other bores of this world to remind them of his superiority."

It is significant that Brummell exaggerated his father's humble birth and cut his elder brother but coalesced into immediate union with the Prince of Wales who was himself in revolt against his own father and who had said that the only gentleman among his ancestors was Charles II.

It is in the reign of Charles II that literary dandyism begins, when Etherege put Rochester on the stage and set the tone for Congreve who evolved the dead-pan man-and-valet relationship improved on by Brummell and perfected by Wilde. Brummell's fall was occasioned by his antisocial instinct rounding on the royal benefactor from whom he could no longer conceal his sense of superiority. Miss Moers exhumes a forgotten novel, T. H. Lister's *Granby* (1826), which portrays Brummell as Trebeck.

> There was a heartlessness in his character, a spirit of gay misanthropy, a cynical depreciating view of society, an absence of high-minded generous sentiment, a treacherous versatility, and deep powers of deceit.

Little survives in his wit today but the aggression, for we are too used to the ploy by which trifles are taken seriously and serious things made light of. Wilde overdid it. As Hazlitt wrote, "We may say of Mr. Brummell's jests that they are of a meaning so attenuated that nothing lives 'twixt them and nonsense—they hover on the very brink of vacancy: he has touched the *ne plus ultra* that divides the dandy from the dunce. But what a fine eye to discriminate."

Eternal inferiority of the dandy—this is my regretted conclusion; for, being committed to clothes and externals, he is committed to stupidity and physical ageing; spiritually opaque, he reigns for ten years and decays for forty more, while mind and body rust. The dandy is but the larval form of a bore. "Brummell had too much self-love ever to be really in love," wrote his biographer, Jesse, and even self-love withers without an audience. Perhaps his greatest saying (new to me) was to the anonymous military gentleman stopping at Caen who recognised him in the shabby old man at the door of the Hotel d'Angleterre. Brummell acknowledged his expressions of sympathy: *"On est bien changé,"* he said, *"voilà tout."*

What was at stake in dandyism was more than a pose, it was privilege and male selfishness, the right of the drone to be fed without the hazards of the nuptial flight. The middle-class protest followed and has continued ever since, though seldom as clearly put as by Maginn (editor of *Fraser's Magazine*) in an article on Bulwer.

> It is a favourite notion with our fashionable novelists, to sacrifice the middle classes equally to the lowest and highest . . . There is a sort of instinct in this. The one class esteem themselves above law, and the other one too frequently below it. They are attracted then by a sympathy with their mutual lawlessness.

Meanwhile Dickens and Thackeray, the two anti-snobs, were to perform their parabolas, and Miss Moers writes very well about their preoccupation with class. She shows how Thackeray's financial reverses made him oversensitive to problems of status, how Dickens's later success disillusioned him until he was creating "grey men"—sympathetic characters who were failures and fallen: dandies, culminating in Sidney Carton and Eugene Wrayburn, who says of the bees: "Ye-es they work—but don't you think they overdo it?"

These chapters on Victorian novelists, on Dickens, Thackeray, Disraeli and Bulwer (with D'Orsay on close terms with them all, constantly propagating his dandyism) are of great interest and combine research with originality. The French field is better known, though Miss Moers has some new things to say about Barbey d'Aurevilly who arrived in Caen in 1829, a year before Brummell's appointment as consul.

By 1832 Brummell's Boswell, Jesse, had turned up, who was to bridge the gap between French and English dandyism through Barbey's friend Trébutien. Barbey's *On Dandyism and George Brummell* appeared in 1845, hence Baudelaire and Huysmans whose *A Rebours* enchanted Dorian Gray, and so to Wilde. Beerbohm began by making fun of Oscar Wilde and by eulogising the dandies and George IV. "My gifts are small," he wrote to a biographer. "I've used them very well and discreetly, never straining them." Brummell said much the same to Lady Hester Stanhope.

(1960)

THE DANDY: 3

GRONOW* belongs to the little cluster of sources for Regency high living. For this period Greville is the Saint-Simon, Jesse's life of Brummell, the memoirs of Princess Lieven and various lives of D'Orsay help out with *Vanity Fair* as an historical novel and "Childe Harold" and "Don Juan" for verse. Harriet Wilson supplies the *demi-mondaine* approach. There are also copious memoirs and letters about the Devonshire House Set.

Gronow, however, is the epitome of the Regency male; his limitations confine him to the world of French and English club-men. Not for him Greville's high politics, or Creevey's jobbery, nor the elevated tone of the ladies' journals. He writes best about gamblers, dandies and soldiers. One might say "heroes," for so many of these characters took part in the Napoleonic Wars. They fought in the Peninsula or on the field of Waterloo and we owed a century of peace and world leadership to their courage and initiative, from Wellington downwards. Paris, in defeat, remained the centre of fashion as it had always been, and French resorts other than Paris the chosen haunts of ruined gamblers. One did one's living in St. James's, and one's reminiscing in Boulogne or Calais for the remainder of our gouty span.

At one time I started to calculate what would have been the most interesting life span. There are several possible favourites but one of the best is to have been born between 1760 and 1770 and to have died about 1850; thus getting a glimpse of France before 1789, living through the Napoleonic Wars and Romanticism, and seeing the beginnings of modernity with Flaubert and Baudelaire. Few famous men qualify, yet one might call it the period of Wellington, Talleyrand, Beckford, Wordsworth and Chateaubriand. I further narrowed it down to the long lives of Samuel Rogers and Henry Luttrell and finally decided that

* *The Reminiscences and Recollections of Captain Gronow,* abridged and with an introduction by John Raymond (New York, 1964).

Luttrell (so much happier an epicure than Rogers, though so much poorer) was the fortunate individual who most fitted this golden age.

"I consider him to have been the most agreeable man I have ever met," wrote Gronow. "In his eighties he still took the greatest interest in everything that was going on in Paris (1849) and had lost none of the fire and eagerness of youth. We all thought him quite delightful." About Rogers, Gronow works off his best phrase: "One might have compared the old poet to one of those velvety caterpillars that crawl gently and quietly over the skin, but leave an irritating blister behind."

What was Gronow like? Member of an old Welsh family, he was a soldier, an unreformed Member of Parliament, a dandy of the quiet variety, a duellist, a good Parisian, a man of poor concentration and conventional culture, a worshipper of the right thing. If he had only wished to tell all—like Harriet Wilson—or all about himself—like Greville—or been able to compose a proper narrative rather than a succession of scattered jottings.

His military virtues did not make a Tacitus; he is arch or sentimental when depicting women, too impressed by rank and wealth when describing men. One longs for a real revelation. Perhaps his criticism of the dandies comes nearest to this. "How unspeakably odious . . . were the Dandies of forty years ago. They were generally not high-born, nor rich, nor very good-looking, nor clever, nor agreeable . . . they were generally middle-aged, some even elderly men, had large appetites and weak digestions, gambled freely and had no luck. They hated everybody and abused everybody . . . a motley crew with nothing remarkable about them but their insolence."

They make, however, very good copy and anecdotes about them form the bulk of his book apart from military reminiscences and glimpses of forgotten warriors. The world of St. James's Street, its clubs, its gambling, its tradesmen, its eccentrics is an earthly paradise that one can touch and see, which depends for its magic on the relationship between a few luxury tradesmen and a few regular customers who require each other for a male ritual connected with the choosing of wine, cigars, and leather.

The dandy can be interpreted in a Freudian sense; he is also an economic necessity, an illuminated advertisement for a whole combination of "exclusive" purveyors who, nevertheless, will never exclude new custom. Gronow's gallery is like a Fortnum's catalogue with Lord Petersham's brands of snuff and tea, Lord Saye and Sele's omelette of golden pheasant's eggs, some other dandy's secret recipe for blacking.

What a terrible moment in a dandy's education when he is first constrained to cut his father:

In London in bygone days a worldly man or woman would, without scruple, cut their father or mother did they not belong to the particular set which they considered good society.

Riding in the park they met a respectable-looking elderly man who nodded somewhat familiarly to S——. "Who's your friend?" drawled Lord C——. "That?" replied S. "Oh a very good sort of fellow, one of my Cheshire farmers." The world's canker had eaten into his heart!

Gronow's *Reminiscences,* covering 1810–60, first appeared in book form in a two-volume illustrated edition in 1889. Many of the illustrations are here reproduced, though not in colour and lacking the charming picture of Lady Jersey, Clanronald Macdonald and the Worcesters leading off in the first quadrille at Almacks—so characteristic of ultra-exclusive fatuity—or the water-colour of Beau Brummell with his friends.

Gronow has, by the way, a charming description of the women of Waterloo days. "How grand they used to look, with their full stately forms, small thoroughbred heads and long flowing ringlets. You could not help feeling somewhat elated and self-satisfied, if perchance one of these side-long glances, half-proud, half-bashful, like a petted child's, fell upon you, leaving you silent and pensive."

(1964)

OPIUM

THIS book* has two meanings: as a study of opium and its effects on the great addicts, Coleridge, de Quincey, Baudelaire; and also as a tract for our times, a general warning against addiction. Thus in Miss Hayter's analysis the three commonest characteristics of the opium-prone, "restless mental curiosity about strange and novel mental experiences," "the longing for peace and freedom from anxiety," and "a delight in secret rites and hidden fellowships, in being an initiate" (*"la vie opiacée"*) are all familiar to us today.

How did the past differ? When the romantic writers took opium or laudanum (pronounced "lodnum" in those days), it was not necessary to have a prescription. Various brands of opium pills were sold cheaply at any chemist's and were favoured by manual workers. It took a long course of trial and error, sometimes a lifetime, to learn of its addictive properties and withdrawal symptoms; and since there were far fewer patent medicines, no tranquillisers, barbiturates, sleeping pills, pep pills or vitamin pick-me-ups, it was the natural remedy or "drug of choice" for gastric upsets, hang-overs, insomnia, gout, rheumatism and cramps of all kinds. Opium pills were carried on many a journey and phials of morphine, bought over the counter, were sent with brandy, pâté and the latest novel to young officers in the First World War in case it were needed to relieve the wounded. The stigma of addiction was no greater than that attached to alcoholism, being less public.

In fact, all writing about drug addiction must take into account the official view of alcohol. The state has never refused alcohol to anyone who could afford to pay for it and, since it takes a rake-off on every

* *Opium and the Romantic Imagination,* by Alethea Hayter (Berkeley, 1968).

bottle, has never discriminated between the addict and the moderate drinker, never presumed to say "you've had enough." As long as the state raises no obstacle to people "going to hell in their own way" through drink, there will be an element of hypocrisy in its treatment of drug addicts. This is particularly apparent in the attitude to cannabis, which is not habit-forming and might well be taken in moderation by many people if it were legally permitted after being tested and developed scientifically.

I can't help feeling that in her book Miss Hayter is too conscious of the contemporary implications of the Brain Report, and so rams home the horrors of opium indulgence and its ugly withdrawal symptoms until we are all sick of them and impatient with her. Nothing irritates one more with middlebrow morality than the perpetual needling of great artists for not having been greater. If Coleridge, de Quincey or Baudelaire had not been neurotics they might not have been artists at all; if they had not been addicted to opium it would have been to something else. Excess and self-oblivion were necessary components of their genius and to rap their knuckles for unwritten or unfinished books or bonds not honoured is sheer presumption.

Miss Hayter is careful to state that she has never indulged in opium herself while nevertheless describing for us her conception of an opium hallucination. "Their paradises may have been wholly or partly artificial; their hells were real," she concludes, ignoring the fact that two of her addicts, Crabbe and Wilkie Collins (even de Quincey), led perfectly normal lives and survived to a ripe old age. It was hard not to become an addict when laudanum was ignorantly prescribed by doctors for painful symptoms brought on by its own excessive use.

Now that we know so much more about it we might sum up. Opium is a loser; it will ultimately bring more pain than pleasure and the withdrawal process will have to be faced from time to time; it is expensive and antisocial and kindles, then dulls, the creative faculties. Like alcohol it creates its own need. Even so, with controlled use, it can be of great benefit to certain temperaments. It is a calculated risk, and nowadays we are better at calculation. It has been largely superseded by chemical substances which provide more effective escapes from external reality.

Yet of all drugs it has the noblest literature; the poppy is the vine's only serious rival. Compared to the opium poppy, cannabis is just birdseed. In Cocteau and Bérard we have had two more opium acolytes, bringing the tradition down to our own day. " 'O just, subtle and mighty opium'—this fatal prayer of de Quincey's," writes Miss Hayter, "echoes back and forth among the accounts of opium addicts, 'vieille et terrible amie' Baudelaire called it, 'my only friend' according to Wilkie Collins."

There must be people alive who knew Hall Caine, Hall Caine to whom Wilkie Collins said:

> "I'm going to show you the secrets of my prison-house. Do you see that? It's laudanum," and he drank the whole glassful.
> "Good heavens, Wilkie Colllins! How long have you taken that drug?"
> "Twenty years."
> "More than once a day?"
> "Oh, yes, much more."
> "Why do you take it?"
> "To stimulate the brain and steady the nerves."

And, at the age of nine, Collins remembered hearing Coleridge complaining to his mother about his vain struggle to shed the opium habit, shedding tears as he spoke. Mrs. Collins's breezy answer was "Mr. Coleridge, do not cry; if the opium really does you any good, and you must have it, why do you not go and get it?" This at once dried Coleridge's tears and turning to Wilkie Collins's father he said: "Collins, your wife is an exceedingly sensible woman."

Apart from harping so much on the hells which depend for their reality, like the paradises, on the subjects' own account of them, Miss Hayter is an admirable literary critic and historian and has an uncanny understanding of the opium syndrome from the outside. She has been able to work out the image clusters, the whole peculiar sensibility which opium confers, its effect on the inner core of imagination, the rigidity of its symbolism.

We see exactly what the great dreamers had in common: the earthly paradise, the visual and tactile hallucinations, the architectural dominations of palaces, pleasure-domes, Piranesi prisons, dungeons, tunnels, caves, coffins; the marble halls, symbols of power and freedom which contract gradually into nightmares of claustrophobia, "the weight of twenty Atlantics was upon me"; and the face-hauntings, the maidens, prostitutes, hags, Malays, and magicians, Memnon and Ozymandias, the damsel with a dulcimer, Anne of Soho, "darkness and lights, tempests and human faces"—all inspired by a seed pod.

Towering over their circumstances is the splendid prose of de Quincey, the genius of Coleridge and Baudelaire, the tales of Poe, Scott's *Bride of Lammermoor,* Collins's *Moonstone,* Crabbe's *Peter Grimes* and Thompson's *Dream Tryst.* Though her range is more limited, one is reminded of Mario Praz's *Romantic Agony* by Miss Hayter's blend of scholarship, imagination and ambivalence: Shadwell, Clive of India, Wilberforce, Bulwer Lytton, Mrs. Browning, Keats, Berlioz, flit through her pages. She does not, by the way, believe that

Coleridge really could have dreamt Kubla Khan (her deduction has since been confirmed by Professor Fruman). Opium dreams crystallise the material for poetry, provide the obsessional images but not the poetry itself. In fact I have never read a better study of dream configurations.

But what are dreams? Have they not shrunk today? "The machinery for dreaming planted in the human brain was not planted for nothing," wrote de Quincey:

> That faculty, in alliance with the mystery of darkness, is the one great tube through which man communicates with the shadows. Of all agencies which assist the faculty of dreaming, beyond all others is opium.

(1968)

SHADES
OF
SPLEEN

ELIOT used to say that one should visit Paris for the place, not the people, as their activities got in the way of the appreciation of the city itself, and the extraordinary hold of its past on all art-lovers. He was right; cities change but there are always backwaters. One can stop the time-clock at will and shut out everything since 1850 or 1950 according to disposition.

Paris change, mais rien dans ma mélancolie
n'a bougé! palais neufs, échafaudages, blocs,
Vieux faubourgs, tout pour moi devient allégorie

I have been to Paris only once in the last ten years, for my trips have been further afield, mopping up more distant corners of the world that I must hurry to win from the jaws of decrepitude. Now for two days in the city which for so long constituted the inspiration of my youth and the delight of my imagination.

Le vieux Paris n'est plus (la forme d'une ville
change plus vite, hélas! que le coeur d'un mortel) . . .

Was Baudelaire right? There are streets which have outlived generations of users; shops and restaurants which seem indestructible, cities like Venice in which an Ostrogoth would feel at home. It is the heart which hardens, falters, fibrillates, stops, while the Grand Véfour still looks much as Baudelaire saw it, or the Hotel du Quai Voltaire or the Ile Saint-Louis.

My hotel has an inner courtyard with an eighteenth-century façade, and was once the home of Lafayette. The long windows open on the gravel as in the days of Henry James who chose Alvin Coborn's photograph of the Saint James et d'Albany to illustrate a volume in his collected edition. In the years after the war it resounded with English voices like an Oxford quad. Now it is rather quiet. My first walk is from the hotel to the Baudelaire exhibition in the Petit Palais, for I have placed my visit under the protection of Baudelaire and Proust, the outstanding geniuses of the last century, with perhaps a side-glance at Palinurus, whose Paris owed so much to them. I discovered those two writers almost simultaneously, in my last year at school and my first at the University, though both are poets whom one cannot truly appreciate before middle age, *"quand une fois le coeur a fait son vendange."*

Soon after leaving the hotel I pass a sign *"Livres rares"* hanging above a Proustian stronghold and then I pass the little bar—Castiglione—where my first publisher, Jack Kahane, used to entertain his authors. He paid me a thousand francs for *The Rock Pool.*

The Place Vendôme meant only one thing, the Ritz, where one used to go on arrival "to see who was in Paris" on the understanding that its Rue Cambon bar would shelter anyone who felt a cut above Montparnasse. I remember seeing Boni de Castellane, Berry Wall and other ancient dandies, the famous maître d'hotel, Olivier, the barman Georges, friend of Hemingway, the discreet commissionaire in his brown uniform with his pomaded cheeks and silken moustaches—and then the English dandies dropping in—Evan Morgan, Napier Alington, Michael Arlen.

It was while staying there in 1929 that my life was changed by a telephone call. I rang up one girl; another husky voice answered, using the expression "you're welcome"—an American commonplace, but which coming from a total stranger to one who had never heard it before, seemed to promise the ultimate alleviation of the heart's hunger. I rushed round and that welcome took care of the next ten years.

The bar has been redecorated; the magic has left it—so has barman Georges, though the *quarts Krug* may taste as good as ever. Out in the Rue Cambon to the Rue Saint Honoré again, which gets subtly more elegant as we approach Hermès and the picture-dealers.

Now we reach the Place Beauvau. Here I register my first loss, the restaurant, La Crêmaillère. It was the furthest west many of us Left Bankers would care to go and was open on Sundays with very pleasant, rather international food and, in summer, claret cup. Clive Bell used to haunt it and the last meal I gave there was for André Gide. Down the Avenue de Marigny, to the Avenue Gabriel. The Petit Palais comes into sight, with its big Baudelaire poster. But it is also Proust country. In these pollarded alleys, black in the wan winter sunshine, Gilberte used to play and set the coil in motion, the heart's periplus.

There are really two separate exhibitions for Baudelaire. One is the great centenary accolade to the first modern art critic, the large rooms panelled with his favourites: David, Ingres, Delacroix, Courbet, Guys, Manet, together with much academic rubbish that he reviewed in the course of duty, and appropriate rooms of sculpture. Viewed in this light, Baudelaire's career was un unqualified success, for so much of the glory of Delacroix and Manet rubs off on him.

The other exhibition unfolds in the small cases round the walls, the story of his life, loves and poetry. It is unbearably sad. The dazzling brilliance of his youth, comparable to that of Byron or Keats, a brilliance already deepened by the note of erotic nostalgia, signature of the Baudelairean resonance running through all his verse—apprehension of beauty, awareness of loss—gives way to what also dates from his childhood: *"Ma plaie et ma fatalité."* The wounds were material. Perpetual insolvency (poverty is too mild a word) and syphilis, both hereditary and acquired, with guilt, remorse, and sloth—a fungus on the will. Debts, which many undergraduates grapple with successfully, plagued him for the rest of his life. For home, a shifting series of rooms, growing ever meaner to end in Brussels in the squalor of the Hôtel du Grand Miroir. His only companion a white Negress of doubtful occupation who sinks with him into syphilis and alcoholism.

For me the most moving object in the exhibition is the manuscript (No. 621) of the four sonnets "Un fantôme," first published in 1860, in which he bids farewell to Jeanne whom he glimpses hobbling through the streets. The poems assert both the poet's "eternising" gift, in superb Shakespearean cadences, and the tragic futility or helplessness of romantic love, of all human love which refuses to regard itself as expendable:

La Maladie et la Morte font des cendres
De tout le feu qui pour nous flamboya . . .

He goes on to describe Jeanne:

qui, comme moi, meurt dans la solitude
et que le Temps, injurieux vieillard,
chaque jour frotte avec son aile rude . . .
Noir assassin de la Vie et de l'Art,
Tu ne tueras jamais dans ma mémoire
Celle qui fut mon plaisir et ma gloire!

Brave words—but his memory was already crumbling and here in the manuscript is the version he sacrificed of the last three lines:

comme un manant ivre, ou comme un soudard
qui bat les murs et salit et coudoie
une beauté frêle, en robe de soie.

I had to look up *manant* (a boor or churl) and *soudard* (an old trooper). Crepet thinks the other ending was adopted as providing more of a "finale" to the series.

The Baudelairean *échec* is summed up in the tragedy of the *Fleurs du Mal* itself. This beautifully produced book, about whose presentation poet and publisher took so much trouble, whose complimentary copies were so carefully apportioned, was delivered over to the Philistines to be mauled and finally eviscerated by the censorship, some pages being torn out and a fine inflicted—within a year of Flaubert winning his case on *Madame Bovary*. I should like to see one of these mutilated copies of the *Fleurs du Mal,* as the official badge or crest of all censors everywhere. "At the sign of the Six Pièces Condamnées."

Among the sculptures is Clésinger's "Femme piquée par un serpent," said to be a representation of the female orgasm. The model was Madame Sabatier, "La Présidente" to whom Baudelaire wrote some of his finest poems, like "Reversibilité," one of them accompanied by a note in English: "After a night of pleasure and desolation all my soul belongs to you."

What haunts one longest is the poet's own face . . .

When I emerge it is sunset and I cross the river, so fast and swirling and alive compared to the Thames, and walk back along the *quais* to the Hôtel du Quai Voltaire. Baudelaire was living here for two years at the time of the *Fleurs* (1856–58). Wagner also. It is the hotel whence the Nancy Cunard-like character penned her devastating anti-love letters in *Point Counter Point.* Up the Rue de Seine is what used to be the Hôtel de la Louisiane—the name is still visible—with the circular room on the first floor where I spent a blissful winter. It now looks unbelievably tiny, noisy and shabby.

> I have quite given up the social struggle, I have scratched from the race of life. I have a room for 400 francs a month and at last will be living within my own and other people's income. I am tired of acquaintances, tired of friends, unless they're intelligent, tired also of extrovert, unbookish life. I am for good talk, wet evenings, intimacy, *vins rouges en carafe,* reading, relative solitude, street-worship, shop gazing, alley sloping, Seine-loafing, exploration of the least-known *arrondissements* and plenty of writing from this table in the window where I can watch the streets light up. I am for the Past, the North, the world of ideas. I am for the Hôtel de la Louisiane. (Autumn 1929)

Now the pendulum swings Proustwards. I attended the presentation by Sotheby's of a Turkish manuscript to the Bibliothèque Nationale, to which it had once belonged, and talked with rare-book experts like M. Berès and M. Heilbrun.

There are Proust letters and Baudelaire mss. in the sale of the Lambiotte collection. Lambiotte, a Belgian bibliophile, once let me look at his material. He had one of the best of all Proust letters, in which he explains to Montesquiou a thousand and one reasons why he could not possibly be intended for the Baron de Charlus. All *romanciers à clef* should get it by heart. And the Valèry-Pierre Louÿs correspondence is also up for sale. At M. Heilbrun's in the Rue de Seine I saw some more Proust letters (to Robert de Billy); one describes a dinner party he gave at the Ritz—the guests, the music, the enormous bill—another about "Les Plaisirs et les Jours," but these were very expensive.

That evening I hit one of the few anti-Proust pockets. A brilliant grandson of Francis de Croisset had found fifty-two letters of Proust, nearly all making excuses, and he recalled his grandfather describing Proust at parties as looking like a *"chaudfroid de corbeau"* while his great-grandmother, the Comtesse de Chevigné (Oriane), summed him up as *"un raseur."* I remembered Miss Barney's "Proust oust!" and the Princess Edmond de Polignac's dislike of him. How fortunate for his fame that he died immediately his work was accomplished, and did not survive through the Thirties (he was younger than Gide)—Proust at Juan les Pins, on Hitler, at the Café de Flore, in Harlem, Palm Beach; Proust in Hollywood . . . he was present at the baptism of modernity and spared the pimples of its coming of age. I talked about him the next day to Paul Morand, whose *Visiteur du Soir* describes their early friendship (Proust wrote his only preface for him). I mentioned Francis de Croisset's fifty-two letters all putting him off . . . "They would be." "I gather he didn't much like Proust." *"D'ailleurs c'était réciproque."*

He described Proust's voice, but did not give me his celebrated imitation. Proust wrote about eight thousand letters, he thinks, of which four thousand are known and more are always coming to light. The Albuféra correspondence has never been published. There is another hoard at Amphion, with the Brancovans. And a parody of Maeterlinck's *Pelléas*. Morand was one of the pleasures of my youth, his *Rien que la Terre* was the first book I reviewed. "Ouvert la Nuit" and "Fermé la Nuit" were blue prints of what a young man might then hope to find in the sleepers, river steamers, bars and night-clubs of post-war Europe. I am glad Gallimard has just reissued them and I have learnt a new alexandrine: *"L'Eternité! Quelle est cette étrange menace?"*

(1969)

FLAUBERT: 1

I CAN'T think of a happier book to slip into a pocket in the VIP lounge than *Flaubert in Egypt**—it will see us through at least one hijacking. For three reasons: Flaubert was a genius, genius is uncommon, if not rare, and everything connected with it is interesting. This applies even to Sartre's three-volume demolition job, *L'Idiot de la Famille;* though the axe may have proved too heavy for the executioner. Secondly, because Steegmuller is no propagandist; he grinds nothing but his own faculties, of which a passionate preoccupation with this great novelist is the chief. Lastly, because so much of his text has been unpublished until recent editions such as Bruneau's two books on the young Flaubert, and Naaman's uncensored edition of the letters from Egypt (Nizet, Paris, 1965).

What Mr. Steegmuller has done is to dovetail the materials for Flaubert's Egyptian journey (his letters, his notebooks and his companion Maxime du Camp's published and unpublished notebooks and *Souvenirs Littéraires*), translate them into up-to-date American suitable for the permissive society and supply us with his own invaluable commentary.

Flaubert was twenty-seven when he went to Egypt at Maxime du Camp's suggestion, "for health reasons" with the consent and financial encouragement of his mother. He was a large, handsome Viking with a stentorian voice and a sensitive mouth, a splendid brow and cold blue eyes, whom a mysterious epileptiform illness had debarred from continuing his legal studies. He wanted to write and read avidly, he dreamt of masterpieces but disdained to publish. He was already the author of "Novembre," the "Mémoires d'un Fou," and other early stories and of the first *Temptation of St. Anthony*. This he had read aloud to du

* *Flaubert in Egypt,* translated and edited by Francis Steegmuller (Boston, 1972).

Camp and his great friend Louis Bouilhet who had brutally advised him to set it aside and concentrate on a work of realism. This was to become *Madame Bovary* seven years later.

Flaubert's early work is marred by undisciplined lyricism. John Cage's dictum "I have nothing to say, I am saying it, and that is poetry" would have been true of Flaubert. His talent was like an oil gusher without a pipe-line; his imagination coloured everything with a slightly morbid romanticism; but his ambition remained insatiable. Shakespeare, Virgil, Dante—he demanded to share their glory. Yet he was the son of a prominent surgeon of Rouen, his background was provincial and professional, his bourgeois virtues included a love of the bawdy, of exact observation, gargantuan appetites, a sense of the ridiculous. He had got himself into a bind by falling in love with a married woman older than himself who could not acknowledge his devotion, and by being ensnared by an ambitious and attractive Parisian authoress, Louise Colet, whose over-eagerness was to drive him away.

His devotion to his mother and his platonic love for Eliza Schlésinger left only one outlet: whoring; and the young Flaubert became a visitor to the brothels which so gripped the mid-century imagination, from Baudelaire to Degas and Lautrec. It was not merely the satisfaction of lust but the link with pagan Rome, with the poetry in the word "harlot" or even *"fille"* and it was easy to extend this interest to the brothels of Cairo and of the Upper Nile to which the dancing prostitutes had been banished. Bouilhet, who seems to have been sexually repressed but with a quite uninhibited intelligence, formed his ideal audience.

Up to the death of Flaubert's niece in 1931 the iron hand of family censorship and Victorian prudery kept both scholars and gossip-writers at bay, and Madame Grout could make amends for her earlier unkindness to her uncle until the time came to sell his manuscripts and even the dressing-gown in which he received Henry James (bought by Sacha Guitry). But one of the foibles of modern criticism is to expose everything which a writer has tried to keep secret for the gratification of a public interested in nothing else. Did Flaubert die of syphilis or epilepsy? Was he homosexual? Did Maxime du Camp fornicate or not on his trip up the Nile? At twenty-seven the human male is outstandingly lustful and in the courtesan Rustchouk Hanem Flaubert was to discover a hieratic quality that his imagination desired as well as a complete satisfaction of his senses. It is fitting that it was not through this temple prostitute but a more casual pick-up in Syria that he contracted the syphilis which a promiscuous tourist in those parts of the world was sure to invite.

The question of his homosexuality depends on more slender evidence. Certainly he loved Alfred Le Poittevin romantically, and Bouilhet sentimentally, but did he actually permit, invite or even welcome intercourse of some kind in the Cairo *hammams?* True, he first repelled an attractive boy, but when Bouilhet asked him "if you consummated that business at the baths," he replied: "Yes—and on a pockmarked young rascal wearing a white turban. It made me laugh, that's all. But I'll be at it again. To be done well an experiment must be repeated."

Sartre thinks all this talk was a smoke-screen and Mr. Steegmuller refers us to the discussion of "the business at the baths" beginning on page 687, Vol. I of Sartre's *L'Idiot de la Famille.* He stresses the ugliness of the attendants which Flaubert mentions. But that may have been irresistible to the connoisseur of bittersweet—like the bedbugs at Rustchouk Hanem's. "Their nauseating odour mingled with the scent of her skin, which was dripping with sandalwood oil. I want a touch of bitterness in everything."

Flaubert was to renounce the world of sex as well as the world of action for the world of art; like James or Proust, he believed that the work of art was the only true and permanent expression of the personality; the Pyramids, the Sphinx taught him that lesson. Meanwhile he was young and privileged, the broad sails and singing sailors carried him along the stream while the panorama of antiquity unfolded along the banks and crude rituals and punishments, tortures and diseases provided him with his emotional roughage. Their notebooks soon filled, for du Camp was an experienced journalist, photographer, and progressive who was to become an academician. He found Flaubert's apparent apathy, his "*oisiveté pleine de pouvoir*" bewildering.

"When we arrived off Thebes," wrote Flaubert,

> our soldiers were drumming on their *drabukehs,* the mate was playing his flute, Khalil was dancing with his castanets; they broke off to land. It was then, as I was enjoying these things, and just as I was watching three wave crests bending under the wind behind us, that I felt a surge of solemn happiness that reached out towards what I was seeing, and I thanked God in my heart for having made me capable of such a joy. I felt fortunate at the thought, and yet it seemed to me that I was thinking of nothing.

POSTSCRIPT: Further reading of Sartre's *L'Idiot de la Famille* has convinced me it is a truly magnificent attempt at exploration in depth which includes some of his greatest writing. He sees Flaubert as essentially passive and feminine despite his virility, a man who literally wished to be changed into water, with its "thousand liquid nipples travelling all over his body" (Letters II, page 209).

(1972)

FLAUBERT: 2

THIS* is the posthumous sequel to Professor Starkie's earlier volume, *Flaubert, the Making of the Master,* which has just been reissued as a Pelican.

Taken together, although there is a little overlapping at the join, we have a treasure-house of information about the greatest novelist between Balzac and Proust, the fertilising genius of writers like Conrad, Joyce, Beckett, Gide (who said Flaubert's letters were his *"livre de chevet"*) and ultimately Sartre. Bloom owes much to Joyce's favourite *Bouvard et Pécuchet,* whose cataloguing for cataloguing's sake was their remedy for the cares of life, leading straight to the enumeration of door-handles in the *nouveau roman.*

Flaubert wrote six major works (a seventh with his correspondence), and they have had their ups and downs; yet all have been totally different in style and purpose and in the influence they have exerted. *Madame Bovary* remains a masterpiece impervious to time. *Salammbo,* greatly admired in the nineteenth century, is almost unreadable in spite of the now fashionable scenes of torture and mutilation. It has gained in probability but the ornate style repels.

The Temptation of St. Anthony was a great success but I would still call it unreadable in all three versions. *Trois Contes* holds its own; if *Un Coeur Simple* has become less credible, the *St. Julien* remains a most moving tour de force, and *Hérodiade* dates as happily as Gustave Moreau.

There remain *The Sentimental Education, Bouvard and Pécuchet,* and the Letters, now swollen to nine volumes, with more to come.

The Sentimental Education, Flaubert's favourite book, belittled by

* *Flaubert the Master 1856–1880,* by Enid Starkie (New York, 1971).

Henry James as "dead" and by many others considered the greatest novel of the nineteenth century, is written in a timeless style. I doubt if it would be possible to improve on the opening of the Epilogue (admired by Proust).

> Il voyagea.
>
> Il connut la mélancolie des paquebots, les froids réveils sous la tente, l'étourdissement des paysages et des ruines, l'amertume des sympathies interrompues.
>
> Il revint.
>
> Il fréquenta le monde, et il eût d'autres amours, encore. Mais le souvenir continuel du premier les lui rendit insipides . . .

One is reminded of Eugène Onegin.

Nevertheless Henry James had a point: there *is* something dead about the novel. Frédéric Moreau (according to Dr. Starkie the first anti-hero) is almost too ineffectual. "It was a mistake to propose to register in so mean a consciousness as that of such a hero, so large and so mixed a quantity of life as 'L'Education Sentimentale' intends" (Henry James). "Readers could not accept the general quality of greyness which pervaded the whole novel and its lack of purpose. Everyone fails, even the most ambitious" (Dr. Starkie).

I am afraid there is worse than that. The one redeeming feature of Frédéric's aimless, drifting life, his frittering of money and passion till he ends up back in Nogent where he started, reduced to spiritual and material poverty, was meant to be his love for Madame Arnoux, the "good woman" whose beauty reflected the overwhelming experience of Flaubert's teen-age infatuation with Madame Schlésinger that began on the beach at Trouville and lasted all his life. Like any Victorian heroine she personifies virtue, and Frédéric loses her through being unable to resist other temptations of desire and vanity, the blandishments of inferior women—Rosanette, Madame Dambreuse—who happen to be on the spot.

But Rosanette the lively, amiable, hard-boiled cocotte, and the coldly scheming woman of the world, the political hostess, Madame Dambreuse, are far more interesting. There is something unconvincing about the *grande passion,* perhaps because Madame Arnoux is less clearly drawn than her rivals.

In real life Flaubert didn't want to marry, he was "wedded to literature," also to his comfortable monastic life at Croisset where he was looked after by his mother. He had syphilis as well. Given all these impediments, to which one might add a considerable social success in imperial circles which involved keeping rooms in Paris and a large expenditure on suits and gloves, the *grande passion* is really a form of religion in which an image is worshipped at odd convenient moments. If Frédéric is futile, Madame Arnoux is a dummy, and this adds a suspicion of humbug to the general episodic looseness of the structure.

The recent production of *The Sentimental Education* on television brought out some of the greatness as well as some flaws in the book. Politically and socially it holds together; the salons, garrets, studios, barricades, the Impressionist landscapes are unforgettable; so is the giant turbot served at the Dambreuse dinner party. Frédéric's Wooster-like charm expands and fades with his money.

Bouvard et Pécuchet, which is very hard reading indeed, does not stand or fall by being readable. Again, what a magical beginning: *"Comme il faisait une chaleur de trente-trois degrés, le boulevard Bourdon se trouvait absolument désert."* Of all *mots justes* sought and found by Flaubert the word "Bourdon," so full of heat and unfashionable monotony, fit setting for his two supremely monotonous and unfashionable scriveners, his Laurel and Hardy, must be the rightest.

The story is well known: the two copyists meet and vow eternal friendship for each has written his name in his hat. A legacy to Bouvard enables them to retire and settle in the country to cultivate their minds. Their education proceeds by trial and disillusion: each chapter being devoted to a subject which they attack with enthusiasm only to be blocked by the difficulties and contradictions inherent in contemporary ignorance. One topic leads on to another: thus, on the verge of suicide, they watch the peasants walking through the snow to midnight mass, they attend it, find solace and almost conversion, then "historic doubts" set in. Finally they are expelled by the outraged community for their experiments in education and their subversive speeches. They get a double desk made and set up copying again. At first they copy anything, then they arrange all the silliest quotations under subjects, finally they come on the local doctor's report on them to the prefect: "A pair of harmless lunatics." They copy that too.

Though the novel was unfinished, a plan survives in which an enormous second volume, a *sottisier* or dictionary of clichés, was to precede the climax. This would have been unreadable and it is better to insert, as in Queneau's edition, the short "dictionary of clichés" as the penultimate chapter. Most of these are still applicable today, for they spring from bourgeois timidity and smugness.

> Railway stations. Gape with admiration: cite them as architectural wonders.

And the *idées chic:*

> Defence of Slavery, or Saint Bartholomew's Day (a "vieille blague"); make fun of intellectuals, admiration of Stendhal (!) Raphael, no talent. Mirabeau, no talent—but his father (whom nobody has read) oh!

Dr. Starkie died before this book was published. With her Baudelaire and Rimbaud it forms a trilogy, a monument to her total devotion to the French nineteenth century. I think there is some fatigue in this last volume and a few minor repetitions, but she gives an excellent over-all account of Flaubert's dedicated life, so infinitely promising, so varied in achievement, so clouded at the last by poverty and death. He went bankrupt to save his niece who, according to Dr. Starkie, wasn't worth the saving.

All Flaubert's other relationships are faithfully dealt with by her; his intense gift of friendship, his attraction for women, both respectable fellow craftsmen, royalties like Princess Mathilde and demi-mondaines like Jane de Tourbey. Only by one figure is she nonplussed. From 1853–64 his horrible niece's English governess was one Juliet Herbert; and Dr. Starkie quotes from Benjamin Bart's *Flaubert* (1967) that she was his mistress and spent passionate weeks in Paris with him in 1872 and 1874. These facts Dr. Starkie does not believe are substantiated. Can anyone remember an ancestress, or relative of one, called Juliet Herbert who lived in London in 1870 and spent ten years with the Flaubert family? It might prove a last foot-note to the patience and curiosity of this indomitable Dublin lady.

(1971)

ARTHUR SYMONS

THIS* is the first production of a reorganised firm of publishers who have a "period" list of eighteen-ninetyish exhumations. I wish them all success. I have lately been taking a quick look at the Nineties myself and I came to the sad conclusion that what destroyed them was not a wrong aesthetic (I am all for "Art for Art's sake" and the "hard gem-like flame") but lack of talent. So many of them had no flame to burn with. Their epitaph is in Pound's *Mauberley:*

> *Likewise a friend of Bloughram's once advised me:*
> *"Don't kick against the pricks,*
> *Accept opinion. The 'Nineties' tried your game*
> *and died, there's nothing in it."*

In fact these *fin-de-siècle* writers all had to undergo a painful adaptation to the twentieth century. Some opted out through drink or early death (Beardsley, Dowson, Johnson), others triumphed by understanding the forces of modernity (Yeats) or by making a work of art out of their own past (Beerbohm). Arthur Symons solved the problem by mere longevity. 1865–1945! Brave dates—they form almost a poem in themselves, comparable to those of Shaw, Pearsall Smith or Berenson, all of whom, however, escaped petrifaction on the altar of decadence.

I once owned a Symons's Baudelaire (the third edition of *Les Fleurs du Mal*), which he had bought and annotated in 1885 when he and it came out. His whole life was to be dominated by this poet, who became an obsession with him through his forties and fifties and whom he has translated so extensively. (He spent one summer tracking down all the hotels Baudelaire stayed at.) To some natures Baudelaire is not an

* *Arthur Symons,* by Roger Lhombreaud (Chester Springs, Pa., 1964).

inspiration but a disease, a morbid growth affecting the will. The godlike youth, the inspired poet of modern times crumbles before our eyes into the prematurely decrepit, shiftless parasite, driven out of his dignity by debt and out of his mind by syphilis, and some readers who come under his spell re-enact his fall or find excuses for their own inertia or take up the cudgels to avenge him, and incur the wrath of society. He can set one back a lifetime.

As a youth Symons, son of a Methodist preacher and something of a mother's boy, escaped to London and the Reading Room of the British Museum to win attention by specialising in the Elizabethans. He soon began to pour out verse and come under the inevitable influences—Pater, Symonds, Swinburne, Verlaine, Villiers, Huysmans, Symbolists and Decadents. The precocious, handsome, lecherous young rebel was both scholarly and imaginative and revealed gifts as an editor and critic as well as a poet, and by 1890 was well launched on his brief career of notoriety as leader, with Beardsley, of the English *fin de siècle* and consequently was much attacked for his licentious semi-autobiographical lyrics indicating promiscuity and for his cult of all things French.

Symons and Beardsley formed the true Nineties; Wilde has stolen their thunder by capturing the public imagination; in fact he was more derivative and less original in his literary work; though enormously talented as a comic dramatist. Both Beardsley and Symons disliked him and the monument of their own co-operation was *The Savoy,* an ill-fated magazine which Symons edited and which is the truest single distillation of the Nineties' spirit. Wilde also disliked Symons and called him an egoist without an ego, with more justice than when he applied the same epigram to the youthful André Gide.

If one had to sum up Arthur Symons, one would have to say "he liked all the right things but he was no good" and then qualify: "Yet he helped us to like the right things by being one of the first to introduce French writers to the English public." He got Verlaine to come and lecture and Eliot has acknowledged that it was Symons's *The Symbolist Movement in Literature* (1899) which introduced him to the poems of Jules Laforgue. Much of the English Nineties was in fact nothing but a harking back to the French Eighties, to Naturalism or Symbolism, and Symons's development was retarded rather than advanced by this influence. His poetry lacks all intensity, and is even more facile than his prose. When he sets out to portray his agony of spirit, as in "Amoris Victima," he communicates it no better than in his Verlainesque "Silhouettes" and "London Nights." As a poet he is memorable only for one or two genre pieces which carry the authentic Nineties' atmosphere of stage-doors and ballet dancers, hansom cabs and prostitutes by gas-light.

> *The little bedroom papered red*
> *The gas's faint malodorous light,*
> *And one beside me in the bed*
> *Who chatters, chatters, half the night.*

The second half of Symons's life (1905–45) dates from his marriage, the familiar trap. "Caught between the desire for perfection and quality, and the necessity for as remunerative a quantity of work as possible, he doubtless became a prey to weariness and dejection." In 1908 he went mad and was institutionalised for several years. His madness was generally thought to be of syphilitic origin, legacy from one of his "Juliets of a night," but in fact Professor Lhombreaud shows it to have been true mania and suggests that Symons was a manic-depressive. He cites the fact that Symons's mother had a brother who was insane, and that Symons had typical manic-depressive traits, a sense of guilt and anxiety alternating with a profound inhumanity. He quotes the ballet dancer of "Amoris Victima," once saying, "Why, Arthur do you so often read of madness, speak of madness . . . ? You are so inhuman, then you become human, then back again comes your inhumanity." "Am I really inhuman?" I queried. "Why not? What's the use of being merely human?"

The proof that his madness was not degenerative was that he recovered and from his stream-lined base at Island Cottage, Wittersham (near to his friend Conrad), was able to navigate the Twenties and Thirties as a minor essayist. It was then that he used to visit the Café Royal and was seen by John Betjeman and several other reviewers of this book, alone and palely loitering. As a prose-writer he was better than as a poet. In his autobiographies and reminiscences his egotism found itself at last and today they make fascinating reading. At the top I put *Confessions,* a privately printed account of his madness (1930), which is very hard to find and which ought to be reprinted, for it is as dramatic and truthful as subsequent revelations by Antonia White and Emily Holmes Coleman.

Next I put *Mes Souvenirs,* also 1930, with its account of Verlaine's Paris (this also deserves reprinting) and the essays on the *Café Royal* and *Parisian Nights,* mostly connected with French subjects.

This may lead the curious on to Symons's travel books, which show a true feeling for places, particularly for Spain in *Cities and Sea Coasts and Islands,* which he dedicated to Augustus John, and of course Venice (where he went mad). His account of Dieppe, where he went for a week-end and did not come back for a whole season, is so persuasive that I have to restrain myself from dashing off to Newhaven. Alas, there would be no Conder, Beardsley, Sickert, Rothenstein or Blanche on that blitz-swept sea-front.

M. Lhombreaud presumably writes in English since no translator is mentioned. Symons would have been fond of his Bordelais biographer, who has amassed an American-style thesis, as far as humourless documentation is concerned, but without the suffocating rawness. He writes with understanding and sympathy and seems unaware of the mediocrity of so many of his quotations from Symons's poems, books and letters, or from those of some of his contemporaries. Symons helped Yeats to understand the Symbolists, he helped Havelock Ellis to love France, he helped Joyce to get his poems published, from Eliot to Hart Crane he introduced many to the joys of Laforgue, Baudelaire, Verlaine, Rimbaud.

POSTSCRIPT: It was Symons who took Yeats to the first performance of Jarry's *King Ubu* which so distressed him. His first edition of *Les Fleurs du Mal* in a grey on grey morocco binding chosen by Baudelaire with the manuscript of "Une Charogne" inserted turned up at a London auction during the war and was bought by Zwemmer for £40 and resold immediately to a Frenchman.

(1963)

ERNEST DOWSON

In his monumental history of the Thirties Sir Grigory Snovis dismisses Connolly in a contemptuous foot-note; in their monumental encyclopaedia of the Forties, Godfrey Wain and Hardly Amis dismiss Connolly in a contemptuous foot-note and spell his name with an "e." In his highly concentrated check-list of the nineteen-fifties Professor Julian Jaffers does not mention him at all. Connolly's own autobiography *I Was One of Them* was contemptuously dismissed in these columns by Sir Evelyn Yeahman. "Connolly? Connais pas."

In January 1965, he discovered himself to be that terrible thing, a man without a decade. In vain he battered on the door of the Twenties where the perpetual party was still in progress (refused admission as out of resonance). The nineteen hundreds had eyes only for Maugham and Masefield and suggested he went away and re-thought his priorities.

The Nineties remained his only hope. That was where he might come in. The Nineties, of course, means a tiny group of people. John Lane and Leonard Smithers, the poets of the Rhymers' Club: Beardsley, Dowson, Lionel Johnson, Arthur Symons and *The Savoy,* hardly even Wilde and *The Yellow Book,* certainly not Beerbohm; only the little Frenchified hard core with a smattering of Celts.

In that world even the famous seemed to breathe an atmosphere of peaceful obscurity compared to the present day; it was a world in which the masses were more philistine and hostile, the great more powerful and aloof from the arts than they are now, in which a poet's best friend might be his landlady or a City clerk, and the love of his life a waitress or a woman of the streets.

It was a world with no critics, its boundaries Paris or somewhere in the wilds of Brittany, or Dieppe—Dieppe in that summer of '95 so well described by Arthur Symons and Jacques Emile Blanche, the Dieppe of Sickert and Rothenstein and Conder and Cléo de Mérode, where

Dowson took Wilde to the brothel after Berneval ("It was like cold mutton, but tell it in England, for it will entirely restore my character"), where Maupassant spread the story of Swinburne and the monkey.

Jacques Blanche, by the way, maintained that Dieppe, rather than Cabourg or Houlgate, was the true original of Proust's Balbec and he listed its hostesses and salons; the British preferred the all-night fishermen's cafés round the harbour while their cottages across the water on the Pollet were Dowson's favourite haunt. In my flight from the present he became my Dante:

> They are not long, the days of wine and roses;
> Out of a misty dream
> Our path emerges for a while, then closes
> Within a dream.

Slight but true—and how unexpected, almost compulsive, is the repetition of the word "dream" instead of a rhyme. It makes one want to learn more about him.

"Ernest Dowson (1867–1900) received a sporadic, mostly French education, after which in 1886, he went up to Oxford, where his indifference to sleep and food was to bring out latent tuberculosis and inherited nervous instability. Going down without a degree, he helped his father for several years to manage a small London dock. In 1892 and 1894 he contributed to the anthologies of the Rhymers' Club. In 1891 he fell unhappily in love with twelve-year-old Adelaide Folkinowicz. His parents committed suicide in 1894. Thrown on his own resources, Dowson began translating French memoirs and *romans noirs*. His first, most accomplished book, *Verses,* appeared in 1896. His life became progressively disorganised, and he died at Catford, London, on 23 February, 1900." (Article by Ian Fletcher from the *Concise Encyclopaedia of English and American Poets and Poetry.*) I add some flesh to the skeleton:

Oxford: He was at Queens's and one of his best-known poems, "Amor Umbratilis," was written on the back of an angry demand from an Oxford tradesman.

The Rhymers' Club—they met at the Cheshire Cheese, drank beer (not absinthe), smoked clay pipes and read their poems. Yeats wrote that he organised the two anthologies so as to get Dowson into print. Soon after leaving the University he became a Catholic.

In 1891 . . . in 1891 his life was practically over; it was the year he wrote "Cynara," his best poem, which was to inspire a popular song by Cole Porter and give a title to a best-seller, *Gone with the Wind,* and of which Eliot writes *"Non Sum Qualis Eram* seems to me the one poem in which, by a slight shift of rhythm, Ernest Dowson freed himself from the poetic diction of English Verse of his time." It is indeed a marvellous poem, an exercise in rhetorical sentimentality which yet comes off and appeals to everyone. The "shift of rhythm" is in the caesura before "in my fashion" and Dowson altered Horace's Cinara to Cynara (Odes 4. 1. lines 3, 4) to show that he wanted the accent on the first syllable. He owed far more to Propertius than to Horace, including the whole feeling of this poem, which first appeared (1891) in *The Hobbyhorse,* the Art Nouveau magazine edited by Horne and Mackmurdo.

Two main sources for Dowson's life are Symons's well-known preface to the *Collected Poems* and Victor Plarr's kindlier *Ernest Dowson* (1914) which contradict each other. According to Plarr, Adelaide married the waiter at her parents' restaurant in Glasshouse Street in 1897, when she would have been seventeen or eighteen. Symons says that "she listened to his verses, smiled charmingly, under her mother's eyes, on his two years' courtship, and at the end of two years married the waiter instead . . ."

This would make the marriage in 1893. Perhaps at that time the courtship was abandoned, though his love continued to mature and simmer. Leaving the restaurant every evening at closing time bred the restlessness which took him through the rest of the night to drinking dens and cabmen's shelters ("Dowson found harlots cheaper than hotels"). By now he was an alcoholic; gentle, diffident, thin-lipped and courteous when sober, a typical academic young poet, but insulting and loud-mouthed when drunk. The only photograph of him shows him in a blazer, looking rather *chétif*. "He fell into furious and unreasoning passions; a vocabulary unknown to him at other times sprang up like a whirlwind; he seemed always about to commit some act of absurd violence" (Symons). Violence! He thought "V" the most beautiful of the letters and his ideal line of verse was Poe's:

The viol, the violet and the vine

Victor Plarr (1867–1929), librarian to the College of Surgeons, was Alsatian by origin and one of the surviving Rhymers to attend the presentation of the poet's casket to Wilfred Blunt; he was an intimate friend of Dowson, who wrote a christening poem for his daughter but who dropped him when his "disorganised life" became too much for Plarr, so that it was Wilde's friend Robert Sherard who took in the dying poet at Catford.

Upon the eyes, the lips, the feet,
On all the passages of sense,
The atoning oil is spread with sweet
Renewal of lost innocence.

How good a poet was he? He seldom broke free from Swinburne and Verlaine, yet there was a desperate craftsman in him even though he used so many "poetical" words. "He achieves a faint wavering music which, however sensuous, is his own" (Graham Hough).

Wine and women and song
Three things garnish our way
Yet is day over long

Unto us they belong
Us the bitter and gay
Fruit and flowers among,
Wine and women and song . . .

What is better than they,
Wine and women and song?
Yet is day over long.

No poet had a stronger death-wish; it fatigues us even in his shortest verses and comes into its own in such extraordinary prose pieces as "The Visit" and "The Dying of Francis Dunne" (*The Savoy*). Rightly were his three books provided with covers by Beardsley. He came in with the Nineties like his fellow-Catholics Beardsley and Johnson and with them he went out. "The gentleman, the kindly, charming boyish friend, the scholar, the exquisite poet . . ." Plarr sums him up in tones long drummed out of current criticism—for Plarr is Pound's M. Verog:

Out of step with the decade
Detached from his contemporaries,
Neglected by the young
Because of these reveries.

(1964)

THE NINETIES

MR. THORNTON* is too young to have come under the Nineties as an early influence, so he enjoys them without ambivalence. For myself, the mood of the Nineties, embracing both the Celtic Twilight and the *Fin de Siècle,* was my most overwhelming experience after Tennyson. I was a schoolboy at the time and Eliot, the rescuer, was still round the corner. To read such an anthology, not too long and so well-chosen, is to bring back the senility of extreme youth:

> They are not long, the weeping and the laughter,
> Love and desire and hate
> I think they have no portion in us after
> we pass the gate.

Yes, the true poets of the Nineties are Dowson and Symons. In this anthology we have seventeen of one and twenty of the other, and seventeen also of Yeats, whose broad stream flows through the period: (*The Wind among the Reeds,* 1899) on its way to join the moderns. John Davidson and Lionel Johnson are runners-up. I have to write off Francis Thompson, whose poetry means little to me, and Henley, a phoney if ever there was one. But John Gray and Theodore Wratislaw (eight each) repay investigation and Housman improves when taken in this context.

The poets of the Nineties, seen at this distance, seem an idyllic group. The London they loved was only just emerging from the nineteenth century, telephones and motor cars were non-existent, Paris and Dieppe beckoned economically. There was always Verlaine, to whom Symons

* *Poetry of the 'Nineties,* edited and introduced by R. K. R. Thornton (Baltimore, 1970.)

dedicated his *London Nights,* the Verlaine of *Jadis et naguère* with the Pierrot poems and *Romances sans Paroles.*

Les roses étaient toutes rouges,
et les lierres étaient tout noirs.
Chère, pour peu que tu te bouges
renaissent tous mes désespoirs . . .

Mr. Thornton prints two translations of this exquisite poem, whose second couplet was Joyce's favourite.

Around were all the roses red,
The ivy all around was black.
Dear, so thou only move thy head,
Shall all mine old despairs awake.

The roses every one were red,
And all the ivy leaves were black
Sweet, do not even stir your head,
Or all of my despairs come back.

The versions are by Dowson and John Gray.

These poets were scholars but not intellectuals: they had never heard of the Objective Correlative, they were content with symbolism; the public thought them decadent but nobody called them stupid or wrote theses about them, nor did they review each other and engender envy and spite. "Companions of the Cheshire Cheese" or absinthe-sippers at the Café Royal, they were mostly penurious members of the middle classes with a leaning to Bohemianism. They either drank and died young or disappeared into steady unimportant jobs, steering precariously between starvation and syphilis.

They were not even original: Swinburne, Pater, J. A. Symonds, Wilde and Rossetti had blazed the trail; the only genius among them was Aubrey Beardsley. But they formed a group, the only group to exist between the Pre-Raphaelites and Bloomsbury. Much of their poetry was personal and rather superficial, life was easier then and so was art; one finds a relief in understanding them so easily, provided they are not dull.

The melancholy common to Dowson, Symons, Beardsley, Yeats and Housman may have been in their characters, or due to their unhappy love-affairs (same thing), or to the influence of Verlaine, or mere fashion. But it makes for good dying falls, especially when combined with the exhilaration of London and Paris. For this was the moment of urban ecstasy, when Baudelaire's Seine is grafted on to Whistler's Thames.

The train through the night of the town,
Through a blackness broken in twain
By the sudden finger of streets;
Lights, red, yellow and brown,
From curtain and window-pane,
The flashing eyes of the streets . . .

Arthur Symons is an under-estimated poet, his book on the Symbolist movement influenced both Yeats and Eliot and he had a genuine erotic vein, nurtured on Verlaine.

Mr. Thornton quotes Eliot on Dowson and Davidson. "The personage that Davidson created in this poem has haunted me all my life and the poem ['Thirty bob a week'] is to me a great poem for ever."

I am not quite happy about Davidson, while Dowson, I feel, had a talent for near misses. Luckily Mr. Thornton prints the newly discovered poem of Dowson's, "Against my lady Burton: on her burning the last writing of her dead husband." This was Burton's great book on homosexuality in various races and she burnt it because she dreamed that he had asked her to. It is the classic case of modern suttee—when the widow throws her late husband's works on the pyre rather than ascend it herself.

Her lean distrust awoke when he was dead;
Dead, hardly cold; whose life was worn away
In scholarship's high service; from his head
She lightly tore his ultimate crown of bay.
His masterpiece, the ripe fruit of his age . . .

The country-side was better described by John Davidson, the expert on poverty, and his "In Romney Marsh" contains the germ of much Georgian poetry: "As I came up from Dymchurch Wall . . ." The Nineties, in fact, like any arbitrarily chosen date, can mean what one wishes.

What in fact they are is a continuation of the Eighties, of Mallarmé, Huysmans, Gautier. The wave formed in Paris rippled out to Synge's Aran Islands, by way of *The Yellow Book.*

Even John Buchan appeared in *The Yellow Book,* so Mr. Thornton is right to stick to poetry written between 1890 and 1900 which can be grouped under his Ninetyish headings; he listens to his own taste and the result is a delightful book with plenty of variety which fits into the left pocket when the *Penguin Book of Socialist Verse,* bulky but less intimate, goes into the other. Only William Morris can bridge the gap between them. Socialism's all very well, but for broody youth and introspective age and for those who still care for word music, give us Dowson.

(1970)

OSCAR WILDE

WILDE is one of our few writers to have won academic honours, positive proof of a first-rate mind. He took a first in both Mods and Greats and could have been a don. This brilliant intelligence, stuffed with classics and philosophy, is obscured in his plays and novels by his delight in the visible world and by his snobbery. In his private life, sex was to usurp the throne of intellect. The public have taken to its heart only his *Dorian Gray, The Importance of Being Earnest* and *The Ballad of Reading Gaol.*

Professor Ellmann is to be congratulated (as usual) on bringing out an edition of the forgotten Wilde to include his major critical works—*Intentions, The Portrait of Mr. W. H.* and *The Soul of Man under Socialism*—as well as some of his book reviews and his apology for *Dorian Gray*. Sprightliness is Wilde's worst fault as a journalist, perhaps because he wrote so much for women's magazines, but there are moments when his classical scholarship and knowledge of French and Elizabethan literature make their appearance and when one wishes that he had been ruled by his head and not his inferior organs; what a waste of a good mind!*

If he were to face a trial it should have been for a book he had written, a premature *Ulysses* or *Lady Chatterley* that dare not speak its name, not for something he had done. He claimed to have put his genius in his life and his talent in his work, and paid for the blasphemy. He should have lived on like Gosse or Saintsbury and performed for literary criticism in its dullest hour what Shaw and Beerbohm did for the theatre. Born in 1854 he could have lived to review *Swann's Way* and even *Finnegans Wake.*

* *The Artist as Critic: Critical Writings of Oscar Wilde,* edited by Richard Ellmann (New York, 1970).

It is clear from some of this writing that he hankered after prison but was quite unprepared for hard labour with its shattering effect on mind and health. He saw it through romantic eyes: the poet, undisturbed in his cell, finding his true self in company with his muse and calling for his tablets. "After all, even in prison a man can be quite free," or "Prison has had an admirable effect on Mr. Blunt as a poet." "By sending Mr. Blunt to jail he (Mr. Balfour) has converted a clever rhymer into an earnest and deep-thinking poet."

Wilde is Wilde in these essays and seldom "Oscar." The change is beneficial. In some cases he is both: thus *The Soul of Man under Socialism* in places seems almost inspired; it is a breath of fresh air in which the idealistic aspects of Socialism (or Christian Democracy) have seldom been so well expressed—in his denunciation of private property for example.

> It is clear then that no Authoritarian Socialism will do . . . Every man must be left quite free to choose his own work. No form of compulsion must be exercised over him . . . The true perfection of man lies not in what man has, but in what man is . . . What a man really has, is what is in him. With the abolition of private property, then, we shall have true beautiful healthy Individualism. Nobody will waste his life in accumulating things or the symbols for things. One will live.

And he goes on, Lawrence-fashion, to describe his "perfect man" as

> one who develops under perfect conditions, one who is not wounded or worried or maimed or in danger. Most personalities have been obliged to be rebels. Half their strength has been wasted in friction . . . It will be a marvellous thing—the true personality of a man when we see it. It will grow naturally and simply, flower-like, or as a tree grows. It will not be at discord. It will never argue or dispute. It will not prove things. It will know everything . . . "Know Thyself" was written over the portal of the antique world. Over the portal of the new world "Be Thyself" shall be written. And the message of Christ to man was simply "Be Thyself." That is the secret of Christ. When Jesus talks about the poor he simply means personalities and when he talks about the rich he simply means people who have not developed their personalities. Personal property hinders Individualism at every step.

Then "Oscar" intervenes. "There is only one class in the community that thinks more about money than the rich, and that is the poor. The poor can think of nothing else."

Freedom from cares and chores, from household management is necessary to the individual (or Christian Socialist) and there must no longer be economic slaves to do the housework. "The proper aim is to try and reconstruct society on such a basis that poverty will be impossible." This means automation and there is a remarkable prophecy (1891) of how machinery will take over domestic drudgery.

> There is nothing necessarily dignified about manual labour and most of it is absolutely degrading . . . Man is made for something better than disturbing dirt. All that kind of work should be done by a machine . . . Machinery must work for us in coal mines and do all the sanitary services and be the stokers of steamers and run messages on wet days.

So thunders Wilde, and yet when I think of "Oscar," it is against a background of servants, of butlers announcing him and footmen with salvers, of a hansom cab hired by the day, the driver nodding under his tarpaulin while Wilde and Bosie display far into the night. And even Mrs. Wilde was pressed into service, bringing round his daily post-bag, weeping, to his rooms with Lord Alfred in the Savoy.

The Soul of Man confuses Socialism with a form of Tolstoyan anarchism in which men are left on their own to allow their natural perfections to expand ("All modes of government are failures. It is only in voluntary associations that man is free"). This is based on adolescent innocence. Such anarchism is exemplary in theory but when put into practice is soon forced to use compulsion and then use it more drastically than any form of government which has had greater practical experience.

Indeed Wilde, as his new "Hellenism" runs away with him, abandons his defence of Socialism for a more typical attack on the British public and an enunciation of the aesthetic doctrines with which we are too familiar.

> What does it mean? What is a healthy or unhealthy work of art? In the old days men had the rack. Now they have the press . . . A true artist takes no notice whatever of the public. The public are to him non-existent.

How hard I am finding it to stop quoting. Wilde was wrong about the machines. Eighty years after he was writing there is still no machine to make beds, polish furniture, clean carpets without human direction, serve meals or clear the table. How he would have enjoyed the telephone!

And Socialism has developed on the lines he deplored. "Authority and compulsion are out of the question," he wrote. "It would be like Russia. No one who lived in modern Russia would possibly realise his perfection except by pain."

As one who has broken many teeth on the problem of Shakespeare's Sonnets I welcomed the re-reading of *The Portrait of Mr. W. H.* in which Wilde produces the theory that the sonnets were addressed to a boy actor, Willie Hughes, for whom Shakespeare wrote all his woman's parts until he left to play Piers Gaveston for the "rival poet," Marlowe.

The Sonnets are like a Yale lock which many keys fit, but none open. How often have we slipped in the key cut to Southampton or Pembroke or any of the other contenders only to find it jam hopelessly. Whoever wrote them wished to leave no evidence. Wilde's theory helps to explain certain passages in the Sonnets in which Shakespeare might have been addressing an actor who was to play his lines in Romeo and so be immortalised as a lover rather than through the Sonnets alone. He is an actor or "shadow."

> What is your substance, whereof are you made
> That millions of strange shadows on you tend?

But the theory surely breaks down over the "Dark Lady" and on the sequence urging the young man to marry. "You had a father, let your son say so" becomes meaningless applied to a counter-tenor. Yet we are reminded by Wilde's theory and his list of boy actors that our desire to wish on Shakespeare nothing but the best and find him fit companions like Pembroke or Southampton will not allow his fancy to roam among the obscure. In this one case Wilde has let his preoccupation with boys override his love of titled dilettanti. His scholarship also shines out in some reviews in which he teases Gosse.

(1970)

OSCAR WILDE AND HENRY JAMES

An Imaginary Transmogrification

MONTGOMERY HYDE* is the author of *The Trials of Oscar Wilde* which wins the praise of M. Jullian† so who better to chronicle Sir Oscar's slow but mellow decline at Lamb House, Rye, where he retired, Congreve-like, in the height of his glory, till the fateful bomb on the garden room ended his life, a mere stripling of eighty-five, in August 1940.

And who better than Philippe Jullian, so worldly-wise and compassionate in two cultures, to describe the meteoric rise and tragic fall of the Cork expatriate and typical product of *The Yellow Book,* Henry James? The years of disintegration on the Paris boulevards attended only by his faithful friend, Robbie Gosse, and his evil genius, Wallie Hewpole (*The Portrait of Mr. W. H.*) and the usual task force of "renters" are now enlivened with much new evidence.

When, on a Sunday afternoon in the late Thirties, Harold and Vita Nicolson drove me over from Sissinghurst to call on Sir Oscar at Rye, I took my courage in both hands and asked him if he'd ever met Henry James. He held his finger to his lips, indicating the parlour-maid who was still in the room.

"Alas, poor Henry," he replied. "Yes—I did meet him. Though I never permitted my boy Cyril or my boy Vyvyan—nor, of course, Lady Wilde, to be present. He had a heart of gold. If only his other parts had been less volatile! He was his own worst enemy. He aspired to the bays and found only the bailiffs. I put all my wickedest fantasies into my work and kept my virtues for private circulation. Hence all this," and he waved his hand at a signed portrait of King Edward in a silver frame. "Poor James never realised literature's a fun thing. He stuffed his books

* *Henry James at Home,* by H. Montgomery Hyde (New York, 1969).
† *Oscar Wilde,* by Philippe Jullian. Translated by Violet Wyndham (New York, 1969).

with morality and stained his private life with satin sins—not that there was anything satin about Hewpole.

"I saw him last in a Montmartre café, his bloated face, tinctured by absinthe, *légèrement cardinalisé,* his pale eyes protruding with unnameable urges, his mouth already in the valley of the shadow while predatory pardine creatures stalked him from the darkness. I motioned Mrs. Wharton and the Bourgets to leave me while I went over to his table: 'I'm Oscar Wilde,' I said, 'if you remember, your *Guy Domville* was taken off for my *Importance of Being Earnest*. It's still running! Naughty, wasn't I?'

"He lifted his great ruined head and indicated the pile of saucers. My purse released a stream of yellow coin. *Ecco il leone!*"

This led me to investigate what the two really did think of each other. Beerbohm got as far as a cartoon of James being cross-examined by Carson. "Come, Sir," says Carson, "I ask you a plain question and I expect a plain answer." Both Mr. Hyde and M. Jullian quote the same passage on the Wilde case from James's letters to Gosse.

> It has been, it is, hideously dramatic and really interesting—so far as one can say that of a thing of which the interest is qualified by such a sickening horribility. It is the squalid gratuitousness of it all—of the mere exposure—that blurs the spectacle. But the fall from nearly twenty years of a really unique kind of "brilliant" conspicuity (wit, "art," conversation—"one of our two or three dramatists" etc.) to that sordid prison cell and this gulf of obscenity over which the ghoulish public hangs and gloats—it is beyond any utterance of irony or any pang of compassion! He was never in the smallest degree interesting to me—but this hideous human history has made him so —in a manner.

They first met in America in 1882 when James called on the visiting lecturer. "When Henry told the apostle of the aesthetic movement" [I quote from Mr. Hyde] "that he was homesick for London, Oscar dismissed him as provincial. 'Really, you care for *places,*' he exclaimed. 'The world is my home.' " Henry subsequently referred to him as "an unclean beast," "a fatuous fool" and "a tenth-rate cad."

The night of the disastrous opening of *Guy Domville* James filled in the time by a visit to Wilde's *An Ideal Husband* (it was the third performance).

> "I sat through it," he told his brother, "and saw it played with every appearance of complete success, and *that* gave me the most fearful apprehension. The thing seemed so helpless, so crude, so bad, so clumsy, feeble and vulgar, that as I walked away across St. James's Square to learn my own fate . . . I stopped in the middle of the Square, paralysed by the terror

of this probability—afraid to go on and learn more. How *can* my piece do anything with a public with whom *that* is a success?" (Hyde)

But Wilde admired *The Turn of the Screw*.

Although during their lifetime James towered morally over Wilde not only because he was the better man—one who completely was a gentleman while Wilde was always using the word to disparage other people ("a gentleman never looks out of the window")—but because he was a dedicated artist, yet he never made money by his books nor knew the delights of fame as Oscar did: not for him the packed house, the royal guffaw, the supper in the private room.

But he had a solid position with great ladies and Cabinet Ministers from Gladstone to Asquith. One would expect by now that the vulgarity, frivolity and lack of originality of Wilde's work would have been exposed and the grandeur of James's *oeuvre* have won its deserts. But there was a grandeur about Wilde as well. He orchestrated his life on a Wagnerian scale and drove himself inexorably towards his trial and disgrace as if fulfilling some secret prophecy. He was a blood-sacrifice on the altar of philistinism. This ritual murder assumes more and more importance in our annals; it preceded the *hubris* of the Boer War which darkened the close of Victoria's reign.

Wilde's sufferings, so articulate and well-documented, dominate his situation. M. Jullian rightly calls him the English Dreyfus. In comparison Henry James suffered nothing worse than boredom and moods of disillusion with the world he lived in. But time has dealt less than generously with his work. Despite the thriving James industry, largely confined to American universities, his later works remain grounded. Do not many of us secretly agree with his brother?

> In this crowded and hurried reading age, pages that require such close attention remain unread and neglected. You can't skip a word if you are to get the effect and nineteen out of twenty worthy readers grow intolerant. And so I say now, give us *one* thing in your older, directer manner.

Against this must be set the encomium by James's secretary, Theodora Bosanquet, with which Mr. Hyde ends the book and which summarises his virtue more than any other.

> The essential fact is that wherever he looked Henry James saw fineness sacrificed to grossness, beauty to avarice, truth to a bold front. He realised how constantly the tenderness of growing life is at the mercy of personal tyranny and he hated the tyranny of persons over each other. His novels are a repeated exposure of this wickedness, a reiterated and passionate plea for the fullest freedom of development.

Mr. Hyde is supremely entitled to call his book *Henry James at Home,* since he has been the tenant of Lamb House and is also related to the James family. He has acquired many treasures for the library and cared for the lovely house with its panelled Georgian rooms and pleasant garden till driven out by increasing expenses. He includes fascinating new information about James (such as the Waterlow diaries, letters to Gosse, etc.), and we end by liking the glorious old fuss-pot more than ever. Beneath the triviality and well-ordered gossip is the constant presence of a great artist and good man with whom it is an alleviation to dwell.

M. Jullian, too, has done his best for Wilde, so has his translator, Violet Wyndham, daughter of Wilde's friend, "the Sphinx." Here, too, is new material, long descriptions of the chaste "Art Nouveau" of Wilde's house in Tite Street, and many new Paris anecdotes, including the now famous meeting with Proust.* Wilde's links with French writers were even closer than James's and lasted to the bitter end.

These would not be enough, did not M. Jullian know how to make use of them. He is both well-informed and charitable; his book on Montesquiou has been a good preparation. Montesquiou could not bear Wilde and I remember Jacques Blanche telling me how vulgar he too found him—in very strong terms for a painter to use of a sitter. Yet Mallarmé admired *Dorian Gray.*

"One should not be moved to pity," concludes M. Jullian, "because he sank so low; he sought obscurity and through it attained exaltation . . . he was dedicated to his own destruction." "The artist's mission," said Wilde to Laurence Housman, "is to live the complete life: success as an episode (which is all it can be): failure as the real, the final end."

(1969)

* Proust asked him to dinner. When Wilde arrived and found he was to be alone with the family, he retired to the bathroom and then disappeared, saying he'd been taken ill.

HENRY JAMES

THIS* is the fourth of Mr. Edel's five volumes and depicts Henry James from 1895 to 1900, when, settled in Lamb House, he is about to embark on his three major novels. I doubt if I shall ever read them again. I can no longer tolerate slow action; some reservoir of patience and concentration has evaporated; there is room only for one difficult writer at a time and Proust has all but eliminated his English counterpart.

My admiration for James the artist persists but I can't read him. The tragic fire smoulders but always at some vapid country-house tea-party. Sex is the trouble; he understood wickedness but not sexual passion; Proust has plumbed both.

But reading about James is another matter. There, one is insatiable and Mr. Edel has produced what is so far his most distinguished volume. We begin with the disaster of *Guy Domville,* the period comedy of renunciation (the hero ends as a priest) with which James sought to woo the British playgoer. Many novelists and poets have wished to shine in the theatre, to hear their words spoken instead of read, and to rake in fame and shekels. Flaubert tried, so did Yeats; Eliot almost succeeded, Joyce failed but Dylan Thomas wrote *Under Milk Wood.* It is easier to name some of the few who have not written plays: Proust, Pound, E. M. Forster, Baudelaire, Graves, Mallarmé.

Like Flaubert, James got it badly; he hoped for a triumphant run with the leading West End company. (The fiasco is well known, and should be read in conjunction with Ada Leverson's account of the first night of *The Importance of Being Earnest* with which Alexander replaced it.) But Mr. Edel has unearthed far more than was known already, including

* *Henry James: The Treacherous Years 1895–1900,* by Leon Edel (Philadelphia, 1969).

the sensational fact that three young critics won their spurs that evening. Shaw, Wells and Bennett were all there; it was practically Wells's first assignment and he met Shaw for the first time; Bennett was writing for a woman's magazine under a feminine *nom de plume*. The younger generation knocked at the door and it fell open.

The stalls and critics were, however, well disposed to the play, it was the gallery that booed it, and James was led on to the stage to face the uproar. "Two members of the cast, years later, said they had never forgotten the expression on James's face as he came into the wings." "It has been a great relief," he wrote, "to feel that one of the most detestable incidents of my life has closed."

This was the first "treachery" of these crucial years, a blessing in disguise, since it held the beginning of the operation which freed him from London and set him up at Lamb House. These were also the years of his best work, excepting the last three novels, the period of *The Awkward Age, The Sacred Fount, The Turn of the Screw, The Spoils of Poynton* and *What Maisie Knew*.

Some kind of sexual explosion seems to have taken place, however subterranean, and the glow reveals the figure of the young Danish sculptor, Henrik Andersen, whom he met in the studios of the Via Margutta. "I hold you close," "I feel, my dear boy, my arms around you," "I draw you close I hold you long," "Lean on me as a brother and a lover" (1902). What does all this amount to? Mr. Edel, quite rightly, is non-committal. The words sound more passionate than they are and he quotes with approval Geoffrey Scott's analysis of the love between Madame de Charrière and Benjamin Constant: "The character of their relationship was abundantly clear—technically the inquiry would be inconclusive."

To sum up, the very frankness of James's language suggests physical innocence and is very different from writing "last night was the best ever." We all like subconsciously to castrate our father-figures. Not only analysts but doctors, dentists, bank-managers should all be celibate. But James's chastity was characteristic of his whole nature both as man and artist, as much as was the perversity of Proust or Wilde of theirs. He may have regretted it; he may have boiled over with platonic emotion or affected a knowingness which he did not feel but it was both his strength and his weakness. Novelists are not priests, they must experience the flesh and the world.

To illustrate these pitfalls I will quote the famous inscription in the Pearsall Smith/Gathorne-Hardy copy of *The Ambassadors*. "To Jonathan Sturges from Henry James. The Inspirer from the Inspired." I always took this to mean that James was in love with him, the original of Chad, and it would be easy to advance this as a proof of his homosexuality. But Mr. Edel supplies the explanation:

> Sturges had met Howells one day in Whistler's garden in the Rue du Bac. Howells was full of sad emotion. He had just arrived. Paris was beautiful and he had to leave, recalled to America because his father was dying. In the garden setting Howells had said to young Sturges: "Oh, you are young, you are young—be glad of it; be glad of it and *live*. Live all you can; it's a mistake not to . . ." and this became the crux of the famous passage in *The Ambassadors*. Sturges was the germ, the donnée—not a Mr. W. H.

Mr. Edel devotes much space to a Freudian—or is it Jungian?—analysis of James's dark period, his childhood fears and disappointments as typified in the many stories about little girls, and the two or three like *The Pupil* or *Owen Wingrave* about the growing male. "Studies of little boys and young male adults as signs of problems in self-assertion particularly in masculine way" the index describes it.

His identification with the little girls seems more tenuous and we will have to wait for Mr. Edel's explanations of the three major novels to see how far this is credible. Yet something was seriously wrong for which Lamb House (a house can give only what we put into it) was an anodyne.

> This is a grey, gusty, lonely Sunday at Rye, the tail of a great, of an almost in fact perpetual, winter gale. The wind booms in the old chimneys, wails and shrieks about the old walls. I sit, however, in the little warm white study—and many things come back to me . . . I feel the old reviving ache of desire to get back to work . . . the divine unrest again touches me.

Against this was London:

> the deluge of people, the insane movement for movement, the ruin of thought, of life, the negation of work, of literature . . . the nightmare.

These quotations from the mysterious *Notebooks* and unpublished letters reveal the James whom we can all follow and are in themselves enough to bring out his moral and intellectual greatness. His estimates of other writers, Kipling, D'Annunzio, Symonds, Wilde, Zola, Meredith, Daudet are invaluable. Most revealing of all is a passage quoted from his letter to Fullerton (1900).

> The port from which I set out was, I think, that of the *essential loneliness of my life* . . . this loneliness, what is it still but the deepest thing about one . . . Deeper than my "genius," deeper than my "Discipline," deeper than my pride, deeper, above all, than the deep counterminings of art.

It is this note which sets him above his contemporaries and above all the malignant and empty non-artists of today whose vanity is their only vocation. Perhaps this Life, when completed, will instigate a "healing process" in some of them and they will find his ghost, like Stevenson's, "waves its great dusky wings between me and all occupations."

By the way, the rare wine which Meredith gave Daudet must have been Côte Rôtie, not Votes-rotiers.

(1969)

EDITH WHARTON AND HENRY JAMES

MRS. BELL tells a fascinating story* in what is also a well-documented work of scholarship. I would include her book in my special series for the insomniac's bedside—books which transport us to a more enchanting world than the present and induce a state of grace. "The Angel of Devastation" was one of James's nicknames for Mrs. Wharton—and the friendship is revealed or rather shown up in all its levels of ambivalence.

First level. Henry James, old and celebrated, meets the rich, talented, admiring and devoted Edith Wharton, twenty years younger and just emerging as a writer herself. A well-balanced couple, they become great friends, and James visits her in America at Newport and Lenox and also travels with her abroad. He helps her to settle into her apartment in Paris and she introduces him to the delights of touring by motor—her "motor-flights" in the great 60 h.p. Panhard with its master-chauffeur, Cook. There are also visits to England, to Lamb House and Howard Sturgis at Windsor, and week-ends in stately homes like Mrs. Hunter's at Hill. In the war, drawn closer together by horror and indignation, they both devote their pens to defending the Allied cause.

Second level. The profession of letters, while appearing to unite them, gave rise to much envy. Edith Wharton was constantly accused of imitating James; one reviewer described her as "a masculine James" and there was a suggestion that she borrowed too much from him. At the same time she was admitting that she could not read his books. "It's a relief to know you can't read H.J.," she wrote to their publisher in 1904. "The efforts I made to read *The Ambassadors*! I broke one tooth after another on it."

* *Edith Wharton and Henry James,* by Millicent Bell (New York, 1965).

She constantly criticised James's theories of how to write novels and he also found considerable difficulty in praising hers. The difference in their ages which should have encouraged mutual admiration was embittered by his failure in the last ten years of his life to hold on to his sales or his public while she received as much as fifteen thousand dollars advance for what he knew to be inferior work.

Third level. Beneath her disguise of friend and adoring disciple, James recognised that Edith Wharton represented a very real threat to his independence and tranquillity. He soon refers to "the poison of the motor." James was a poor man, a moralist and a puritan as well as the most dedicated artist of his generation; he had always been fascinated by the world of the rich because he needed a leisured class to work out, in fiction, ethical problems.

The reality was different; Mrs. Wharton was not noticeably corrupt, she was an artist herself, but she represented the twentieth-century viewpoint that art could be combined with the mobility which wealth confers, with going everywhere and seeing everything, with knowing everyone, collecting eighteenth-century furniture and owning beautiful houses. She was a dynamic all-round perfectionist. If he saw too much of her, he would be gobbled up, he would lose his privacy, his originality, his self-respect, he would re-enact the Death of the Lion. "The rich, rushing, ravening Whartons"—he "only rather thanked goodness" that such fantastic wealth and freedom were not his portion: "such incoherence, such a nightmare of perpetually renewable choice and decision, such a luxury of bloated alternatives do they seem to burden life withal."

Such a negation of his values did Mrs. Wharton represent that he bestowed an almost supernatural nightmarish quality on her. "What an incoherent life! It makes me crouch more dodderingly than ever over my hearthstone." "*Her* power to go and to consume and to enjoy—her incomparable restlessness—leave me more and more 'abasourdi.' "

It was in her motor, on the way from Windsor to Cliveden, that he had a heart attack. "All I want for the improvement" (he wrote to Sturgis) "is to be *let alone,* and not to feel myself far aloft in irresistible talons and under the flap of mighty wings—and about to be deposited on dizzy and alien peaks. 'Take me *down*—take me home!' You saw me having to cry that, too piteously, the other day to the inscrutable and incomparable Cook—rescuer as well as a destroyer."

Rescuer as well as destroyer—that leads to the final level. When the war prevented her from coming to England his fears were stilled and she became for him the friend whose roots were in the same American past but who could take the active part in France's struggle which was denied him, and on which she reported to him almost daily. In the same way, in her hour of need, he had been her rescuer: when her marriage to Edward Wharton was breaking up he had advised her not to run away. "Only sit tight yourself *and go through the movements of life.*" His letters throughout this crisis illustrate his "aboundingly tender friendship" until she finally managed to divorce her husband, when he almost gloats: "Teddy is now howling in space."

The marriage was obviously a mistake and the couple were incompatible: Wharton was a handsome athlete and a man of action whose life became increasingly constricted and finally subordinate to his wife's social and literary ambitions—a not uncommon pattern. She fell in love with Walter Berry, friend of James and Proust, and spent more and more time travelling with him. Meanwhile Wharton grew more and more "neurasthenic" and developed mysterious mental symptoms.

Mrs. Wharton and her friend clearly exaggerated these and what was apparently a mildly manic-depressive cycle with a few psychopathic symptoms was worked up into insanity. He began to speculate and lose money, and Logan Pearsall Smith told me that he would also make love to the maids—in the circumstances quite understandable. Mrs. Wharton most dreaded having to look after a dependent invalid, and so he was "divorced and *incomed* by formal process of French law" and Mrs. Wharton was congratulated on her "definite liberation." One would like to know for how long he lived afterwards and where—but Mrs. Bell consigns him to oblivion even as she fails to answer Edmund Wilson's queries about how much money Mrs. Wharton had (her archive is closed till 1967).

While enjoying every page of this fascinating book one can't help getting rather impatient with the immense fuss made about everything; the dwelling on trifling incidents and the blowing them up to more than life size for the sake of conversation, the harping on minor idiosyncrasies which is part of the give-and-take of salons. When war broke out James wrote: "I find it such a mistake to have lived on—when like other saner and safer persons, I might perfectly have not—into this unspeakable give-away of the whole fool's paradise of our past."

(1966)

MARCEL PROUST: 1

*Contre Sainte-Beuve** was written around 1908 when Proust was thirty-seven, six years before *Swann's Way*. It is not an early work like *Jean Santeuil;* it bears the mark of fully developed maturity and confident genius. I would class it as compulsory reading.

The form is original, though closer to some of Gide's early works than one would expect. We approach the main subject, the attack on Sainte-Beuve, through a series of conversation-pieces between Proust and his mother (who had died four years earlier), which are also imaginative essays like Virginia Woolf's *Mark on the Wall.*

These essays contain the genesis (the Madeleine, the Three Trees) of central metaphysical experiences in *La Recherche,* and the first sentence—"Every day I set less store on the intellect. . . . What intellect restores to us under the name of the past is not the past"—is the key to his whole work. His mother brings him the *Figaro* with his first article in it, and that leads up to a new series of articles, the attack on Sainte-Beuve, which turns out too long. The articles lead on to the position of Balzac and Sainte-Beuve in aristocratic society, whereupon the whole Guermantes family arrive on the scene and give their opinions. One of them, the Baron de Quercy, is a homosexual, and this gives rise to a passionate analysis. "A race accursed." By way of Combray we return to Proust's childhood and his mother, and to a final essay on his theory of literature: "Books are the work of solitude and the *children of silence.*"

This is the kernel of the attack on Sainte-Beuve, which develops on two fronts. Sainte-Beuve's idea of a scientific approach to writers (as a

* *By Way of Sainte-Beuve,* by Marcel Proust. Translated by Sylvia Townsend Warner (London, 1958).

natural historian) is false, his attitude to his great contemporaries (Stendhal, Balzac, Flaubert and above all Baudelaire) is unjust. The attack is fuelled by indignation, particularly over Sainte-Beuve's treatment of Baudelaire as friend as well as critic.

There is only one defence of Sainte-Beuve, that he was a greater critic than he knew, that his "method" was a rationalisation of an instinctive process of identification with his subject which was really a form of genius and which often enabled him to write superlatively well about unimportant people—given the transference—while with others, particularly the successful and the copious as exemplified by the "great novelists," there was often a barrier.

In the case of Baudelaire, to whom he stood as a kind of uncle, there was probably complete incomprehension. Sainte-Beuve's own poetry was dim, cold and inhibited, he was offended by Baudelaire's emotional excesses, and lines which in a poem by Sainte-Beauve would show up like distant summer lightning could be turned out by Baudelaire in their hundreds and used as a soft pedal to mute a flight of genius. Sainte-Beuve's trite descriptions of *Les Fleurs du Mal* as "Baudelaire's Folly" and "a literary Kamschatka" on the map of Romanticism are only a little more banal than Hugo's *"vous avez créé un frisson nouveau."* It is as if Gosse had been the guardian of Dylan Thomas, or George Moore of Beckett. Nevertheless, Proust was right. Incomprehension may excuse Sainte-Beuve's attitude to Baudelaire, but his behaviour during the trial is contemptible and his failure to appreciate Flaubert, Stendhal, Balzac, Nerval and so many others reveals fear and envy. "How often Sainte-Beuve tempts one to cry out 'What an old ass!' or 'What an old blackguard!' "

> Any man who shares his skin with a man of genius has very little in common with the other inmate; yet it is he who is known by the genius's friends, so it is absurd to judge the poet by the man, or by the report of his friends, as Sainte-Beuve did. As for the man himself, he is just a man and may perfectly well be unaware of the intentions of the poet who lives in him. And perhaps it is best so.

Genius in fact is an Atman which transcends the personality, and therefore personal data are of no importance.

"I do not think of literature," replies Sainte-Beuve, "as a thing apart, or at least detachable, from the rest of the man and his nature . . . One cannot provide oneself with too many means or too many objectives if one is to know a man—by which I mean something other than a pure intelligence. So long as one has not asked an author a certain number of questions and received answers to them, one cannot be certain of having a complete grasp of him."

Today a great critic (Valéry, Thibaudet or André Maurois) would apply both methods, as does Proust himself in his novel, where Elstir, Bergotte and Vinteuil are seen in their element as painter, writer and composer and also in the grip of their personal problems, painful in the case of Vinteuil and directly connected with his genius. The importance of Proust's attack is that it is a reaction against everything that is frivolous, superficial and patronising in a certain method of criticism.

This leads him to praise Sainte-Beuve's poetry for its "austere refinement" as "the only genuine thing about him," and to condemn the "Lundis" as superior hack-work owing to "his shallow conception of the creative mind."

We can argue the other way round: the Sainte-Beuve who failed as a creative artist both with his poems and his novel *Volupté,* found his greatness as a critic with *Port Royal* and his essays on the seventeenth and eighteenth centuries. Few Romantics have been presented with a second chance.

Miss Townsend Warner, whose translation is a labour of love and therefore so natural as to appear unnoticeable, points out that in *Contre Sainte-Beuve* "the writing conveys an effect of force and pace and commandingness which Proust never again repeated," and she thinks the influence of Balzac is the cause. It is certainly the most vivid and rapid of all his books. The intelligence and sensibility seem at white heat, the relationship with his mother exposed, with his preoccupation with social values. In these first sketches he seems almost to foam dithyrambically at the mouth when the Guermantes are mentioned.

Incidentally the Duc de Guermantes appears here as the "Count," an amiable antisocial Balzac-lover: "Only when there was a question of relationship did the Count blaze into animation. At the utterance of some name he would cry out: 'But she's my cousin!' as if this were some unhoped-for stroke of luck." Madame de Villeparisis is shown in her prime as an intolerable old humbug:

> To begin with, he never set foot in it, he was invited nowhere, what could he have known about it? Sainte-Beuve, yes! Now there was a charming man, so witty, such a gentleman, he never put himself forward and one never had to meet him unless one wanted to. Not like Balzac. There's no good feeling in what he wrote, there are no nice people.

All true Philistines like art.

I hope I have said enough to encourage Proust-lovers to descend on this book. It is alive with intelligence, rarest of qualities in combination with the artist's vocation, and the frankness of the childhood scenes is revelatory: "The unbearable recollection of the distress I had caused her brought back an agony that only her presence and her kiss could heal . . ." The mother is ubiquitous, sole witness of the expansion of his genius, fountain of love and whimsy. Sex seizes him through auto-erotic experiences in the lavatory where a lilac flowered through the window: then comes the sea-side, and a love-affair with the Countess which merges into literature. The erotic, the mystical, the metaphysical, the literary—all combine into a kind of visual ecstasy: the emotional security which the mother provided became in retrospect a spring-board for adventure.

(1958)

MARCEL PROUST: 2

THERE is always room for a new book about Proust. One has only to pronounce this sentence to know that it is untrue; we are utterly satiated with books about Proust, his hostesses, his cork-lined rooms, his boy friends, his creepy correspondence, the new anecdote, the pilgrimage to Illiers, the defence of snobbery . . . So let us write: "There is room for exactly one more book about Proust, and it is Mr. Painter's* for he has digested all the others."

The publication of *Jean Santeuil* made all biographies of Proust out of date, and our first debt to Mr. Painter is for bringing all the autobiographical evidence supplied by these three posthumous volumes—and also *Contre Sainte-Beuve*—into line with the rest. Next we must be grateful to him for giving us a fully documented life of Proust, and for not using the life as a peg on which to hang preconceived theories.

Mr. Painter has only two theories; the first is that *A la Recherche du Temps Perdu* is not a novel so much as an autobiography recast as a work of art—consequently the relationship between the work of art and the raw material of the artist's life is all-important; the second is that nothing in this relationship is simple.

He gives Proust's mind and character full credit for its complexity and subtlety. What took a lifetime to conceive must need a lifetime to unravel. Proust has been fortunate in that most of his biographers have been intelligent, but at this stage what is needed is a mixture of intelligence, imagination, scholarship and humility, for by his searching self-examination Proust provides a touchstone on which his commentators are judged.

Let us take the example of Proust's snobbery. There is no doubt that

* *Proust: The Early Years,* by George Painter (Boston, 1959).

the young Proust was an unmitigated social climber, and that there was in his snobbery a strong element of aggression against his family and of guilt, both sexual and racial: he genuinely believed that the Faubourg Saint Germain was a better world, like the kings and queens who enter our dreams, by whom our merits are appreciated and our enemies excluded.

"I will talk with your Majesty," says the Duke of Brittany to the King of Portugal at the Opéra in *Jean Santeuil;* and "No, Brittany," replies the affable monarch, "I'd rather go with my young friend Jean; he can finish telling me about the libel-suit between Ruskin and Whistler, which fascinates me, and, besides, it will be one in the eye for Mme Marmet."

And one in the eye for Dr. Proust . . . But beyond this amicable approach (which persisted in the first draft of *A la Recherche*) Proust's intelligence and critical sense were at work, also his homosexuality and asthma, and he begins to realise that affable monarchs do not give a damn for Whistler and Ruskin, and that his enemy, Madame Marmet, will get as far as he has; the cruelty and ruthless egotism from which he is flying were enthroned—as the Dreyfus case proved—in the heart of the sanctuary.

This disillusion generally appeals to the Anglo-Saxon critic who takes a puritanical view of the Guermantes in the first place. But disillusion is not everything. Beyond the selfishness and stupidity, the terrible ordinariness of people of fashion, so shallow compared to the spiritual depth of the artist or the selfless goodness of his grandmother, remain the agreeable ambience of an upper class, the system of good manners evolved as a lubricant by many cynical generations, the courage and gaiety which were to be pressurised by the First World War; and to this ambience Proust remained faithful all his life.

He had run away to the salons as sterner young rebels run away to sea, pursuing the white whale of perfect exclusiveness. Mr. Painter understands all this and more, and his generalisations are a delight, even as his molehills of fact, which he seems to throw up so casually, form a mountain of information.

> Perhaps, however they choose, the young are right, for the highest, whatever it be, is not of this earth, and it matters little in which of its earthly symbols they may seek it in vain. A drawing-room, it seemed to Proust, was itself a work of art. . . . He must be accepted where acceptance would be most difficult and failure most humiliating, in the company of the elect, in the Faubourg which was on earth the image, whether real or merely blasphemous, of the blessed saints in heaven.

With even greater understanding, Mr. Painter enters into the convolutions of Proust's sexual desire. Although he does not skimp a detail of

Proust's homosexuality he gives full value to every impulse in the opposite direction, showing us how long it took him to discover his true proclivities, "how nearly his inclinations towards young girls were fulfilled."

> Ability to love a person of the opposite sex, and of one's own age, is the only valid escape from the prison of the family, and that way was now barred . . . When he migrated to the Cities of the Plain he took with him a prisoner crushed beneath the weight of Time and Habit, a buried heterosexual boy who continued to cry unappeased for a little girl lost.

Mr. Painter writes admirably about Combray, Illiers, and Proust's Ruskin phase. He peppers his account of the Faubourg with amusing anecdotes, and brings dead wits and forgotten hostesses to life. I have compared his book with four or five other documentaries to find evidence that he has selected wisely from them all; he is perhaps a little unfair to Madeleine Lemaire's illustrations to *Les Plaisirs et les Jours,* which contain a portrait of Proust at dinner; he is sometimes too inclined to sit in judgement.

But he never loses sight of the abstract beauty of Proust's life, which was a ceaseless quest to gain material for his novel, and which required several minor novels and much illness and suffering before the vision of eternity which would make it finally different from all other novels—a unique work of art—was vouchsafed to him.

We must now wait two intolerable years for Mr. Painter's second volume.

(1959)

MARCEL PROUST: 3

I REMEMBER pleading that there should be no more books about Proust after Painter. But there is just room for this one.* Not only because it is intelligent, imaginative and well-written but because it is exactly what it says, a Baedeker which conducts us through the great novel and will send those who can spare the time scurrying back to it.

I believe that *A la Recherche du Temps Perdu* is the greatest literary achievement of the century. Proust is the one writer we can mention in the same breath as Balzac, Stendhal, Baudelaire, Flaubert. As novelist laureate he was preceded by Henry James who just lived to read *Swann,* succeeded by Joyce who met him once but, without disputing their greatness, one feels Proust surpassed both by drinking just that much deeper of human nature at the springs of creativity and suffering. I was fortunate, while still at Oxford, to have read the later volumes as they came out. With *The Waste Land* and the later poems of Yeats (collected at the same moment), I was intoxicated for several years. I tried to talk like Proust, think like Proust, and write like Proust and had to destroy it all later.

I mention this to show how difficult I find it to be objective about him. Of course he bored me too. There are hundreds of pages of pseudo-scientific analysis which seem to take away more than they add by encapsulating character-traits and deforming the action. But now I do not find them so boring as when I was half in love with Swann, Saint Loup, Gilberte and Albertine. And even now I cannot read about the sea-side world of Balbec without a personal pang of tragedy and loss as if it had belonged to my own youth, as indeed, through my first reading, was the case.

* *A Reading of Proust,* by Wallace Fowlie (Garden City, N.Y., 1964).

Meanwhile, what does Proust offer to the generations who did not come of age with his novel? How many people under forty have dined with the Guermantes or laughed at Charlus or wept for Swann? Proust's world lies about us in ruins and though he prophesied its ruin, some of him has perished with it. The society which he took as subject for his novel was also the environment which he breathed and went on breathing the moment he laid down his pen. Time has destroyed his habitat and the salons have to be reconstructed by a feat of the imagination before we can appreciate his treatment of them. Drawing-rooms, boudoirs, dandies, blackballing club-men, coachmen, footmen, valets, great cocottes—they still exist but shorn of their importance. Elstir, Vinteuil, Swann, Bergotte, the painter, composer, connoisseur, and writer—their lonely and neglected genius today might find itself herded into "Late Night Line-Up" or a campus in California. As Proust himself wrote:

> Sans doute mes livres, eux aussi, comme mon être de chair, finiraient un jour par mourir. Mais il faut se résigner à mourir. La durée éternelle n'est pas plus promise aux oeuvres qu'aux hommes.

Looking back at Proust from this distance one can see that the first half of the novel (as far as the end of *Sodome et Gomorrhe*), the half which appeared in his lifetime, contains most of the action while the last three volumes, *The Captive, The Fugitive* and *Time Regained,* are far more subjective, the pages flowing on unsullied by dialogue or happenings. Mr. Fowlie has helped me to appreciate these volumes and to see them as less of an anticlimax. The narrator's love for Albertine, he explains, is the deepest feeling in the book and here it takes full effect while the dominant motive, the growth of a literary vocation, gathers force until it emerges triumphantly in the last pages.

As he points out, the novel has three themes: the nature of art and the artist, the meaning of love, and the structure of society and the laws which govern it. "Other novelists, Stendhal for example, emphasise either society or the individual. At no point in the closely woven texture of Proust's writing is any demarcation visible between society and the individual's interacting within the society."

"La vocation invisible dont cet ouvrage est l'histoire," is that really the main clue, as Mr. Fowlie maintains, or is the purpose of the novel set out in the title, *A la Recherche du Temps Perdu* with its conclusion in the last chapter of *Le Temps Retrouvé?* We have to waste time first before we can win it back and the footling, philandering dilettantism of the sheltered Marcel is to be seen and understood in relation to deeper forces through the controlled use of subconscious memory. The vocation grows like a honeycomb but the novel is about the gathering of honey.

The two operations are simultaneous. In that sense Proust is the completely self-conscious novelist as Mallarmé is the completely self-conscious poet.

In the case of an even more self-conscious poet, Valéry, and novelist, Gide, the dual process cancelled itself out. The poem about the poet writing a poem, the novel about the novelist writing a novel, nearly defeated them. Proust triumphed becaused his marvellous intellect was combined with a Baudelairean understanding of love and suffering and a Balzacian avidity for the Comédie Humaine. Like Freud or Einstein he will always be a little over our heads—over everybody's head—and that is why we shall always return to him.

"Proust belongs to that lineage of artists who bear within themselves an entire world: Dante, Shakespeare, Balzac, Joyce. Their work has a largesse, a prodigality, a part of their nature which is inscribed on their pages as forcefully as the nature of their characters . . . the other aspect of his writing always present but infinitely more difficult to define, is the poetry he discovers at every moment in life"; and Mr. Fowlie concludes, "Proust is the greater for the scope of his poetry, for the epic impact of some of the great passages, and for the power of his thought in which another universe is seen, or half-seen, to exist behind the familiar lineaments of whatever world he describes."

In such a complex analysis of the texture of the work I think Mr. Fowlie has neglected Proust's comic genius. One couldn't enjoy him as a novelist if there was nothing there but analysis of aesthetic experience and social decay. Proust is a master of the humour of cross-purposes, of the ironical nuance, and the broadest farce.

When the blatantly homosexual Baron de Charlus is making up to Madame de Surgis because of her two handsome sons beside her, the fatuously ignorant guests at the party remark "When you think of all the women he's had, he might leave his brother's mistress alone"; and such incidents as the spying on Morel through the supposedly one-way mirror in the brothel are pure Chaplin. I respect Mr. Fowlie for deliberately side-stepping Proust's own private life, about which we still know relatively little, except that he genuinely loved his adventurous chauffeur Agostinelli who may have been an original of Albertine as the ex-footman Albert Le Cuziat certainly was of Jupien.

An interesting aspect not often noticed are the curious omissions in the novel. There is hardly any mention of alcoholism, for instance, which is the scourge of Western society, nor of debt—so dear to Balzac—nor of real social changes of the war years like the arrival of Americans everywhere or the impact of jazz. How remote Proust seems from the movements which surrounded the end of his life, from Cubism,

Fauvism, Surrealism, night-clubs, the cinema, the ballet, psychoanalysis, Bolshevism or Eng. Lit. after Ruskin. Was it an instinct of self-preservation that kept Orpheus looking back?

(1968)

3

Nothing if Not Critical

THE MODERN MOVEMENT

I SUPPOSE this exhibition* makes me one of the few writers who have seen their dream implemented by reality, who have rubbed a magic lamp and beheld a huge djinn turn the contents of an imaginary bookcase into the living word, the word made flesh through photographs, letters, manuscripts, association copies, so that every error of judgement is magnified as well as every correct guess, making clearer every secret influence or unsuspected affinity. Only the University of Texas has had the will and the means and the erudition to raise this memorial to the writers of our time, and I hope it will bring new hope and happiness and inspiration to everyone who loves literature and who owes a debt to these life-enhancing figures.

I would like to say something about how this book, originally titled *One Hundred Key Books in the Modern Movement* and not *The Modern Movement,* which would have been presumptuous in a check-list, nor *The Hundred Best Books,* since a "best book" implies other criteria than "key," came into being. One must first go back to my school-days, when, an only child in rebellion against a conventional home and an even more conventional classical education, I first came to awareness. My adolescence, 1918–23, coincided with a larger First-War phenomenon. I was, without knowing it, in search of a father—or father-replacement. This search for a sympathetic spiritual authority is one of the least understood yet most persistent of the emotional drives, though it is common enough in other gregarious animals. A French teacher at

* This article first appeared as the catalogue introduction to an exhibition held in March–December 1971 at the Humanities Research Center of the University of Texas, Austin, U.S.A., to illustrate the author's book *The Modern Movement: One Hundred Key Books from England, France and America 1880–1950* (New York, 1966).

school raised a corner of the curtain on Villon, Verlaine, Mallarmé, Baudelaire, but the cult of Flecker, Housman, and the Georgians still lay heavy. It was not until I got to Oxford in 1922 that I met a young don who shared my love of literature and who introduced me to the contemporary ferment. That is why *One Hundred Key Books* is dedicated to Maurice Bowra, through whom I came to love and appreciate early Eliot, later Yeats, Edith Sitwell, E. M. Forster, Proust, and Valéry. Later on I went to work for Logan Pearsall Smith (another father) who made it possible for me to spend a winter in Paris (1928). There I fell in love with an American girl whom I found reading Ronald Firbank, and there I met Sylvia Beach, who introduced me to Joyce, Gide and Hemingway. I identified with the Paris-American pack and was accepted by them, writing some of the first articles on Hemingway, *Finnegans Wake,* and the Surrealists for *Life and Letters* and *The New Statesman.* Even as I read and got to know these Paris expatriates, I came to see them as part of the explosion of my own emotional life as I wooed and won my American girl, Frances Jean Bakewell of Baltimore, then in her nineteenth year. Joyce and Hemingway, Cummings and Fitzgerald, *transition* and Sylvia Beach joined up with Eliot, Yeats, Huxley, the Sitwells and Wyndham Lewis and with the great succession of French writers, Baudelaire, Flaubert, Proust and Valéry to build the Pantheon from which this book came to be chosen. The one great gap was Pound, whom I did not come upon till Sylvia Beach—once more—introduced me to his *Mauberley* many years later—*mea sola et sera voluptas,* my late and only pleasure. I write of these personal feelings to try to show what an upheaval underlies my passion for poetry, of which this list is merely the aftermath. Many new writers then became my friends; Evelyn Waugh, Elizabeth Bowen, Auden, Spender, Isherwood, Dylan Thomas, but none have been sufficient to obliterate the discoveries or the irrecoverable intensity of the year 1928 and the winter/spring of 1929, of 12 Rue de l'Odéon, 30 Rue de Vaugirard, when I found myself in love at the hub of three cultures.

My book, *The Unquiet Grave,* tried to evoke that profound experience; I rather wished someone had suggested that it should have been included in *The Hundred Books,* particularly in view of its extensive quotations from so many authors in this selection, but there was never a murmur. In fact my *One Hundred Key Books* met with a frigid reception from most reviewers and has had to make its way chiefly through booksellers' catalogues. "First they'll crab you, then they'll crib you," as Desmond MacCarthy used to say. This treatment might have been expected for a very idiosyncratic anthology but in fact I have tried very hard to be objective, weighing the claims of country against country, group against group, and allowing for my own weak spots. My worst defect is a blind eye for the grand, an inability to swallow larger than life extravaganzas on a colossal scale. I could reel off a long list but here I will mention some of the most significant. Dreiser, *An American Tragedy;* Gertrude Stein, *The Making of Americans;* Wyndham Lewis, *The Apes of God;* E. E. Cummings, *The Enormous Room;* Claudel, *The Satin Slipper;* St. John Perse, *Anabasis;* Faulkner, Thomas Wolfe, Malcolm Lowry, James Agee, Djuna Barnes, Jules Romains, Roussel, Henry Miller (most regretfully). On the other hand I have included one or two very slight books which should perhaps have made way for some of these titans and twice I fear my judgement has been at fault. I decided on 1880 as the beginning and 1950 as the terminus; even so, 1950, which is marked by the deaths of Shaw and Orwell, with Dylan Thomas's soon to follow, is perhaps too arbitrary.

It has meant excluding several writers whom I should like to have included such as Beckett, Anthony Powell and Robert Lowell. Beckett could have got in on the strength of *Murphy* (1938), with *Watt* on the border-line; *Waiting for Godot* was not yet published. It seemed to me that only the last would have merited his inclusion. Anthony Powell's earlier comic novels, even *From a View to a Death,* are nothing like as important as his novel-sequence, *The Music of Time,* which began with *A Question of Upbringing* (1951), and Robert Lowell's *Lord Weary's Castle* is still based on somewhat monotonous versification from which he only escapes in *Life Studies,* a far more significant book (1959).

I do not know if it is due to old age or to the overwhelming tempo of current events, but I form an impression of hurrying flood-waters carrying everything away in a muddy spate of torn trees, huts, hen-roosts rushing past, of monuments of culture now buried and forgotten, even in the few years since this exhibition was planned and the book written. To compile lists and catalogues is an anxious occupation which suggests a morbid preoccupation with the flight of time. Flaubert, Joyce, Thomas Wolfe were dabs at it, Ezra the Scribe (though not the poet) and I feel my list came just in time. Already a hundred new critical works have accumulated round the corpus of Eliot, Joyce, Yeats, Pound, Proust, Lawrence, Hemingway and even Auden, still so very much with the living. And yet literature, never so well taught as now, is perhaps never so little read; I mean that the literary experience, the shock of recognition, the cross-fertilization between minds of which this exhibition gives such wonderful examples, is severely threatened by the distractions of other media and by economic pressures. These writers, many of whom I knew, lived in an emptier world; no one saw Joyce on television or even heard him on the wireless, his voice survives on one gramophone record.

Yeats also; and though Eliot received modern coverage, we know nothing about Nathanael West or Hart Crane except from one or two snapshots; even a writer very famous in his time like George Moore is physically elusive, and the only man living who can imitate Proust (Paul Morand) is in his eighties. For this reason the association copy, which plays such a large part here, antedates the radio and television interview as a manifestation of personality, a chain reaction. Before the days of the media, writers were unselfconscious and did not "sit" to posterity or sign books for collectors. Hardly anyone collected them. They could also be poor and obscure, and there was no campus spread under them to catch them if they fell. Apart from their powers as trail-blazers, as architects of our own sensibility, I think this modest isolation forms part of their beauty, even as Claudel reminded Gide of seeing Verlaine and Villiers "with destitution in their eyes."

For visitors who have no time for the introduction to *One Hundred Key Books* or its captions, I would like to repeat that I use the "modern movement" loosely to mean what we all know, but cannot define, the revolt against nineteenth-century materialism; "The modern spirit was a combination of certain intellectual qualities inherited from the Enlightenment: lucidity, irony, scepticism, intellectual curiosity, combined with the passionate intensity and enhanced sensibility of the Romantics, their rebellion and sense of technical experiment, their awareness of living in a tragic age." The word "modernity" was first used by the Goncourts, then by Gautier. Technical experiment without imagination is not enough, but neither is imagination with an unimaginative attitude to form.

I suspect Robert Frost, Max Beerbohm, Galsworthy, Wilde of being anti-modernists and have left them out with many other traditional writers (Walter de la Mare, Kipling). I have not included translations from languages I do not know—German, Russian, even Italian and Spanish. Exceptions, Waley's *Chinese Poems,* Koestler's *Darkness at Noon* (written in German but first published in English). I have left out philosophical, historical and other subjects whose frontiers march with literature. My method was to go through lists of books under the years they were published, from 1880–1950, and put together all the significant, then slowly weed them out. If some well-known book is not here, there is, I hope, some good reason.

To come back to this exhibition, it is the embodiment of a dream, the incarnation of the dry bones of my catalogue. One would like it to exist in perpetuity like so many side chapels in a great cathedral, each with their images and ex-votos and paintings where the onlooker can meditate and where time stands still. Hemingway's letter to David Garnett—

what a treasure that is*—and Hart Crane's message to E. E. Cummings to buy the Graves-Riding *A Survey of Modernist Poetry*—"it has more gunpowder in it"; *The Waste Land* with its eliminated line "(The ivory men make company between us)," and many writers expressing their doubt and despair about books which were to prove seminal. I suppose no critic, bibliophile or maker of a literary litany has had such satisfaction as the summoning to this exhibition of the living genius. As Mallarmé said of Debussy's setting to music of his *Après-midi d'un Faune:* "Your illustration goes even further *dans la nostalgie et la lumière, avec finesse, avec malaise, avec richesse*"—in nostalgia and light, with subtlety, with inquietude, with luxury. May these books in turn stimulate the visitor to go home and do better.

(1971)

* He had written the book (*A Farewell to Arms*) so many times trying to get it as he wanted that finally it made no sense to him.

W. B. YEATS

It is significant that Yeats was born in the same year as Kipling. Who could foretell, when both attained their half-century in 1915, the reversal of fortune which would relegate the universally acknowledged laureate (in prose and verse) of the world's greatest empire to semi-oblivion when his hundred was up, while the long-haired floppy-tied survivor of the Celtic Twilight, the last Pre-Raphaelite "companion of the Cheshire Cheese" who refused to write a war-poem, would have amassed yet another bibliography (published in *In Excited Reverie**) solely of books about him since 1950? Wells, Bennett and Galsworthy incidentally were all born within two years of him and cannot expect much from their centenaries at their present showing.

About Yeats, indeed, as about Joyce, it is quite impossible to say anything without being immediately conscious of the enormous bulk of criticism already in print. How fortunate is Mr. Charles Madge who in 1962 "solved once and for all the iconographic origin of 'Leda and the Swan.'" Is there anything one can possibly contribute to the greater glory of this poet whom I have loved since introduced to the *Later Poems* of 1922 by Sir Maurice Bowra?

One feels, incidentally, that there is still scope for a fuller account of Yeats at Oxford (and of Oxford's influence on him) than is given in Hone's biography or the reminiscences of L. A. G. Strong and others. Perhaps a symposium on the lines of W. R. Rodgers's *Dublin Portrait,* which opens the Macmillan memorial volume. It was the general cattiness of some of these Dublin wits which aroused Mr. Henn, he tells us, to sufficient anger to undertake *The Lonely Tower.*† Some of this malice

* *In Excited Reverie: A Centenary Tribute to W. B. Yeats,* edited by A. Norman Jeffares and K. G. W. Cross (New York, 1965).
† *The Lonely Tower,* by T. R. Henn (New York, 1965).

persists in the *Dublin Portrait,* which has, however, the fascination of genuine small talk about the great. One longs for more of it. "As far as the younger generation of poets are concerned here in Ireland," said Frank O'Connor, "Yeats was rather like an enormous oak-tree which, of course, kept us in the shade. We always hoped we would reach the sun, but the shadow of that great oak-tree is still there"—this, and some anecdotes of Yeats's life at Coole formed, I believe, the genesis of Auden's opera *Elegy for Young Lovers.*

His first detractor was George Moore; and Moore, who seemed before the First World War to have all the advantages, lost the public's favour even before Yeats could administer the *coup de grâce* in his autobiography. Here, I think, is scope for an essay charting the Moore-Yeats relationship, especially if Moore's point of view could be sympathetically stated. Beerbohm was another disparager. But an unfavourable impression in the Dublin symposium is dispelled by Lennox Robinson's touching personal tribute:

> An "unbuttoned" Beethoven is often spoken of, there was no unbuttoned Yeats either in his work or in himself, and that is why I deny that he was guilty of pose. He was fastidious in his person and his choice of friends; he loathed pretentiousness in others and so had none himself. The only art to which he was almost wholly insensitive was music.

With painting it was different. Yeats's father and brother were painters and Mr. Henn has a fascinating chapter (now revised) on "Painters and Poet" with reproductions of some of Yeats's archetypal works of art. His covers and title-pages (many by Sturge Moore) were a forest of symbols. The beautiful and very late poem "News for the Delphic Oracle" with the lines

> *Slim adolescence that a nymph has stripped*
> *Peleus on Thetis stares . . .*

is an exact description of a Poussin in the Dublin National Gallery (now renamed "Acis and Galatea") down to Pan's "brutal arm" and the nymphs and satyrs who "copulate in the foam"—I had always wondered how a man of over seventy could have managed to express so much sexual excitement ("belly, shoulder, bum"), but his contemplation of this painting explains it. The "Leda and the Swan" is a relief in the British Museum. Blake, Calvert, Pater's Mona Lisa, Moreau are among other pictorial influences "and but so much music as he can discover on the wings of words." Here a wonderful anecdote from Dr. Gogarty's last memoir (1962) is quoted by Mr. Henn (in the Macmillan volume). The Spanish doctor who treated Yeats in Majorca reported to his Irish colleague, "We have here an antique cardiosclerotic of advanced years." Gogarty tried to slur over this death sentence. " 'Read it slowly and distinctly,' Yeats ordered. There was no escape, so I read slowly and distinctly. He inclined his head. 'Read that again.' He followed the cadence with his finger. As the sound died away he exclaimed: 'Do you know, I would rather be called "Cardiosclerotic" than Lord of Lower Egypt.' "

The most impressive contribution is Conor Cruise O'Brien's seventy-page *Passion and Cunning,* an essay on Yeats's politics. For the first time Yeats's prolonged political activity is viewed as a whole, from his early republicanism to his ultimate fraternising with the Blue Shirts and Mussolini. Mr. O'Brien makes it quite plain that Yeats did sympathise with Fascism, and that he expected England to lose the coming war. It is doubtful how much he was aware of the crimes against humanity which Hitler was carrying out, being blinded by his desire for a stable authoritarian government which would preserve old families and great houses and discomfit England at the same time. (He had refused a knighthood—but accepted a civil list pension.) "What is equality? Muck in the yard," he wrote for the Blue Shirts; and Homer, Virgil, Dante, Shakespeare would have agreed with him. At the end of his life he returned to an early passion and wrote poems in praise of the O'Rahilly (shot in 1916) and Roger Casement. "Why then," asked Dorothy Wellesley, "in the twentieth century and when the Irish are freed from their oppressors the English, does he dislike us and despise us increasingly? Because he dislikes the stuffed lion and admires the ranting, roaring oppressors."

Mr. O'Brien sums up, and rightly, that Yeats became most politically active at the time of the Parnell split in 1891, the Sinn Fein split of 1920–22 and the abortive Fascist movement of 1933; otherwise retiring into lofty neutrality:

> It is probably fortunate for his future reputation that he died in January, 1939. . . . He defended the liberty of the artist, consistently. In politics, true to his duality, he defended the liberty of Ireland against English domination and the liberty of his own caste—and sometimes, by extension, of others—against clerical domination. Often these liberties overlapped and the cause of artist and aristocrat became the same. . . . But his objection to clerical authoritarianism is not the liberal's objection to *all* authoritarianism. On the contrary he favours a "despotism of the educated classes" and in the search for this, is drawn towards Fascism.

"His own caste" is beautifully analysed in "The Great House," the first chapter of Mr. Henn's book. The Great House, Coole, was his only by adoption; you will seek him in vain in Burke's *Landed Gentry* though you would have found him in their stronghold the Kildare Street Club, and Austin Clarke (and even Lennox Robinson) was somewhat satirical on this point.

A book which deserves to be much better known is Jon Stallworthy's *Between the Lines* (Oxford, 1963) which examines the manuscript versions, some almost illegible, of a few of Yeats's poems. To the Macmillan volume Mr. Stallworthy has contributed a chapter on Yeats and the *Oxford Book of Modern Verse* which is enthralling, and full of unconscious comedy. Yeats was chosen to select the *Oxford Book* after Lascelles Abercrombie had proved a broken reed. Charles Williams proposed Dylan Thomas. "We rather reluctantly declined some very modern poems of his some time ago." (This was in 1934, when he had published only one book.) But a name was thought necessary and Eliot, de la Mare, Huxley were suggested as well as Yeats. "He is sixty-nine but when I met him last year he was vivid and entertaining." Sisam and Chapman voted for Yeats, who worked away with much advice from Dorothy Wellesley.

His comments are devastating on his exclusion of Owen; on Pound, "the sexless American professor for all his violence." "T. E. Hulme" (wrote Williams) "may not be important but he was the first of or the leader of a movement, and I think might be desired." "Hulme I have left out precisely because he was the mere leader of a movement." The anthologist Laura Riding on the other hand refused Yeats and so did Graves. The longest extracts were devoted to Yeats's own friends, Dorothy Wellesley, Gogarty and W. J. Turner (plus Edith Sitwell). Lord Alfred Douglas sent insulting telegrams all round the old Bosie network, quoting a disparaging letter from Yeats's contemporary, Quiller-Couch: "Lord—*What* an anthology and *what* a preface."

Yeats took it all calmly. "Most of my critics are very vindictive, a sure sign that I have somewhere got down to reality." "You must be prepared for silly reviews until you are so old that you are beyond caring and then they will only take another form of silliness." But in this case the critics were right.

The last chapter of *In Excited Reverie,* the *catalogue raisonné* of books about Yeats, provides the answer to the snipers of the first chapter. Yeats appears like a dead bird covered by ants, each bearing off a thesis in its jaws. Somewhere buried beyond all this scholarship and conjecture are the poems—the greatest lyrics of our time written by a great and infinitely complicated man. "He was the most brilliant conversationalist I have ever known, at once witty and profound" (Robinson). "Yeats wrote not only poems and plays but also two of the most remarkable books of his time—the *Autobiographies* and *A Vision*"

(Adams). This last is well described in Miss Stock's *W. B. Yeats: His Poetry and Thought* which has just been reprinted.

In fact the main difference between the enthusiasm we felt about Yeats in 1922 and the attitude now is that we tended to dismiss the contents of the mind which had produced the poems as a side-issue, because they were so unfamiliar. Byzantium seemed to us much the same as the Georgians' Babylon—a romantic noise. The fortunes of *A Vision* illustrate the improvement. The greatest single lacuna in the Yeats canon is a new edition of his letters to include those to Synge, Shaw, Joyce, Pound, Gordon Craig and Mrs. Yeats, "which would, if released for publication, swell the volume to more than three times its present size" (Cross). There are also twenty-three letters to Lady Gregory in the *Review of English Literature* (1963, July) and twenty-one, unpublished, to Mabel Beardsley. The *Letters to Dorothy Wellesley* are now available in paper-back and so is Hone's excellent *Life*, now far too brief, though supplemented by Mr. Jeffares's *W. B. Yeats: Man and Poet* which goes much deeper. Like Mr. Henn, Norman Jeffares is another Anglo-Irishman, and the "indomitable Irishry" still hold up against American champions like Richard Ellmann and Hugh Kenner. In India more critics are blossoming and the topography of County Sligo is being studied from Simla to Ceylon.

(1965)

T. S. ELIOT: 1

"WHATEVER happens read 'The Waste Land' by T. S. Eliot—only read it twice. It is quite short and has the most marvellous things in it—though the 'message' is almost unintelligible and it is a very Alexandrian poem—sterility disguised by superb use of quotation and obscure symbolism—thoroughly decadent. It will ruin your style . . ." So I wrote as an undergraduate at Oxford to another at Cambridge in the winter of 1923–24, shortly after the appearance of the Hogarth Press edition.

For what can convey the veritable brain-washing, the total preoccupation, the drugged and haunted condition which this new poet induced in some of us? We were like new-born goslings for ever imprinted with the image of an alien and indifferent foster-parent, infatuated with his erudition, his sophistication, yet sapped and ruined by the contagion of his despair. Housman, Flecker and the Georgians all melted away overnight. At that time his earlier poems were hard to come by and I still have the transcript I made of "La figlia che piange" from Sir Maurice Bowra's copy of "Ara Vos Prec."

By early 1925 the first version of "The Hollow Men" had appeared in *The Criterion* and later in that year came the *Poems 1909–25* which marked the culmination of early Eliot, the handsome pagan from Harvard with his Harlequin good looks, his luminous Luciferian expression, of whom one could find out nothing but that he was poor and unhappy and had worked in a bank and sometimes stayed at nearby Garsington. His favourite poets were clearly Dante, who supplied so many of his epigraphs, and the minor Elizabethans. It was not known then how much he owed to Laforgue (he was so much better than Laforgue).

Then in 1926 and early '27 the two dramatic "Sweeney" fragments appeared in his *Criterion,* followed in August 1927 by his first religious poem, "The Journey of the Magi," and—in 1928—by two sections of "Ash Wednesday." During 1927 he became a British subject and proclaimed his conversion to the Church of England ("A Song for Simeon" and "For Lancelot Andrewes," 1928).

Eliot's literary span has lasted fifty years, from 1915 when "The Love Song of J. Alfred Prufrock," "Portrait of a Lady" and the Preludes and "Rhapsody" were published in little magazines ("Prufrock" in Pound's *Catholic Anthology*) up to his death.

He was born in St. Louis, Missouri, on September 26, 1888, the seventh and youngest child of Henry Ware Eliot, president of the Hydraulic Press Brick Co. of St. Louis, and Charlotte Chauncy Stearns of Boston, author of a dramatic poem on the life of Savonarola. The Eliots came over *circa* 1650 from East Coker, Somerset, and were mainly merchants of Boston: but the poet's grandfather, the Reverend William Greenleaf Eliot, had gone west to St. Louis and established the first Unitarian church in that city.

Two of his four sons entered the ministry. Eliot went to Harvard where he was Bertrand Russell's most brilliant pupil; he continued a post-graduate course in philosophy which took him to Paris and in 1914 to Germany on a travelling fellowship until the war. By the winter of 1914 he had got to Merton College, Oxford, through his thesis on Bradley—but Merton and its married dons made him long for London. "Come, let us desert our wives and fly to a land where there are no Medici prints, nothing but concubinage and conversation. Oxford is very pretty, but I don't like to be dead." And so, for the rest of his life, London it was.

I suppose no great poet since Johnson has been so much a Londoner or written so elegantly about it; one could never imagine him with a week-end cottage. It has often given me satisfaction just to think that he was somewhere around, as loyal subjects feel when they see the Royal Standard floating from the Palace. In Russell Square one might run across "his set imperial face" or near his club in Pall Mall or in Gloucester Road or Chelsea. I believe that his devotion to London shortened his life, for two winters ago he put off going abroad for so long that he went down with acute bronchitis in the first bad fog.

"Pound is rather intelligent as a talker; his verse is touchingly incompetent," he wrote to Conrad Aiken before falling under the spell of "il miglior fabbro" (it was Pound who took over from Aiken the task of getting Eliot published successfully). Critics have been so occupied in recognising Eliot's debt to Pound that they have ignored Pound's debt to Eliot. Surely the change from the epigrams of "Lustra" to "Homage to Sextus Propertius" owed something to the academic seriousness of the younger mind and Pound's "Mauberley" to the dazzling rhymed quatrains of the Sweeney poems of 1919?

I find I keep returning to the early Eliot and his poetry; it was after all the moment when the key fitted the lock, when the time was ripe for a poetical revolution incorporating urban life and its new vernacular; and he and Pound made it, only to look back, over the corpses of the slaughtered Georgians, to their own vision of the traditional past—Dante and Cavalcanti, or the French nineteenth century—and fall backwards to embrace it.

In addition there is something deeply enigmatic about the youthful Eliot with his intellectual gifts; it is seldom that a mind with so elastic a grasp of mental concepts can turn out such haunting poetry, or that such a mind should inhabit that formal and elusive body, which took boxing lessons and affected a discreet dandyism.

Professor Kenner called his book on Eliot *The Invisible Poet,* partly in allusion to the way in which all his tracks had been covered. I know of no lyric poet who has so completely disguised the clues, leaving only the harrowing sense of personal grief and loss lurking in the poems—"the last twist of the knife." This withdrawal of any affirmative personality, according to Hugh Kenner, "has allowed his work to be discussed as though it were the legacy of a deceased poet and, like such a legacy, it invades the reader's mind and there undergoes an assimilation which soon persuades us that we have always possessed it." It is this assimilation of such a completed life-work of poetry and criticism that makes his death less difficult to bear.

In 1915 Eliot married Vivien Haigh-Wood and moved to London. It was a most unhappy marriage and is likely to figure largely in many future accounts as an explanation of so much of his reticence. *The Waste Land* was written in Switzerland recuperating from some kind of break-down ("the nightingale sings of adulterous wrong"), and the marvellous penitential sequence of "Ash Wednesday" was dedicated to her. She became mentally deranged and remained ill for many years, dying in 1947.

> The golden foot I may not kiss or touch
> Glowed in the shadow of the bed
> Perhaps it does not come to very much
> This thought this ghost this pendulum in the head
> Swinging from life to death
> Bleeding between two lives
> Waiting that touch . . .
>
> —From a poem in *The Tyro,* 1921

Eliot's middle period covers his dominating years as a critic and editor, his lectures, his best essays, his first verse plays: *The Rock, Murder in the Cathedral,* and *The Family Reunion* (1939) (to my mind the loveliest and the most original, though not the most actable), some of his own favourite short poems like "Virginia" and "Cape Ann," and his two masterpieces, "Ash Wednesday" and "Four Quartets." One might include his two prose masterpieces *Selected Essays* (1930) and *The Use of Poetry and the Use of Criticism.*

"He introduced a severity and astringency into criticism which were long resented, but which eventually compelled respect when backed by the prestige gained by his work in poetry" (Robson). He planted many a stiletto, painlessly, in a fatal spot—and some of his early definitions, from *The Sacred Wood* onwards, have the perfection of his best lines of verse. As, of the poet, "What happens is a continual surrender of himself as he is at the moment to something which is more valuable. The progress of an artist is a continual self-sacrifice, a continual extinction of the personality."

As the years went by, the astringent, sparkling quality deserted Eliot's prose, which was apt to become arid and sometimes pontifical, bowed down by the honours and ex-cathedra authority which society had bestowed on him. During the war he suddenly found himself accepted as something we were fighting for, like the Four Freedoms or Big Ben. In the Thirties the image had been formed of the cat-addict and cheese-taster, the writer of pawky blurbs, the church-warden, the polite deflater.

But all this time "Four Quartets" were in gestation, the greatest single poem of the first half of the twentieth century. The Quartets are still baffling and few possess the philosophical training as well as the critical equipment to unravel them, but one can read them again and again discovering new consonances, familiar truths and fresh meanings. No one has written, throughout a long life, so movingly about death, ever present from Phlebas to the serene passing of the Elder Statesman, and no poet has so elegantly mocked human pretentions and the trappings of fame, orders and decorations, honours and emoluments.

Yet he has been carried through time and death to a state of mystical rapture where "fire and the rose are one." The rose-garden has always been his symbol of happiness.

In 1957 Eliot married his "confidential clerk," Miss Valerie Fletcher, and gained the human happiness which by a tragic mistake he had for so many years been denied. In what I believe to be the last poem he wrote, the dedication to his last *Collected Poems,* he comes back to the rose-garden:

No peevish winter wind shall chill
No sullen tropic sun shall wither
The roses in the rose-garden
which is ours and ours only.

I would like to quote from a letter of last autumn so typical of his humility and candour:

> I was particularly touched by the way in which you referred, in reviewing my *Collected Poems,* to my last dedicatory poem to my wife. You were the first sympathetic reader and critic to call attention to the unusual fact that I had at last written a poem of love and of happiness. It would almost seem that some readers were shocked that I should be happy.

Like many admirers of Eliot I could never see enough of him. One longs for his Letters to get to know him better. I suppose my crowning moment was at a party I gave when he had won the Nobel Prize and where the poet, John Hayward, and myself read "Sweeney Agonistes" at a late hour, Eliot singing "Under the Bamboo Tree" for us. Although by his reserve he carried the prestige of literature far into enemy country he relaxed into gaiety when he could. His three last plays brought him an enormous audience and lost him some of his earlier admirers—unjustly, for in its way *The Cocktail Party* is just as original as *The Waste Land*. I am reminded of what Valéry, Eliot's closest French counterpart, once wrote about Mallarmé.

> Our beloved Mallarmé, the great event of our youth, always present and always perceptible and recognisable in the minds and judgements of everyone who approached him and revered him, and who accepted him as different from anyone else whom they would ever meet, martyr and confessor of the will to perfection.

(1965)

T. S. ELIOT: 2

LONG awaited and well worth the waiting, the new edition of *The Waste Land: A Facsimile Transcript,* edited by Valerie Eliot (Faber), with all its corrections and the "lost" excisions, is a joy to hold and to behold; a monument to the dead poet and the *vatis amici,* Ezra Pound and Valerie Eliot, who come to breathe upon his ashes. Indispensable to all lovers of poetry, students of the early twentieth century, and survivors like myself.

The Waste Land first appeared in Number One of *The Criterion,* at the end of 1922, then in *The Dial* (Chicago), then in the American edition and finally from the Hogarth Press hand-set by Leonard and Virginia Woolf. I read it as an undergraduate when it came out and since then have never looked forward. John Quinn, the New York lawyer and friend of Pound and Joyce, the Maecenas of the "Mouvemong," helped Eliot with the American publication which netted him the Dial Prize of two thousand dollars. Eliot presented Quinn with the manuscript as a token of gratitude and that passionate bibliophile (who also owned most Conrad manuscripts and the bulk of *Ulysses*) was about to help Eliot off the hook in Lloyds Bank when he died suddenly in 1924.

The manuscript disappeared and was not in the Quinn sale. It had reached him in Januay 1923 and formed part of the estate inherited by his sister whose daughter Mrs. Conroy only discovered it in storage in the early 1950s. In April 1958 she sold the manuscript to the Berg Collection of the New York Public Library for eighteen thousand dollars. "The purchase remained private, neither Eliot nor Pound being told about it." Mrs. Eliot was not informed till 1968.

The manuscript is partly in holograph but largely typewritten and there are some fair copies; besides her introduction and notes Mrs. Eliot also includes the first edition as it originally appeared.

In this presentation all Pound's corrections and suggestions are printed in red to distinguish them from Eliot's own alterations and from a few remarks by Vivien Eliot, usually confined to "Wonderful, wonderful."

Eliot submitted the poem to Pound because he regarded him as *"il miglior fabbro,"* his literary mentor and fellow-rebel, the best critic of his time. As Eliot was undergoing a mild form of nervous break-down he probably felt that he needed Pound's judgement to tell him what the poem lacked. Pound had already purged Yeats's later verse of abstractions: he was, as Eliot said, "a marvellous critic because he didn't try to turn you into an imitation of himself. He tried to see what you were trying to do" (interview, *Paris Review*).

Donald Gallup has pointed out a very important difference between the two men which does affect the Pound deletions: "At least part of what the central poem gained in concentration, intensity and general effectiveness through Pound's editing was at the sacrifice of some of its experimental character." In 1942 Eliot wrote: "In a poem of any length there must be transitions between passages of greater and less intensity, to give a rhythm of fluctuating emotion essential to the musical structure of the whole." In Mr. Gallup's opinion this was particularly true of the long sea-piece, of which only the last eight lines were used, in the Phlebas episode of "Death by Water."

More light from the *Paris Review* interview:

> *Interviewer: What sort of thing did Pound cut from "The Waste Land"? Did he cut whole sections?*
>
> Eliot: Whole sections, yes. There was a long section about a shipwreck. . . . Then there was another section which was an imitation "Rape of the Lock." Pound said, "It's no use trying to do something that somebody else has done as well as it can be done. Do something different."

Three long sections were omitted, along with "Gerontion," which Eliot wished to print as Prologue, and some short lyrics from the end. These would have turned the book into one of those compilations called "The Waste Land and Other Poems" and this would have robbed it of its element of surprise.

After "Gerontion" the poem opened with the description of a night out in the vein of "Sweeney Agonistes," designed to show the mastery of the vernacular which Eliot felt a modern poem required. This was already clear in the pub scene and may have owed something to Joyce. Anyhow it is a tame affair.

This excision of fifty-five lines was made by Eliot himself and has no marks by Pound. The "Rape of the Lock" stanzas consist of seventy lines of urban pastiche describing the toilette and levée of "Fresca"—

one of the fashionable arty young ladies of the period. It's good fun and some of it was rescued as an in-joke in lines by "Fanny Marlow" (Vivien Eliot) in *The Criterion* for January 1924. It formed the beginning of the "Fire Sermon" and was deleted by Pound, I think correctly. Pound also cut some stanzas, a Baudelairean invocation to London and some further details about the "young man carbuncular." (Pound's comments here are particularly instructive.)

The shipwreck passage (based on Ulysses in Dante and Tennyson) is eighty lines long, in blank verse or rhyming stanzas with echoes of Rimbaud and Conrad. Here Eliot wished to draw upon his New England boyhood, spent among sailing men at Gloucester, Massachusetts, and his knowledge of the sea. He even mentions the "Dry Salvages."

I feel it is better out, for it provides an elaborate setting for the Phlebas verses which however gain enormously by their being isolated as the whole of Section IV. (Eliot, by now down-hearted, proposed to cut them as well, but Pound would not have it.)

As for the last section, "What the Thunder Said," it was Pound's turn to give up. "OK from here on," he pencils, and suggests only a few small alterations.

The short poems at the end should really belong to the earlier volume, "Ara Vos Prec." About the many verbal suggestions and small deletions by Pound there can be only one verdict: they are nearly all improvements. Particularly good are his rearrangements of word order. As Pound wrote to Eliot: "Complimenti you bitch. I am wracked by the seven jealousies." And he sent him his delightful:

Sage Homme
These are the poems of Eliot
By the Uranian muse begot:
A man their mother was,
A Muse their Sire.

How did the printed Infancies result
From nuptials thus doubly difficult?

If you must needs enquire
Know diligent Reader
That on each occasion
Ezra performed the Caesarean operation.

Mrs. Eliot's editing tidies it all up. Her notes and introduction benefit from access to her husband's correspondence.

The final *Waste Land* leaps from passages of immense talent to those, like the last section, of sheer genius where Eliot seems to rise above and out of himself, as in "Ash Wednesday." What was that self, so austere, so arrogant, so prim and whimsical, so tragic?

The late Robert Sencourt, a New Zealand expatriate high churchman, has tried to explain it in his memoir *T. S. Eliot,* edited by Donald Adamson (Garnstone Press), defying Eliot's injunction that he did not wish for a biography. The book has been completed, annotated and expanded by Mr. Adamson, who seems to possess Sencourt's notes, letters and photographs. There is a formidable array of acknowledgements, although Mrs. Eliot has issued a list of twenty-five factual inaccuracies, an unusual proceeding.

It is not difficult to find further inaccuracies in Mr. Sencourt. What is wrong is the general tone. I am sure the late Robert Sencourt had many interesting things to say, particularly on Eliot's religious life, but the way he said them is creepy, mealy-mouthed, and crypto-malicious. Heaven preserve one from such a biographer. And he writes in fulsome prize-giving journalese, a special style for padding out insufficient data. He would call God by his Christian name.

The main interest of his book, apart from its religious data, is in the light it throws on Eliot's first marriage. Here I can throw a small grenade. Logan Pearsall Smith told me, many years ago, that Eliot had compromised Miss Haigh-Wood (a school-teacher from Southampton, according to Leonard Woolf) and then felt obliged, as an American gentleman, the New England code being stricter than ours, to propose to her. This would account for the furtive nature of the ceremony, and for a subsequent recoiling from his conjugal privileges.*

It is clear that Vivien's temperament, so closely resembling Zelda Fitzgerald's, was quite unsuited to Eliot's, once her initial pleasure in dancing and poetry had worn off. When she had an affair with Bertrand Russell Eliot must have been almost grateful. She wrote some charming, light-hearted pieces for *The Criterion* (as Sibylla—see *The Waste Land* epigraph) but became destructive and self-destructive, then took to ether (corroborated by Grover Smith and also by Leonard Woolf in conversation), and finally went mad. Eliot in his turn suffered from guilt and remorse, uncertain how much he was to blame for what might well have happened anyhow.

The Waste Land in fact is a poem of a broken marriage, where love survives amid the craters. In Vivien's own hand is the line "What you get married for if you don't want children," which Eliot interpolated

* Mrs. Eliot has contradicted this.

before "Hurry up please its time"; while after "Good night, sweet ladies" she wrote: "Splendid last lines."

He still loved her at the time of writing "Ash Wednesday" (1930). But by 1932, the situation was hopeless.

More controversial points are raised over the break with John Hayward, by which time Mr. Sencourt has lost much of his credibility.

Meanwhile we await Mrs. Eliot's edition of the Correspondence, and perhaps the publication of the other Quinn notebook.

(1971)

EZRA POUND: 1

I SUPPOSE I must be one of the few people who listened to some of Pound's broadcasts from Italy during the war. They were delivered with a rather cranky homespun small-town accent. "This is Poun' speakin' "—and I remember him attacking Churchill and warning us that we paid interest to the Jews on the very air we breathed. Some of the literary talks—on Joyce, Cummings, "Blast," Cocteau and Céline—have been collected in a rare pamphlet, *If This Be Treason* (Siena, 1948), by his lifelong friend the musician Olga Rudge. It deserves reprinting.

Pound's "treason" lay in these broadcasts, which he continued after the United States was at war with Italy, and in which he went on to attack the Jewish element behind Churchill and Roosevelt that he considered had obtained mastery of the world and which had defrauded the American people through manipulating the currency. When one thinks of what was being done then to the Jews, to the humblest as well as the powerful, by Italy's ally, the greatest crime in history, of which Pound must have known, there seems no moral excuse for such opinions, treasonable or otherwise, and this may have been a factor in Pound's persistent remorse.

But it was for his criticism of the American government that he was brought to trial,* for "giving aid and comfort to the enemy." Pound maintained that "the treason was in the White House, not in Rapallo." The penalty for treason was electrocution; but there is also a minimum penalty—a fine of ten thousand dollars and five years' imprisonment. One wonders if that sentence would not have been the most merciful in contrast to what actually took place. Pound was sixty when he gave

* *The Trial of Ezra Pound,* by Julien Cornell (New York, 1966).

himself up (May 1945), he was kept for seven months in solitary confinement (a roofless cage made of air-strip material) in a military detention camp at Pisa. His only companion was a Negro prisoner who brought him his meals. Here he suffered a severe nervous break-down ("his mind gave way") which led to slightly better conditions (a cot) and here he wrote his "Pisan Cantos." In November he was permitted half-hour visits from his wife and daughter.

> Hast thou swum in a sea of air-strip
> thru an aeon of nothingness
> Immaculate, Introibo
> When the raft broke and the waters went over me.
> for those who drink of the bitterness . . .
> Les larmes que j'ai créées m'inondent
> tard, très tard, je t'ai connue la Tristesse. . . .

In late November Pound was taken to Washington to stand his trial. When arraigned he remained mute and a plea of "not guilty" was entered. Mr. Cornell had by then been appointed his counsel through his publisher James Laughlin. He questioned not only Pound's sanity but his ability to stand trial. Pound was examined by four psychiatrists, three of them appointed by the government and all of the highest standing. All four doctors testified that Pound was insane and mentally unfit for trial, that he was suffering from a paranoid state and should be cared for in a mental hospital. He was therefore removed from prison to St. Elizabeth's Hospital for the Insane, where he remained for anoher thirteen years, till 1958.

In 1949 he received the thousand-dollar Bollingen Prize for his *Pisan Cantos* but it was not till 1956 that Robert Frost, aided by Eliot, MacLeish, Hemingway, Auden and other writers was able to set his release in motion. By 1958 Frost was victorious and Pound returned to Italy; in 1961 he suffered a severe illness. He came to London for Eliot's memorial service and was acclaimed with great enthusiasm at the Spoleto Festival in 1965 where he made some fine recordings.

> He now lives in a flat at Sant' Ambrogio, a tiny settlement in the hills overlooking Rapallo which is reached only by a mule track. The winter months find him in Venice . . . Now eighty years of age, Pound is still physically vigorous. But the years have taken their toll. The old ebullience and fire have faded. Now there is the sweet, gentle quiet old man, who is still writing what many consider the finest verse of our time. (Cornell)

I have just come back from spending two days with him. In Rapallo he is looked after by Olga Rudge, who also acts as interpreter to

Pound's private language, for he is almost totally silent. In the twelve hours I spent with him I do not suppose he uttered more than twelve words. His villa stands high up on a mountain shelf commanding breath-taking views of sea and hill, cypress and olive, Italian certainly but with a suggestion of a Chinese landscape in the early autumn haze. The rooms are few and simple; within walking distance is the church of St. Ambrogio and a rustic trattoria where we ate out under the planes.

Pound is physically tough and likes to walk or take the bus down to Rapallo. He is contemplating an immediate journey to Canada to open a poets' festival at Montreal. He is thin and wiry as a grass-blade, extremely frugal in his appetites (I can think of no living poet who has made fewer mentions of food and drink), and his whole being seems concentrated in his eyes, which are of a particularly cold shade of blue. When we met he held my hand for a long time and fixed me with this penetrating gaze while I felt layers of ugliness and insincerity peeling off me like an onion revealing even deeper layers of insincerity and ugliness within. In another moment I felt sure the ultimate *nada* would be reached and the onion dissolve into the floor. My whole face by now was one hideous simper (I am an eye-evader at the best of times) and I withdrew my hand and turned away. Mr. Pound spoke and said what sounded like "There's the artist." I looked behind to see whom he meant but we were still alone.

Those who know don't speak
Those who speak don't know . . .

The lines from the Tao I felt summed up his attitude and I could not be sure if he preferred one to remain silent too, like Carlyle and Tennyson, or to go on chattering until the cistern had emptied. Mr. Pound notices everything and understands everything: it was like lunching with the recording angel. I spent my afternoon siesta looking at Miss Rudge's collection of his first editions. There was a "Cantos" of 1930 with the missing names in his Inferno (14, 15) filled in and I noticed that Churchill, Wilson, Balfour and Zaharoff were already there. I re-read "Mauberley" and more Cantos and came out for tea.

"Tear up everything; start again; try to be more serious," had been the conclusion of this respite, I told them. "Why, that's what Ezra's always saying . . ." A young Italian visitor appeared, one of a TV team who had been recording him, and played over some of the Spoleto tapes. We sat listening, two of us following from the book, while the magic of the early Circe Cantos rolled out, and some of the Pisans in which Pound had written his way out of the abyss.

Nothing matters but the quality of the affection—
in the end—that has carved the trace in the mind
what thou lovest well is thy true heritage
what thou lovest well shall not be reft from thee.

Another Canto with which I was unfamiliar came out as an original Chinese poem. In fact these later, even latest Cantos are full of surprises, and as I contemplated my frail host listening to his early poetry read in his present voice, which occasionally mumbled a word and then went back to it for correction, I realised that his working hours are probably spent entirely in composition, that his silence is fed by this landscape and covers an unending panorama of words and music, *un homme au rêve habitué,* as we can see from the fragment of 1962 reprinted in the last edition of the *Faber Book of Modern Verse* (Canto 115).

When one's friends hate each other
how can there be peace in the world
Their asperities diverted me in my green time,
A blown husk that is finished
But the light sings eternal
a pale flare over marshes
Where the salt hay whispers to tide's change
Time, space,
neither life nor death is the answer.

Pound's attitude to his own work distressed me. He claims it is all rubbish, that the Cantos have no basic structure; he suffers from despondency and anxiety about trifles. I read him an article of mine, "The Breakthrough in Modern Verse" from *Previous Convictions*. He denied, by the way, having thrown Frost over his back by ju-jitsu in a restaurant (Frost's story) but his only comment was "I'm sorry you gave yourself the bother of so much trouble." "Well I'm the best judge of that," I answered, and reminded him that if he had not existed, Yeats might be remembered only for Innisfree, Joyce have lived and died in the Berlitz School, Eliot remained in his bank, Hemingway at his sports column, Confucius, Cavalcanti, Provençal and the East-West synthesis indefinitely postponed: he had given the world a *frisson nouveau* and taught us a new way to look at water.

When they came down for a coffee the next morning to see me off, I had become an habitué of his silence; it had become indispensable, a balm to be preferred to all other conversation. From the station window I watched them walk away after we had said good-bye; two delicate

Bustelli figures among the horde of German holiday-makers, leaving behind them an acute sense of loss like the sun going down on a winter day.

It was in the knowledge of this happy ending that I read the *Trial*. It was, of course, the four psychiatrists who were really on trial since they alone were cross-examined. Pound sat in the back of the court and interrupted only once:

"Did he give you in his general history anything about his belief in Fascism?" Dr. Overholzer: "I did not discuss that with him particularly." The Defendant: "I never did believe in Fascism, God damn it; I am opposed to Fascism." The jury retired for only three minutes.

What emerges from the trial are some admirable definitions of paranoia and some accurate statements of Pound's involvement in it, stemming, according to Hemingway and others, from long before the war. "We are dealing now with the end-product of an individual who throughout his life-time has been highly antagonistic, highly eccentric; the whole world has revolved round him . . ." (Dr. King).

It is clear from this most interesting and very sad book that Pound's incarceration in St. Elizabeth's was not a ruse on the part of powerful friends, as has sometimes been assumed, to protect the poet from the consequences of his political activities but a natural and inevitable step in the legal process. The four psychiatrists were undoubtedly right but they can hardly have expected that Pound would be kept a prisoner for thirteen years. Despite the protests of Eliot, Auden, Hemingway, MacLeish, and Dag Hammarskjöld, only Frost possessed the influence to "clear it with Sherman." "None of us can bear the disgrace of our letting Ezra Pound come to his end where he is," Frost wrote. "It would leave too woeful a story in American literature . . . I rest the case on Dr. Overholzer's pronouncement that Ezra Pound is not too dangerous to go free in his wife's care though too insane ever to be tried—a very nice discrimination."

(1967)

EZRA POUND: 2

It was after some letters about the *Pisan Cantos* and a suggestion from Olga Rudge, that I found myself on my way to Venice to attend Pound's eighty-fourth birthday (October 30, Scorpio). I knew Venice only in spring and summer and was unprepared for the overwhelming beauty of the city at this last moment of sunshine with all tourists gone. Pound's references are surprisingly few. He published his first book there (rarest of all the moderns), at his own expense when he came to Europe in 1908. *A Lume Spento* (*With Tapers Quenched*) has since been reprinted, with additions, in both Italy and America. According to his daughter, Mary de Rachewiltz, Pound lived at that time at Calle dei Frati, 942, in the San Trovaso quarter near the Accademia.

> I sat on the Dogana steps
> For the gondolas cost too much that year,

he wrote in Canto 3, but his best evocation of Venice is in the *Pisan Cantos* (No. 76). I might say in passing that I think the *Pisan Cantos* are among the greatest poems of the last war, indeed of our time, a *canción del prisoniero* in which the war is seen like the reflection of distant cloud-shadows, in which the detail of daily life gives way to the blaze of memory, memory operating without books, friends, letters or any outside assistance. I prefer them to "Four Quartets" and cannot praise them higher than that.

> Under the two-winged cloud
> as of less and more than a day
> by the soap-smooth stone posts where San Vio
> meets with il Canal Grande

between Salviati and the house that
  was of Don Carlos
shd/I chuck the lot in the tide-water?
Le bozze "A Lume Spento"
And by the column of Todero
shd/I shift to the other side?

Trovaso, Gregorio, Vio . . .

The blue soap-stone posts are still there on the corners of the Canal San Vio and the Palazzo Loredan, where we were lunching. Everything in Venice is still there: if one was set down there five hundred years ago, we would still find our way. "The House that was of Don Carlos" is now Count Cini's Loredan.

Our host, Count Cini, was an old friend of Pound's, an outstanding octogenarian whose fortune is devoted to his foundation on the island of San Giorgio. I had not seen Pound for two years. He seemed if anything younger. He was not so thin, he was not so depressed, he did not pick at his hands; he wore a well-cut light blue suit, a felt hat and carried a malacca cane. He was silent as ever, silent as the lanes of Venice after London traffic, but the silence held no more terrors; it was of two kinds, benevolent or else simply abstracted, like a light switched on or off. It did not prevent him from jumping in and out of launches and vaporettos or striding about Torcello. I bought him a pocket Virgil as a birthday gift and suggested he open it at random and take a "Sors Virgiliana." "Bello," he said and showed me with his finger:

. . . Caesar dum magnus ad altum
Fulminat Euphraten bello . . .
Illo Virgilium me tempore dulcis alebat
Parthenope, studiis florentem ignobilis oti.

"While great Caesar was smiting the wide Euphrates with war," I translated, "Soft Naples was nourishing me, Virgil"—and then suddenly I stuck, unable to parse the rest. Pound waited, with mild blue eyes fixed on his Boswell. I skipped hastily and went on to the last line, *"te patulae cecini sub tegmine fagi."* "Singing of you, Tityrus, under the shade of a spreading beech." (What in hell was *"patulae"?*)—Pound waited. Was he going to correct me? Why was I translating for him at all? It was a bad moment.

Luckily it was time to go. The Count was a gourmet. The meal was a celebration. We had place-cards and menus and rows of gold-engraved glass goblets. I shall never forget the white truffles in cheese sauce and it took them a long time to forget me. We ate persimmons and local muscats and white figs while the Count's beautiful Roman wife cut up an apple for Mr. Pound. After luncheon the guests gathered round and the Count toasted the Maestro in Marc de Bourgogne and he drank back. The sun streamed through the huge windows of the piano nobile; children appeared, poets, beautiful women, coffee, chocolates—footmen looked genially on. Boswell blundered around getting in the way.

I went to Pound's home for his own birthday party, a mixture of Americans and Italians, painters, sculptors, writers. Peter Russell, once editor of *Nine* and a devoted Ezraphile now living in Venice, read a poem in his honour; we drank champagne, and a cake arrived with eighty-four small candles. I realised he was the same age as the ageless Duncan Grant. The patriarch gave two great puffs like the Cyclops' bellows and blew them all out.

I soon found myself back on the old problem. Where would one live in Venice, or even in which hotel? Was it not Leslie Hartley who had plumped for the sunny Zattere? The churches of this magic area of Dorsoduro began to fall into place. San Trovaso with its slightly down-at-heel canals and mystery, the Gesuati, the gayer residential quarter of San Gregorio and finally the never-failing miracle of the Salute, with the Dogana Steps at the point. Across are the bristling dollar strongholds, from the Gritti, urbane as ever, to the windows of Harry's Bar.

It was here we met the next morning to take the launch for Cipriani's at Torcello. The sun raised a tan on the cheek, danced over the immeasurable peace of the lagoon, islands covered with reed-beds, before the launch drew up at the restaurant steps. Fish soup, grilled scampi, more muscats. In the garden the pomegranates were ripe, a scarlet flush on each little tree, it was hot enough to lunch out; the campanile and ochre bricks of the church (the oldest in Venice) glowed against the blue sky. We talked of the book of essays, *New Approaches to Ezra Pound* (they liked Christine Brooke-Rose's contribution) and the new edition of Charles Norman's biography. I mentioned that Norman thought Frederick Manning had attended the poet's luncheon at Wilfred Blunt's and Pound shook his head indignantly. We talked about the six poets; of Aldington's verse he said "I don't remember much of it"; of Henry James, and Eliot's letters, of the forthcoming edition of *The Waste Land* with Pound's emendations from the mss. He ate very little and was afraid that Miss Rudge, most abstemious of Bostonians, would drink to excess.

One had the feeling that everywhere he went Pound was a revered and popular figure. To the Italians he is not a traitor but a martyr or rather a loyal friend who had stood by them in bad days. His enemies would one day be as forgotten as Dante's. I say "we talked about," "we discussed," but in fact Miss Rudge, his daughter and I talked while Pound either bestowed on us the elixir of his silence or absented his being altogether.

After a walk in the Basilica where the German television had recently made a film of Pound we sped back over the green water. More hotels . . . Miss Rudge recommended the Riva del Schiavoni in winter. In summer the noise and trippers were terrible. The pigeons had turned the piazza into a chicken run, tourists lay swigging on the ground. They should all pay an entrance fee. I went back before dinner. Pound was playing records of early music. He has a studio at the top of the house, a bedroom below, a salon on the ground floor. We returned to my favourite topic, who's who in the *Pisan Cantos.* Restaurants in the *Pisan Cantos*: Dieudonné, London; Mouquin, New York; Voisin, Paris; the Greif, Bolzano; Schöners, Vienna; Robert's, New York; La Rupe, Rome. "No longer, *finito.*" "But the Taverna—is it the Taverna here?" "No," barks Pound. "Where then?" "I can't remember."

Next morning I went round to say good-bye; Pound was sitting up in bed; the ladies produce biscuits and a *canarino* (a decoction of lemon rind) for me. Ideal beverage! I bring tuberoses, the last of the season, and some of the little black grapes which taste of strawberries. We talk of Beckett (Pound is very happy about his Nobel Prize) and about his "Jewel Box," Santa Maria dei Miracoli, which on their recommendation I had just seen for the first time. The carved "sirens" of Tullio Lombardo are in the Cantos, too. I bid farewell to the poet-friend, this wisp of history, to the solace and the sunshine. The bells ring out

"Trovasco, Gregorio, Vio . . ."

Miss Rudge comes with me to the airport launch. She tells me Pound's latest dream. "He lost all his money so he got a job as a builder's labourer carrying two long planks over his shoulders. He was much younger then."

(1969)

EZRA POUND: 3

Mr. Pound is eighty-five, and his life falls into a series of compartments: Growing up in America (1885–1908); Illumination in Venice (1908); Life in London (1908–20) and Paris (1920–24); after which he settled down in Rapallo till his capture by the Americans in 1943. He was held in St. Elizabeth's Hospital, Washington, from 1945–58 when he returned to Italy again, Tirolo, Rapallo, Venice.

We are now most likely to find him in Rapallo in summer or Venice the rest of the year; he has a son, Omar, a daughter, Mary, with two grandchildren, Patricia and Walter de Rachewiltz. The first great milestone in his life was when he settled in Europe and seemed to be becoming for the Georgian literary scene what Whistler had been to English painting; the next was his meeting with the economist C. H. Douglas and introduction to "social credit" (1918).

Somewhere around the mid-Thirties, with the first forty Cantos behind him, he became totally obsessed with economics and poured out from his base at Rapallo the torrent of articles and letters on that subject by which he was chiefly known till the war directed his energies to broadcasting, the only way in which he could still communicate with his public. By then his long residence in Italy had made him pro-Mussolini, and he was fatally ignorant of the true nature of Nazism or the virtues of Anglo-American democracy. He was engaged in a one-man propaganda battle with Roosevelt, Churchill and other war leaders and with Morgenthau and Baruch, from which, given the official attitude to collaborators, he was lucky to escape with his life.

His life was spared because he was considered unfit to plead. His messianic mission to convert the Pentagon to Confucius was considered further proof of mania, and the subsequent twelve years' incarceration as Washington's antipope in St. Elizabeth's was not wholly a misfortune for he was able to rest his mind and yet exercise considerable influence from his cell which became his Patmos, his Magic Mountain. The last ten years have seen a mellowing of world opinion in his favour and a mellowing of his own character as well. In drawing up his balance-sheet Mr. Stock* is inclined to the theory that Pound is a great lyric poet who has been consistently false to his genius, led astray by a compulsive need to teach and preach economic theories, goaded by political ambition.

But man cannot live by beauty alone, and great lyric poets who sacrifice everything to their muse can be badly let down. Even Yeats could not travel without a quantity of excess ideological baggage. "Pure" poets like Cummings and Frost found their talent subject to the law of diminishing returns. Pound was the kind of American who had to get things done, who wanted results, who saw himself negotiating with world leaders like his heroes of the early days of Independence. Even in his English days he was an editor and impresario as well as a poet, and he was always looking for magazines to take over.

Dante, Milton, Marvell, Byron, Hugo, were all politicians as well as poets. Pound belonged to the last generation, almost, when to be a "young poet" was also to be somoene who could legislate for mankind. It was his tragedy to wish to legislate through economics, in particular through questions of currency, and to have clung to an arrogant anti-democratic attitude at a time when it was politically fatal. Eliot may have shared some of Pound's prejudices (see *After Strange Gods*), but he drew back in time and wrote "Four Quartets."

On the other hand a confirmed Poundian might reply: "E.P.'s strength is that he is the only major poet to see that the human problem is one of economics; nobody blames Marx for saying so. Must Pound be far behind? Instead of picking your way among the Cantos looking for sixpences and thimbles admit that the pudding is made of Adams and Jefferson and Douglas and innumerable bankers with theories of credit and money. A critic-aesthete who cannot follow this will soon be left behind by the Cantos when the public they are intended for grows up and the theses get under way." The Cantos may not be a great epic poem or even a great didactic poem; they are, however, a personal anthology of a lifetime's reading and meditation, an elegiac record which includes both verse and prose and some outstandingly beautiful lyrics.

What sort of a Life is Mr. Stock's? Comprehensive, for he has had access to innumerable papers in the Pound archive and has also been able to consult Pound, Mrs. Pound, Olga Rudge and her daughter Mary

* *The Life of Ezra Pound,* by Noel Stock (New York, 1970).

de Rachewiltz; deferential, for he does not express more than a minimum of impatience with some of the material. The result is a book which will immediately become indispensable as source material but which cannot be called a great biography because it is weighed down by excess of information and because Mr. Stock, an Australian who became an economist disciple of Mr. Pound and then his secretary, cannot step aside and view his subject dispassionately. One would have to have something of Pound's greatness to judge him as he deserves: to assess the mixture of egotism and humility, genius and bigot, wit and warmth: the combination of technical virtuosity with lyrical insight. No poet has written so unfailingly well of water from the pagan springs of simplicity and wonder beneath his clear-eyed gaze.

"Exhibitionist, egotistic, self-centered and self-indulgent" he once seemed to a colleague (age twenty-three); "one of the gentlest, most modest, bashful, kind creatures who ever walked the earth" (Aldington six years later).

Looking back on Pound's phases one can see that he was absolutely right to quit America when he did but perhaps wrong to forsake England. Herbert Read told me once that he thought Pound would have done better by remaining to lead us—but such questions are purely speculative. Four years was probably as much of Paris as he could take. Italy was his spiritual home. In becoming an economist he neglected not only lyric poetry but his other love, music; and had he given up the same amount of time to Vivaldi as he did to Douglas he might have escaped making the political pronouncements which were his undoing.

It is sad to see him rounding on authors like Eliot, Joyce, and Hemingway for whom he had done so much, because they were so little preoccupied with the national debt. When his time of trouble came it is equally reassuring to see how generously the same writers behaved (Joyce was dead but replaced by Cummings), and Pound repaid them by coming to London for Eliot's memorial service and going on to Dublin to call on Mrs. Yeats. Mr. Stock sums up his—to me—enthralling account by pointing out his "generosity of spirit which caused him to yearn and work for beauty and justice and to dream of a realm in which perfect beauty might be fused with perfect justice."

To build the city of Dioce
whose terraces are the colour of stars.

(1970)

JAMES JOYCE

THESE two volumes* come to nearly a thousand pages and complement Volume I (a mere four hundred pages) edited by Stuart Gilbert. The arrangement is most unsatisfactory for one has to keep checking up with Volume I to see what has already been said to a correspondent.

Either the three volumes should have been re-issued with all the letters in chronological order—or, if this proved too difficult, owing to their having separate editors, then the last two volumes should have mentioned in brackets the references to letters already in Volume I. So much of Joyce's correspondence deals with set issues—the *Dubliners* row, the *Exiles* row, the Roth row, his eye trouble, or his daughter's illness—that one wants to get at the top copies, the key letters on these main themes, or at least to be referred to them.

Otherwise, I have nothing but praise. Richard Ellmann is a marvellous editor—he works hand in glove with Joyce; one never knows which to read first, the text or the foot-notes. Stuart Gilbert's role is as a friend and explainer of Joyce and his work—he is one of the twelve disciples; Ellmann is the indefatigable researcher and inspired commentator who tops up the cask with his own spirit to prevent evaporation.

Since Gilbert's work some vast correspondences have tumbled into the public domain of the American university libraries. The most important is Stanislas Joyce's correspondence which Gilbert was hoping to use for his biography's final version. Nearly three hundred family letters turned up this way; also the fascinating correspondence with Mrs. Joyce (Nora Barnacle).

To read all these letters is an overwhelming experience. That is true

* *Letters of James Joyce,* Vols. II and III, edited by Richard Ellmann (New York, 1966).

in the case of any character, but Joyce's crabbed obstinate genius, outcropping like a slab of granite all through his life, is unlike any other. He writes about small things; money, publishers, printers, proof-corrections, finding apartments, promoting his wares, propounding questions about local lore and gossip, narrating eye operations, with an occasional feast or frolic leading to more promotion (of the singer Sullivan)—nothing disturbs the harsh uneven tenor of his way.

Therefore one is grateful for his unbendings, as in the letters to his brother, his first and last correspondent, and in the remarkable group of love letters to Nora Barnacle. These show the author very much *"du côté de chez Bloom."* I have always been fascinated by the analogies between Joyce and Proust. George D. Painter has described their one meeting from Proust's angle and Ellmann from Joyce's. Here comes a new reference, in a letter to Miss Weaver:

> His name has often been coupled with mine. People here seem to have expected his death but when I saw him last May he did not look bad. He looked, in fact, ten years younger than his age.

That was also the Schiffs' impression. I wish that those who had known both had made a comparison—Edmond Jaloux, for example, or Curtius, or Valéry Larbaud. I know only one man living who could do it—Philippe Soupault, who as a very young man met Proust in Cabourg and afterwards became a member of the Joyce circle. *Entre Deux Maîtres*—I beseech him to write it.*

In his early twenties—as with many a genius—Joyce's correspondence took wing and the complete man stands revealed. To Nora Barnacle, age twenty-two, 1904:

> My mind rejects the whole social order and Christianity—home, the recognised virtues, classes of life, and religious doctrines. How could I like the idea of home? My home was simply a middle-class affair ruined by spendthrift habits which I have inherited. My mother was slowly killed, I think, by my father's ill-treatment, by years of troubles, and by my cynical frankness of conduct. When I looked on her face as she lay in her coffin—a face grey and wasted with cancer—I understood that I was looking on the face of a victim and I cursed the system which had made her a victim. We were seventeen in family. My brothers and sisters are nothing to me. One brother alone is capable of understanding me.
>
> Six years ago I left the Catholic Church, hating it most fervently . . . I cannot enter the social order except as a vagabond . . .

* There are, in fact, essays on both Joyce and Proust in Soupault's "Profils Perdus" (*Mercure de France,* 1963).

And to that brother, he writes, a year later, parodying Renan's prayer:

> O Vague something behind Everything. For the love of the Lord Christ change my curse-o'-God state of affairs. Give me for Christ's sake a pen and an ink-bottle and some peace of mind and then, by the Crucified Jaysus, if I don't sharpen that little pen and dip it into fermented ink and write tiny little sentences about the people who betray me and send me to Hell . . .

Although at this very early stage Joyce met Yeats and Arthur Symons, who were to stand by him all through his life, his reputation was not made till Pound, at Yeats's suggestion, took him up in 1913. Through Pound he came to *The Little Review* and *The Egoist* which serialised his books, and to Miss Weaver, most generous and modest of all patrons—who in fact settled a fortune on him. He made her the recipient of every complaint about his health and she was given, besides the manuscript of *Finnegans Wake,* an invaluable treasure of gloomy reading, including long reports by his secretary, Paul Léon, in which the tale of woe arises to a howl (or hwyl rather), plus the particular mortification for her of watching Joyce selling his capital to provide more income until, by the end of his life, he was nearly destitute.

Although fortunate in patronage and helped in many ways by those who believed in him or were grateful to him, he remained uncorrupted and punctilious in the discharge of his own obligations. He might have had a happy life if he had escaped some of his major vexations. First his eyesight—then his daughter's madness, the incomprehension of his wife (this did not constitute infidelity or disloyalty), and the nagging imbroglios with censors, publishers and agent. These pile up in the correspondence but are absent in the long rock-like relationship with his brother Stanislas, or with trusties like Eliot and Pound. Incidentally George Moore proved a good friend and so did Lady Cunard, whom it is the fashion to snipe at.

As to the love letters: "A new generation does not confirm the privacy of a dead author's conjugal life," explains Professor Ellmann as a justification for seeking to publish this batch, written when Joyce was twenty-seven, "expressly for mutual sexual excitement." At least two have had to be omitted and others to be cut.

"A new generation does not confirm" . . . What a priggish argument! A new generation is even more determined to know the sexual facts at all costs, like the popular press. It is up to living authors to protect themselves and somehow get their love letters back even if their wives should treasure them. Presumably the Joyce heirs are not embarrassed by such passages as his ardent request for a flogging so there is no reason why we should be. We don't mind identifying Nora with Mollie: "Do you notice how women when they write disregard stops and capital letters?" (to Stanislas, 1906)—so why boggle at Joyce as Bloom? ("I wish you were strong, *strong,* dear, and had a big full proud bosom and big fat thighs. I would love to be whipped by you, Nora dear." "Some of it is ugly, obscene and bestial, some of it is pure and holy and spiritual: all of it is myself.")

Lovers of Joyce and also lovers of the period will find endless new glimpses. Moore writing: "One eye is quite sufficient; a man is as well off with one eye as with two," or the luckless Sherwood Anderson introducing "my friend Ernest Hemingway" or the new Finnegans Wake Circle forming round the bewildered *Ulysses* fans.

Buy a book in brown paper
From Faber and Faber
to see Annie Liffey
trip, tumble and caper.
Sevensinns in her singthings,
Plurabelle on her prose
Seashell ebb music wayriver she flows.

(1966)

RICHARD ALDINGTON

Richard Aldington (1892–1962) is a writer who has been undeservedly neglected. This "book of reminiscence"* was first published in New York in 1941 and has only just reached us (still with no index) six years after his death. The publisher explains that it was not issued here at the time because of the feeling against expatriates, but spoils it by adding: "Aldington remained in the United States, where he died on July 27, 1962."

In fact he returned to Europe in 1946, and he spent the remaining sixteen years of his life in Montpellier, Aix, and Le Lavandou, and died near Sancerre in a cottage lent him by his devoted Australian admirer, Alister Kershaw, after his return from a triumphal visit to Russia where he obtained the recognition denied him here. An excellent memorial volume was published by the Southern Illinois University Press with contributions from his friends, including Herbert Read, Henry Williamson, C. P. Snow and Lawrence Durrell.

Why is he so neglected? There are three reasons. He outlived his creative powers, he was anti-Establishment in the wrong way (from the Right rather than the Left). The Durrells' nickname for him—which he relished—was "Top Grumpy." He was an expatriate with a permanent chip on his shoulder, and his rather complicated love-life forced on him a series of withdrawals, from England to France, from France to America, which involved a certain amount of boat-burning, unnecessary by present standards, but which led him to a rejection of society and consequent suspiciousness.

He certainly had a paranoid streak, and this lay behind the exercises in debunking which made him so unpopular. But, though a man of the

* *Life for Life's Sake,* by Richard Aldington (New York, 1941).

extreme Right, he was not a Fascist. He may have been prejudiced, but he had much common decency and a large and generous nature when not clouded by persecution mania. He was a romantic idealist with a second-strike armament of satirical weapons ready for his inevitable disillusion. By 1930 he had announced his amibition, in an American questionnaire, "to tell England what I think of it."

He has three grounds for consideration: as a novelist and poet; as a biographer and translator; as a case-history, a key minor figure in a major movement, the friend of Eliot, Yeats, and Pound, the friend and biographer of D. H. Lawrence and Norman Douglas, the young man who abandoned the Georgians for the Imagists, the Imagists for *The Criterion,* and a job on *The Times Literary Supplement* for Paris. For many years he ran a short head behind Graves in the anthologies and his war novel, *Death of a Hero,* was reviewed simultaneously with *Goodbye to All That,* and *A Farewell to Arms* (1929).

> They sell primarily as war books, though actually the war interest is only the jam in which they make the public swallow the pill of their discontent. . . . Aldington, however, is really too uncontrolled to be entirely palatable. His book comes ten years too late, it is too bitter, too much like the first flush of embittered war poets. It is a promising novel rather than an important one. (Connolly, 1930)

Both *Death of a Hero* and its successor *All Men Are Enemies* (1933) are largely autobiographical and contain much about his love-life as well as portraits of Pound (disguised as a painter), Eliot, Lawrence, Wilfred Blunt, Ford and others. On the whole his novels are sentimental, petulant and long-winded and his poetry facile.

Although a clever man and a fine scholar and translator, Aldington was an anti-intellectual. He was on the side of Lawrence, of life, emotion, feeling, sensuality as against the pale glow inside the dome of the mind; he enviously accused Eliot of lack of emotion. Aldington in fact was a neo-pagan, a lover of the body, of nature, of the Mediterranean; a troubadour who revealed his personal autobiography through his poetry. *A Dream in the Luxembourg* and *The Eaten Heart* celebrate his long love for Brigit Patmore, even as *The Crystal World* (1937) describes its end with his flight to America with her daughter-in-law and subsequent marriage. *Life for Life's Sake* barely alludes to these upheavals; it is a book about the rest of his life through childhood in Kent, literary London, the War, the Twenties and Provence to his settlement in America. It is a good-humoured book almost without a trace of paranoia, the last to be written by the old successful Aldington, if we except his *Wellington.* One has only to compare the glowing pages about

D. H. Lawrence ("the most interesting human being I have known"), Eliot, Pound, Douglas, the publisher Charles Prentice and many another, to see that we are still in the Golden Age. "That camaraderie of minds—how can one express it?"

Connoisseurs of the Pejorative Process might compare the anecdote about Douglas and Athenaeus on page 334 with the treatment accorded to it later in his *Pinorman*. In fact his enthusiasm for these older men (Aldington was the youngest poet to join in the pilgrimage to Blunt on his seventieth birthday) is, as he says, "like trying to describe the perfume of a flower which has vanished from this earth."

The war was, of course, as for so many young poets, the main experience in Aldington's life. Others who fought, Sassoon, Sitwell, Read, Williamson, got over this; Aldington claimed to do so by writing *Death of a Hero* and working the death-wish out of his system. In fact he never recovered; he was permanently browned off (see *Last Straws*) and embittered with post-war England. No one has written more feelingly about Europe before it committed suicide in 1914. We enjoy the excitement of his best-seller and are spared the agonies in which it was conceived.

This autobiography is, in fact, a curiously light-weight book and one which grows progressively lighter as the central experience recedes. This may be a penalty of serialisation in the *Atlantic Monthly,* or due to Aldington's gentlemanly reticence. Luckily Aldington was a poet, and the book is full of poetical feeling—the discovery of Wilde on Keats and so of Keats, his first trips abroad to France and Italy, butterfly-hunting in Kent, his visits to Barfreston Church, his years at London University and his first excursion into literary London, where he met his salon-Sappho wife "H.D." (Hilda Doolittle). Only a poet could analyse the significance of certain smells:

> The smell of old wood burning brings back to my lungs and nostrils the hot frowsty air from a dug-out on a winter's night. I can see the rough chalk steps going down through darkness to the candle-glimmer, the trench in which I stand, the dark patient sentry beside me, and overhead the cold stars dimmed suddenly by a Véry light. The scent of new-mown hay is no longer delicious to me. It is like phosgene, and brings up a picture of dawn over a ruined village and stretcher-bearers bringing down gasping foam-mouthed bodies. In the vaults of the Escorial I smelt again the awful stench of corrupting corpse.

However, as the title suggests, this is a cheerful book, a natural for the literary historian. If only to so much intelligent and agreeable observation had been added the quality of intellect which he affected to despise!

Aldington's later years were marred by poverty and unsuccess, while his books on T. E. Lawrence and Norman Douglas affronted both the general and the high-brow public. How he would have enjoyed being proved right about Lawrence by the recent articles in the *Sunday Times!* He was the first to quote the now famous letter to Mrs. Shaw about Lawrence's humilitation in Deraa. All the disappointment of these last years is summed up by Lawrence Durrell in his contribution to the *Portrait:*

> With the trouble caused by these two volumes (on T. E. Lawrence and Norman Douglas) the whole of the rest of his admirable life-work went out of print and out of public demand—some seventy titles in all! This was of course catastrophic for a man living on his books, and he was facing up to it gamely, but the tide had turned against him. . . . He was a difficult, touchy, strange, lonely, shy, aggravating and utterly delightful man . . .

And incidentally, very good looking: his publishers might have run to a photograph.

(1968)

LYTTON STRACHEY

"O such a plunge into the past—and so many pasts"
—LYTTON STRACHEY

A GOOD biography should not just present us with a central character who is more intelligent, more gifted, more civilised than ourselves, but with a milieu which is more intense, more spacious and more loving.

Bloomsbury was such a society, matriarchal despite the brilliance of the courtiers, and at the centre of the maze sat the unwobbling pivot, Vanessa Bell.

Lytton Strachey, besides having a special Solomon and Sheba relationship with her sister Virginia Woolf, admired Vanessa, the only true Bloomsburian who could raise a family without forfeiting the respect of the others.

Once one gets the hierarchy straight and knows where the tribal altar stood, Lytton is revealed as a parallel centre, a rival court where an almost purely male society sought sanctuary from maternal domination. Carrington was a page, the Knave of Hearts, never the Queen. The wonder is that Lytton's Berkshire homes, defenceless as the kingdoms of the Morea or the empire of Trebizond, endured for so long in the world of rapidly shifting homosexual allegiances and barbarian invasions.

That Tidmarsh and Ham Spray should have lasted from 1917, when Carrington gave up Mark Gertler for him, to Lytton's death in 1932 was due to her complete devotion to his interests and to his resolute refusal to be spoiled by money and fame, to abandon the essential simplicity of his country way of life for the temptations of Mayfair and Chelsea.

His fundamental goodness, his unremitting industry in the service of his intellectual curiosity, his streak of Victorian frugality kept the extraordinary relationship alive. The men in both their lives never quite overwhelmed it, and just as it seemed most in danger, Lytton's fatal illness brought it prematurely to an ending of antique beauty when the inconsolable Carrington committed suicide after ending her commonplace-book with an epitaph by Sir Henry Wooton:

He first deceased, she for a little tried
to live without him, liked it NOT, and died.

In many biographies the "years of achievement" signify a general decline in spiritual values as love, integrity and mental growth are jettisoned for the sake of ambition. Here* it is the reverse. I would not say that Mr. Holroyd's first volume is the weaker—it may well represent a more difficult investigation—but it is certainly the more depressing and leaves his hero frustrated in love, denied a Fellowship and forced to retire to the bosom of his family to eke out a living by weekly journalism.

In the sequel Strachey acquired fame and freedom and the platonic devotion of a lifetime from his young Cordelia, followed by two love-affairs with fascinating ephebi. He becomes distinguished through his own grotesqueness and also a social success. His two well-meditated masterpieces, *Eminent Victorians,* 1918, and *Queen Victoria,* 1922, between them pleased everyone. His biographer, having navigated the dismal channels of Volume I, now gains the open sea with the wind behind him. "A large leisureliness descends upon one." Everybody has kept everything. Letters, journals, eyewitnesses abound. There are often three or four descriptions of a single incident. "I'm afraid my biography will present a slightly shocking spectacle," wrote Lytton to Mrs. Hutchinson in 1927.

Above all this is Carrington's volume, the girl whom we first came to know through *Crome Yellow.* There is no doubt that she carries the book on her dumpy shoulders—not only because of her fifteen-year stint running his two houses but through the complexity of her character, particularly in relation to younger men for whom she was the innocent baby-faced Medusa; and, above all, by her prose style, for her letters, with their capitals at the end of words, their sensuous naïvety and directness, are as original as her paintings and far more numerous. Her talent was genuine and just missed being whimsical or arty. I used to meet her at parties but never suspected this inner wealth until Gerald Brenan showed me his journal many years later.

If Carrington was the Knave of Hearts, her husband, Ralph Partridge, was the King, since he was loved by both of them. There were also the trio of young men, all closely involved with each other, who illuminated Lytton's last years. I knew these charmers well: George Rylands, Roger Senhouse, Philip Ritchie. To the first two he left his library. The third died young (see Bowra's autobiography).

* *Lytton Strachey: The Years of Achievement 1910–1932,* by Michael Holroyd (New York, 1968).

I rate Mr. Holroyd very high as a biographer, almost in the Painter class. With the great set pieces he has an easy time, but the evaluation of so much sexual and sentimental inflation requires an exercise of judgement. Unforgivable things are said, terrible decisions are taken, and after the explosion everyone is still there. The deadly irresistibles—Rupert Brooke, Duncan Grant, Henry Lamb, Augustus John—are like predators who strike at night and are then seen drowsing peacefully beside the herds.

Perhaps Bloomsbury can be criticised in that the creation of "Bloomsbury," the imaginary country of intellectual integrity, aesthetic appreciation and personal relations—first envisaged at Cambridge in the philosophy of G. E. Moore—took so much out of the creators in self-criticism and conversation that not enough energy was left for works of art. Compared with the Impressionists or even the Surrealists, their *oeuvre* is rather slight. Perhaps the subscription was too high.

Taken as a group it is about the best we've had; yet, considered as individuals, uncreative in comparison with Joyce, Yeats, Lawrence, Pound, Eliot, Auden or Henry Moore. Lytton, who undermined the Victorians and renewed the art of biography, also propagated the dignity of letters in the French style and the virtues of the French eighteenth century—tolerance, urbanity, measure, discipline—which inhibit originality. Nothing grew in his shade.

"I prefer Joyce to you," wrote Gerald Brenan in 1921. "He does not taunt me, but leads me on, points to very far horizons, and shows me a way that leads there. He promises new discoveries, new methods, new beauties—you don't promise anything. You just are." Eliot also drew a comparison between the two. "As for *Ulysses,*" wrote Lytton to his brother, "I *will not* look at it, *no,* NO."

Mr. Holroyd draws his comparison between Strachey and Lawrence; when one is out of fashion, he claims, the other is in, and we have lived too long under the Lawrence banner. To end this involves a dismissal of Dr. Leavis and his pupils, which is accomplished in Volume I with some of the contempt which they have made their own weapon. He backs this up with long and considered judgements on Strachey's six books. But Lytton will not stand too much limelight; a writer who sought to interpret the present solely through the past cannot inspire the young, except for the few who already approach him with a built-in nostalgia. This does not diminish his power and originality as a biographer, summed up in a marvellous letter from Freud about *Elizabeth and Essex.*

> You are aware of what other historians so easily overlook—that it is impossible to understand the past with certainty because we cannot divine men's motives and the essence of their minds and so interpret their actions.

Mr. Holroyd is aware of this too: he is an inveterate gossip and so has recorded everything he has found out, leaving the reader to decide whether, for example, David Garnett knew Lytton and Carrington well, as large extracts from his admirable autobiography (not always here acknowledged) lead us to think, or whether Brenan's statement: "Garnett was never a close friend of hers or Lytton's" (page 440) is more correct.

How accurate is Mr. Holroyd? One can only speak of what one knows. He describes a house where I spent many months as "having a view of the Sussex weald as far as the South Downs and Chanctonbury Ring"—not very easy from sea-level on Southampton water. He is rather unfair to Desmond MacCarthy, he quotes me three times and drags me into a foot-note which contains an inaccuracy, but does not include me in the voluminous index. One quotation from me describes Lytton: "using the method of Bayle [sic], Voltaire and Gibbon." Why the [sic]? He will find Bayle summarised on page 135 of Strachey's *Landmarks in French Literature.*

(1968)

DON GERALDO

GRANADA is the most northerly city of southern Europe. Between the elms of the Alhambra and the sugar-cane of Motril towers the Sierra Nevada; beyond them lies the network of valleys known as the Alpujarras, where the Moors retired after the fall of Granada. Among their remoter villages is Yegen, home for some ten years of Mr. Gerald Brenan* who first arrived there in 1920, a war veteran of twenty-five, a refugee from the English middle classes, determined to educate himself among books and peasants on a few pounds a year.

Mr. Brenan was thus the first of the post-war Spanish expatriates, his arrival in Yegen anticipating Mr. Hemingway's epiphany at the Pamplona Fiesta by several years. I did not reach Granada myself till Easter 1925, a magical moment for an undergraduate, for all the Sitwells and Richard Wyndham and Sir William Walton were staying in the same hotel. By 1923 I had got as far as Almeria, the other city which framed Mr. Brenan's world and which played Naples to Granada's Florence, his own village being almost Alpine.

I long to know what readers will make of this book, and how much my admiration for it should be discounted by my long affection for the author and by my early enthusiasm for this region of snow and chestnut woods, fig and almond and cool, cheerful guttural towns; Orgiva, Ugijar, Lanjaron. For me *South from Granada* is the best of Mr. Brenan's books, and as a travel book almost in the same class as *Old Calabria.* Like Norman Douglas, Mr. Brenan has a true and proper knowledge of the culture he describes, a sense of composition and an original point of view; he is a poet and romantic preserved by his irony and scholarship from inflationary looseness, about to take his place, I prophesy, as a major writer in our age of nickel.

* *South from Granada,* by Gerald Brenan (New York, 1957).

Consider this description of "coming down to Almeria," the Venusine sea city, goal of generations of mountain peasants:

> Two things combined to give Almeria its special character—animation and monotony. It was a hurdy-gurdy. Every morning and every evening the miraculous act would be put on—but it was always the same one. The Spanish pattern of culture is so tight and rigid and the need for keeping up appearances so strong, that in a small provincial capital such as this there could be no variations. Courtship led to marriage, marriage led to children, and children landed the parents in a groove of narrow economic restrictions from which there was no hope of ever emerging. The monotony that descended like the sunlight was untempered by even the ghost of an illicit love-affair. So it came about that the individual with his hopes and daydreams had withered by the time he was thirty, a cog in the chain of births and deaths, and by the time he was forty looked like a pressed fern in an album. The only gainers were the children, because the parents put all the illusions of their own youthful days on to them and treated them like heirs to a kingdom. Thus the spectacle of heightened life and animation, which so impressed the person just arriving from his village, was a mirage. The routine of a peasant with its quiet variation of crops and weather, was a good deal more satisfying than that of a white-collar worker in this city of ritournelle, though the peasant was the last person to know it.

This blend of meditation, poetry and disillusion with an unexpected interest in botany, sociology, anthropology and the picaresque constitutes the Brenan mixture: one of the most satisfactory Flaubert-derivatives:

> It is the usual fate of shepherds—those sailors of the wavy sierras, condemned to long absences from their families—that their wives should be unfaithful to them.

You recognise his touch?

South from Granada is dedicated to "Ralph Partridge" and Mr. Brenan's first book (already brimful of *Brenanismo*) was called *Dr. Partridge's Almanack;* and one of the wiles of his story-telling-cum-sociology is to insert accounts of the visits of friends like Virginia Woolf and Lytton Strachey or the Partridges themselves among his shepherd's calendar in contrast with the Spanish peasant-characters who form the chorus. We thus get a most sensitive analysis of the Gods of Bloomsbury and their orchestrated conversations to relieve the chick-pea monotony of peasant life and I wonder again whether, if it had been my fate to have encountered High Bloomsbury in Almeria on their visit in 1923 rather than the Sitwells in 1925, I should have been purged of that taint of Oxford dandyism which brought down the epithet "cocktail critic" on me in Virginia Woolf's journals many years later.

The beauty of *South from Granada* is that the young man who fled to these remote uplands was healed by them; he found the ancient rhythm, the beliefs, the folk-lore, the pagan survivals, the Virgilian purity, the life-cycle that he had craved and he emerged with a philosophy as well as an education: "The picture I formed of this place," he concludes, "was not an illusion." There are of course some dull moments; it is difficult to bring alive a great many simple souls to a sophisticated reader and one needs a map of the characters as well as of the places; and when Mr. Brenan returns after the civil war there is an inevitable disillusion, even as I find the Granada of today very different from that of Mr. Temple wearing his two hats or the Sitwells in their capes or de Falla, or that great lady the Macleod of Macleod, for it is no longer a city one would wish to live in, and Almeria also has lost the magic which Mr. Brenan and Mr. Aldous Huxley discovered.

The sense of expectation diminishes with age: the multiplication of machines and human beings destroys the contour of places, especially of those city-states like Granada, Seville or Cordoba which had retained their exquisite proportions of old and new, rich and poor, grave and gay for twenty centuries and which only *el Brenanismo* can restore.

(1957)

ALDOUS HUXLEY: 1

LAURA ARCHERA was the second wife of the widowed Aldous Huxley: a violinist and film cutter interested in psychotherapy whom he met in 1948 and married in 1956. Her book is a record of his last years, rendered tragic by his first wife's death from cancer, then by his own.

O miserable and fatuous humanity which still squanders on armaments and space trips the fortunes which might help to find a cure for the most ruthless, painful and humiliating of ailments, that destroys the finest minds and bodies in their prime and denies old age the privilege of natural death!

Mrs. Huxley's book* is not depressing; she is convinced that love is stronger than death; she is one of those wives whose devotion to an ageing artist is a "gratuitous grace," to use Huxley's phrase for psychedelic drugs (he coined the adjective in 1957). The arrival of such a latecomer on the final scene always seems something of a miracle yet in some degree it is the reward of being an artist and of remaining accessible to the world of love. Huxley left a record of his first wife's last hours when he sat with her describing their past happiness and literally talking her down into the ultimate silence; his widow performed the same service as well as giving him at his own request an LSD injection.

This drug, in which he was one of the first to experiment, has been tried in Canada as a terminal remedy which dissociates the mind from the agony of the body and lasts much longer than morphia in its analgesic effects. Huxley wrote of Maria:

> I told her to let go, to forget the body, to leave it lying there like a bundle of old clothes, and to allow herself to be carried, as a child is

* *This Timeless Moment,* by Laura Huxley (London, 1969).

carried, into the heart of the rosy light of love. "Peace now," I kept repeating, "Peace, love, joy, *now, Being now.*"

And Laura Huxley used similar words to him. "Breathing came slower—and slower—and slower; the ceasing of life was not a drama at all, but like a piece of music just finishing . . ."

In fairness it must be said that she allows some of us an alternative.

> There are two diametrically opposite views about dying. One is that the best way is to go without knowing it, to slip away—hopefully when sleeping. The other view is that one should die as aware and clear-minded as possible; that death is one of the great adventures of life. Aldous believed in the latter.

"Aldous"; that unique Christian name has reverberated through my life. A scholar like myself, of Eton and Balliol, he had ten years' seniority and infinitely more application. I read his books as a schoolboy, I settled in Sanary to be near him and one of my happiest moments was when his red Bugatti first swung into the drive. But in the Thirties I found his books a great disappointment and it was not till *Time Must Have a Stop* that he regained my devotion.

I saw him in California in 1946, and interviewed him later in London. Gone were the silk suits and suave manner of his European heyday when he lived in Paris or Rome, travelled round the world and wrote for *Vogue* and *Vanity Fair*. The sage who reappeared, triumphant over his blindness, had now an otherworldly quality; one could not meet him without being aware of this extraordinary perceptiveness and goodness, yet his purely intellectual brand of verbal humour never deserted him. How rare is a healer better-read than oneself! Perhaps he was somewhat over-obsessed with world famine and the population-explosion, yet the fragment of the new novel which Mrs. Huxley prints shows a return to his bourgeois Anglo-Indian background, his mother's kiss, his initiation by a German governess.

> Sixty years later, as I rasp the grey stubble off my chin and cheeks, I find myself asking the same question. Am I that alien presence in the glass, that hardly recognisable caricature of the man who used to climb mountains and go to bed with beautiful women? Or am I this still active mind, this hardly impaired capacity to feel and think, this God-like awareness that has created all the worlds in which successively or simultaneously, I have lived?

The Huxley of this book is totally engrossed in mysticism, in the psychedelic experience—hypnotism, LSD, mescalin, psilocybin, tape-recorded trips and trances—ending with a séance in which he claims to prove by a book-test his existence in another sphere. This is not a work for those who prefer a concrete personality like Stravinsky's in Craft's conversations, or Gide's, or Bertrand Russell's autobiography. "Human beings cannot stand very much reality," particularly in the form of interlocking planes of love and light, or the Tibetan Book of the Dead. Some of this drug-induced writing seems complete nonsense. The mystical experience is notoriously hard to communicate: the soul falters.

> Along with many scientists, he considered the discovery of psychedelics one of the three major scientific breakthroughs of the twentieth century, the other two being the splitting of the atom and manipulation of genetic structures.

The last two are discoveries whose importance can be demonstrated; the first is valid only if we also assume that cosmic bliss surrounds us and that the psychedelics connect us to it, reopening the valve which consciousness shuts down. But supposing there is no joy in the Universe except what we ourselves bring there; supposing ceasing to be means what it says? Then these drugs are just hallucinogens and the breakthrough is illusory. No wonder he dismissed the Freudian theory that mystical experiences are "simply the revivals of some obscure memory of infantile bliss," as "utter bosh"! The "God-like awareness" can brook no challenge.

A merit of this book, besides the author's love and understanding, are her excellent quotations from unpublished essays and letters. Everything of Aldous was obliterated by the fire which wiped out his Hollywood home and all his possessions, his complete archive, except for the manuscript of his novel, *Island,* and three suits he took with him. His wife saved only a statuette and her violin, and let his love-letters burn. Her account of the total paralysis and bewilderment which affected them and prevented them from taking any action though there was a full swimming-pool nearby is baffling. Did the magnitude of the disaster (of which they had full warning) make all action seem derisory, or were they immobilised by guilt at having any personality or possessions, regarding the fire as purgative of egotism? *"Aun aprendo,"* "I am still learning," was the motto Huxley borrowed from Goya. "The process goes on from the cradle to the grave and doubtless beyond," he said.

This book should be read in conjunction with the memorial volume which includes his last essay on "Shakespeare and Death" that he finished in great pain three days before he died (on the same day as Kennedy). He wrote to his children announcing his second marriage in 1956 in words that Laura Huxley can well now apply, "Tenderness, I discover, is the best memorial to tenderness."

(1969)

ALDOUS HUXLEY: 2

THAT wonderful Chinese allegory, 'Monkey,' which Waley translated a few years back, gives a very forceful account of that blessing and curse of cleverness with which the Fairy Godmother, who is also the Wicked Fairy, endowed me, and with which, as a young man, I was in considerable measure identified. However, there is, let us hope, Evolution and a Descent of Man; and I have tried to drop the old tail and trick or at least to make use of them for better and less malicious purposes than in the past."

So wrote Aldous Huxley to the once despised Middleton Murry, the humbug Burlap of *Point Counter Point* with his "slug's-eye view" of Lawrence. I have quoted it because it contains in a nutshell the whole spiritual progress of Huxley, from Ape to Essence, from Monkey to Mystic.

Was his journey really necessary, as the war posters used to say? Cleverness had to be sacrificed for Compassion; it is perhaps an ingredient which must be dissolved to make way for that much overworked word. Was the sacrifice of so much intransigent and sceptical brilliance rewarded, in terms of art, by the end-product, the later novels, the final compendium of belief, synthesis of Oriental detachment and Western action? If we take a typically unregenerate writer like Norman Douglas we notice that his end and his beginnings are much of a muchness: style, point of view, cleverness are there in *Siren Land* or *South Wind,* and hardly altered in *Looking Back* or *Late Harvest*. But the Huxley of *Time Must Have a Stop* or *Island* is as different from that of *Crome Yellow* or *Antic Hay* as the "Four Quartets" from "J. Alfred Prufrock." Different, yes, but better? Perhaps his letters* supply the answer.

* *Letters of Aldous Huxley,* edited by Grover Smith (New York, 1969).

There are a thousand pages of them, representing 943 letters out of 2,500 examined, a quarter perhaps of all he wrote. The letters which represent his deepest emotions are lost or withheld. This means that there is little or no passion in the book. An enormous number of letters are to his brother Sir Julian, and a quantity to his father. Anyone who has had any experience in writing to fathers must know that they are not the best recipients for confidences; one writes what they would like to hear, and even a brother must be presented with a façade of unfailing masculinity.

The two Huxleys (a third brother, Trev, hanged himself aged twenty-four) are somewhat similar in temperament to the two Jameses, the younger visionary and introverted, the elder pragmatical and scientific, avid of recognition, determined to help mankind. The missing factor is the mother who died when Aldous was twelve.

> You never knew my mother—I wish you had because she was a very wonderful woman. Trev was most like her. I have just been reading again what she wrote to me just before she died. The last words of her letter were "Don't be too critical of other people and love much" and I have come to see more and more how wise that advice was. (1915)

Huxley's career falls into several natural divisions but there are no abrupt transitions. There is little cleverness after *Antic Hay* (1925), and mysticism already "undercuts" cynicism in *Those Barren Leaves*. He became an expatriate almost by accident around 1923 and remained one the rest of his life, emigrating from Italy to Paris and Provence, from Provence to California to provide a safe home for his son Matthew in 1937. There he remained, with visits to Europe, for the rest of his life.

The letters make heavy going; so much family jocularity, so much labouring of the same points to different correspondents, so much hammering home of favourite beliefs and authorities.

"There can, I think, be little doubt that the deflection of attention on to sexuality in adolescence makes it very hard for young people to think of other matters."

One cannot dismiss the correspondence of a lifetime on the weakness of a few platitudes. The trouble is that there are so very few letter-writers of genius. Lawrence was one, and we somehow expect the editor of Lawrence's letters to possess a similar gift. Huxley's letters are typical of a most intelligent polymath and novelist of talent. Depth and intellectual tenacity are no substitute for genius but they have a quality of their own. His letters are invariably kind, they disdain triviality, exude something of Sir Julian's philanthropy, they are humorous without being witty, and are all readable, even the numerous missives to publishers, editors, agents and stray enquirers.

In the later American phase the texture thickens considerably and I confess to preferring the much scantier section (O for a change of heart from Lady Ottoline's executors or Mrs. Hutchinson) which deals with the Teens and Twenties, with the early Garsington, with Gilbert Murray as a telepathist, with Evan Morgan's party (in a letter to Carrington) or the war-poets' reading (1917).

Gosse in the chair—the bloodiest little old man I have ever seen—oh what a performance. Eliot and I were the only people who had any dignity. Bob Nichols raved and screamed and hooted and moaned his filthy war poems, like a Lyceum villain who hasn't learnt how to act: Viola Tree declaimed in a voice so syrupy and fruity and rich, that one felt quite cloyed and sick by two lines, the Shufflebottoms (Sitwells) were respectable but terribly nervous: Gosse was like a reciter at a penny reading.

Or the Oxford volunteers (unpublished)

Some have piles and some have goitres.
Most of them have Bright's disease
Uric acid has made them flaccid
And one gouty hero loiters
Ankylosed in toes and knees.

The letters contain many good phrases and pleasant surprises. Huxley could pick winners. He enjoyed *Ulysses* as far back as 1918, and, of course, Eliot. He found David Cecil, "though only sixteen, the most brilliant conversationalist, has written one or two uncommonly good poems." He fancied Edward Sackville-West; he thought Graham Greene's *The Man Within* much better than Virginia Woolf's *To the Lighthouse.* "It's the difference between something full and something empty" (1930). He can administer the *coup de grâce:* "It is full of that kind of exquisitely good writing, that is, one feels instinctively, only another kind of bad writing. Santayana is the most perfect specimen of the type."

Occasionally he misfires, as on Lawrence before he fell under the spell: "The slightly insane novelist was analysed for his complexes, dark and tufty ones, tangled in his mind. The complexes were discovered, and it is said that Lawrence has now lost, along with his slight sexual mania, all his talent as a writer" (June 1920, year of *Women in Love*!).

His attitude to England is typical of the expatriate: "How is England? My trouble is that there never seem to be any new people . . . the same old set, slowly putrefying in their own juice. But I suppose there are young people; Only one doesn't see them" (1926). This becomes grotesque twenty years later.

> Not much news from England, and what comes is unutterably drab and weary. Dishonesty is everywhere rampant . . . sexlife like Sodom and Gomorrah. Government tyranny is complete.

Such outbursts are rare. The Sanary period in which I knew the Huxleys best was perhaps his happiest. It lasted seven years; they owned their house, they toured, they swam, they worked, their friends came from England and America (including Gerald Heard), they visited the local grandees: "tho' nice, they have the rich person's inability to conceive that other people have anything better to do than eat lunches and teas in their houses." He was economically independent, free of *Vogue* and *Vanity Fair.*

> I've declined Beaverbrook's offer. Writing against time once a week and—worse—having to read contemporary literature. Also the certainty, if I'd been really honest, of quarrelling with all my literary colleagues. For, after all, at least 99.8 per cent of the literary production of this age—as of all other ages, for that matter—is the purest cat-piss.

The letters are well-edited, with most useful foot-notes which err on the side of compassion rather than cleverness where the living are concerned. Do we really need so many erasures and dots? For example, page 629 Cyril Connolly: (. .) "one likes him *malgré tout.*" I've known him too for sixty years and that's just how I feel. (. . .)

(1969)

THE SITWELLS

As I write I have before me a long and eulogistic account of Edith Sitwell by one of her oldest friends, Allanah Harper. "Perhaps one should write in an objective way about even those one most admires but it is not in my nature to do so . . . Do you think any English magazine would be interested in it?" . . . Such is the current unpopularity of the poet who was treated on equal terms by Yeats and Eliot that one cannot firmly say "Yes."

As early as 1934 Edith Sitwell named her three enemies: "Dr Leavis, Mr Grigson, and dear Mr Wyndham Lewis" and they or their disciples were still active thirty years later; puritan roundheads tilting against the element of privileged silliness which formed, however, but one aspect of the talented trio. Class hatred can be just as misguided as the aristocratic frivolity which kindles it, and is often an alibi for envy. Even so, the Sitwells did exploit an unsuspected talent for publicity through their counter-attacks on the philistine.

What is left when the dust settles? Mr. Lehmann* cannot really tell us; he has had too much encouragement from the family to be unbiased and he is also by nature disinclined for home truths. This animated and astringent conversationalist always seems to me to put on a morning coat to write; sometimes he sounds like a schoolmaster distributing prizes on parents' day, sometimes like a solicitor breaking bad news.

> Nevertheless, Dylan's increasingly Dionysiac impulses caused awkward moments and she [Edith] became more and more aware of the dangers he was running unless the fatal circle of habit could be broken.

We take the point.

* *A Nest of Tigers,* by John Lehmann (Boston, 1968).

The world, as the saying goes, was their oyster, and they savoured what they found inside with insatiable relish.

It is, I think, a matter of fairly general agreement among Osbert Sitwell's admirers that they value him, and believe he has made his distinct contribution to the literature of his time, as a writer of prose.

These seem innocuous enough, but the cumulative effect of so many guarded statements is to produce a kind of White Paper, so that we are quite shocked when Edith refers to her middle-class education or comes out with "I often wonder how many of them (her Left-wing critics) at the age of seventeen have been sent out to pawn false teeth—parental false teeth!!! You get ten shillings on them. And whisky was then twelve shillings and sixpence." Incidentally the whole incident of Sir George allowing his wife to be sent to prison for a financial irregularity is barely touched on in spite of its devastating effect on the children. It is extremely important in understanding their attitude that it be known that their father was a monster, not just a *monstre sacré*.

Nevertheless once we accept Mr. Lehmann's bedside manner there is much to admire and enjoy in his interim report. It makes good reading, it quotes good literature, it sets the extraordinary family before a generation who may know little about them. I think he might have pointed out to us that the Sitwells were enormous fun, though he does quote Evelyn Waugh aptly to that effect.

In the Twenties they represented the rush towards pleasure and aesthetic enjoyment characteristic of the intelligent young who had come through the war; they were the natural allies of Cocteau and the Ecole de Paris, dandies, irreproachably dressed and fed, who indicated to young men down from Oxford and even Cambridge that it was possible to reconcile art and fashion, as an alternative to Bloomsbury. Dandyism is the prerogative of the youthful male in many bird and animal species. Why should this display be suspect only in the human? Even Dr. Leavis must have been young once and worn a tie.

I first met all the Sitwells together in Granada in 1925 when I was still an undergraduate, and was bowled over by them. I was pitched into outer darkness four years later on account of "information received" and only forgiven for something I had never said many years after, with a royal banquet in my honour at which the whole clan welcomed me as if I had only just left the room. But I had been mulcted by then of many years of their invigorating company and sartorial splendour.

Mr. Lehmann moves nimbly from one set of achievements to another, collating their autobiographical experiences, the Scarborough and Renishaw of *All Summer in a Day* (S.S.), *Left Hand, Right Hand* (O.S.) and *Colonel Fantock* (E.S.). What emerges?

The background of the Sitwells was conventional Edwardian upper-class, though darkened by domestic tragedy. The three were quite uniquely gifted with a poetic and satirical imagination and a quickened visual and olfactory sense. They were romantic rebels who developed weapons of verbal self-defence. They were largely self-educated. Unlike their contemporaries they were drawn to the artificial, the poetry of Pope, "mannerism" in painting and architecture, the eighteenth century, rococo and baroque. They were quick, especially Sacheverell, to recognise kindred spirits among the emerging obscure or the neglected dead; they set a high value on loyalty and on fighting their own and other people's battles, but were too apt to suspect treachery and avenge insults better ignored.

Friends of their parents were the first philistines they encountered. Later on the term was extended to cover all those who seemed unaware of their existence. They had strong supporters. As to their performance, I can vouch for the magical effect of Edith's early poetry and I am saddened when poets and critics of poetry whom I admire cannot appreciate it. Some of it is artificial, some of it wildly gay, most of it impregnated with mysterious sadness; it is not intellectual poetry like Eliot's, but the intellect operates behind the scenes through technique and word-play; it is a poetry of walled gardens rather than of the Georgian country-side, of constricted and frustrated Marianas.

It is all included in her collected poems of 1930, which has the fine ending to "Gold Coast Customs" not in the original. The 1930 volume would be enough to assure her a place equal to de la Mare or Graves in a normal critical climate. Then after a long interval came the war-poems of which Mr. Lehmann writes: "In Edith, I am profoundly convinced, the hour and the poet were matched" and he quotes Sir Kenneth Clark and Sir Maurice Bowra in support. These included "Street Songs," "Green Song" and "The Shadow of Cain." I would also like to add to the canon some of her latest lyrics, down to her very last book.

Sir Osbert's poetic output is by no means negligible and he is expert at the verse portrait in which eccentric characters from his past are set in their natural environment. "Inquilinics," with its collection of Florentine expatriates, is one of my favourites. Two travel books, Osbert's *Discursions* (1925) and Sacheverell's *Southern Baroque Art* (1924), are of great significance in the history of taste: they rediscovered and rehabilitated the baroque and rococo for succeeding generations.

I personally owe a lot to Sacheverell's *British Architects and Craftsmen* and to his books on South German rococo which are not listed in Mr. Lehmann's bibliography. In these fields the Sitwells are forerunners rather than scholars but no scholar can rival them in the poetic appreciation of painting, music and architecture. "Anyone who can afford to visit Angkor and doesn't, is mad" (O.S.).

Sir Osbert's novels and stories stand up well, in particular *Triple Fugue,* an admirable comic piece. His autobiography, I have elsewhere suggested, is too overweighted by ancestor-worship: it was an act of leisurely defiance which grew out of war-time frustration. It should be cut down from five to two or three fat volumes and reissued in paperback: that much would still present the essence of that grand and generous character.

One last tribute to Mr. Lehmann: his eyewitness accounts of Sitwell readings and celebrations are a joy. No one else could have described them so well and they indicate how much closer to all of them he was than his modesty has allowed him to say.

(1968)

ERNEST HEMINGWAY: 1

POSTHUMOUS works are seldom well written. *A Moveable Feast** is an exception, like *Between the Acts*. It seems to have occupied Hemingway from 1958–60 and to have been carefully revised and in it he returns to the wonder of his early Paris years—the Paris which Joyce called "a lamp lit for lovers in the wood of the world"—even as Goya returned to the Madrid of the Fair of San Isidro, or the bull to his *querencia*.

It is one of the best books Hemingway wrote and one which he had to write. Having read it we could not imagine the *oeuvre* of Hemingway without it, for, although one felt one knew a lot about his early days in Paris, this was almost entirely by hearsay, through the favourable accounts of Sylvia Beach, Ford Madox Ford, Sisley Huddleston and the less favourable pictures of Gertrude Stein, Harold Loeb, etc. Hemingway himself alludes to the scene briefly in *The Torrents of Spring,* while the good beer and the sawmill come through in *Green Hills of Africa.*

The Paris of the early Twenties was very different, however, from the Paris of the early Thirties and it is easy to confuse them. If one wants to perform a Hemingway memorial ritual it is still possible to eat exactly the same meal as he describes in *A Moveable Feast* in precisely the same surroundings by going to—but why should I tell you? I am fond of the place myself.

I have read and re-read *A Moveable Feast* and enjoyed it more—except for the racing chapters—on a second reading. "Ernest Hemingway is a very considerable artist in prose-fiction. Besides this, or with this, his work possesses a penetrating quality, like an animal speaking." So Wyndham Lewis opened his famous (though by now almost unread-

* *A Moveable Feast,* by Ernest Hemingway (New York, 1964).

able) "Dumb Ox" chapter. The animal which speaks, so irresistibly and with such consummate art, is the human subconscious and that is what makes *A Moveable Feast* so entrancing. Not a word is wasted, not an emphasis misplaced; a magical directness flowers in the first sentence: "Then there was the bad weather."

"All of the sadness of the city came suddenly up with the first cold rains of winter." A pause to try if the phrase would have sounded better without the first "of"—surprisingly, it wouldn't. But it is the last pause. Another page and the critical faculty is totally suspended. What a writer!

> It was where Joyce ate with his family then, he and his wife against the wall, Joyce peering at the menu through his thick glasses, holding the menu up in one hand; Nora by him, a hearty but delicate eater; Giorgio thin, foppish, sleek-headed from the back; Lucia with heavy curly hair, a girl not quite yet grown; all of them talking Italian.

Perhaps another writer could put together such a vignette, but certainly only Hemingway could write (of *mutilés de guerre*):

> I watched how well they were overcoming the handicap of the loss of limbs and saw the quality of their artificial eyes and the degree of skill with which their faces had been reconstructed. There was an almost iridescent shiny cast about the considerably reconstructed face, rather like that of a well-packed ski run . . .

One must not think of this as a sentimental, nostalgic book; much of it is about as sentimental as a Mafia-killing. When Hemingway says what he really thinks of someone it becomes a verdict against which there is no appeal. Ford's halitosis, Wyndham Lewis "with the eyes of an unsuccessful rapist," the portraits of Fitzgerald and Gertrude Stein . . . That is how they were, one feels, and they are left utterly devastated. Each fired first, Lewis with his "Ox" essay, Ford with his bumbling criticisms of Hemingway's handling of the *Transatlantic Review,* Stein with her rabbit punches, Fitzgerald with his unconscious patronage and now, from the grave, the coffin lid rises, and on these once malicious dead a dead hand deals the last irrefutable clout.

I have said before that Hemingway's fault was "a sadistic facetiousness with a tendency to sentimentality." This comes out at moments in the book, especially in his puerile remarks on Eliot and his baiting of a nameless homosexual admirer. He is the bully of the Left Bank, always ready to twist the milksop's arm, "Take your dirty camping mouth out of here." ("In those days we did not trust anyone who had not been in the War.") He tells Miss Stein that he had to carry a knife and know how to kill a man in order to protect his virtue from tramps and sailors on Chicago lake boats.

Perhaps he uses his knife too freely. It is sad to contrast Fitzgerald's many friendly references to Hemingway in his letters ("a peach of a man etc."), his efforts to get him more remuneration, his perceptive review of *In Our Time* (republished in *Afternoons of an Author*) with Hemingway's ferocious though not altogether unfriendly portrait. Fitzgerald remarked that he was Hemingway's private drunk even as Ring Lardner was *his* private drunk—but he reckoned without Hemingway's animosity to Zelda, which also rubbed off on him. Sentimentality creeps in as well as sadism.

> "We'll come home and eat here and we'll have a lovely meal and drink Beaune from the co-operative you can see right out of the window there with the price of the Beaune on the window. And afterwards we'll read and then go to bed and make love . . ."
> "And we'll never love anyone else but each other."
> "No, never."

At this point we all listen for our private tumbril. The attack on the rich, however, is perfectly delivered—besides, it is always convenient to blame them.

"Then you have the rich, and nothing is ever as it was again."

Here, for a tail-piece, is how Hemingway describes himself in January 1925 ("It was the year that the rich showed up") in an unpublished letter to Ernest Walsh, who fares so hardly in this book:

> As near as I can find out, I am twenty-seven years old, six feet tall, weigh 182 pounds, born in Oak Park, Illinois, served in war on Italian front, wounded, profession newspaper correspondent . . . Amusements, Boxing, Trout-Fishing, Skiing, and Bull-Fighting. Prefers to do the first three and watch the latter. State of health good. Very fond of eating and drinking. Lives in France for that reason among others. Believes Gertrude Stein to be a great writer. Friend of Ezra Pound. Believes Pound greatest living poet. Believes other great living poets would admit it. Few great poets living. Fond of horse-racing.

(1964)

ERNEST HEMINGWAY: 2

SEVEN hundred pages of authentic Hemingway, weight around 210, blood-pressure on request (watch that diastolic), innumerable illnesses and accidents, four wives, three divorces, two suicides (father and son), battles in three wars, houses amid palm and pine, a lifelong holocaust of animals, birds, fishes in various seas and continents (only the whale got away), about twenty books, innumerable articles, many quarrels, rows, fights, insults, total recall, a physical presence close as the man in the next berth, anecdotes on every level covering some sixty years, and how about another drink? Three scotches before dinner, tequila for the helm, daiquiris in tall frosted glasses, half a dozen beers, good red wine for breakfast (bring me another half-dozen beers), anis, pisco, Chinese wine and Bloody Marys for Christmas morning. How do you like it now, gentlemen? More words than Flaubert, better sales than *Gone with the Wind,* a tommy gun for sharks, six-ounce gloves for critics. "Without exception the most courageous man I have ever known, both in war and peace" (General Lanham).

He described his submarine hunting in the Caribbean and boasted that he had bedded every woman he had ever wanted, and some that he hadn't. He said that his hatred of his mother was non-Freudian, that she was an all-time, all-American bitch, and that the first big psychic wound of his life had come when he discovered that his father was a coward . . .

"Any man who allowed himself to suffer from women," said Ernest, "had a disease as incurable as cancer . . . a man ought to shoot any woman he planned to leave, even if it got him hanged. A less drastic solution would be to get so that no one could hurt you. But by that time, as a rule, you were dead . . ."

His novel was very likely to be a better book than any son of a bitch, alive or dead could write . . . "Am trying to knock Mr. Shakespeare on his ass."

I don't think anyone can get through these seven hundred pages* without a deepening distaste for Hemingway the man. With anecdote piled upon anecdote over some forty years of maturity, even though some of them be trivial or biased, the indictment stands; he was not a nice guy. But it is not as simple as that; in the eyes of many, and over long periods, he was not only nice but a demigod.

He had the gift of leadership, of resolution in a crisis, of intense personal magnetism, "poise and strength—a persuasive and inescapable force of personality," that made him worshipped by what an officer could call his men, but, since he was not an officer, that meant his women, his loaders, his bearers, his beaters, his drivers, his waiters, his head waiters, his barmen, his tackle-makers, gunsmiths, pilots, taxidermists, picadors, boatmen, etc., but with some reservations from his publishers, editors, tailors, colleagues, wives, sons, even his friends. His friendships were full of uncharted reefs, the most durable being with men of action, such as white hunters or professional soldiers, who were specialists in some field which he admired but could not dominate.

Once the demon of competitiveness rose up, his rivalry would destroy the friendship, particularly with sportsmen and other writers (Fitzgerald, Dos Passos, Sherwood Anderson, MacLeish), but he could be kind for a long time to younger and humbler admirers like Hotchner. One should say rather, not a nice man and progressively less so, especially at the end, but, when he chose to be nice, totally irresistible.

He radiated health and wit like Don Giovanni. As a child he wanted to be a king and he became one, with the mysterious aura of a king in exile, determined to excel in all pastimes and cultivate the bloom of giving, but also cruel and capricious, tainted with envy and the terrible American success myth that propels the victim up the steps of the pyramid to where the priests wait to cut out his heart and fling it on the steaming pile.

Most artists have bodies like cheap cars, perfectly adequate to the demands made upon them; Hemingway's was a Rolls-Royce or a Bentley, a Bentley tested to destruction, shabby with dents and scars, yet capable of infinite, elegant endurance.

His prowess as a marksman, as a boxer, as a sailor and swimmer and guerrilla leader were unique among writers; there is no one to compare him with:

> Hurrying into a surgeon's gown and a face-mask, he made the intern probe for a vein, cleared the feed-line of a bottle of plasma, inserted the needle,

* *Ernest Hemingway,* by Carlos Baker (New York, 1969).

and stayed at Mary's side until her pulse resumed, her respiration returned to normal, and the surgeon appeared.

In fact he saved his wife's life, for the intern had already given it up. When one was with him one never wanted to be anywhere else.

Of all modern writers, Hemingway was the most individual, the most ruthlessly hedonistic. He was determined, after his first narrow escape from death in the 1914 War, to live every day as if it were his last, to enjoy the present and extract every ounce of pleasure and excitement from his "one life." Every summer was so much raw material for his body to exploit, every autumn a challenge to write; the winter brought new physical pleasures in the game reserves or the snow. Fish had no close season. Nor had war, and war for Hemingway produced the ideal conditions of danger, camaraderie, feats of endurance and legitimised killing. It got the women reshuffled, too.

Professor Baker does not attempt a literary estimate, he is concerned only with the books through their impact on the life; he is as interested in unfinished, unpublished work like his novel *The Garden of Eden* as in the great set pieces. Yet for the connoisseur in lives who has learnt from many biographies to evaluate the parabola, the trajectory of an artist's life, it is clear that something went out of Hemingway in the early Thirties; Italy and the war, the Paris of the expatriates, Key West, Spain, had provided his undying themes. But not only his art but his life begins to silt up with the return to America and the years of fame. There are too many people, dollars, rows, marlins, retainers, editors and film stars. Life is no longer an adventure but a visitors' book; youth curdles into success.

There were, of course, many summers left, from the summer of the Liberation, to the "dangerous summer," that is to say, the summer particularly dangerous for two rival bull-fighters, Ordoñez and Dominguin ('59); there was Africa and the Spanish War. A truly selective biographer would have pared down the wealth of anecdote and perhaps have given the isolated inner Hemingway more chance to emerge, a man who did try to reconcile the physical life with the life of the artist and very nearly succeeded.

Hemingway alive was not a bore; he knew the virtues of compression and elimination, of leaving the important things unsaid. Now he is dead, he cannot defend himself. The Lilliputian anecdote-makers clamber over him like camel fleas on his shot kudu; the scourge of everything with four feet, two wings, or a dorsal fin is now at the taxidermist on permanent loan.

Professor Baker means well. He supplies a year-by-year chronicle, he avoids moral judgements, his introduction is a brilliant summary of the character as he sees it, he includes a wealth of quotation from Hemingway himself, much of it unpublished, like his letters to Berenson. He does not tone down the unpleasantness, yet the fact that Hemingway was a marvellous writer is never in question.

Several times when reading I felt saturated, that I could not go on any more, only to be clawed, cajoled or hoicked by the hair; the ancient mariner or old man of the sea is off again and one has to follow.

Incidentally, Harry Crosby shot himself in New York, not Paris, the index omits the account of Eric Dorman-Smith on pages 79 and 81, Duff Twysden was Lady Twysden not Lady Duff Twysden (page 183). The Davises home, "La Cónsula," is near Churriana, not Coin.

The last agonising year of Hemingway, who was never the same after his crash in Uganda, is better described by Hotchner. The paranoia and depression which drove him to take his own life were implicit in early youth, despite his romantic defiance of death and age. *"Mens morbida in corpore sano,"* wrote his Russian translator.

(1969)

A FITZGERALD ENTERTAINMENT

I THOUGHT I had reached saturation point about Scott Fitzgerald. He is becoming an American imposition and I am beginning to want to deny him his pinch of incense, to refuse to sacrifice at his altar. I never want to read about another alcoholic; alcoholism is the enemy of art, and the curse of Western civilisation. It is neither poetic nor amusing. I am not referring to people getting drunk, but to the gradual bloating of the sensibilities and the destruction of personal relationships involved in such long-drawn-out social suicide. The greater the artist, the deadlier the process. "There was a terrible deliberateness about the way Fitzgerald dosed himself with gin."

However, Mr. Turnbull knew Fitzgerald when he was a small boy, and the Fitzgeralds were his father's tenants on their estate outside Baltimore. (Fitzgerald was one of nature's Baltimoreans.) He developed a cult for him, and is besides a professional writer so that the result is a most sympathetic and entertaining volume* worthy of all that the Bodley Head are doing for Fitzgerald. Mr. Turnbull concentrates on the man and does not provide a critical exegesis of all the novels and stories.

Besides reading all the documents, he seems to have interviewed all the surviving friends. This gives added freshness, for not only does he revere Fitzgerald but he admires and tries to understand Zelda. He does not accept the Hemingway view that she was bent on ruining Scott out of envy and ran up bills to force him to write worse stories. The whole harrowing tale is retold from the beginning to Fitzgerald's pathetic funeral, aged forty-four, and Zelda's horrible death by fire in her asylum three years later.

I am also an admirer of Professor Mizener's biography of Fitzgerald

* *Scott Fitzgerald,* by Andrew Turnbull (New York, 1962).

(*The Far Side of Paradise* published ten years ago by Eyre & Spottiswoode) and I wondered how Mr. Turnbull would manage with so much of the spade-work already done for him. I would have expected a stream of references to Mizener's work but there is only one, tucked away in small print among the notes at the end. "Among previous books on Fitzgerald the most useful for my purposes were Sheilah Graham's memoir *Beloved Infidel* and Arthur Mizener's pioneering biography, *The Far Side of Paradise.*"

Both draw extensively on Fitzgerald's daughter, Miss Lanahan, Harold Ober (Fitzgerald's agent), the Murphys and Mr. Turnbull's mother, and of course from Fitzgerald's own copious archive, but Professor Mizener is more sympathetic to Hemingway and Budd Schulberg and Edmund Wilson. Mr. Henry Piper and Judge Biggs are also common to both. I found in many anecdotes they run neck and neck. Sometimes there are differences. Here are two examples. Mizener's account of the first Fitzgerald-Hemingway quarrel over Fitzgerald's time-keeping in the fight with Morley Callaghan is more full and accurate than Turnbull's, and he gives three different sources. Turnbull, on the other hand, is better on the earth-shaking tea-party with Edith Wharton. Here is Professor Mizener:

"Mrs. Wharton," Fitzgerald demanded, "do you know what is the matter with you?"

"No, Mr. Fitzgerald. I've often wondered about that. What is it?"

"You don't know anything about life," Fitzgerald roared and then, determined to shock and impress them—"Why, when my wife and I first came to Paris, we took a room in a bordello. And we lived there for two weeks."

After a moment's pause, Mrs. Wharton, seeming to realize from his expression how baffled Fitzgerald was, tried to help him.

"But Mr. Fitzgerald," she said, "you haven't told us what they did in the bordello."

At first when Zelda asked him how it had gone he answered her that it had been a great success, they had liked him, he had bowled them over. But gradually the truth came out, until—after several drinks—Fitzgerald put his head on his arms and began to pound the table with his fists.

"They beat me," he said. "They beat me! They *beat* me!"

["I owe this anecdote to a careful note of it by Mr. Robert Chapman immediately after hearing it from Richard Knight," notes the Professor.]

And Mr. Turnbull:

Arrived at the Pavillon Colombe, Fitzgerald and Chanler were ushered into a salon where Mrs. Wharton, the confidante of Henry James, sat behind her tea-set in shy majesty. There was one other guest, an American-born Cambridge don named Gaillard Lapsley . . . Since Chanler and Lapsley were unable to break the ice, Fitzgerald descended to such platitudes as "Mrs. Wharton, you have no idea what it means to me to come out here!" Finally, in desperation, he suggested telling "a couple of—er—rather rough stories."

Permission having been granted by a queenly nod and a smile, he began one and switched to another about an American couple who had spent three days in a Paris bordello, which they mistook for a hotel. As he faltered to a conclusion, Mrs. Wharton said "But Mr. Fitzgerald, your story lacks data"—whereupon he tried to patch it up without success . . . Mrs. Wharton wrote "Horrible" beside his name in her diary. ["I have described the encounter between Fitzgerald and Edith Wharton," notes Mr. Turnbull, "as it was told me by Theodore Chanler, who was there."]

I am myself undertaking a brief thesis of one hundred thousand words for the literary department of the University of Spittoon on the great bordello controversy and would welcome any further information on it. What did Lapsley think? What did Mrs. Wharton really say?

(1966)

Scott Fitzgerald and Edith Wharton

(to the *Times Literary Supplement*)

Sir,

There has been some comment on a discrepancy between the version of an anecdote about Scott Fitzgerald and Edith Wharton that appears in my *Far Side of Paradise,* Revised Edition, pages 202–203 and the version that appears in Mr. Andrew Turnbull's *Scott Fitzgerald,* pages 153–154. I am happy therefore to have the permission of Mr. Roderick Coupe to send you a copy of a letter about this occasion that he wrote Cyril Connolly when Mr. Connolly commented on the discrepancy between my version and Mr. Turnbull's.

44 Rue du Bac,
Paris, 7

Dear Mr. Connolly—

I have just been reading your piece on Scott Fitzgerald in *Previous Convictions.* As concerns Edith Wharton and "the great bordello controversy" Professor Mizener's version is much more accurate than Mr. Turnbull's. Esther Arthur (Gerald Murphy's sister and John Strachey's ex-wife) and not Theodore Chanler accompanied Fitzgerald to the famous luncheon at Pavillon Colombe. I have heard her version of it many times and I couldn't possibly do her justice in retelling it but it went something like this:

Fitzgerald, terrified of the impending meeting with Mrs. Wharton, had gone on the wagon a week before and naturally fell off the night before. Zelda declined at the last minute unable to face it, and Esther drove off with Scott. The latter, she said, stopped in every cafe en route throwing down innumerable mahogany brandies and they arrived an hour late. There were twelve or fifteen to lunch, Paul Claudel, lots of blue-stocking French duchesses (do they still exist?), Fitzgerald and Esther. Mrs. Wharton put Fitzgerald on her right—as étranger and guest of honour. The bordello dialogue then ensued. Fitzgerald also became ill and was taken into another room by Walter Berry, who according to Esther, behaved impeccably (probably his snobbish American side coming out), smoothing things over. [Oh, also, Claudel, as E was about to raise a glass of Pouilly fumé to her parched lips, said in a not too inaudible voice: "Que les Américains boivent."] Fitzgerald pulled himself together sufficiently at the end but in the car returning to Paris he collapsed in tearful rage: "They beat me."

Yours sincerely,
Roderick Coupe

13 July
1964

Something at least of what Mrs. Wharton thought about all this can be deduced from her treatment of Vance Weston in *Hudson River Bracketed*. Much of Vance comes from elsewhere, of course, but the pastless middle-westerner with the vivid imagination owes a good deal to Fitzgerald; Mrs. Wharton as good as says so when she refers to Fitzgerald in Chapter XXXII.

Arthur Mizener
Department of English,
Cornell University,
Ithaca, New York

167 Brattle St.
Cambridge, Mass.
September 19, 1966

Dear Mr. Connolly:

You may have seen Arthur Mizener's letter in the *Times Literary Supplement* of July 7, 1966 in which he quotes Roderick Coupe's letter to you saying that Mizener's version of Scott Fitzgerald's encounter with Edith Wharton is more accurate than mine. I have decided to answer

Mizener and enclose a copy of my reply. Perhaps you may feel that it vindicates your original statement on this matter in your review of my biography, *Scott Fitzgerald.*

Sincerely yours,
Andrew Turnbull

167 Brattle St.
Cambridge, Mass.
September 19, 1966

To the Editor
The Times Literary Supplement
The Times Publishing Co. Ltd.
Printing House Square
London, EC4
England

Sir,
I have read with interest Mr. Arthur Mizener's letter which appeared in your issue of July 7, 1966, concerning the discrepancy between his version of Scott Fitzgerald's visit to Edith Wharton (*The Far Side of Paradise,* Revised Edition, pages 202–203) and my version (*Scott Fitzgerald,* pages 153–154). I would like to explain why I believe mine to be the definitive version of this celebrated rencontre.

Mine was told me by Theodore Chanler, the composer-son of Mrs. Wharton's close friend, Margaret Winthrop Chanler. The first time I interviewed Mr. Chanler he said it was he and not Esther Arthur, as some people seemed to think, who drove Fitzgerald to the Pavillon Colombe one afternoon in the spring of 1925. I see no reason to doubt Mr. Chanler's word.

He said that immediately after he returned to Paris from the Pavillon Colombe he reported to Mrs. Arthur what had occurred. Mrs. Arthur, a gifted and witty raconteur—a "trumpeting monologuist" as Thornton Wilder once described her—was also known for drawing a long bow and embroidering the truth to make a better story. It seems likely that the version which she told Mr. Roderick Coupe, and which Mr. Mizener cited in his letter as reinforcing *his* version, was Mrs. Arthur's "treatment" of what Chanler had told her. She evidently allowed others to think that she had accompanied Fitzgerald and may have come to believe it herself after telling the story a great many times. But she did not tell me so during my two lengthy interviews with her the fall of 1959. I do remember her mentioning a luncheon where Fitzgerald had come up against some French intellectuals—Claudel, Bourget, and others—but Mrs. Wharton was not of the party. Mr. Coupe, in his recollection of what Mrs. Arthur told him, seems to have telescoped these two separate occasions.

It is my understanding that Mr. Mizener never wrote or interviewed Mr. Chanler or Mrs. Arthur. According to a footnote in *The Far Side of Paradise* he got his version from "Robert Chapman who made a note of it immediately after hearing it from Richard Knight" who probably heard it from Fitzgerald's wife, so Mr. Mizener thinks.

In May, 1959, to make sure I had Mr. Chanler's version straight, I sent him a transcript of Mr. Mizener's version about which Mr. Chanler wrote me as follows:

> Thank you for showing me Mizener's account of the Wharton visit. It shocked me somewhat less than when I first read it years ago when the only thing that stood out for me was the gross mistake of representing Fitzgerald as having been cocky on this occasion. He was, as I have told you, anything but. He fawned and flattered and made himself as well as everyone else acutely uncomfortable. The only other guest was Gaillard Lapsley, an American-born Cambridge don who, being a don, knew what was the matter with Fitzgerald, whereas Mrs. Wharton couldn't make it out at all. Fitzgerald never of course said "Do you know what's the matter with you?" to her. But the flow of talk kept stopping up (Lapsley never opened his mouth) and in one of the embarrassed pauses Fitzgerald in desperation suggested telling "a couple of—er—rather rough stories." (Permission to do so was granted by a queenly nod of the head, a fixed imperturable smile.) But even this I don't think Fitzgerald did with the kind of aggressive intent that Mizener ascribes to him. It was just *anything* to start the ball rolling. Nor was it he and Zelda who stayed at the bordello (which doesn't sound at all probable anyway) but some couple he did not name. Fitzgerald did not "flee" after Mrs. Wharton's mordant comment. On the contrary, it passed right over his head and he started humorlessly and clumsily to try to answer it—he was possibly too thoroughly anesthetized by alcohol to have felt the shaft.
>
> Otherwise Mizener's account is approximately correct; though the business with Zelda afterwards—who reported *that?*—and his "They beat me! They beat me!" sounds like a bit of cheap dramatizing. Fitzgerald knew the occasion had been a fiasco but I doubt if he took it as a personal one. Mrs. Wharton was socially so shy and ill at ease with new people that it would have been only natural to put a good share of the blame for it on her. Esther [Arthur's] elegant epigram asserting that "Mrs. Wharton has the grand manner that triumphs over a situation where another woman's might save it" was, in this connection, Esther's comment on *her* equally unsatisfactory call on the great lady. It might have been Fitzgerald's so far as his reaction went.

In April, 1961, two months before his death, I sent Mr. Chanler the description of this incident which appears in my *Scott Fitzgerald,* and he gave it his entire approval save for one adjective which I deleted before the biography went to press.

Andrew Turnbull

F. SCOTT FITZGERALD

WHAT is the book that takes a lifetime to write and which the author will never read? His collected letters. I have now reviewed those of Joyce, Pound, Yeats, Wilde, Lawrence, Lewis and Thomas Wolfe, and feel like one who watches at a glacier, and sees a whole man pass every few months, complete with friends and family, faults and foibles, talents and tantrums, then as suddenly crumble away.

Now it is Fitzgerald's turn and soon, I hope, it will be Hemingway's. When one has known the writer, there is a sensation of eavesdropping, of prying into friendships from which one was excluded, but Scott Fitzgerald is surprisingly remote—was remote even in his lifetime, perhaps because he came only once to England and because the last years of his life were passed far away from literary circles.

I think if one knew him only through these letters* one would be conscious of an enigma. The missing item is, of course, alcoholism, for he seldom refers to its effects on his work or his friendships or even his finances, though constantly mentioning that he is on the wagon. As early as 1922 he asks Edmund Wilson not to refer to it; already its shadow has fallen across the sun of that stupendous early success. One of the tragedies of alcoholism is that, while it destroys dignity and self-respect in the personal relationships of the addict, the personality somehow continues to ripen and develop beneath the addiction and to demand its legitimate expression.

> I am not a great man, but sometimes I think the impersonal and objective quality of my talent and the sacrifices of it, in pieces, to preserve its essential value, has some sort of epic grandeur . . .

* *The Letters of F. Scott Fitzgerald,* edited by Andrew Turnbull (New York, 1963).

> I am too much a moralist at heart and really want to preach at people in some acceptable form rather than to entertain them.

In the last four years of his short life Fitzgerald, self-exiled to Hollywood, had only his daughter on whom he could exercise responsibility and to whom he could release the pent-up wisdom and experience of the man within. The result is one of the strangest sequences in literature, fit to rank beside Halifax's *Advice to a Daughter,* or Lord Chesterfield's *Letters.* "You are a poor girl, and if you don't like to think about it, just ask me."

Applying what he had learnt at Princeton to his daughter's career at Vassar, he dispenses worldly wisdom, pocket-money and literary advice, his accumulated bitterness brimming over, as if he were writing to a son. Coming as it does at the start of this volume this sombre colloquy of a sick, bitter, extremely perceptive parent with his one satisfactory link with the future (his wife during this time was in a mental home) gives no idea of the light-hearted chapters to follow. "In my end is my beginning."

The arrangement of letters always presents a problem. Should it be chronological or should it be listed under the recipients? Mr. Turnbull has chosen the latter method, and from the letters to his daughter we pass on to those to his wife, his publisher, his agent, and his literary friends—Hemingway, Wilson, Bishop, etc.—winding up with a miscellaneous collection which contains some of the most interesting pages. Fitzgerald was a natural letter-writer, no genius like Yeats or Lawrence, but with a fresh incisive spontaneity and a way of keeping to the point. He does not rant and orate like Pound or Wolfe, or bumble like a trapped wasp like Lewis or wear a mask like Joyce. He casts a cold eye.

You will enormously enjoy his letters. They show him as suddenly maturing around 1925 with the first summer in the South of France, the appearance and success of *The Great Gatsby* (fortunately not in the end called "Trimalchio" or "Gold-hatted Gatsby"), the emergent competitiveness of Zelda, and the friendship with the Murphys—a friendship much criticised at the time, for the Murphys were rich, but which proved to be one of the most lasting of his life. Before this *annus mirabilis* his letters are delightful but typical of any brilliant youthful charmer suddenly become a best-seller (he names Michael Arlen his successor!).

By far the most rewarding group of letters are those to his publisher, Maxwell Perkins of Scribners, a name also immortally involved with Wolfe and Hemingway. Here too one can watch the emergence of Hemingway:

This is to tell you (1924) about a young man named Ernest Hemingway who lives in Paris (an American), writes for the *Transatlantic Review* and has a brilliant future . . . He's the real thing.

Further letters throw light on the way Hemingway was able to break his contract with Boni and Liveright by presenting them with a book which they could not publish, a parody of their own favourite author, Sherwood Anderson.

It is *biting* on Anderson—so Liveright turns it down. Hemingway's contract *lapses when Liveright turns down a book, so Hemingway says.* But I think Horace will claim this isn't a book (it was only 28,000 words) and fight it like the devil, because he's crazy to get Ernest's almost completed novel *The Sun Also Rises* . . . Meanwhile Harcourt and Knopf are after him . . . You won't be able to help liking him, he's one of the nicest fellows I ever knew. I'll tip you off the moment he arrives. (1926)

Disillusion is not far away. "There has always been a subtle struggle between Ernest and Zelda." "You haven't been in the publishing business for twenty years without noticing the streaks of smallness in very large personalities." "He is quite as nervously broken down as I am!" In 1936 came Hemingway's slighting reference to him in the *Snows of Kilimanjaro,* which Fitzgerald never got over, even as he never got over his admiration for Hemingway's style and intensity of feeling or his personal courage, though he held no brief for *For Whom the Bell Tolls.* It is also as well that he never read Hemingway's chapter in *A Moveable Feast* since he blissfully refers to his trip from Lyon with Hemingway as a success. But the great interest of the letters to Perkins is in what they reveal of the writing of *The Great Gatsby* and *Tender Is the Night.* I was impressed by Fitzgerald's comment on the latter.

Its great fault is that the *true* beginning—the young psychiatrist in Switzerland—is tucked away in the middle of the book. If pages 151–212 were taken from their present place and put at the start, the improvement in appeal would be enormous.

The alteration has since been made, at least in one edition, but it is not an improvement. The original beginning is one of the most worked-over passages Fitzgerald wrote, a magical piece of writing which sets the mood for all the rest. The true chronological beginning comes in the slipshod weary style of the latter part of the novel which Fitzgerald admits to have written "entirely on stimulants."

Once again I am forced to the conclusion that Fitzgerald is overrated as a writer, that his importance, apart from *Gatsby* and a few stories, lies in his personality as the epitome of a historical moment. That is why one would always rather read his letters (which imply other desirable letters by the Paris expatriates of the post-war movement) rather than the correspondence of greater novelists like Faulkner or poets like Frost and Stevens. One likes to hear what he thought about everything, but he thought tantalisingly little.

Of course any apologia is necessarily a whine to some extent; a man digs his own grave and should, presumably, lie in it, and I know that the fault for this goes back to those years, which were really years of self-indulgence . . .

A whole lot of people have found life a whole lot of fun. I have not found it so. But I have had a hell of a lot of fun when I was in my twenties and thirties . . .

It was fun when we all believed the same things. It was more fun to think we were all going to die together or live together, and none of us anticipated this great loneliness . . .

(1964)

SCOTT AND ZELDA FITZGERALD

ERNEST scrawled a thank-you note to Scott and Zelda. He was more than ever convinced of what he had recently told Max Perkins—that Zelda was her husband's evil demon" (1928). "Zelda must die" (1933). A charge to which he returned again and again, and which plays an integral part in the Fitzgerald myth.

Mrs. Milford* would not agree. She feels it was the other way round, and she has had access to the later correspondence from Zelda to Scott, which was believed lost. She has also interviewed all the Fitzgerald circle including the Murphys and the first Mrs. Hemingway. Zelda disliked Hemingway from the start and called him "bogus." "He's a pain in the neck, talking about me and borrowing money from you while he does it. He's phony as a rubber check and you know it."

I have written so many times about the Fitzgeralds that I can hardly bear to grapple with the tragedy again when the revolving doors whirl and once more precipitate the two talented self-destroyers, drunk and garlanded, into my lap. Surprise, surprise, it's us! And a high kick from her sends his opera hat flying. "Save me the schmaltz," he cracks back and soon she is sitting on her trunk on the sidewalk, altogether elsewhere.

This definitive biography is precisely documented. Mrs. Milford writes with understanding and sympathy, retells the oft-told story and includes new evidence from her letters and her doctors. "I made one of those mistakes that literary men make," wrote Scott to Zelda. "I thought I was a man of the world, that everybody liked me and admired me for myself . . . I remember wondering why I kept working to pay the bills of this desolate ménage I had evolved."

* *Zelda,* by Nancy Milford (New York, 1970).

Things were always the same. The apartments that were rotten, the maids that stank . . . ("Well if you want a better apartment why don't you make some money . . .")

> You were going crazy and calling it genius [he wrote]. I was going to ruin and calling it anything that came to hand. And I think everyone far enough away to see us outside our glib presentations of ourselves guessed at your almost megalomaniacal selfishness and my insane indulgence in drink. We ruined ourselves . . . I have never honestly thought that we ruined each other.

And Zelda replies from the clinic:

> You will have all the things you want without me. You will have some nice girl . . . For us there is not the slightest use . . . Blame does not matter. Try to understand that people are not always reasonable when the world is as unstable and vacillating as a sick head can render it . . . I was semi-imbecile when I arrived here.

Mrs. Milford quotes Zelda's accusation that Scott was homosexual and having an affair with Hemingway. Several months later Robert McAlmon told Hemingway that Scott was a homosexual. Hemingway passed this on and Fitzgerald reacted strongly. When Zelda returned to the charge, in the Rue Palatine, Fitzgerald threatened to leave her. One cannot help feeling that all these writers of the Twenties, Hemingway, Fitzgerald, Lawrence, were too busy leaning over backwards to deny traces of an element which nowadays would have needed less excusing.

This is the third time Zelda's novel* has been published. It first appeared in America in 1932, then in London (Greywalls Press, 1953) and now having failed with the Thirties, Forties and Fifties, it is being tried on the Sixties. The tenacity of this by-product of the Fitzgerald myth and genius must have some justification, like the paintings by a painter's wife or the snapshots from a photographer's consort. Has it more than documentary value?

At first I thought not. The early purple passages are like a knife scraping on a plate. But in telling her story the novelist grows up. Europe seasons her, marriage refines her, we take leave with affection and sorrow of the character whom we detested when she first pranced into the room. We will save her Gatsby's "neat sad waltz" much as we dislike waltzing.

I first heard of Zelda in the early Thirties from Joe Hergesheimer, a friend of my wife's family. Joe, with his round frog face and gravel voice, his suède polo coat from Charvet (one hundred dollars, then an

* *Save Me the Waltz,* by Zelda Fitzgerald (Carbondale, Ill., 1967).

enormous sum), was the picture of the successful novelist, and like most successful novelists inordinately vain and consequently envious.

One day he was going through his rivals with us, dismissing them as being no danger to the author of *Three Black Pennys* and *Java Head.* "Scott Fitzgerald?" I asked Joe. "A nice chap—and *Gatsby*'s a good book—but poor Scott—he's finished. He's married to Zelda and Zelda's a very deleterious woman."

The effect on me was electric. I wanted a deleterious woman, too, for I could not imagine her otherwise than as a *femme fatale* spurring one to death through sexual exhaustion. "Zelda" suggested a languid Baudelairean night-hag. When I saw her picture I was deeply disappointed: she was pretty and vivacious; in fact her self-portrait on this jacket is astonishingly like Melinda Maclean's. It was Hemingway who explained that her harmfulness lay in her extravagance. "Zelda was constantly making him drink because she was jealous of him working well," he wrote, looking back. "Money went through her fingers like water," said Scott's publisher, "she wanted everything; she kept him writing for the magazines."

Zelda was in fact the worst form of wife, the Hostile Witness, the "Anything you can do I can do better (except provide for me)," a classic case of penis envy. She was Pasteurella Pestis as a Southern Belle. And Scott was neurotically dependent on her, the worst combination.

Despite his great abilities and his popularity it was only her approval that counted. She had refused him when he had no money and accepted him only after the success of *This Side of Paradise* in 1920. She came from Montgomery, Alabama, where her father Judge Sayre was highly respected. Marriage to such women is a rehearsal for suicide; in a parasitic interdependence, infidelity is only skin-deep and alters nothing, except the content of the indictment. And no one has suggested that the Fitzgeralds really loved anyone but each other or hurt anyone but themselves. Her novel unwittingly reveals "Alabama's" insensibility to both her parents and her daughter which is typical of the egomaniac and there is only the sketchiest understanding of "David" himself, who is seconded from novel-writing to decorative painting: "You heard his name in bank lobbies and the Ritz Bar." He seems only visible in his own right in the courtship scenes.

Zelda's story must be told in brief. She met Scott when she was eighteen and he twenty-one (he was posted South) and they were married in 1920. By the time they reached Europe via New York they were already drinking heavily, jumping into fountains, stripping on café tables, fighting in public. They had a villa near St. Raphael where Zelda had an affair with a French airman. "Eager to match her husband's celebrity" (i.e., eager to castrate everything but his cheque-book), Zelda took up painting, wrote a little, then tried desperately to become a dancer . . . Scott was now a confirmed alcoholic and Zelda had developed schizophrenia . . . She wrote *Save Me the Waltz* in six weeks (1932) while he was working on *Tender Is the Night*; her last years were spent in various sanatoriums; in one of which in 1947 she was burnt to death.

Much of her book runs parallel with *Tender Is the Night*. It is unfortunate that we do not know what it was like before Fitzgerald removed some of her worst digs. In her account of the affair with the French airman it is left unclear if intercourse takes place; while Fitzgerald's account leads up to one of the most moving rejection-scenes in modern literature. At first Zelda seems steeped in the Firbankian hit-or-miss impressionist method with a fashionable eye for expensive accessories; yet her glimpses of Southern scenery and later of the South of France in summer are authentic; so is her psychology where she herself is concerned.

Like many married couples the Fitzgeralds committed the sin for which there is no forgiveness. They outgrew each other. This makes the last half of the book—the part which describes Zelda's search for self-realisation and independence through the ballet—the most interesting. Scott's biographers dismiss her ballet ambitions curtly, as an alcoholic diversion; it is clear that she took them intensely seriously and the result is an excellent account of the Diaghilev ensemble in the late Twenties (period of *La Chatte*) and of her struggles to outdo yet get on well with her professional colleagues. From here to the end is a good novel, even as the Paris parties and Riviera infidelities also make good reading.

After finishing the book one can see what Fitzgerald must have found in her—an indispensable gaiety and quality of mind, a lightness of touch he could not get elsewhere and without which the life of pleasure revealed only the crass and sordid. When exhibitionist pairs with exhibitionist the resulting works of art are few indeed; "all olive-brine and wood-ash" like the ship's bar in Zelda's storm at sea. Yet over nine years Fitzgerald wrote seventeen drafts of her epitaph, *Tender Is the Night,* and she too was capable of patient craftsmanship and some tragic intuitions even while her mind was going. *Brevis hic est fructus homullis,* as Lucretius makes his roisterers exclaim.

O moon of Alabama
We now must say good-bye.

(1969)

THOMAS WOLFE

How can one write the life* of someone who was larger than life—and who earned his living by writing his life? Wolfe put it into his novels, then into his letters (usually about his novels), then into *The Story of a Novel* and the remainder into drink and conversation. He was larger than life and somehow flatter than life; a giant writing-machine with considerable metal fatigue (expressed as persecution mania), but, given the right breakfast (one dozen eggs, two quarts of milk, a loaf of bread), he could average ten thousand words a day.

He also kept a diary. "He would get up in the middle of the night," he wrote,

> to scrawl down insane catalogues of all that he had seen and done . . . the number of people he had known, the number of women he had slept with, the number of meals he had eaten, the number of towns he had visited, the number of states he had been in . . . Then he would begin another list full of enormous catalogues of all the books he had not read, all the food he had not eaten, all the women he had not slept with, all the states he had not been in, all the towns he had not visited.

Some of these lists are still to be found among Wolfe's papers, symptoms of the compulsive hunger which he brought into the subtitle for *Of Time and the River*. The six-foot-six romantic was prepared literally to destroy himself by writing, and his early death from tuberculosis of the brain was due partly to overwork, partly to alcohol and the total neglect of his health.

It is possible to maintain that he was no good, and I notice large tracts of silence about him in the best critics of his time, for example Mr. Edmund Wilson. He himself loathed adverse criticism, and sophisti-

* *Thomas Wolfe: A Biography,* by Elizabeth Nowell (Garden City, N.Y., 1960).

cated expatriates (except Joyce), and he loved to pull out all the loudest stops on the American organ, though he came to Europe seven times in eleven years.

But somehow the assumption that he was no good does not fit the facts: it is like saying the Ancient Mariner was a bore. So what? He held his audience. And Thomas Wolfe holds his audience, he communicates his hunger, his own brand of romantic egomania—perhaps because he is young—even as Mr. Henry Miller, another compulsive egoist, often fails to communicate because he is not so young, and therefore stands back to admire his own effects.

It is better to assume that Wolfe was a genius, and after reading Miss Nowell's excellent biography I retract my description of him as a young man "who looked like a genius but had nothing but talent," which I used in reviewing her equally excellent edition of his letters. Talent heated by so much vocational energy becomes genius.

Wolfe was a Balzac, a Tolstoy, a Dickens who remained in the larval, provincial-adolescent stage. In this stage he could not see other people except through the blurred lens of his own emotional conflict: he sought a mother and a father, and thought he had found one in Faulkner. But he belongs in their company. Of course he blamed others, and was an adept at a kind of humourless self-pity with a sting in its tail.

> In Christ's name, Max, what is wrong with us in America? The whole world—not myself alone—wants to know. The English ask me, everyone asks me, why do we cry out that what we want is life, and then try to destroy and kill the best people that we have? Why do our best writers, poets, men of talent turn into drunkards, dipsomaniacs, charlatans, cocktail-cliquers, creatures of Pop-eye horrors, pederasts, macabre distortions, etc? I tell you it is not I alone who ask the question, but everyone here—all Europe knows it. Why is it that we are burnt out to an empty shell by the time we are forty . . . Men in England also ask me, they all want to know. And then how easy for them all, when we *are* done for—when we have been driven mad, when we are drunkards, dipsomaniacs, perverts, charlatans, burnt-out-shells—how easy it is for the whole pack to pull the face of pious regret, to sigh mournfully, to say "what a pity! We had hoped once—He looked so promising at one time! What a shame he had to go and waste it all!"

I have left out two more pages of invective and one long paragraph in the middle, and I wish I had space to compare it with a similar diatribe by Hemingway in *Green Hills of Africa* beginning:

> We do not have great writers. Something happens to our good writers at a certain age. You see we make our writers into something very strange, we destroy them in many ways.

It will be seen that Wolfe slips quickly into a they-we mood: "they" are the majority, the public, the expatriates, the critics: "we" are the little band of doomed writers—reduced in the last sentence to "he." But "he" does not stand alone: he has the whole of England indignantly behind him; all Europe has a right to know. I have said before that his diatribes are almost Hitlerian. Hemingway, on the other hand, uses "we" alone to include both the public and the writers, the hunters and the hunted. There is no hysteria. And notice the youthfulness of Wolfe's style, the strange assumption that an unfavourable review can turn one into a pederast or pervert.

His audience, he was convinced, was always longing for his disgrace. First his neighbours in Asheville, next his colleagues in the university where he taught, then the critics, the "Hemingways, Fadimans, Waste-Landers—their idea of helping you is to kick you in the face," and finally betrayal from within, when even his publisher *"unconsciously* by some kind of *wishful* desire wants me to come to grief." When one wants to fail as much as that it can usually be arranged.

The central drama of Wolfe's whole life was his relationship with Maxwell Perkins. It is unnecessary to point out that American publishers are a dedicated group: they are loyal, generous and infinitely painstaking, they live for their authors and not for social climbing or the books they want to write themselves; they know how to be confessors, solicitors, auditors and witch-doctors, and Maxwell Perkins was all of these, combining patience, taste, industry and unselfish understanding.

He was forced practically to adopt Wolfe and for years they struggled with *Of Time and the River* after he had published *Look Homeward Angel*. The book was far too long and as fast as he and Wolfe could cut it in their evening sessions, the human writing-machine would turn out ten thousand words more. The situation was driving both of them mad and when Wolfe was off on one of his trips Perkins took the unprecedented step of "taking the book away from him"—i.e., sending it to the printers rather than waiting for that extra six months which Wolfe was always demanding.

"There are limitations of time, of space, and of human laws which cannot be treated as if they did not exist," wrote Perkins in desperation. His action was justified. The book was a complete success—but Wolfe's publicly expressed gratitude for Perkins's share caused some critics, particularly Bernard de Voto, to sneer and talk about "the Scribner assembly-line" and suggest that it was Perkins who had supplied the real genius.

Although this was at once disclaimed, Wolfe's subconscious grabbed the straw and began to distil its own poison. Why cut books? Nobody cuts large pictures, or said to Rubens or Veronese, "You don't need this, old boy—much too much of that"—slash—"out she comes—you'll be better for it in the end etc.," he joked in his diary at the National Gallery.

But the harm was done, and, after protracted wrangling and increasing bitterness ending in a fist-fight, the pilot was dropped. Without a publisher Wolfe was helpless as a young cuckoo. Who would provide the requisite gesture of faith and love? A young editor from Harpers offered spontaneously an immediate advance of ten thousand dollars on the next book unseen. It was the miracle Wolfe wanted and by another miracle Saxton and Cass Canfield, "two good publishers, and great gentlemen," backed up their young editor. Wolfe survived a year and left his new firm with three more books.

(1961)

E. E. CUMMINGS

MR. CUMMINGS is now sixty-five, and entitled to a full-dress biography.* He is, however, one of those baffling subjects who live entirely for their vocation, to whom nothing happens for many years at a time and to whom whatever does happen—being imprisoned in France or visiting Russia—goes straight into autobiography; he is one of the wily ones, he has cheated time, and therefore eludes his biographer who must content himself with quoting reviews and analysing books of poems. I imagine a life of Robert Frost or Walter de la Mare would present the same problem. It is, of course, the right way for an artist to live.

But the nature of Cummings's genius also offers little scope to the biographer for he was and is a lyric poet (and also a lyric painter) who never writes long poems and who never strays from his personal theme. For forty-five years he has been writing about the moon, about love and spring and snow and prostitutes and politicians—"man's mighty briefness." He is closer to a Chinese poet or a Greek epigrammatist or a troubadour than to a modern bard. He develops, but internally, like a gem-cutter, through greater precision or deeper charity and has now discarded many of his typographical eye-twisters.

Typography, I feel, was a false trail and responsible for much unnecessary grittiness in his work. Poetry is surely meant to be recited, in silence perhaps, but not to be expressed by the shape of the printed word. Cummings achieves many effects by a sparse use of his typographical invention, as a means to point emphasis, reveal allusions, destroy cliché or bring it out by droll spelling, but in some books, like

* *The Magic-Maker, E. E. Cummings,* by Charles Norman (New York, 1959).

No Thanks, his feverish distortions and deformations of the Word appear compulsive. It would be possible to argue that Mr. Cummings is a neurotic who has been treating himself quite successfully for the past fifty years, and whose passionate belief in the freedom and integrity of the individual is a form of self-protection, the cone of smoke hanging above what had been a violent adolescent eruption.

Mr. Norman is an utterly devoted and pious eager-beaver of a biographer; he even seems to be photographed in the same tie and pipe on the back jacket as his hero sports on the front; he records only the sunny hours and takes most things for granted. But some of what he tells us is very strange. The clue is the poet's father, the Reverend Dr. Cummings, the most famous Unitarian minister in Boston, and master of many other crafts and skills. "This son of a famous minister," Malcolm Cowley tells us, "was in revolt against ministerial standards, so that his father's car, with its clergyman's license plates, was found parked outside a famous joint near Scollay Square, to the embarrassment of the Boston police."

This situation foreshadows the far greater embarrassment a few years later when Cummings and his friend Brown, another rebel New Englander, were in France with an American ambulance unit. Brown sent some mildly defeatist letters home, but the French censorship took a serious view and both were arrested. A word would have saved Cummings, who had written nothing, but he would not give it and preferred to be interned with his more violent friend; this caused the Reverend Dr. Cummings practically to initiate an international upheaval (he even appealed to the President) before his son was released. In gratitude the son sat down—or was made to sit down—and write *The Enormous Room.*

Cummings, of course, adored his father, as his famous poem "My father moved through dooms of love" was to prove—but he also belonged to that heady and rebellious generation whose coming-of-age celebrations began in the trenches and ended after Prohibition in America or many riotous Quatorze Juillets in France. He was part of the great American overthrow of nineteenth-century convention and provincialism. Thus as an undergraduate his poetry had already revealed his divided nature: many of his early poems are languorous evocations of Keats and Swinburne and one in this vein ("All in green went my love riding") is particularly successful.

But there is also a vein of erotic realism, owing something to "Prufrock" and Pound, which yet emerges in complete mastery of the sonnet form and the *objets trouvés* of American low life. It was these poems which enraptured Harry Crosby and so many others, including myself—

séduisants climats, when the poet's own youth coincided with the youth of the liberated world.

Some of these last poems are so dry and metallic that Mr. Cummings seems to be setting up as a verse Hemingway, but the romantic vein is never far away. And he is also a metaphysical poet with a talent for asking himself unanswerable questions, and a turn for vitriolic abuse.

But poets who follow a profession can be as forceful as those who, like Cummings, insist on living a poetical life and who perhaps dissipate some of their energy in the daily celebration of beautiful things. Back in 1923, after *The Enormous Room* and *Tulips and Chimneys,* his father had capitulated: "Well, Stewart, I'll never be known as anything but the father of my son," and perhaps a stimulus was removed. Certainly a sameness of theme has been held against him, a tendency to combine sentimental love poetry with a vein of esoteric word-juggling. Randall Jarrell sums this up by describing his *Poems,* 1923–54, as

> Not a feast but a picnic—a picnic which goes on for yard after yard, mile after mile, of hot dogs, rat cheese, soda crackers, boiled ham curled into imitation rose petals, Valentines, jokes and fans from the Jokes and Magic Shop, warm chain-store beer . . . What I like least about Cummings' poems is their pride in Cummings and their contempt for most other people . . . All his work thanks God that he is not as other men.

This sentence seems to me to betray a total ignorance of Cummings the man who is one of the least snobbish human beings alive and of the nature of his poetry which is a permanent anarchistic revolt against industrialisation, totalitarianism, ugliness and humbug:

When skies are hanged and oceans drowned
the single secret will still be man.

(1959)

POSTSCRIPT: These two volumes* of Cummings break at 1935, after which his muse hung fire for a year or two. I must say at once that such an important collection which includes everything he ever wrote including *73 poems* first published in 1963 and *95 poems* first published in 1958, surely deserves a proper introduction. Instead there is no introduction to Volume I and Volume II is fobbed off with the somewhat tendentious preface he wrote for his collected poems of 1938.

The great influence in Cummings's early life were (1) his father, a

* *E. E. Cummings: Complete Poems 1913–62.* 2 vols. (New York, 1972).

popular Unitarian minister (Boston); (2) Harvard; (3) the war; (4) Paris, where he lived from 1921–23. By 1920 he was publishing poems and drawings in *The Dial* and from that year *Tulips and Chimneys* was going the rounds of the publishers.

Cummings referred to "six years of acute activity" (1916–23).

These years cover a veritable explosion of personality of Keatsian proportions. One gets the impression from eyewitnesses like Dos Passos that Cummings was in a perpetual manic state. He could talk all round the clock. This is the period of his most violent feeling, his sexual instincts fused with the poetic imagination. Where lust led, poetry followed, illuminating the speakeasies and brothels, the boulevard tarts, the girl art students in their cafés, with a corresponding aggressiveness against prudes and censors which lasted him through life.

Anarchists are not reactionary but, politically ineffectual, they may fail to impede reaction. Cummings was an Orwellian with pacifist leanings whose passion for the underdog led to many fine outbursts. The fact remains that his typographical inventions, while producing some occasional felicities, can also slow up the perception of a poem for the reader unless he be an acrostician.

Having now read or re-read all his later poems I am afraid I find very little improvement. He sailed to no Byzantium and had to make do with lovers, the moon, stars, snow, birds, flowers, children and the spring: the lyrical poet's limited octave.

Nevertheless the poems from his last two volumes ('58 and '63) are full of surprises. Technique ripens, aggression mellows, "only the game fish swims upstream."

(1968)

WILLIAM CARLOS WILLIAMS: 1

WILLIAM CARLOS WILLIAMS, a hard-working general practitioner, was born in Rutherford, New Jersey, in 1883, and spent most of his life there. He never gave up medicine any more than Wallace Stevens gave up selling insurance and this lifelong experience of the troubles and ailments of simple people, of birth and death—as an executive, not a spectator—forms the background of his poetry.

One should have spotted him in 1923 when that refreshing poem appeared in *Spring and All* ("By the road to the contagious hospital . . .") or, a few years later, with "Nantucket" (1929):

Flowers through the window
lavender and yellow
changed by white curtains—
Smell of cleanliness—
Sunshine of late afternoon—
On the glass tray
glass pitcher, the tumbler
turned down, by which
a key is lying—And the
immaculate white bed

Or, to get the complete flavour of his originality even in his orthodox Imagism, here is the end of "This Florida" (1924):

let me examine
those varying shades
of orange . . .
Orange of topaz, orange of red hair
orange of Curaçao

orange of the Tiber
turbid, orange of the bottom
rocks in Maine rivers
orange of mushrooms
of Cepes, that Martial loved
to cook in copper
pans, orange of the sun—
I shall do my pees, instead—
boiling them in test tubes
holding them to the light
dropping in the acid—
Peggy has a little albumen
in hers—

One can see Williams in fact as an antidote to Eliot, growing up with him like the dock-leaf by the nettle. His attitude to Eliot is severe. He blamed him for starting a revolution (the new poetry) and then betraying it by his intellectual academicism as if only dons were qualified to join the revolution. Williams, a quiet active man with capable hands, was as unintellectual as de la Mare or Ralph Hodgson, but being an American he suffered from the questing modern spirit—"nothing is good save the new."

For many years no little magazine was complete without the inevitable self-effacing little poem by him. He majored late in life in his long poem *Paterson,** in the lyrics of *The Desert Music* and *Pictures from Breughel.* At the University of Pennsylvania as a young man he had come across Pound (a lifelong friend), Wallace Stevens, a neighbour, and H.D; he went to England and met Yeats, he studied medicine in Paris and turned on the expatriates ("Kora in Hell"). He must be the only writer to consider Eliot a kind of devil and has called him "an archbishop of procurers to a lecherous antiquity." This is almost his first book to be published in England (though I have a feeling that his first book, *Poems 1909,* may have been published here—like Frost's).

Paterson (= Rutherford, New Jersey) is both a man and a city, and undergoes experiences common to both, like H. C. Earwicker as the Hill of Howth. Books One to Four were published as complete in themselves (1946–51) and then the fifth book was added in 1958. I have read the whole poem (first published by New Directions) twice. It is something one does not understand and does not get tired of because the general *matière* is so pleasing, like the brush-work of Bonnard. It is flat but not

* *Paterson: Books 1–5,* by William Carlos Williams (New York, 1963).

dull and enlivened by long quotations from letters from friends like Pound or Ginsberg, while suddenly the descriptive verse takes wing into something which no one else could have done and which justifies the whole experiment. MacGibbon & Kee have also published *Pictures from Breughel* where the poems are written in "the triadic stanza" and "variable foot" he first used in *Paterson II* and there is a special number of the magazine *Agenda* (November 1963) devoted to him. "Poetry is language charged with emotion. It's words rhythmically organised. A poem is a complete little universe. It exists separately. Any poem that has worth expresses the whole life of the poet" (from an interview).

Williams had a caustic sense of humour and *Paterson* bursts suddenly into an extremely funny love idyll (Corydon and Phyllis, in Book Four); at other times Paterson (he, it) is genuinely erotic. "Sunday in the Park" (Book Two) is a composite picture of a suburban holiday like "La Grande Jatte."

> A cop is directing traffic
> across the main road up
> a little wooded slope toward
> the conveniences:
> oaks, choke-cherry,
> dogwoods, white and green, iron-wood:
> humped roots matted into the shallow soil
> —mostly gone, rock out-croppings
> polished by the feet of the picnickers:
> sweet-barked sassafras . . .
> NO DOGS ALLOWED AT LARGE
> IN THIS PARK.

It is inevitable that we should compare *Paterson* with Pound's *Cantos*. Williams incorporates a few historical anecdotes about Paterson and the falls of the Passaic into his text to situate it (him) in the American tradition, but he has none of Pound's historical sense or his ability to live himself into the present through fragments of parchment. Williams lives anyway in the present (i.e., the horde of poor patients—something no other poet has to put up with). He uses no proper names to evoke, no medievalism, his poem has no incantations. "No ideas but in things," he proclaims, and "no ideas but in the facts." History leaves him cold: "Leadership passes into empire: empire begets insolence: insolence brings ruin." He prefers his verse still-life.

> Tenement windows, sharp-edged, in which no face is seen . . .
> Things, things unmentionable

the sink with the waste farina in it and
lumps of rancid meat, milk-bottle tops: have
here a tranquillity and loveliness . . .

One is always thinking of painting perhaps because Williams thinks of it too; he dedicated early books to Paul de Muth, he mentions Pollock and Ben Shahn, his *Paterson Five,* with its glorious invocation to old age, is dedicated to Toulouse-Lautrec. "In old age the mind casts off rebelliously, an eagle from its crag." Even so, I am not sure that I do not prefer Paterson in four books, ending with the river's journey to the sea which recalls *Finnegans Wake* and *The Dry Salvages:* "the sea that sucks in all rivers, dazzled, led by the salmon and the shad . . ." But "the sea is not our home," he tells us, and signs off with the Miltonic line:

Then headed inland, followed by the dog.

I hope those who search for what is both exciting and peaceful in modern poetry—*le repos éclairé*—will find it as I have done in *Paterson.*

(1964)

WILLIAM CARLOS WILLIAMS: 2

A MONTH ago, through a book-shop in Capetown, I obtained a volume I had been seeking for years, ever since I panned it in 1938: Robert McAlmon's *Being Geniuses Together*—I suppose it must have been one of those books whose stock was destroyed in the Blitz.

McAlmon, who married "Bryher," the Ellerman heiress, befriended many writers and published the Contact Editions, became a sharer in the golden age of American expatriation, and the friend of Joyce and Hemingway before drifting off into alcoholic obscurity. He stood for a certain cold-eyed never-blot-a-line literary realism and was a menace at parties, where he would scream and brawl.

However he must have been different with his friends and *Being Geniuses* contains descriptions of little-known aspects of Joyce, Hemingway and others. I believe Joyce described the book as a "What the butler saw" through a Paris keyhole. It tails off into name-dropping and superficial depreciation, but is worth republishing here as a documentary.

The one friendship which emerged unclouded from McAlmon's reminiscences was that with the poet William Carlos Williams,* and for several chapters the two autobiographies are closely interwoven—McAlmon, like the hare, with his money and his brilliant marriage, forging ahead while the modest unostentatious New Jersey GP plods after.

McAlmon published two of Williams's early books—*The Great American Novel* and *Spring and All,* but Williams, who had known McAlmon before his marriage in New York, and indeed had brought him to the fatal meeting with H.D. (Hilda Doolittle, afterwards Mrs.

* *The Autobiography of William Carlos Williams* (New York, 1967).

Richard Aldington) and Bryher at the Belmont Hotel which led to her proposal and who had been his crony in Paris, got over his expatriate fever and returned to practise medicine in Paterson, from which his great poem of that name was born. McAlmon remained behind and foundered.

One other figure dominates the Williams story: Ezra Pound. Williams knew him in their early days in Philadelphia, when Pound courted Professor Doolittle's daughter H.D. and the mysterious "Mary Moore from Trenton." He knew him as a poet in London, he knew him as a composer in Paris, he visited him several times in St. Elizabeth's Hospital, he incorporates chunks of his letters into *Paterson* though he always kept well within the bounds of idolatry.

> He was the livest, most intelligent and unexplainable thing I'd ever seen, and the most fun . . . usually I got fed up to the gills with him after a few days. He, too, with me, I have no doubt. I could never take him as a steady diet. Never. He was often brilliant but an ass. But I never (so long as I kept away) got tired of him or ceased to love him . . . And he had, at bottom, an inexhaustible patience, and infinite depth of human imagination and sympathy.
>
> What I could never tolerate in Pound, or seek for myself was the "side" that went with all his posturings as a poet. To me that was the emptiest sort of old hat. Any simpleton, I believed, should see at once what that came from; the conflict between an aristocracy of birth and that of mind and spirit—a silly and unnecessary thing. The poet scorning the other made himself ridiculous by imitating that which he despised. My upbringing assumed rather the humility and caution of the scientist. One was or one was not *there*.

I quote at length so as to show the kind of mind Williams had, so completely without pose or rhetoric, so devastating in its clarity, for the shaft about artists trying to assume the mantle of aristocracy (the poet as *grand seigneur,* lord of language, etc.) hits also at Yeats at a weak spot, and even Joyce (whom Hemingway called "Duke of Joyce") as well as Pound. Williams's type of craftsman's humility we find in some only of our artists—Forster, perhaps Henry Moore.

In his quiet way Williams was a revolutionary. From Imagism he went on to aim at a simple and direct all-embracing kind of poetry; limpid, apparently formless, but setting out to dethrone the iambic pentameter—the metre of all the bigwigs from Shakespeare to Eliot. He was deeply upset by *The Waste Land:*

> the great catastrophe to our letters . . . Our work staggered to a halt for a moment under the blast of Eliot's genius which gave the poem back to the academics, we did not know how to answer him.

and later he returns to it:

> It wiped out our world as if an atom bomb had been dropped on it . . . I felt at once that it had set me back twenty years, and I'm sure it did. Critically Eliot returned us to the class-room just at the moment when I felt we were on the point of an escape to matters much closer to the essence of a new art form itself—rooted in the locality which should give it fruit.

In Williams's case this meant not just Paterson, New Jersey, but his life as a doctor. There have been very few doctor-poets but Williams's career as a much loved, hard-working, fee-scorning general practitioner both provided him with themes and kept him in moral training as an active humanist; his whole life was *dans le vrai,* he never stopped writing poetry or treating patients, his last book, *Pictures from Breughel,* is one of his best.

> As a writer I have never felt that medicine interfered with me but rather that it was my very food and drink, the very thing which made it possible for me to write. Was I not interested in Man? There the thing was, right in front of me. I could touch it, smell it, it was myself.

Unlike McAlmon who could not really be bothered with other people, Williams was profoundly interested in women; his judgement of Nancy Cunard, Iris Tree, Adrienne Monnier, the perennial Nataley Barney, Marianne Moore and others are vignettes in depth, and he writes of them from his own depth, as a poet.

> What do I look for in a woman? Death, I suppose, since it's all I see anyhow in these various perfections. I want them all in lesser or greater degree.

And though happily married for forty years he craves permanent extra-marital satisfaction and receives it—he discreetly tells us:

> It is my instinctive affection for these "lost" girls that is the best part of me—and them. I loved them all. Like Toulouse-Lautrec I would gladly have lived in a brothel.

I wish I could stop quoting: It seems a lazy way to review a book; yet I am trying to give a picture of this complicated and so unfamiliar type of American with his throwaway simple style. He is no Hemingway, his is not a shining simplicity, nor is he Dos Passos with his lurking vanity. He hits people off in a phrase:

> Ford Madox Ford the lumbering Britisher, opening his mouth to talk, his napkin in one hand, half-stammering but enjoying the fun, a mind wonderfully attractive to me, I could see that.

Two of his great friends, Marsden Hartley and Charles Demuth, were painters. He was pursued by that grotesque iron maiden, Baroness Elsa von Freytag-Loringhoven (who sank Ford's *Transatlantic Review* by her gibberish) and he learnt boxing to defend himself from her. But O for some illustrations! Where is the snapshot he describes of an avant-garde party during the first war? His art is like a glass of Perrier with a slice of lemon in it on a hot day. He fills an indispensable square in the Paris of the Twenties. The pieces of that puzzle are now pretty well complete.

(1969)

HENRY MILLER

THIS BOOK* was first published by the Obelisk Press, Paris, in 1934. In his autobiography Jack Kahane describes his joy in receiving it, his meeting with Miller and his difficulty in selling the first thousand copies. I have never been able to find the first edition with its lurid jacket, but a tribute from me (with another by T. S. Eliot) occupies the back wrapper of the third. This is what I said:

> A gay, fierce, shocking, profound, sometimes brilliant, sometimes madly irritating first novel by the American Céline . . . Apart from the narrative power, the undulating swell of the style perfectly at ease with its creator, it has a maturity which is quite unlike the bravado, the spiritual ungrown-upness of most American fiction. Miller's writing is more in the nature of a Whitmanesque philosophic optimism which has been deepened and disciplined but never destroyed by his lean years in a city where even to starve is an education.

Miller was in his early forties when he wrote the book and I in my early thirties when I reviewed it. England was still the smug sanctuary of Joynson Hicks who was busy banning everything. How do we feel about it now, author and reviewer, as we approach the sere and yellow? Too often when a critic says a book has not kept, it is he who hasn't kept. When sex plays a large part in a book a critic must take into consideration his personal bias. The other day I went into a famous French book-shop and I found what I can best describe as a sex counter, corresponding to the cosmetics counter in a high-class chemist's. One had to pass the display of paper-backed erotica to reach the solid material at the back. But how many would want to pass it? I hope more and more. I hope that, through the free circulation of all the books which

* *Tropic of Cancer,* by Henry Miller (New York, 1961).

had to be read surreptitiously, this section of human experience which took on such undue emphasis in the years of bannings and prosecutions and the hounding of Joyce and Lawrence by mouth-foaming Sunday journalists, will one day occupy its proper place in our culture, an essential ingredient in most works of art but of decreasing aesthetic significance in proportion as it is isolated from the rest. Art is larger than sex although without sex there would be no artists.

When I reviewed Durrell's anthology of Miller I said no one had tried harder to write pornography or more signally failed. I was thinking of later books for there is nothing pornographic about *Tropic of Cancer,* though it sometimes disgusted me. Miller is here a typical Anglo-Saxon romantic in love with the French capital, i.e., with liberty and with himself, a refugee from American puritanism and Prohibition. He, like so many romantics, is fascinated by the Latin non-romantic attitude to sex, by prostitutes and brothels, by the paradox of the whore—i.e., the paradox that she is just like anybody else.

This leads on to a more frightening conclusion. Sex is just like anything else. The descriptions of the sexual act in *Tropic* are realistic, unimaginative and cynical like descriptions of hiccoughs or sneezing; the only erotic moments take place in fantasy. "All that mystery about sex and then you discover that it's nothing—just a blank."

Where I disagree most with my original verdict is in the estimate of Miller's prose. It goes into overdrive like a car. This overdrive is an interminable rhapsody deriving from Lautréamont, Whitman, Joyce, Lawrence and Céline, a Left Bank prose essay on life, art and Miller; and which now leaves me cold. It is not profound, it is adolescent egomania much of which could be cut. "I have made a silent compact with myself not to change a line of what I write. I am not interested in perfecting my thoughts nor my actions." What a bully! Apart from the overdrive Miller has a terrible second gear and can write as clumsily as a debutante on her first wild party.

> The Russian girl had dropped in after we toddled on to bed and Yvette had insulted her promptly, without even waiting for an excuse. They had commenced to pull each other's hair and in the midst of it a big Swede had stepped in and given the Russian girl a sound slap in the jaw—to bring her to her senses. That started the fireworks. Collins wanted to know what right this big stiff had to interfere in a private quarrel. He got a poke in the jaw for answer, a good one that sent him flying to the other end of the bar. "Serves you right!" screamed Yvette, taking advantage of the occasion to swing a bottle at the Russian girl's head. And at that moment the thunderstorm broke loose. For a while there was a regular pandemonium.

Strong meat! But as Miller puts it, "This is not a book. This is libel, slander, defamation of character. No, this is a prolonged insult, a gob of spit in the face of Art, a kick in the pants to God, Man, Destiny, Time, Love, Beauty . . . what you will"—and he is off in overdrive.

The "Cancer" element in the title is illustrated by diatribes against Europe and Western Civilisation. Everything is dying or dead or has halitosis, except Miller. (I believe he wrote the Introduction himself.)

> Side by side with the human race there runs another race of beings, the inhuman ones, the race of artists who, goaded by unknown impulses, take the lifeless mass of humanity and by the fever and ferment with which they imbue it turn this soggy dough into bread and the bread into wine and the wine into song. Out of the dead compost and the inert slag they breed a song that contaminates . . . A man who belongs to this race must stand up on the high place with gibberish in his mouth and rip out his entrails.

A purely rhapsodic journal could not survive. But there is also a comic novelist in Miller, if he could but have submitted to the discipline of the novel. The central frame of the book is occupied by two or three other characters mostly working on an American newspaper in Paris, like Miller himself. These characters are well observed. Miller writes with poetical feeling about hunger and about Paris, and he describes his cronies with sympathetic gusto. The book is carried along by a deep sensual enjoyment of living: "walking along the Champs-Elysées I keep thinking of my really superb health. When I say 'health' I mean optimism, to be truthful. Incurably optimistic."

I suppose his chief characteristic is really randiness. It is a ranting randy book which seems to obey no rules, but which is in fact a series of episodes from a "journal in time." Since then Miller has written much better. He is, after all, self-taught and this is his beginning. The four-letter words he is determined to set down are the normal vocabulary of the kind of Americans he is describing, and the sex-life is their normal sex-life; his rhapsodies too are the normal rhapsodies. It is a work of innocent realism and undisciplined imagination, a typical expatriate's first book—an expatriate who was also, in this case, a premature G.I. and a premature beatnik.

(1963)

MARY McCARTHY

THE KEY to Miss McCarthy's new novel* is her admiration for Zola. She has applied the Zola method, the conception of the novel as primarily a sociological document in which the individual is not sacrificed but rather exposed, stretched out on an accurate historical framework as on an operating table. Being not Zola but a clever American-Irish girl, a *docta puella,* the result is completely herself, the rigidly objective purpose is cloaked in her own language, style, sensibility.

It was conceived as a kind of mock-chronicle novel. It is a novel about the idea of progress really. The idea of progress seen in the female sphere, the feminine sphere. You know, home economics, architecture, domestic technology, contraception, childbearing, the study of technology in the home, in the play-pen, in the bed. It is supposed to be the history of the loss of faith in progress, in the idea of progress, during that twenty-year period.

Interviewer: Are these eight Vassar girls patterned more or less after ones you knew when you were there in college?

McCarthy: Some of them are drawn pretty much from life, and some of them are rather composite. I've tried to keep myself out of this book. Oh, and all their mothers are in it. That's the part I almost like the best. (From *Writers at Work*)

My only complaint about the novel is that the print is too small and that on page 32 "He took her hat and furs" sounds rather odd on Midsummer Night. Otherwise I have no fault to find for she achieves exactly what she has set out to do: she has employed the heavy chronicle technique of the sociological novelist (of all those novels which have titles like "Oil," "Cement," "The Cheyne-Stokes Family," "The

* *The Group,* by Mary McCarthy (New York, 1963).

Prufrock Saga") to produce a completely feminine pastiche—as if Zola had written *The Waves* or *The Years*.

Although she calls her book a mock-chronicle, there is no mockery; she applies the method conscientiously and stands at the opposite pole from an impressionist poet-novelist like Virginia Woolf. She is not concerned with life's magic or mystery.

I understand that some critics have been shocked by certain passages. This can only be because they have failed to see the debt to Zola, who was shocking too. These passages occur in the first sixty pages and include a very factual description of the deflowering of a virgin and an essay on the pessary with a realistic description of being fitted for one. Here the point is to describe an age-old and unchanging experience and then contrast it with the new modern phenomenon which belongs exactly to the period of the novel: "The new device recommended by the bureau had the backing of the whole US medical profession; it had been found by Margaret Sanger in Holland and was now for the first time being imported in quantity into the USA."

This historical method is then applied to the kind of cooking which was considered fashionable in the early Thirties and passes "the death sentence on Boston lettuce, Boston baked beans and the Boston School Cookbook." Breast-feeding v. bottle is another typical period controversy.

Originality is not enough. These digressions, half dialogue, half essay, on such topics as breast-feeding, toilet training, psychological impotence, decoration, party-giving and marital infidelity give one a privileged insight into a purely feminine world in the exciting Thirties, from the Depression and Roosevelt to Hitler and the outbreak of war, but this would never make a novel, which must in this case stand or fall by the eight Vassar girls. (We can assume for purposes of assessment that such girls, in such a time, were as she claims the salt of the earth.)

The novel takes place in a series of episodes each centred upon a different girl although they all come together for the opening wedding and the final funeral. The girls are loquacious, and very soon we begin to see them separately and to distinguish between their backgrounds. In many "collegiate" novels there is a tendency to idolise the prominent figures in a group and sentimentalise about them (a fault of most school-stories). But Miss McCarthy is a realist and is writing a comedy.

We know how the girls look and which are the prettiest but they keep their distance from their creator. Libby, the enthusiastic literary moll with her mixture of high-brow and campus slang, is the only one to live in a world of fantasy about herself, and her relationship with the publisher who employs her is hilariously funny. Perhaps Miss McCarthy is too resolutely comic, for she has got hold of a tragic theme in the marriage of Kay and Harald—where one of the top-flight Vassar girls is gradually got down and driven round the bend by a thoroughly specious and obnoxious coxcomb of a husband who contrives continually to put her in the wrong. ("A chronically unfaithful man who has to have a faithful wife; otherwise it's no marriage.") Miss McCarthy lifts the curtain on the tragedy and quickly drops it again.

Then there is Dottie, the Bostonian, who never recovers from her one night's experience with her first lover, and whose subsequent engagement forms another episode, and Polly (the poorest of the eight) who has an affair with Libby's publisher only to find he is being analysed at his wife's suggestion because he had been jealous of her promiscuity. His analysis results in a "block" which his wife suggests will only be removed by his coming back to her.

> He drained his sherry disconsolately. "Every day it's the same story. I go in. 'Good afternoon, doctor.' I lie down on the couch. 'Any dreams?' says Bijurf, picking up the notebook. 'No.' He puts down the notebook. Silence. At the end of fifty minutes, he tells me the hour's over. I hand him my five bucks. 'So long, doctor' and I leave . . ." "But you can free-associate to *anything,*" said Polly. "The word 'fire' for instance. What does it make you think of?" "Water." "And water?" "Fire." She could not help laughing. "You see," he said darkly. "That's what I mean. I'm blocked."

Polly's next episode concerns her keeping house for her father, a gentle manic-depressive who has suddenly insisted on a divorce and become a Trotskyite.

> "All neurotics are petty-bourgeois. And vice-versa. Madness is too revolutionary for them. They can't go the whole hog. We madmen are the aristocrats of mental illness."

The girls' mothers are indeed brilliantly done, from those who are themselves Vassar girls, progressive and ageless, to the rich New York dowager (mother of "Pokey") totally dependent on her English butler. "She did not care for shopping: fittings fatigued her: matinees made her cry (there were so many sad plays nowadays) and she had never been able to learn the bidding for contract bridge."

This is a novel which should certainly be made into a film, for the reward of creating eight characters in the round is to be allowed to project them into the flesh. It may be a little difficult for English readers to transport themselves into the American scene, into the Roosevelt New Deal as exemplified by these young, eager, sophisticated beauties whose folk-lore, beliefs and superstitions are so prodigally recorded, but it will be worth it for the warmth and laughter dispensed with the package. Miss McCarthy's style adapts itself fluently to each character but otherwise bubbles on in an unwearying catalogue of significant detail interrupted by ironical asides and outrageous speculations; it is brilliantly contrived, extremely funny and totally adult—by far her best book.

(1965)

THE GIDE-VALÉRY LETTERS

THE SUMMER before last I spent an ecstatic week reading and annotating these letters* in French. It seemed to me then one of the key books of the century. First published in 1955, they have taken eleven years to reach us in English in a book two hundred pages shorter than the original. Inevitably something is lost by both abridgement and translation. Letters are most alive when freshly delivered in the sender's handwriting, something perishes when they are typed, more when they are printed, most of all when they are translated. Finally we are left with a well-pressed flower from the original blossom, a silent film of a life-long tennis match without the sound of the rallies, the oaths and the endearments.

Reading them again, I am not so sure if they form a key book after all. What had these two sacred monsters really to give each other? Advance, retreat, advance, retreat, an admission here, a concession there, an increasingly stonewall attitude to Gide's work on the part of Valéry, who must have found that prodigious output of adolescent treacle hard to swallow: an increasing difficulty, on the part of Gide, in following Valéry's algebraic definitions and summary analyses. Exception made for *M. Teste* and *La Jeune Parque* and for the early poems.

Their egotism advances under the same banner of Mallarmé and Symbolism, then is separated by their different temperaments and station in life. Gide, a homosexual with a considerable private income and an estate in Normandy, can afford to pick and choose while remaining outside the normal struggle. Valéry, with a family to support, must enter for the *cursus honorum,* giving lectures, writing prefaces, accepting

* *Self-Portraits: The Gide-Valéry Letters 1890–1942,* edited by Robert Mallet, abridged and translated by June Guicharnaud (Chicago, 1966).

secretaryships until he ends up an Academician with a street named after him and a state funeral.

> You don't see me any more. It's because I don't see myself any more. I get up between five and six. I find a confused pile of obligatory things, a lot of foolishness that is promised, due, and I labour over these dreary works, written to order without ever coming to the end of it. At eight o'clock the confounded postman. A prime minister's mail but without the minister's offices and secretaries. At ten begin the visits. Until one o'clock I have to receive and talk, talk, talk. And by lunchtime I'm dead. Then I have to rush around for one must "live" and I fly from one publisher, library, etc., to another. At that point I'm *done for* . . . Lectures help me to flee, to change fatigues . . . I'm being eaten alive. I was a hundred times freer when I was not free at all.

This is but one of several dazzling self-portraits which Valéry paints of himself.

> I have tried to think what I thought, and I have done so with persistent naiveté. I am said to be *subtle* and it's absurd. Rather I am brutal, but I have, or did have, a mania for precision. An enormous portion of my work, half-lost, half-useful, was to make definitions for myself. To think by means of my own definitions was for me a kind of goal.

Elsewhere he writes: "And finally, of greatest importance and my true pride—*I owe to my friends almost everything I am.* They believed in me, who didn't believe in myself."

This, in fact, is the redeeming feature, the deep and genuine affection between the two men which enabled their egotism to be paraded without a single jarring note, and which gives the correspondence its fascination. For it really is a study in the development of two talents, two personalities, and has but little truck with the outside world. Both get married but one would never detect from these letters that Valéry's marriage was genuine, Gide's the cake-eater's pious fraud in which a permanent solicitude for his bride's ailing health replaces sexual intercourse. Valéry is at first ignorant of this, then ignoring.

The two young men were brought together by Pierre Louÿs, who had run into Valéry by accident at Palavas-les-Flots, the *plage* of his native Montpellier, scene of innumerable *"fornications avec l'onde,"* as he described swimming. It is a great pity that a Gide-Louÿs and Valéry-Louÿs correspondence is not available (but see page 64), for his role is similar to Lady Ottoline Morrell's in Bloomsbury letters, that is to say he is the impresario who brings together people who will cement their friendship by abusing him. Louÿs had a jealous, imperious, feline and ceremonious nature, more vanity and malice than his two fellow students, and a profoundly erotic but otherwise more external and superficial talent than theirs, as they quickly found out. It is typical that Wilde should feel so much more drawn to him than to the admiring Gide. (Valéry disapproved of Wilde completely and thought him a waste of Gide's time.)

One cannot but feel that Louÿs is dealt with rather hardly by Gide, even as life would deal hardly with him. His deepest relationship was, of course, with Debussy. The trio of obscure young bourgeois plunged into the Nineties through their admiration for Mallarmé and the crop of esoteric magazines to which—as to the salons connected with them—they became habitual contributors. Valéry was the special friend of Mallarmé and of Huysmans, who persuaded him to enter the Ministry of War to combine security with leisure. Louÿs married Hérédia's daughter; Gide broke with him in 1895.

After their first meeting, Gide is clearly platonically in love with Valéry, "his angelic choir-boy" whose simple existence and bourgeois innocence contrasts with his precocious intellectual genius and extraordinary imagination, as if he combined the incandescence of the youthful Keynes with the sensibility of the early Yeats. Some letters (omitted here) in which Gide vainly tries to persuade Valéry to spend a night at Les Baux, indicates his ardour. Hence the jealousy of Pierre Louÿs (reciprocated). Gide is the first to assault the literary salons of Paris, Valéry remaining a provincial.

> This afternoon at Hérédia's! I was really terrified by that ferocious scramble known as "the literary world." They furiously eat each other up. Ah! what selfish hate one feels in those souls. Everything becomes a matter of journalism and the making of reputations—Hérédia's salon is like an advertising agency.

The exception, of course, was Mallarmé's, where Gide went and sang its praises to Valéry—unaware that Louÿs had sent some of Valéry's poems to the great arbiter, who wrote at once to welcome him.

I find on the re-reading that, though the correspondence is not as wonderful as I had thought—too much of the early part is windy nonsense and literary growing-pains, too much of the later confined to names and dates—it remains of overwhelming interest. Nearly all my exclamation marks are for Valéry. Gide is content to return his service and await the next rally—though in every respect he is a worthy partner. "If I were kept from writing, I should kill myself," he said to Valéry in the gardens of Montpellier, to which Valéry replied: "And I should kill myself if I were forced to write." This sums up the stance they were both to adopt for the next fifty years.

I am convinced that these letters have a particular meaning at the present moment. They reveal the explosion of talent and cultivated narcissism of the Parisian Nineties and early 1900s—the period of *M. Teste* and the *Vers Anciens* of Valéry, of *Là-Bas* and Huysmans, of Gide's *André Walter, Paludes* and *Les Nourritures Terrestres.* And again they came to life, in the second moment of the French Renaissance of 1913–22; the period of *La Jeune Parque,* and *Le Cimetière Marin,* of *Les Caves du Vatican* and *Si le grain ne meurt,* of Proust and Cocteau.

Just before his death, in 1945, Valéry noted: "Gide, Cocteau . . . after all, men of the 'ancien régime' along with me"—but, above all, these letters show the value of a dedication to the inner literary life, the reward of constant meditation and brooding. These two sages span the whole of that period—they were brilliantly entertaining and stimulating before we were born; they continued to be so when I last saw them both, in 1945. Their world is "wiser and kinder" than our own, they are still, thank heaven, too clever for us—

Le Temps est fait d'un tas de choses
C'est un Océan qu'on a bu!
De mille merdes et de roses
Monte dans l'âme le rebut . . .

—From an unpublished poem of Valéry's in the French edition

(1966)

MEMORIES OF GIDE

I FIRST met Gide through Sylvia Beach in 1929. He had already had a great influence on me, especially his *Nourritures Terrestres,* and I had reviewed him in *The New Statesman.* I remembered the physical impression; the massive head with its look of Easter Island, the Bloomsbury black hat, the rather clerical manner. He asked me what I thought of *Point Counter Point* and we were both rather pleased when I said "*mais c'est un faux* Faux-monnayeurs." He told Sylvia Beach afterwards that "it was not *une amitié* but an *amour*"—and that was the last I heard of him. I never followed up his invitation to the summer debates at Pontigney where I might have met him again. Our first meeting, so important to me, was never recorded in his Journal. Nor were any of the others. The next time I saw him was towards the end of the war at the British Embassy in Paris. I was allowed to arrange a luncheon party for Duff Cooper to meet some of the French writers like Paulhan, and Gide came too. As he entered he flung his arms wide and exclaimed:

> *"O nimium coelo et pelago confise sereno*
> *nudus in ignota, Palinure, jacebis harena."*

The Ambassador and his august colleagues thought he had taken leave of his senses. I suppose this quotation, in public, from *The Unquiet Grave,* was as fine a compliment as an older writer can pay a younger. It was unfortunately the last and he went on to find considerable fault with the vein of defeatism which he diagnosed. He came to lunch with me then on two occasions and I met him for the last time staying with Lord Berners after taking his honorary degree at Oxford. We drove back to London with Robert Heber Percy and he asked to be shown Eton. It was summer and I remember how interested he became at lunch in a miniature daddy-long-legs on the window-pane. It was a fly, he said, that was not found in France, only in England. He was horrified by the uniform of the Eton boys, their tail-coats and stiff collars. *"Mais qu'est ce que c'est que cela? Est-ce une punition?"* On the other hand he revelled in the choir practice and pointed out that these trained altos to whom we were listening could hardly be found anywhere else. He always looked to me exactly the same as in his photographs and the same at all ages. If I had only made notes of his conversation! He was benign rather than friendly. I had published his "Imaginary Interviews" in *Horizon* and we talked about them, but it's all gone out of my head except that he disapproved of radio announcers sounding both l's in "Hollande." Buried in the memory-store are about twenty hours of his conversation, all told. I would willingly submit to any truth drug that would bring them out.

He spoke French with a Bloomsbury accent, pronouncing *"em-merdant"* like they said "ex-cru-ci-at-ing!" He smoked non-stop and wore many mufflers.

(1970)

JEAN COCTEAU: 1

In the last war a leader of the French Resistance took refuge in a lunatic asylum. When the Vichy doctors made their round he set up a great din to convince them. He was interrupted by a sombre inmate of frightening appearance: *"Taisez-vous, simulateur!"* In his long career at the not-at-all-still centre of the turning art world a persistent whisper of *"simulateur"* has clung to M. Cocteau. Though he has contrived always to be coupled with those authentically inspired—Picasso, Stravinsky, Apollinaire, Radiguet, even Gide—his work will not stand up to theirs; his variety is considered weakness, his originality borrowed.

He seems not so much an artist as a showman; but a showman who steals the show. His youthful love of the limelight has become a journalist's passion for publicity; we are as tired as he ought to be of his whole bag of tricks, the *voix d'airain,* the star signature, the stone in the snowball, the poet and Death, the monotony of narcissism, neoclassicism, juvenile delinquency and the Boeuf sur le Toit.

Miss Crosland, however, in her close and careful presentation* of his numerous activities, has done a great deal to dispel this impression. Cocteau had a very difficult beginning: he was born in 1889, into an easy-going, artistic, but thoroughly conventional family of the Parisian *haute bourgeoisie,* a cousin of Admiral Darlan and General Catroux; there was no pressure on him to exert his talents or earn his living; he was a delightful prodigy, an irresistible young man (as can be seen in the full-length portrait by Blanche), a poet, a talker and a fashionable declaimer of verses in the Nineties' tradition who seemed destined to *refaire Oscar en maigre.*

The turning-point in his career was the visit of the Russian ballet and

* *Jean Cocteau,* by Margaret Crosland (New York, 1956).

Diaghilev's disturbing encouragement, *"Jean, étonne-moi"* (1912), which led him to understand that art could not be constructed out of cleverness, charm and frivolity. The *Sacre du Printemps* revealed to him the challenge of modern art, the inevitable unpopularity of the true artist. His admiration for Picasso and Satie led him further afield, and the young Radiguet, so gifted and uncompromising, had the same stimulating effect (without the poison) as Rimbaud had on Verlaine.

He now knew how art ought to be made: it remained to be seen whether he had anything to say. His lucid and imaginative cleverness has all his life given rise to a series of critical epigrams and aesthetic maxims. *"Un peu trop, pour moi c'est juste assez!"* is one of my favourites. As a poet, however, he seems always to have been short of themes: the schoolboy drama of *Les Enfants Terribles,* the Orpheus myth, opium and the dreams of disintoxication, beauty and sudden death, youth's cruelty; his repertoire is brief. He had, however, an extraordinary gift, which even now is insufficiently appreciated, that of projecting poetry into original visual images, so that his work for the cinema, when he has been able to find the right backer, is among the most exciting of our time. *Orphée,* despite some bad patches, is a landmark and shows what the cinema might have become as an instrument of magic guided by a poet's imagination. *Le Sang d'un Poète* and the ballet, *Le Jeune Homme et la Mort* have also something of this hallucinatory quality.

One of his plays, moreover, *Les Parents Terribles,* is a brilliant combination of wit and intensity, and is surely a superb contribution to the theatre. The opium drawings, the two autobiographies, *Portraits-Souvenirs* and *Le Difficulté d'Être,* and the early novels like *Le Grand Ecart* are all outstanding, and in their different ways reveal that phosphorescent melancholy which hovers over his crisp, limpid style and proclaims a true poet.

By discipline and fierce discarding the *"simulateur"* has achieved a genuine frenzy. Despite his egotism and insincerity (Miss Crosland quotes Claude Mauriac, after weeks of interviewing, as saying that there should be a word, *"un cocteau,"* introduced into the French language, meaning a hypocrite), his personality gives out a rare benignity, and I have seen him, when booed on the stage, behave with much dignity.

Falsely accused of collaborating during the war, he is now something of a national figure, for quite apart from his work his personality is a symbol of fifty years of aesthetic appreciation, manifestations and manifestoes, of the aura of wonder and brightness which hangs round those golden years of creation between 1905 and 1915, and of those silver years of enjoyment that followed.

To a young poet about to join the Resistance he said: *"Vous avez tort. La vie est plus grave que ça."* He meant that to be a poet was already to belong to such a movement. It is a wise remark and makes one wonder if we could not develop some ampler form of criticism which could estimate not only the published work but the whole impact of a writer's personality on his contemporaries and through them on what is written after.

(1955)

JEAN COCTEAU: 2

I SET OUT on this book* about Cocteau determined to like it more than the last one, that is to overcome my prejudice against Cocteau as an artist, for one could not fail to like him enormously as a man. I felt that there must be some book of his I should read that I had missed. I remembered that the Oxford Dictionary of European Literature (which gives his birth as 1891 instead of 1889) praises his first prose work, *Le Potomak,* written before the First World War though not published till 1919, as a "fantastic medley, an exploration of the subconscious attended by gloomy forebodings." Mr. Raymond Mortimer overheard and immediately provided a copy together with a personal tribute to Cocteau and the love he inspired in all his friends.

What a coincidence and how Cocteau must have enjoyed it that the two families in the *"humour noir"* strip which occupies most of *Le Potomak,* the amiable Mortimers and the cannibalising Eugènes, should have prefigured a similar relationship between the youthful Mortimer (Raymond) and MacCown (Eugene), the Irish-American painter-pianist at Cocteau's night-club Le Boeuf sur le Toit who reacted so destructively to those who tried to help him. The book is enchanting not only for the "Eugènes" who remind me of the Ubus' descent on Achras in Jarry's *Ubu Cocu* (which Cocteau could not possibly have seen) but for the devastating portrait of Catulle Mendès, who made the mistake of inviting him to lunch and forgetting. Cocteau was then fifteen. The book owes much to the Gide of *Les Nourritures Terrestres,* too much for either Gide's or Cocteau's liking.

* *Jean Cocteau: The Man and the Mirror,* by Elizabeth Sprigge and Jean-Jacques Kihm (New York, 1968).

From that moment off they go. Proust, Gide, Diaghilev, Cocteau, the four great homosexual trail-blazers of our time, creative artists who avenged Wilde's fall on the bourgeoisie which had humiliated him. *"Jean, étonne-moi,"* was Diaghilev's command (not *"étonnez"* as in the recent TV programme): and it was the signal to cut the safety-belt which this prince of the good address and good address-book, the versatile Edwardian charmer, had worn; a safety-belt fastened with his mother's love and bulging with the family shekels.

Tout ce qu'il-y-a de plus beau
La Vénus de Milo,
La Belle Otéro,
Le Petit Cocteau.

sang the pre-1914 chansonniers. "I met a young man of nineteen or twenty," wrote Edith Wharton many years later, "who at that time vibrated with all the youth of the world . . . It is one of the regrets of later years to have watched the fading of that light." (It was Cocteau, by the way, who ran round the shelf behind the banquettes of Larue's restaurant to fetch Proust's cloak, not some sprig of nobility.)

The Sprigge/Kihm collaboration is most fortunate. Between them they have got the record straight besides presenting a most sympathetic picture. The Cocteau I knew, emerging somewhat crest-fallen at the end of the war and made nervous by accusations of collaboration, was perhaps a more human and endearing person than he afterwards became; in fact even the two biographers suggest that his vanity and egomania in the last two years grew almost insupportable. He seemed to live only for incense and burnt offering. Perhaps that is all a *vieillard auguste* can digest. And for public appearances, preferably in his Academician's costume: "In this strange insatiable state of mind that seemed a result of his serious illness and which endured till his death Jean Cocteau coveted two things he knew to be incompatible—glory and honour!"

His uniform was made by Lanvin and his Academician's sword subscribed for by the Gallimards and his great friend Madame Weisweiller. "The blade was wrought by Toledo gipsies after a design by Picasso and the hilt was made by Cartier. This was designed by Cocteau himself, showing Orpheus's lyre, the Oedipe-Roi profile, which was also the profile of the angel and of Raymond Radiguet, the twisted cord of a theatre curtain, the star with a great diamond in its centre and a ruby at each point, the monogram JC and the Palais-Royal *grille* to join the hilt to the blade. Certainly no such sword had ever been seen before." It should have been pulled out of a tree by Jean Marais to music by Auric, then stolen by Genet.

Cocteau wrote several autobiographies, of which the best-known are *Portraits-Souvenirs 1900–14* (1935), a collection of worldly reminiscences with revealing drawings, and *The Difficulty of Being* (1947), translated by Elizabeth Sprigge (Peter Owen, 1966), which some think his best book. He achieves here a marmoreal detachment and simplicity in the footsteps of Montaigne. The authors transcribe freely from both, including the error that Apollinaire died from fat round the heart rather than Spanish flu. After considerable reperusal of his writings I come to the conclusion that from 1918 to 1930, i.e., till he was forty, Cocteau was indeed a creative genius, though two-dimensional and superficial as a novelist compared to Proust and Gide or as a poet compared to Valéry.

But subtract him from the French literary scene and his absence is immediately felt. He was the thin man's Oscar Wilde, living dangerously, talking incessantly, dominating the theatre, the cinema of the avant-garde, with Radiguet as his Douglas, Jean Desbordes as his Ross and Dargelos, the schoolboy who threw the lethal snowball, as the symbol of injurious beauty. With Radiguet he made the Bassin d'Arcachon smart, with Desbordes he put the Hotel Welcome at Villefranche on the map, and the quais of Toulon and Saint Mandrier. He was the incarnation of the Twenties, the period that ends with his *Opium* (1930) and his *Enfants Terribles* (1929).

The period also covered his ballets, *Parade* and *Train Bleu,* his *Sang d'un Poète* (film), *Orphée* (play), and *Oedipe Rex* with music by Stravinsky. Satie, Stravinsky, above all Picasso were his early influences. He intervened in the theatre from the ballet to the monologue (*La Voix Humaine*). His drawing was at its best, his industry unflagging. His talent was ubiquitous, as if Apollinaire were to merge with Cecil Beaton, Ashton and Noel Coward. After Radiguet and Desbordes, he let opium choose his friends until Jean Marais, his good angel, gave him a greater preoccupation with the stage which led to much brilliant team-work with Bérard and Auric. He had an easy war. It was not till the Fifties that he began to repeat himself or rather that his variations on the theme of having been Cocteau became monotonous.

Because he knew he was young within he resented those who saw he was old without. Polishing his legend became the only decent means of communication. For such vainglorious arbiters praise is like the gongs beaten to frighten off demons, there must be no letting up. He could never quite get enough. There was always the implacable André Breton and the new surrealists or the audience who booed him at the revival of

Oedipe. It is very hard for a critic to accept excellence or originality in so many different fields. But it existed.

"Cocteau is not a dilettante, as he is often regarded: the variety of his expression is not a dissipation of his talents: he is essentially an avant-garde artist." Such is the verdict of Dorothy Knowles in her new and excellent book on the French theatre from 1918–39, *French Drama of the Inter-war Years* (Harrap). An *oeuvre* without a *chef d'oeuvre* perhaps?

(1968)

THE SPANISH CIVIL WAR: 1

THE Spanish Civil War was a tragedy and, like the Athenian expedition against Syracuse, can only be recorded by an historian with a sense of tragedy. I know nothing about Mr. Thomas* but I deduce him to be very young (or he would have cluttered up his book with allusions to events in the last war), and therefore, if he lacks this tragic sense, it is a defect of youth rather than an indication of superficiality; it may well come later.

But it is a certain flippancy which seems to me to mar this otherwise memorable book. Many of his jokes are good ones and I do not suppose that anyone could master such a mass of material, or tell such a sad story, without a certain necessary hardening of the heart or a desire to remain readable. But, as an eyewitness of some of the events which he describes, I can say that, while I now understand them better for reading his book, there is a deeper feeling about the human personality which is lacking.

Mr. Thomas, for example, gives more space than an impartial historian should to the activities of the British sections of the International Brigade and writes what is in effect a patriotic gossip-column about them. But he fails to grasp, or rather to portray, the extraordinary elation which animated them or, subsequently, the corresponding disillusion; even as he cannot set the magic of the early days of the revolution in Catalonia against the increasing gloom of defeats and purges.

He recalls the atrocities of both sides, but lacks the imagination to see how appalling they were; or how vast was the reversal of fortune which despatched 200,000 men who had fêted their independence in their

* *The Spanish Civil War,* by Hugh Thomas (New York, 1961).

native Catalan into the fearful squalor of the concentration camps of Argelès. Here one found—shivering on their strip of sand—the ministers in whose ante-rooms one had been kept waiting, in pleasurable anticipation, a few months before; here languished a beaten army; here ended youth, under the Senegalese sentries, for a whole generation of the world's most courageous, poetic and sanguine working-class; here vanished the dream of an international intelligentsia.

Mr. Thomas grasps the essential tragedy of the contrast between the aspirations of the Spanish people and their defeat. I think it is the human element on which he is weak. One has to have seen hatred in action to believe in it. His pen-portraits of leaders on both sides are lifelike up to a point, but they lack understanding, they verge on caricature. His Azaña is an example; for if he were as ineffectual as Mr. Thomas makes out it is inconceivable that he could have risen to or maintained his position as President, or made such a speech as he quotes in his last sentence.

I think one abandons each portrait with a slight sense of disappointment. (The exception is his defence of Negrin.) Thus Durruti was more than a bandit, Companys more than a lawyer, Millan d'Astray more than a military buffoon, Largo Caballero better than a vain old windbag. And I remember that we were not allowed to visit José Primo de Rivera in prison because his eloquence was considered by his gaolers irresistible.

There is one very minor point which if I do not make no one else ever will. Mr. Thomas quotes from the pamphlet "Authors take Sides on the Spanish War" (published by the *Left Review* not *Left Wing*) and credits me with the intolerable slogan "Intellectuals come first, almost before women and children." What I wrote was that under Fascism they came first in the order of elimination and I went on "It is impossible therefore to remain an intellectual and admire Fascism for that is to admire the intellect's destruction." (Let us hope this is his only misrepresentation.) "Spain is an emotional luxury to a gang of sap-headed dilettantes," wrote Ezra Pound. "The real enemy of mankind is not the Fascist but the Ignorant Fool," wrote H. G. Wells. "My sympathy is for the non-combatants in Spain," said Malachi Whitaker. Perhaps it is time the pamphlet was reprinted.

Let us turn to the credit side: Mr. Thomas has written a book of seven hundred pages which I have read from cover to cover with enthralled interest (especially for the foot-notes); reading time two days. He means to be impartial but cannot escape being on the Government side because he cannot, like Millan d'Astray, cry *"Viva la Muerte, Abajo la Inteligencia"* and because he is allergic to Hitler and Mussolini and the "craven indolence" of British Appeasers. Within those limits he is impartial, and I do not believe a Nationalist could accuse him of a single distortion of fact, only of failing to be appropriately kindled by their ideals.

He has two great gifts; one for untangling political complications and presenting them clearly and another for describing battles: he is fascinated by campaigns, by the names like Jarama, Brunete, Guadalajara, Belchite, Teruel which once fascinated so many: and he has the historian's most important quality, a tremendous appetite for detail and a grasp of the essential. He makes half-a-dozen key statements throughout the book which show his wisdom.

Such is the admirable statement of the alignment of forces on the eve of the struggle (pages 110–12), from which it is clear that the Republic had failed because it had from the start not been accepted by the most powerful forces of the Left or the Right and also had estranged many of its supporters. Or his account of the fatuous complacency of Azaña and Quiroga on the eve of the insurrection; or of the Non-Intervention Committee or of the race for arms from Italy and Germany, and the later deals with Russia.

He analyses why both Russia and Germany wanted the war to go on, and so explains a fact which had always baffled me—the German arms I was shown towards the close of the war going through for the Republican side.

He seizes the crucial moments of the war: the failure of the Government (through fear and complacency) to arm the working-class parties in time to put down the insurrection (this was a matter of hours); the failure of Blum's Cabinet to carry out their original intention of selling arms and planes to the Spanish Government at the outbreak (they were dissuaded by the British and by pressure from their own Opposition); the formation of the Non-Intervention Committee which was "to graduate from equivocation to hypocrisy and humiliation": the massive aid from Russia which saved the Republic but dictated so many unfortunate political consequences, and the equally massive aid to Franco from Germany in return for the Basque-Asturian mineral concessions which won for him the decisive battle for the Ebro.

We know now that Germany regarded Spain as "a private Aldershot," that Blum justified sending his fighters as a means of testing them, that the Russian experts sent there were on their first stages to liquidation, that the *Blitzkrieg* was first tried out there—but against the Germans, who, however, took it up even as they experimented in the various patterns of aerial bombing.

I have said it was a tragedy because I do not believe that if the Nationalists, who had hoped to take over an acquiescent country after the pattern of so many coups d'état, had known of the three-year struggle awaiting them they would have undertaken it, and because I now have a much greater respect for human life than I had then: nor am I so certain that the Spain which would have arisen out of a Republican victory would have been what we had hoped for or that a European war would have been averted: and also because I am more aware of tragedy, of the unhappy people I saw, the misfits, the luckless soldiers of fortune, the lukewarm bourgeoisie, the politically suspect. It is to Mr. Thomas's credit that almost no aspect of the Civil War, however painful or unpopular, escapes him in this splendid book.

(1961)

THE SPANISH CIVIL WAR: 2

THIS BOOK* is subtitled "The Literary Impact of the Spanish Civil War" but, despite a wealth of material quoted, it is confined to a specialist study of six outstanding writers: Malraux, Hemingway, Orwell, Koestler, Regler and Bernanos. They are not treated in separate chapters but move in procession through the various headings, "Writers Take Sides," "Political Commitments," "Writers in Arms," "War of Ideas," "The Holy War," "The Pornography of Violence," "The Great Crusade," and so forth.

This does these novelists a great disservice for there is no mention of the construction and plan of Malraux's *Espoir* or Hemingway's *For Whom the Bell Tolls* although there are numerous quotations giving views of individual characters and the novelists' own opinions. One longs for a summary of the novels and a judgement on them as works of art.

I haven't read *Espoir* for many years and I would regard being made to re-read *For Whom the Bell Tolls* as an ordeal. I still enjoy the autobiography in Orwell's *Homage to Catalonia* and Koestler's *Spanish Testament* though not the political analyses. Koestler comes out of it all very well; he asks and answers the permanent questions, how does it feel to be under sentence of death, in a city that falls to the Fascists (Malaga), in solitary confinement and so on, and Orwell, too, never forgets that he is a human being. Hemingway's eighteen-year-old love-affair with Spain stood him in good stead despite his overblown, overwritten characters and their barbarous employment of the second person singular which in English, I feel, should be confined to the Ten Commandments.

Bernanos's position as a disgruntled Left-wing Catholic and French patriot is affected by his rather limited experience of the Civil War as a

* *Writers in Arms,* by Frederick Benson (New York, 1967).

resident of Palma, Majorca, which fell immediately to the Fascists. He saw no fighting. What a pity Camus was never in Spain; he would have been an ideal observer.

One fact was neither envisaged nor mentioned in any of those accounts of the Spanish War. Franco's triumph has proved itself the most enduring coup d'état since the Russian revolution. It is now thirty-three years since he landed from the Canaries and he still governs. Either, therefore, the triumph of might over right, the flourishing of the wicked, must be regarded as semi-permanent (only Salazar has ruled longer) or there must have been much more right in his might than we Left-wing intellectuals were prepared to admit.

At the time of writing *For Whom the Bell Tolls* Hemingway's love-affair with Spain was eighteen years old, my own was fifteen, since I first visited Burgos and the monastery of San Domingo de Silos in my twentieth year. Yet for both of us our happiest times in Spain were still to come under the regime of the hated Franco who provided us with the same facilities as if we had been his supporters: Hemingway in particular making a triumphal come-back.

When one looks back on the politics of the Civil War one sees that an immediate victory of the Spanish Government, which would have been possible if the democracies gave it the military aid which it was entitled to purchase, would have been the ideal solution, requiring only a little more courage on the part of Blum, a little more wisdom from Baldwin and Chamberlain, and rendering a European war much more unlikely, but that an eventual victory of the Communist-controlled Negrin Government might have been worse than what actually happened.

The war-correspondents who would forgather for lunch at the Spanish Embassy in Belgrave Square for a last civilised glimpse of the old Spain would find themselves being grilled in Valencia a few days later by sinister agents of the Comintern, themselves to be liquidated on their return to Russia.

I remember pooh-poohing their absurd questions, like the significance in one's passport of an exit stamp from Lisbon three years earlier, and reassuring a worried Spaniard with: *"lo que vale es la inocencia"*—sublimely priggish utterance. (Innocence is what counts.)

It was in Spain, as a matter of fact, that I first came across really frightened people: bourgeois trembling for their lives, men whose hands shook, a group of mercenary pilots in a Barcelona hotel drinking in the evening before taking up their obsolete planes on doomed missions, men who had flown with Rickenbacker and lost their nerve or whose wives had left them, sending back last messages to London with their handsome pay-packets.

The war-correspondents wandered with charmed lives through the blacked-out city while the anarchist cars tore through the Ramblas to pick up suspects and bear them off to the lonely execution grounds. Civil war . . . brother against brother, the most deeply satisfactory of all explosions of aggression.

Trials of suspected Fascists—business men, ex-officers, Fifth-Columnists pouring out their life-stories (they were allowed many words to defend themselves) before the impassive judges, one an almost silent anarchist, the conclusion foregone. The arms stacked in night-club cloak-rooms, the Party banners and slogans, the painted trains, the workers' processions, Durruti's funeral, the interviews with optimistic ministers; Prieto, Largo Caballero, García Oliver, Companys, the International Brigades singing revolutionary songs—*"La Santa Espina"*—hopes destroyed, lives lost, youth wasted, hundreds of millions of words spouted by orators, written by journalists, argued in cafés or London dinner parties while the Fascist line advanced inexorably over the map like water rising in the *Titanic*. "How long will it last?" "Do you still think we can win?" I had my exit permit. Tomorrow I would be in Toulouse.

I do not find Mr. Benson's book nearly as interesting as Hugh Thomas's *The Spanish Civil War* for at this stage one really must be told about the literary activities on both sides; Franco had his intellectuals too and some of the most interesting books about the Civil War were written outside Mr. Benson's chosen six. Barea and Sender, to name two Spaniards, Brenan's *Spanish Labyrinth* and *Face of Spain,* Borkenau's *Spanish Cockpit, Poems for Spain* (ed. Spender and Lehmann), Gamel Woolsey's *Death's Other Kingdom,* Humphrey Slater's *The Heretics,* Chalmers Mitchell's *My House in Malaga* . . . Mr. Benson singles out one work of imagination from the other side for praise: Stefan Andres's short novel *Wir Sind Utopia* (Berlin, 1943).

The writers who plunged deepest into the Spanish Civil War, despite the psychological damage involved in prolonged association with failure all went on to other things: Hemingway's involvement with the Second World War was complete, Koestler became an authority on world Communism, Orwell's anti-totalitarian crusade had barely started. Malraux went from strength to strength.

But some of us barely recovered. The defeat of the Spanish Republic shattered my faith in political action. I doubt if I have written a single political article since.

(1969)

LORCA

Lorca was shot because he fell into the power of an element which detested spiritual reality. Yet Lorca fell into that power because he lived in Granada. Had he lived in Barcelona or Madrid he would be alive today like Sender or Alberti. But he lived in reactionary Granada, a city of the past, of gipsies and bull-fighters. That element in him which sought the past, which drew him to the mediaevalism of Andalucia, contained the seed of his own death, placing him who was no friend to priests or feudal chiefs in a city where the past one day came to life and was deadly.

The quotation is from my *Enemies of Promise* (1938), and I make no apology for quoting it, because it makes a point which is borne out by Ian Gibson in his excellent work of fact-finding.* Lorca in fact was in Madrid up to the day before the Civil War broke out and went into a mood of profound irresolution before he booked his sleeper to Granada on the night of July 16, 1936, and returned to the house of his parents in the country-side outside the city. The poet who had rejected the West in his *Poeta en Nuevo York* had returned to his roots and entrusted his fate, unwittingly, to the forces that would destroy him. On that same train went his Nemesis, the Right-wing deputy and printer, Ramon Ruiz Alonso, who was to engineer his downfall; although, "still alive and kicking," he will admit now only to having arrested him, and taken him to the civil governor's. From there, three days later, he was driven off to execution in the pit at Viznar, near an old Moorish beauty-spot, the well of Ainadamar.

"There's a storm brewing and I'm going home," Lorca told his old schoolmaster, from whom he borrowed his fare from Madrid, "I'll be out of danger there." The next afternoon he said to his friend Nadal, as

* *The Death of Lorca,* by Ian Gibson (Chicago, 1973).

they drove back to the city from the Puerto de Hierro: "Rafael, there'll be bodies over all these fields. I've made up my mind, I'm going to Granada. God's will be done."

Lorca, who had been in a mood of great depression, asked his friends what he should do.

> It has been said that among those who recommended his return to Granada was Luis Rosales, who pointed out that there Lorca could count on the protection of both the Left and Right, and, in the event of the town's falling into the hands of the Nationalists, would be able to depend on the Rosales' family to guarantee his safety. Another friend, the deputy Diez Pastor, was insistent that the poet should remain in Madrid.

The Republic would have taken good care of him.

One must go back to the past, to that summer of 1936, to understand his dilemma. Granada was his passion, and anyone who loved it before the age of char-à-banc and cement would know it was a good place to live and die in, whether one worked, like the composer Manuel de Falla, in a hidden hill-side garden, or, like the writer Gerald Brenan, on the wildest spurs of the Sierra Nevada.

It was in conjunction with de Falla that Lorca had written his *Poema del Cante Jondo*. In an interview in *El Sol* he was asked for his opinion on the capture of Granada in 1492 by Ferdinand and Isabella:

> It was a disastrous event, even though they say the opposite in the schools. An admirable civilisation, and a poetry, architecture and delicacy unique in the world—all were lost, to give way to an impoverished, cowed town, a wasteland populated by the worst bourgeoisie in Spain today . . . I am totally Spanish, and at the same time I am a brother to all men and I detest the person who sacrifices himself for an abstract nationalist ideal just because he loves his country with a blindfold over his eyes. I don't believe in political frontiers . . .
>
> At this dramatic point in time the artist should laugh and cry with the people.

Who were the "worst bourgeoisie in Spain," who were to seize power in Granada within a week of Lorca's return?

Among their first victims was Lorca's brother-in-law, the Socialist mayor, Dr. Montesinos, who was arrested and executed. A brother had married the daughter of Fernando de los Rios, the brilliant Socialist minister much hated by the Right in Granada. Even if he had not expressed Left-wing opinions or written for Left-wing papers, Lorca belonged, through these connections, to the Left-wing establishment. In Granada he would be a marked man, and everything would depend, as with so many artists under dictatorships, on the protection of powerful friends. How powerful were they?

He would, of course, have been saved if Granada had remained loyal to the Government. That it did not was largely due to the incompetence of the Civil Governor, Torres Martinez, and the ineptitude of General Campins: they refused to distribute arms to the workers or to take measures to nip the rising in the bud. The "resistance" crushed by the Nationalists was no resistance at all—"which made the subsequent repression of Granada one of the outstanding crimes of the war."

Although he met and got on well with José Antonio Primo de Rivera (a man of irresistible eloquence and charm), founder of the Falange, Lorca's friends were poets and intellectuals. But among these poets Rosales was a prominent member of the Falange (the Fascist organisation) in Granada, as were his two brothers. It was with him that Lorca lodged in semi-clandestinity when his family's country-house (through the Montesinos connection) became too dangerous. But the Rosales brothers could not protect him from other Right-wing organisations, or from Ruiz Alonso, once letters of denunciation had begun to flow in to the Governor, Valdes, who was a ruthless exterminator of doctors, lawyers, freemasons and university professors; responsible for thousands of deaths against the Cemetery Wall.

There was also a recurrent charge of homosexuality which, as is always the case, inflamed the ignorant and made more difficult the role of his defenders. One must imagine Hart Crane in the grip of the Ku Klux Klan. Above the Falange and the black assassination squads, the torturers and informers, among whom Ruiz Alonso functioned, were the high military authorities, the Governor, the impassive Archbishop, and, in Seville, General Queipo de Llano himself who, according to Mr. Gibson, authorised the execution.

> Valdes, on his radio told Queipo that Lorca had been arrested. "What am I to do with him?" he asked. "I've already had him here for two days."
>
> "Give him coffee," he rasped, "plenty of coffee."

It was the savage general's favourite euphemism when ordering an execution.

Everyone who has written about the death of Lorca seems to think that it was a particular blunder to execute a great poet. But the satisfaction in executing a great poet (or painter, composer or any other man of genius since Socrates and Archimedes) is increased by the pre-eminence of the subject, and the defence has always been, "Why should he think that because he's a poet (painter, composer, physicist, etc.) he's better than anyone else?" As eyewitness accounts put it:

I was one of the people who went to get Lorca from Rosales' house. We were sick and tired of queers in Granada . . .

We've just killed Federico Garcia Lorca. We left him in a ditch and I fired two bullets into his arse for being queer. . . .

We bumped off your friend the poet with the big fat head this morning.

Since Lorca's death there has been no great poet in Spain. Machado survived only long enough to lament him. There have been few great poets anywhere else. The Franco regime, after various attempts at evasion, must now accept full responsibility for the deed, which is the best thing to do provided people today can understand something of the passions, the blind worship of violence and brutality, the panic and intolerance, which are let loose by a civil war.

The leader of the group that took Lorca from his house and killed him was the Right-wing deputy and ex-typographer Ramon Ruiz Alonso. He is still alive and kicking and nobody molests him, in spite of the fact that the crime was stupid and unjust and that it did us great harm, for Lorca was an outstanding poet. (Serrano Suñer, Franco's Foreign Minister, in an interview in 1948)

Lovers of poetry, lovers of truth, lovers of Spain should all read this exemplary piece of literary research which brings up to date the investigations of Gerald Brenan and Claude Couffon.

(1973)

STEPHEN SPENDER

"EVEN today it often disgusts me to read a newspaper in which there is no mention of my name," writes Mr. Spender. *World Within World,** the private world within the public world, is certainly his most considerable prose achievement, admirable as picture of an age and fascinating as an autobiography. Mr. Spender's method is to reconstitute the period from journals and letters and then to provide a summing-up in the form of an essay. In fact we have two styles, anecdotal and analytical which vary the tempo and complement each other.

The essays carry the analysis to a deeper level than that of the literary and political anecdotes until there emerges the voice of an authentic poet—often gnomic and somehow impersonal, like the hollow reverberations of a Bofors gun. We benefit by seeing a typical Left-wing career of the Thirties interpreted by one who has shed all political labels and lost neither humanity nor integrity, not so much retreating from the Left as burrowing beneath it.

Mr. Spender has always seemed to me two people. Let us call them S I and S II. S I is the youthful poet as he appears in Isherwood's *Lions and Shadows,* and to others who knew him in the early Thirties. An inspired simpleton, a great big silly goose, a holy Russian idiot, large, generous, gullible, ignorant, affectionate, idealistic—living for friendship and beauty, writing miraculous poems, expecting too much from everybody and from himself on whom he laid charges and responsibilities which he could never carry out. S II was shrewd and ambitious, aggressive and ruthless, a publicity-seeking intellectual full of administrative

* *World Within World: The Autobiography of Stephen Spender* (New York, 1951).

energy and *rentier* asperity, a young tiger sharpening its claws on the platforms of peace.

Spender's life has been a beautiful imposition of S II on S I until—both lovable and formidable—a complete man is formed: the fruit of his inner personality happily ripening inside a protective armour like a lichee in its shell. One must compare him to Goethe and Gide, artists who combine sensuality with puritanism, loving with willing, innocence and guile.

His book opens with a charming and ironical picture of his Hampstead home—"comfort against a background of calamity" and "puritanism in decay," and then switches to Oxford. He presents a Left-wing-Innocent's case against the University but settles down to admirable portraits of Auden and Isherwood, followed by an essay on the aims of Auden's poetry and his own which is as good as anything in the book. Auden rules over Oxford, Isherwood over Germany, where we are given another fascinating disquisition on Hamburg and Berlin in the pre-Hitler days.

Spender never forgets that it was the Hitler in all of us that permitted Hitler's success; he is consequently more poetical when writing of Fascism than of Communism. Hamburg and Berlin, coming between Oxford and London, contribute an original twist to the conventional literary story so that the account of Bloomsbury which follows has certain reservations. Spender's social success with his discerning elders does not prevent him from judging them politically in a way in which they had never been judged before. He was their first Marxist critic.

Soon he is living in Vienna where he becomes much more involved in the Socialist movement, from which he is driven on to Communism by the Spanish War. Once a Communist, his confrontation with human values and political values where they touch personal relationships is inevitable. Communism is found wanting in the sphere of personal relations even as Bloomsbury was felt to be inadequate by the requirements of a social conscience—and so a slow retreat from political engagement follows, though morally he still remains involved.

The book closes with a revealing glimpse of childhood and of his childish ambition "to be a naturalist, an old man with a long white beard." Alas, this doesn't explain Mr. Spender, nor can Mr. Spender explain himself. We don't know and he doesn't know why he loves A and B or why they love him. What he thinks of freedom or justice or responsibility or Communism or Bloomsbury we know, but even the gleams of his own dark lantern are deadened by the darkness of the human abyss.

"What a writer really needs is a success of which he then purges himself." "When I had known him a short time, I was also surprised to find that he knew most of my own poems by heart." "She, on her side, surprised me when my *Trial of a Judge* was produced by knowing long passages of it by heart." "During this time when I had meals almost every day with him (Isherwood) we ate food such as horse-flesh and lung-soup, which for some years ruined my digestion and for all time my teeth as they had long ago ruined his" . . . An observer with scientific detachment might be able to deduce from these flashes the hidden operations of the poet's thunder.

The long whip-like sentences roll out, flicking and cracking, like the Bofors shells in the night; the distance between the writer and his model is scrupulously maintained as in a self-portrait by Degas. But the solution is withheld. Mr. Spender's noble, hunted profile, I am sure, will one day look up at us from the first metric-penny stamps of the new world-state. But his thoughts? Deep and dangerous as those of his "red-haired Judas," affectionate as St. Francis's, artful as Rousseau's, stern as Savonarola's, impulsive as Verlaine's, they will prove forever unmintable; philosopher's gold.

(1951)

LOUIS MacNEICE

OVER 550 pages* as compared with Auden's *Collected Poems* (340)—but what a difference! Reviewing a poet like Auden who is still alive one is conscious of his presence in every line; why has he left out this, why has he changed that? Perhaps he can tell us.

But here is a rudderless ship; the pilot is gone; nothing can be added or subtracted. It is a memorial, and Professor Dodds can only indicate what poems are left out (being left out by the author from his earlier collected poems in 1949), which have been rescued from a small group of translations, hitherto excluded. The collection ends with his last book, *The Burning Perch,* and "Thalassa," his last poem, published posthumously in the *London Magazine.*

> Put out to sea, ignoble comrades,
> Whose record shall be noble yet;
> Butting through scarps of moving marble
> The narwhal dares us to be free!
> By a high star our course is set
> Our end is life. Put out to sea.

I wish we had known this poem at his memorial service where Auden preached the funeral oration:

> You know the worst: your wills are fickle
> Your values blurred, your hearts impure
> and your past life a ruined church
> But let your poison be your cure.

* *Collected Poems of Louis MacNeice,* edited by Professor E. R. Dodds (New York, 1967).

"With its stoical reaffirmation of his underlying faith in life it makes a fitting conclusion to his life's work" (Dodds).

How does MacNeice's complete opus strike one? Talent, not genius, but talent unfailingly set to work and well-husbanded; a dogged determination to make the most of it; great metrical facility, varied images, vivid imagination but much difficulty in sustaining poems, many of which are uneven. Besetting sin: Journalism. With Day Lewis, his real preoccupation was with everyday life in bohemian London ("A smell of French bread in Charlotte Street"), and holidays in Scotland or Ireland.

I do not feel at all sure that the BBC, as a source of regular employment, is very good for poets; it drains off too much talent and imagination in ephemeral team-work. I have never thought radio drama great literature and the life is inbred and wearing. What poet has come out of the BBC better than when he went in? MacNeice could, of course, have chosen an academic career: he was perfect campus material: or he could have been a publisher-poet, or an all-round man of letters (hack) or starved in a cottage; the BBC was what he preferred. But it took its toll.

Another limiting factor was his common sense, his rationalism. MacNeice was an *homme moyen intellectuel* with Celtic sympathies. His father was a Bishop of the Church of Ireland in Ulster, he went to Marlborough and Merton. Unlike the chain of twentieth-century poets—Yeats, Eliot, Auden—he was without religion or fanaticism, "brought up to scoff rather than bless," he was not Dionysian like Dylan Thomas; nor, like Spender, a mystic and political crusader. By temperament and formation he should have been a critic or commentator. I think it all the more remarkable that, with this outlook, he was a dedicated professional poet, but he lacks intensity and a kind of poetry he wished to write came too easily to him.

An exception is his love poetry; love, at three—no, four—periods in his life filled his sails and resulted in some of his best lyrics. Disillusion added some more, and he was also a good war-poet ("Holes in the sky"). What this volume leaves behind is a climate of the mind, an enriching communication with a sensitive, ironic, wary spirit, an aura of humanism. Beneath that lay a permanent melancholy expressed in his long face, his gentle eyes and sardonic mouth, his throwaway conversation. Like other intellectual humanists he knew that most of the compensations of life were so many liana bridges slung over the indifferent void.

MacNeice wrote two long poems, "Autumn Journal" (1938) and "Autumn Sequel" (1953), which includes his famous and lovely poem on Dylan Thomas. In addition there were the long poems of his post-war volume, *Incantations*. "Autumn Journal" is a success. It will be required reading for unborn students who need to study the Slough of Despond which thinking Englishmen lived through between Munich and the last war. It has a lilting manner of its own, a meditative music like Omar Khayyam. (Journalism is just round the corner.) "Autumn Sequel" is more ambitious, the texture is thicker, the poem is loosely constructed round the portraits of a group of friends like Elgar's *Enigma Variations*. (MacNeice loved his friends, had no enemies, his love poems are without lust, his political poems without rancour.)

I don't feel the poem as a whole carries conviction, but it is interesting to compare his moving lines on Oxford (Canto XII) with the earlier references in "Autumn Journal" (Canto XIII) and the friends are defined with great clarity. Who is Devlin? Who was Gavin?

Let me conclude with a few examples of what MacNeice did better than anybody else: *Indoor Sports,* four short poems on darts, shove-halfpenny, vingt-et-un and crossword puzzles. Then poems of satirical brilliance—"Pet Shop," "The Satirist," "The Libertine," "Bagpipe Music," "Alcohol"—and the poems manifesting his scholarship: "Suite for Recorders," "Cock o' the North" or his translations from Horace, Aragon and the mediaeval Arch-poet.

But, above all, the love poems and those connected with Celtic places ("In doggerel and stout let me honour this country"). Sometimes love and Ireland combine as in the Eleanor Clark cycle of "The Last Ditch" in which the poet is revealed, like Horace, throwing away his shield before returning to the Blitz and the BBC. They combine also in the so characteristic "Flowers in the Interval," four poems to his wife which are the essence of MacNeice.

> Because you intoxicate like all the drinks
> We have drunk together from Achill Island to Athens,
> Retsina and Nostrano, pops and clinks
>
> Through snow or mist or mistral, aquavit . . .
>
> Because, like each of these, you reprieve, repeat
> Whether dry or sweet your newness, with or without
>
> Water, and each one ray of you distils
> A benediction and an end to doubt . . .

It is convenient to imagine that poets die at the right time. MacNeice did not. He was writing some of his best lyrics and the pneumonia he contracted from going down a cave for a radio programme could have been cured if taken earlier. He seemed about to take out a new lease of song. "His last, and, as many think, his best volume, *The Burning Perch,* went to press in January 1963 and he died in September of the same year" (Dodds).

These last poems show a preoccupation with death which he told us had no significance:

> Your health, Master Yew.
>   My bones are few
> and I fully admit my rent is due

has haunted me ever since I read it—as poetry should.

> More power to the Makers. Of
> whom, he made as well as any.

(1967)

W. H. AUDEN

SINCE he does not propose to write an autobiography, Auden told me, he regards *A Certain World* (Faber) as the nearest he will come to one—and attaches considerable importance to it. Besides being an anthology of his favourite writing and influences, it includes many passages by himself which introduce his themes, which are arranged alphabetically.

Thus we find, as we should expect, "jackdaws" and "justice" but not "jealousy" which is an emotion from which his genius may have protected him; we find a continuous spanning of the two cultures, no landscape without a dab of geology, not just "dreams" but how we dream, and a splendid (apparently unpublished) account of the feelings of an anaesthetist by Yanovsky. Icelandic sagas and theological tracts are freely drawn upon, though only Goethe occupies four lines of index.

Several writers little known or unknown to me emerge as of great interest. As Auden gives no book titles for his extracts, one has to search among the acknowledgements to discover such desirable volumes as *The Changing Face of England* by Anthony Collett, an admirable topographical writer (Nisbet), or *The Empty Fortress* by Bruno Bettelheim (Macmillan, New York), *An Alphabet for Gourmets* by M. F. K. Fisher (Viking, 1948) and the poems of Ivor Gurney, a sensitive nature poet (Hutchinson):

> *Larches are most fitting to small red hills*
> *That rise like swollen ant-heaps.*

What is the general impression? This is indeed one of Auden's most important books, and as one gets into it his presence is directly felt, as if he had come to stay with us for a week-end—which is about the time it takes to read him. One is loth to say good-bye and grateful for the brief

"Addenda" which is not in the American edition and which adds a lyric by W. E. Henley to the "Death" section, John Davidson's "War Song" and a wonderful account by Thoreau of a battle between black and red ants; also a poem on windmills by Lord de Tabley, Moore's "Meeting of the Waters," so melodiously perfect, and Bridges's long piece on a parrot in his English hexameters: "Our temple of Christian faith and fair Hellenic art . . ." How far we have wandered since 1930!

I mention these names to show the variety of Auden's taste. He manages to avoid all well-known pieces (there is no Eliot, Pound, Yeats, or Joyce in his anthology) and to supply others of almost equal interest, if only by their unfamiliarity. Many of the longer extracts are in prose, the kind of prose which supplies information. Some of his authors I dislike, or just can't read: Chesterton, Kierkegaard, C. S. Lewis, Dag Hammarskjöld, Simone Weil, and it's no good clamouring for one's own favourites—they simply aren't there.

The fact is that Auden, both as man and poet, is a very different animal from any of his contemporaries. I can't think of anyone, from Graves, at one end, through Spender, Day Lewis, Betjeman, Larkin, who is even remotely like him. The only living poets whom he cites are Betjeman (whom he quotes twice), Malcolm de Chazal (surely overrated), Graves (once), Marianne Moore and Vozhnesensky.

Two plugs: The greatest long poem written in English in this century (*The Anathemata* by David Jones); the only first-rate volume of poems specifically about the Second World War (*Rhymes of a PFC* by Lincoln Kirstein).

The self-portrait of Auden which slowly emerges is endearing if rather professorial. A benign, austere, somewhat solitary man who is seldom contradicted, with a whimsical humour and a taste for the scatological; deeply religious, wayward, tolerant, with a fastidious aversion to passionate love, love poetry and emotional confidences, surprising in the man who wrote "Lay your sleeping head . . ." Sometimes one is reminded of the puritanism latent in Aldous Huxley's anthology of 1932, *Texts and Pretexts*.

Thus Huxley: "If it were not for literature, how many people would ever fall in love? Precious few, I should guess."

And Auden:

No notion of our Western culture has been responsible for more misery and more bad poetry than the supposition, initiated by the Provençal poets, that a certain mystical experience called falling or being "in love" is one which every normal man and woman can expect to have . . . I must confess that I find the personal love poems of Dante, Shakespeare, Donne, for all their verbal felicities, embarrassing.

The Auden addict will enjoy the catalogue of the books in his nursery library. This included Sopwith's *Visit to Alston Moor* and the Stationery Office's *Lead and Zinc Ores of Northumberland and Alston Moore* (see *New Year Letter*), and only three poets, Hoffmann's *Struwwel Peter,* Belloc's *Cautionary Tales* and Harry Graham's *Ruthless Rhymes for Heartless Homes.* He tells us he was not frightened by the "great, long, red-legged scissor-man" as he himself was a nail-biter, not a thumb-sucker, but the scissor-man does occur in a nightmare he relates, from August 1936:

> . . . very different is the fear aroused in me by spiders, crabs, and octopi, which are, I suspect, symbols to me for the castrating "Vagina Dentata." I believe I belong to the first generation which resolved, once we left school and got to the university, that we would never take a cold bath in our lives again.

At times his punctilio seems exaggerated. "To people that one does not know personally, one should speak only of the authors and critics one is fond of"—so we are never to be allowed to hear his "black list," only some of his favourite writers "from whom I have learned most."

Poets: Brecht, Bridges, Cavafy, Frost, Graves, Hardy, David Jones, D. H. Lawrence, de la Mare, Marianne Moore, Wilfred Owen, Laura Riding, Edward Thomas, William Carlos Williams (in his last period). Critics: Valéry and Karl Kraus are those most quoted.

It is not enough for an anthology not to cloy, to possess a tranquillising quality, there must also be flashes of genius which strike from a single line. Here are one or two: "If you are afraid of loneliness, don't marry" (Chekhov). "The only end of writing is to enable readers better to enjoy life or better to endure it" (Dr. Johnson). "By all means let a poet, if he wants to, write *engagé* poems, protesting against this or that political evil or social injustice. But let him remember this. The only person who will benefit from them is himself; they will enhance his literary reputation among those who feel as he does. The evil or injustice, however, will remain exactly what it would have been if he had kept his mouth shut" (Auden). "Men are not punished for their sins but by them" (E. G. Hubbard). "The day of individual happiness has passed" (Hitler).

I don't know who E. G. Hubbard was but he is responsible for one other epigram: "I am not sure just what the unpardonable sin is, but I believe it is a disposition to avoid the payment of small bills." This is endorsed by Auden's magnificent defence of the bourgeois: "It was the middle-class who first practised, if it did not invent, the virtue of financial honesty." He made this point in his funeral oration on Louis MacNeice, who is represented by his admirable translation of Horace. There is another good Horace translation here by James Mitchie, but, except for a paragraph on infancy, of truly Freudian insight, by Saint Augustine, the classical authors are little cited. Nor are the Romantics, except Byron, nor the Moderns except for some telling extracts from the diaries of Virginia Woolf.

"Surtout point de zèle" might be Auden's motto for this golden book. We can dip, gently, but not too deep, or we can mull over every quotation; in neither case will we be disappointed for we have been admitted to the company of one of the most vigorous, reflective and delicate minds of our time, and few of us will ever get as close again.

(1971)

GEORGE ORWELL: 1

FIVE or six years ago I had a visit in my Sussex farm-house from the authors of this book* and I suggested they went on to interview Mrs. Vaughan Wilkes, the former headmistress of St. Cyprians, the preparatory school where Orwell and I were educated. Although she was then in her lucid eighties no one had thought of doing this before. In their book on Julian Bell and John Cornford, scions of Bloomsbury killed in the Spanish War, the authors had mastered the sociology of the Thirties (no easy task for Americans), and now they have tackled an even more remote and sophisticated period, the England of 1910–30, "the fresh green lap of good King Edward's land." I was there, born three months after Orwell, although owing to the complexities of the educational system he always seemed a year senior. From St. Cyprians I followed him to College at Eton, after that our ways parted and our friendship was not resumed till the middle Thirties when it lasted till his death. It begins with his comments on a poem I wrote when I was thirteen on the death of Lord Kitchener and ends with the label on a basket of fruit sent to University College Hospital in 1949. Since this book is about Orwell while he was Eric Arthur Blair up to the appearance of *Down and Out in Paris and London* under his new pen-name in 1932, there is much about the years we had in common; they are described with so much tenderness and insight that I am often persuaded the writers were there, that Peter and William ran over the Downs to Birling Gap in the green jerseys and corduroy knickers calling to Mr. Sillar, "Please sir, may I have an arm, sir" as they trotted beside him before becoming Stansky K.S. and Abrahams K.S., two of

* *The Unknown Orwell,* by Peter Stansky and William Abrahams (New York, 1972).

the most difficult Collegers in that difficult election. Then suddenly they refer to Orwell as "an Etonian Old Boy," instead of "an Old Etonian" and the fraud is discovered. And where did they pick up the expression "a handle to his name" for a title, a vulgarism long obsolete, like "are you in the Stud Book?" From Mrs. Wilkes!

When I read this account of Orwell's school-days, drawn so largely from his and mine, I was at first enchanted as by anything which recalls one's youth but when I went to verify some references from my old reports and letters I was nearly sick. Memory selects and varnishes, heightens what is reassuring, obliterates what is harsh, like the long monotony of growing up when the artist and the adult surface for a moment of vision or comprehension before sinking back into the triviality, facetiousness, ignorance and drudgery of adolescence, herded from form room to form room, dormitory to playing field, chapel to gym. In the case of St. Cyprians and the Wilkeses whom I had so blithely mocked I feel an emotional disturbance. I received a letter of bitter reproach from Mrs. Wilkes after *Enemies of Promise* which I have never dared to re-read and when, after the death of my own parents, their papers descended to me I found evidence of the immense trouble she had taken to help me win my scholarship to Eton despite the misgivings of my father which had to be overcome. The Wilkeses were true friends and I had caricatured their mannerisms (developed as a kind of ritual square-bashing for dealing with generations of boys) and read mercenary motives into much that was just enthusiasm. When Mrs. Wilkes died (1875–August 1967) I went to her funeral in Eastbourne. The church in the Old Town was nearly empty, the service was conducted by her son, John Wilkes, a clergyman and ex-headmaster. Nobody spoke to me. Remorse was there, yet a kind of stoniness as her son intoned "except the Lord keep the house," even as the two feelings cancelled out in those harrowing sessions when I was a small boy. "It wasn't very straight of you, Tim, was it. It's not as if we hadn't . . ." I think the authors should take a look at Henry Longhurst's autobiography *My Life and Soft Times*. He must be the first writer to have praised St. Cyprians and he prints the only photograph I have ever seen of Mrs. Wilkes, the Mum and Morragem round whose "favour" (or displeasure) we all revolved.

"September 26, 1914 . . . I like St Cyprians very much though I feel rather homesick sometimes. I know the names of nearly all the boys. There are seventy-nine. I am longing to see you. There are lots of more things different as we have to unpack our own bags and get things out ourselves and we get up at quarter past seven and then have a cold bath and then get up and have breakfast and about five boys have baths at a

time. I like the chapel very much we go there directly we have dressed before breakfast. I like going on the Downs very much, there is a very nice view on top of them. I went to the Devonshire baths yesterday. I liked it very much. I am in Lower Sixth for most lessons.
With love to you all. Cyril" (To my mother.) Age 11.

"December 19, 1914.
Dear Major Connolly,
I am *very* pleased with your boy. I consider that he has made an admirable start in his new surroundings. He has good abilities—works well and is very pleasant to deal with: and I feel sure he will be a credit to us. He has kept fit and well all the time and is popular with both masters and boys. I have nothing but what is nice to say of him.
L. C. Vaughan Wilkes (Headmaster)"

"June 4. Days more 55 days past 26
I found a place where there are lots of magpies and gold-tail caterpillars but as they are the kind which give you a rash I left them and brought home a 'magpie' which chrysalised the next day. We have an awful lot of nobility this term, i.e. one Siamese Prince, the grandson of the Earl of Chelmsford, the son of Viscount Maldon who is the son of the Earl of Essex, a grandson of another earl and the nephew of the Bishop of London (Winnington Ingram). I have not been homesick lately except when the band played one of the tunes from that roundabout at Easter and when I shut a door which made a noise like winding up the gramophone.
With love to all, from Cyril"

"An awful lot of nobility." The authors tackle this question in depth—was St. Cyprians more snobbish than other schools of the England of that time or were boys like me more snobbish than anybody else? And what about Orwell who appears in *Such, Such Were the Joys* as an anti-snob but one who certainly knew the score.

Something that does come out throughout Orwell's life is that he enjoyed every moment of it, he liked fives and football at school, he liked walking and "natural history," he liked reading, arguing and debunking, his eyes were made to glitter with amusement, his mouth for teasing, his schoolboy chubbiness persisted until his face grew cavernous from two pneumonias. And he was emotionally independent, with the egotism of all natural writers; his friendships were constant but seldom close. The authors mention this detachment and I was reminded of it by purchasing Roger Senhouse's copy of my *Enemies of Promise*. Senhouse, who was at Eton with us was also his publisher (Secker and Warburg) and had written on the end paper about my greatest friend and one of Orwell's chief protectors in his own election.

Bobbie Longden, headmaster of Wellington was killed on leaving his house in an air-raid October 10, 1940, the sole casualty. When I told George Orwell this on 22nd (He had been in the country for ten days without papers, recovering from a poisoned hand and general fear of return of his weak lungs owing to late and strenuous Home Guard duties) he said: "He had just completed *The Lion and the Unicorn.*"

Orwell's Eton days are fairly well documented, Collegers are long-lived and articulate; Denis King-Farlow, Sir Steven Runciman and myself have all aired our views and Mr. Gow who wrote Orwell's reports and whom he went to see when he returned from Burma is still with us. The authors give an accurate description of life in College at that time and of the battle between the Liberals and the Reactionaries which still reverberates. Although the Reactionaries came back again under Lord Hailsham's captaincy the Liberals have had their way where beating, fagging, bullying and sexual inquisitions are concerned. *Enemies of Promise* is no longer a banned book. My parents, when I had bad reports calling me "cynical and irreverent," suspected the influence of Orwell though we had drifted apart in his last year at Eton. When he returned from Burma in 1928 he looked up one or two of his contemporaries. This is perhaps the obscurest period of his life when he was briefly a schoolmaster.

"It is suggestive of his state of mind at this period that he should not have got in touch with Cyril Connolly who was also starting out on a literary career. It is suggestive too that the friendship with Connolly should have been kept in abeyance until the 1930's by which time Blair was already a published author with two books to his credit . . ." It was also suggestive that we spent the winter of 1929 a few streets apart in Paris (myself, Rue de Seine—Orwell, Rue de la Pot de Fer) but we simply did not know of each other's existence. When Orwell came back from Burma he did not care for Oxford and Cambridge intellectuals, the easy livers, the "Pansy Left" as he called them and it was quite natural that he got in touch with me only when he settled properly in London some years later. The definitive action was my review of *Burmese Days* in *The New Statesman* (1935) which led to an invitation to dinner, a *bifteck aux pommes* cooked by himself. I then put him in touch with King-Farlow and the former captain of his election and captain of the school, Denis Dannreuther, a brilliant lawyer engaged in drafting bills for Parliament.

The Burmese chapters are fascinating. If only Orwell's official reports and the reports on him could be made available! Incidentally King-Farlow could not have been at the dinner for Orwell in 1928 as Orwell's 1935 published letter to him begins "Of course I remember you." At the back of my mind lurks some recollection of an earlier communication with Orwell than my own first published letters (1935) but I can't put a date to it. King-Farlow refers to my helping Orwell in 1928 but I think that must have been later or I would have known that he was in Paris. By the way I am sure the ex-policeman would never have broken a restaurant window to steal a peach for her as suggested by Loelia Westminster; his earlier version that it was a German colleague at the Hotel Lotti must have been the correct one. She has since confirmed that he *did* steal it. I don't think *Down and Out in Paris and London* is more than agreeable journalism; it was all better done by his friend Henry Miller. Orwell found his true form a few years later.

Where I think the two collaborators have succeeded is in facing up to the difficult problem of not only "how" but "why" Eric Blair with his shabby-genteel background and Establishment education (intended for the higher branches of the Civil Service) threw it all up to become the proletarian champion, George Orwell. "But it was not the name that mattered, it was the self, the essential second self which had been set free."

(1972)

GEORGE ORWELL: 2

SIR RICHARD REES* was a close friend of Orwell and an editor of the *Adelphi* for which he wrote and therefore one of the people best qualified to bring out a book about him. It is a short book and a simple one; Sir Richard does little more than present Orwell's character as it seemed to him and then take us through his books from *Down and Out in Paris and London* to *1984* and the last essays.

But he does this very well: one feels that his conception of Orwell's complicated nature is the right one and makes sense when applied to his books; and that Sir Richard could have written three times as much if he had chosen. This is the book on Orwell I have liked the best: and he is someone delightful to read about because his personality generated a certain casual intimacy which was very endearing.

The tragedy of Orwell's life is that when at last he achieved fame and success he was a dying man and knew it. He had fame and was too ill to leave his room, money and nothing to spend it on, love in which he could not participate: he tasted the bitterness of dying. But in his years of hardship he was sustained by a genial stoicism, by his excitement about what was going to happen next and by his affection for other people: and these are the years when Sir Richard was closest to him.

He explains that there were four separate strains in Orwell: the Promethean rebel, "a profoundly serious and tragic pessimist"; the second "sympathetic to authority at least as long as it is benign and paternal"; the third an eighteenth-century rationalist "debunker of spurious idealism and spirituality"; the fourth a romantic, a lover of the past, of "old-fashioned virtues, old-fashioned customs and old-fashioned

* *George Orwell: Fugitive from the Camp of Victory,* by Richard Rees (Carbondale, Ill., 1962).

people." Another way to express this would be to say that he suffered from a typically English form of the Oedipus complex, by which, having dealt his father's authority a swingeing blow he would rush up to say "Have I hurt you?"

I once wrote that he was a revolutionary in love with 1910. This England of 1910, the London of *Riceyman Steps,* the country-side of Henry Ryecroft, the nation of village shopkeepers, of little tobacconists in urban alleys, and of decency and individualism, was the damsel in distress to be rescued from the dragon of the ruling class, the monster of Church and State, the capitalist oppressor.

Sir Richard draws an interesting parallel between Orwell and Conrad although I do not remember Orwell expressing early enthusiasm for Conrad so much as for Shaw, Wells and Samuel Butler. Gissing came later.

Both Orwell and I were dominated by the headmistress of our private school: it was this remarkable woman who dished out rewards and punishments, who quoted Kipling and inculcated patriotism, who exalted character and moral courage and Scottish chieftains in kilts. We learnt the father values from a mother, we bit the hand that fed us, that tweaked the short hairs above the ear. But it was a woman's hand, whose husband's cane was merely the secular arm. Agonising ambivalence!

Orwell, too, felt bitterly that he was taken on at reduced fees because he might win the school a scholarship; he saw this as a humiliation, but it was really a compliment.

In any case, I would say that his character was already formed by the time he had arrived at Eton and I regret that the volume of *Collected Essays** still does not include the extraordinary *Such, Such Were the Joys* which is the key to his formation and which has only been published in America. (Mrs. Wilkes refused permission.)

Personally, I think that the secret of Orwell's reduced school-fees (a secret, incidentally, perfectly kept) caused Orwell to adopt a prematurely economic diagnosis of society which does not allow for the many "grace and favour" apartments of which the Establishment disposes. The real heroes of his preparatory school were not peers and plutocrats but kilted charmers who were good at cricket (perhaps their fees were reduced too) and who afterwards sometimes got into trouble.

Another point I would raise with Sir Richard is this assumption:

> When one considers how many of the first intellectuals, in this century alone, have died early from consumption—Chekhov, Katherine Mansfield,

* *Collected Essays of George Orwell* (London, 1961).

D. H. Lawrence, Simone Weil, and Orwell, for example—it seems reasonable to ask whether this disease may not sometimes be connected with the strain and effort of swimming against the stream.

I do not think there was anything psycho-somatic about Orwell's illness. Although he told me he found the disease interesting, I think he most bitterly longed to be well. As a small boy he was always sneezing; he was big and strong but obviously "chesty" and a sufferer from one of the two English diseases, bronchitis (rheumatism is the other), inherent in the climate. This was made much worse by the pneumonia which he caught in Paris and by his experiences in the Spanish War, but he was never an incandescent character like Lawrence or like those frail, highly strung individuals who "go into a decline."

"My starting point is always a feeling of partnership, a sense of injustice," he wrote in 1947: but also "So long as I remain alive and well I shall continue to feel strongly about prose style, to love the surface of the earth, and to take pleasure in solid objects and scraps of useless information . . . a good prose is like a windowpane."

(1961)

GEORGE ORWELL: 3

THIS splendid monument* is erected by Sonia Orwell and Ian Angus, who is in charge of the Orwell archive at London University. Orwell made a request that no biography should be written; this constitutes the nearest equivalent, since so many of his letters are included. Thus, of nine letters to me which appeared in the hundredth number of *Encounter,* seven are reproduced here and two "non-vintage" ones are left out, while two paragraphs omitted from the *Encounter* versions are restored, and rightly. I mention this to illustrate the quality of the editing.

There is not much wholly new material in this book, yet sixty per cent of it is unfamiliar—articles and reviews retrieved from forgotten publications. The Wigan Pier diary, the complete war diary, the notes on the Spanish militia and the Orwell revealed by the hundreds of letters may be considered as new material, which alone justify the outlay on these four volumes. Volume IV includes *Such, Such Were the Joys,* hitherto available only in America. It is, to my mind, his most important autobiographical fragment and perhaps his best essay, running to forty pages, written in 1947:

> I am sending you separately a long autobiographical sketch which I originally undertook as a sort of pendant to Cyril Connolly's *Enemies of Promise,* he having asked me to write a reminiscence of the preparatory school we were at together . . . It is really too libellous to print but I think it should be printed sooner or later. (To F. J. Warburg)

What is important about this essay is the picture it gives of Blair (his real name) as a boy; his account of the school can be verified, the

* *George Orwell: The Collected Essays, Journalism and Letters,* edited by Sonia Orwell and Ian Angus. 4 vols. (New York, 1968).

remainder not. The effect is magical: one enters the antechamber, shrinks, slips through the "windowpane" of his prose and there one is, back again, among the cramming and the hunger and the smells, a little boy in corduroy knickers and a green jersey.

> That was the pattern of school life—a continuous triumph of the strong over the weak . . . Life was hierarchical and whatever happened was right. There were the strong, who deserved to win and always did win, and there were the weak who deserved to lose and always did lose, everlastingly . . . I had no money, I was weak, I was ugly, I was unpopular, I had a chronic cough, I was cowardly, I smelt, I was an unattractive boy . . . But this sense of guilt and inevitable failure was balanced by something else: that is, the instinct to survive.

I have reported, in reviewing George Woodcock's *The Crystal Spirit,* a certain softening in my own attitude to St. Cyprians. This was due to getting possession of my school reports and the headmaster's letters to my father, and some of my own letters home. They revealed a considerable distortion between my picture of the proprietors and their own unremitting care to bring me on. At this point I hear Orwell's wheezy chuckle. "Of course, they knew they were on to a good thing. What do you think was our propaganda value to them as winners of Eton scholarships—almost as good as being an 'Hon.' "

Orwell claims to have been taunted by the headmaster for paying reduced fees—but we had no inkling of this. History, if it can be bothered, will probably show Mr. Wilkes to have been an extremely conscientious, though unimaginative and perhaps unlovable man; and Mrs. Wilkes to have used too much physical violence and emotional blackmail, and to have vented some personal bitterness on the boys. Yet she was warm-hearted and an inspired teacher. The worldliness and snobbery of the Wilkeses which Orwell so much condemns was characteristic of the competitive middle class of the period, not a singular aberration. "A couple of silly, shallow ineffectual people, eagerly clambering up a social ladder which any thinking person could see to be on the point of collapse."

Half a century ago it had not collapsed, nor does it show all those signs of collapsing even now. A knighted grocer still cuts more ice than a writer on most social occasions; the Cavendishes, Capels, and Mildmays, or the Scotch lairds at whom the Wilkeses set their caps so successfully, are still a draw in the world of scholastic private enterprise. So many children enjoy pageantry that the supply of snobs is constantly renewed. It has been suggested by Mr. Gow that Orwell and I were rebels who would be bound to criticise any educational institutions; but this is to underrate the voodoo-like quality of St. Cyprians. Gavin Maxwell found it unchanged ten years later and I have heard of old boys who taught their children to shake their fists at the now deserted playing-fields, as they drove past.

England is the most class-ridden country under the sun. It is a land of snobbery and privilege ruled largely by the old and silly. (1940)

Orwell was a political animal. He reduced everything to politics; he was also unalterably of the Left. His line may have been unpopular or unfashionable, but he followed it unhesitatingly; in fact it was an obsession. He could not blow his nose without moralising on conditions in the handkerchief industry. This habit of mind informed everything he wrote. *Animal Farm* and *1984* are political novels, *Homage to Catalonia, The Road to Wigan Pier* and all his essays ask a *cui bono* and try to unseat the profit-makers, whoever they be. This ruling purpose is the secret of his best writing but far too evident in his worst. If we look dispassionately at his achievement, we notice the enormous proponderance of journalism in these four volumes.

Orwell slipped into the last war as into an old tweed jacket. He settled down in 1939, to the BBC or the Literary Editorial chair of *Tribune,* or as London correspondent to *Partisan Review* (New York) to watch his dream come true—a People's War. He had seen it nearly happen in Spain, now it seemed inevitable. This time the gamble must come off, *Revolution or Disaster.* A series of defeats would topple the British ruling class; in the nick of time the People would kick them out and take control, snatching victory at the last moment, as happened in revolutionary France. Churchill must go, even Cripps must go. Red Guards in the Ritz! Long live the People's Army and the Socialist Home Guard.

This point of view, apart from not being borne out by the facts, limited Orwell. He was anti-Churchill, anti-Stalin, anti-Beaverbrook, anti-American, except for the Trotskyites of *Partisan Review.* He felt enormously at home in the Blitz, among the bombs, the bravery, the rubble, the shortages, the homeless, the signs of rising revolutionary temper.

But the political crisis he "expected for the better part of two years" never materialised. Churchill remained, so did top-hats, titles, officers, the Ritz, Margesson, money, all the bad old things. By 1945 it was too late. Socialism had become respectable. Orwell admitted this, but it is doubtful if he ever admitted what a vast quantity of words he had wasted.

My idea of Hell is a place where one is made to listen to everything one has ever said. But if this punishment be more than one could bear, then to listen to everything one said during the war would be hell enough. The war confined many ambitious, articulate and frustrated publicists to a small space with no outlet but discussion. As Orwell's editor puts it, "he must have written hundreds of thousands of words during those years." Being Orwell, nothing he wrote is quite without value and unexpected gems keep popping up. But O the boredom of argument without action, politics without power.

What is the importance of these four volumes? First, the letters. We are never likely to get such an opportunity again, for though not one of the best letter-writers Orwell was certainly candid. In his letters to women friends, like Brenda Salkeld or Eleanor Jaques, we hear him speaking, as in his letters to friends like Geoffrey Gorer, Julian Symons or Jack Common, who appears out of the blue, or rather the pink, with an enormous bundle. As I wrote about his letters to me, "He was a man, like Lawrence, whose personality shines out in everything he said or wrote."

Next, the non-political essays and reportage—or rather those in which his literary gifts outweigh his political message. Some of these are well known, but it is no bad thing to have them all together. Such are *Why I Write,* the letter about *Ulysses,* the review of *Tropic of Cancer, Shooting an Elephant* and *A Hanging* in Volume I or *Boys' Weeklies* which I published, with Frank Richards's unexpected and admirably written reply. Volume II gives us his memories of the Spanish War, and his fascinating war diary, so much better than the journalism he spun from it. Volume III has the Wodehouse article, the Dali assault.

Volume IV contains his famous rules for writing ("if it is possible to cut a word out cut it out," etc.); his autobiographical letter to his old tutor, Professor Gow; his gloomy but delightful article on book reviewing; and also *Books and Politics, How the Poor Die, The Falling Off of Writers.* ("Many writers, perhaps most, ought simply to stop writing when they reach middle age")—and of course, *Such, Such Were the Joys.* His illness clouds his later letters with his account of hospitalisation and his removal to a sanatorium; and we catch only an echo of his contemplated article on Evelyn Waugh. Of Graham Greene, Orwell wrote: "I have even thought that he might become our first Catholic fellow-traveller."

Waugh was a different matter. I arranged for Evelyn to visit him at Cranham, near his Cotswold home, and he reported that Orwell "was very near to God." Orwell's conclusion: "Waugh is about as good a novelist as one can be while holding untenable opinions."

His last diary concludes with a devastating analysis of upper-class English voices which must have haunted him from St. Cyprians School

Sports. "No wonder everyone hated us so." How typical to shoulder the blame for them!

(1968)

Letters to Orwell are so rare that I append one of which I appear to have kept a copy, with two from him which precede it: the second came out only in *Encounter*.

Sanatori Mauria
Sarria
Barcelona
8.6.37

Dear Cyril,
I wonder if you will be in town during the next few weeks. If you will and would like to meet, you might drop a line . . . If I can get my discharge papers I ought to be home in about a fortnight. I have been nastily wounded, not really a very bad wound, a bullet through the throat which of course ought to have killed me but has merely given me nervous pains in the right arm and robbed me of most of my voice. The doctors here don't seem certain whether I shall get my voice back or not. Personally I believe I shall, as some days it is much better than others, but in any case I want to get home and be properly treated. I was just reading one of your articles on Spain in a February *New Statesman*. It is a credit to the *New Statesman* that it is the only paper, apart from a few obscure ones such as the *New Leader,* where any but the Communist viewpoint has ever got through. Liston Oak's article recently on the Barcelona troubles was very good and well balanced. I was all through that business and know what lies most of the stuff in the papers was. Thanks also for recently telling the public that I should probably write a book on Spain, as I shall, of course, once this bloody arm is right. I have seen wonderful things and at last really believe in Socialism, which I never did before. On the whole, though I am sorry not to have seen Madrid, I am glad to have been on a comparatively little-known front among the Anarchists and P.O.U.M. people instead of the International Brigade, as I should have been if I had come here with C.P. credentials instead of I.L.P. ones. A pity you didn't come up to our position and see me when you were in Aragon. I would have enjoyed giving you tea in a dugout.

Yours,
Eric Blair

12.10.37

Dear Cyril,
I wonder if you are back in England. I haven't seen your name in the *New Statesman* lately. When in town I enquired after you but was told you were abroad. As far as I remember I wrote to you from Spain but not many letters were getting through at that time . . . I wonder if you have been back to Spain and how things are going there. It is almost impossible to get any real news. Owing to having served in the P.O.U.M. militia I had to leave in haste with the police on my heels and most of the people I knew there were in jail, or were when I last had news. We were there about six months and had a most interesting time, but it is heart-breaking to see the way things have gone, nearly a million men dead in all, they say, and obviously it is going to be all for nothing. I was about four months in the line, got badly wounded at Huesca but am now completely all right. My wife really had the worst time, being in the middle of that awful nightmare of political intrigue in Barcelona. Richard Rees was on the Madrid front with an ambulance and got back recently, but I haven't seen him yet. I am doing a book on Spain, of course, and writing against time to try and get it done to come out in March. It doesn't do one any good to have been mixed up with the P.O.U.M.—I have already had to change my publisher, among other things. The only decent book on Spain I have seen hitherto was that one by Franz Borkenau called the *Spanish Cockpit*. I dare say if Jellinek does one it might be good. Do you know where he is? He has left Spain and the *Manchester Guardian* couldn't tell me the address.

Write if you get time . . .

Yours,
Eric Blair

312A King's Road,
Chelsea,
S.W.3.
13 October, 1937

Dear Eric,
Thank you so much for your letter. I have been abroad all the summer in the Balkans, and only got back last week. I heard you had been badly wounded, and I am so glad to hear you are all right again. I tried to come and see you on the Aragon front when I was there, but could not get beyond Fraga, and when I tried again there was only a car going to the other end of the front.

I would very much like to talk to you about Spain as I was very depressed by the treatment of the P.O.U.M., which seemed to me to bear no relation to what they actually were like, but to be purely Russian dogmatism. I suppose it was necessary that Government Spain should swing to the Right in order to obtain more French and English support, but that doesn't alter the fact that they had to put down what was obviously a genuine revolutionary situation to do it. The moment one expresses any anti-communist feelings or shows any sympathy with anarchist or Trotskyist down and outs who are far more interesting and also far more Spanish than the people who replace them, it gets increasingly hard to find a publisher or an editor who will print one.

I haven't got my car at present, but if there is any chance of your coming to London, do let me know at once as I would particularly like to see you.

I enjoyed *The Road to Wigan Pier* enormously, and thought it much your best book. If you have any difficulty about a publisher, I am sure Secker would jump at you. I know them if you want me to suggest it. I haven't heard from Frank Jellinek for ages.

I shall be in London all the winter, so do ring me up if you come up. When I get my car back I will write to you.

Yours ever,
Cyril Connolly

IAN FLEMING

When one has had a friend for nearly thirty years it is natural to suffer extreme impatience when reading his biography* by a journalist who by comparison hardly knew him. After a few pages of Mr. Pearson's book, however, it was I who discovered that I had not really known Ian at all and was learning more and more about him.

The book is very skilfully compiled from reports, opinions and evaluations by this most intelligent and perceptive biographer, who never oversimplifies his subject or under-estimates his complicated mental and emotional processes. I deplore a tendency to end each chapter with a pay-off line as if it were an instalment of a serial, but otherwise I have nothing but praise for a book which engrossed me for two days and a night alone in a Tunis bedroom, immured by the sirocco. During this enforced isolation Ian's life took shape before me and he became my constant companion. I soon began to realise that he had never really confided in me, or rather never spoken to me about large areas in his life or people with whom I was unfamiliar. This was particularly true of his war experiences and many of his friendships.

Thus, although we first met in Kitzbühel in the summer of 1938, I had no idea that he had already lived there, a pupil of Forbes Dennis and his wife Phyllis Bottome, in 1927–28, and that Graf Schlick, the local grandee whom he pointed out to me, was the Bluebeard of a horrifying saga constructed by him on his first visit. At one of our last meetings, just before his death, he talked mostly of Kitzbühel, of the marathon bridge game we played all day, and even mentioned Graf Schlick again. He was there with Ivor Bryce and it would be hard to imagine two more distinguished-looking young men; a Greco-Roman Apollo and a Twelfth Dynasty Pharaoh.

* *The Life of Ian Fleming,* by John Pearson (New York, 1966).

As I came to see more of Ian, the qualities which impressed themselves on all his friends soon became apparent: a determination to succeed at everything he undertook without seeming to be trying, an almost neurotic diffidence especially in intellectual matters, a quick eye to detect failure or humbug and tread on the idol's clay corns, an underlying puritanism which permitted luxury and excess, but soon reacted against them, in the proportion of about nine days' desert to three days' flesh-pots, a defensive/offensive attitude to women, a genuine gift for friendship—that is to say of putting himself out to help and please his friends. Mr. Pearson skirts around his faults, though he drops a few hints about his parsimony which was not unlike Hemingway's.

In fact, their careers have certain resemblances. Both were romantically inclined to the life of action while being constantly hauled back from it by too much imagination and sensibility and even intellectual discipline: both had their moments of being men of action in the late war (Fleming in Germany, Hemingway in France) while otherwise relying on sport—golf, cards, skiing and underwater fishing for one; shooting, hunting and spectator bull-fighting for the other. Both had dominating mothers and had experienced woman trouble: both made large fortunes and were dragged protesting by the Bitch Goddess into ever wider areas of limelight. Both died prematurely. In fact I began to imagine a composite character, Ernest Flemingway, author of a macabre thriller, *The Scum Also Rises.* And both were excellent company.

Mr. Pearson brings out the curious circumstances of Ian's childhood: his difficult position as the second son of a paragon who was killed in the First War leaving an elder brother, the redoubtable Peter, as head of the family. The mother was intensely ambitious for her four sons' success, and inaugurated a reign of "get on or get out." I have heard, on good authority, that she encouraged competition and favouritism among the brothers who would otherwise have settled down amicably enough. Ian, at Eton, excelled at all the sports his brother left him room for, but academically fell far behind him.

One can detect a similarity of predicament as between Alec and Evelyn Waugh and Peter and Ian Fleming, but one can strain Adlerian principles too far. Without Peter (or Alec) the second brothers might have done just as well. The monstrous father-figure who is the villain, in various shapes, of all the Bond books bears no resemblance to Ian's doting father or immaculately dapper elder-prefect brother; M. is already monster enough without Blofeld and Le Chiffre and Dr. No. These have in common a total absence of pity or attraction; they are as hostile and unmalleable as the dragons of old, manifestations of anti-human natural forces whom only the Hero can outwit.

Page thirty-two: "There was a girl in Camberley he had grown quite fond of"—a wild understatement. As well say there was a Miss Juliet in Verona . . . I think a little more research at this point would have uncovered a tale of passionate first love inextricably woven into his unfortunate period at Sandhurst. In this affair, and in his engagement to a girl at Geneva, Ian was far from being the cynical philanderer who emerges from all the later romances. He was not born incapable of deeper relations with the other sex but was forced prematurely to abandon them. Blame the parents.

In reading biographies and autobiographies one is sadly conscious of the point of no return, the moment when the life-shaping forces begin to recede, when the actors are acted upon. Such a moment comes with Ian at the end of the war when he buys his dream plot in Jamaica, leaves the Naval Intelligence, starts up as foreign manager to the Kemsley newspapers (a job which brings increasing frustration instead of fulfilment), begins the James Bond novels and bows his broad shoulders to the yoke of marriage. If we compare the Fleming of the late Forties and Fifties with the right-hand man of Admiral Godfrey, the youthful Naval Commander who had organised the evacuation of Bordeaux, the developer of a unique intelligence-commando, the man who retrieved some of Hitler's most dangerous secrets and captured the complete files of the German Admiralty before they could be burnt, we can hardly believe that the sardonic best-seller, log-rolling for reviews, engrossed in publicity and percentages, hungry for Hollywood, bent on an even louder and tawdrier brand-image, was the same person.

Yet the Fleming of the Thirties was in some ways an equally unsatisfactory figure. After digesting all the many facets brilliantly revealed by Mr. Pearson, one still can't be sure what he really wanted from life, and if that was what he got. He collected first editions—then lost interest in them. He was a perfectionist in matters of detail, he was faithful all his life to coffee and scrambled eggs, he had the beginnings of a pattern-mania, he dreaded *accidie,* he wanted to use women without being used by them, he loved his wife because he could never mentally possess her, he wrote a memorandum for General Donovan which he believed to be the charter of the American Intelligence Service, he carried a tear-gun fountain pen and underwent a stringent course in spy-training and unarmed combat.

"His zeal, ability and judgement are altogether exceptional" (Admiral Godfrey). "He just hadn't got the temperament for an agent or a genuine man of action. I'm not saying that he lacked courage—he had a great deal. But he had far too much imagination" (Sir William Stephenson). "If I had lived in Edgar Wallace's day or in Somerset Maugham's I should be a rich man by now, but, alas, I just missed the boat" (to his mother). Maugham, Simenon, Chandler, Eric Ambler are among the writers he admires. In his youth he corresponded with Jung and collected little magazines. He thought his illness was the punishment of youthful excesses. "The strain on his heart of all that damned underwater fishing" (Stephenson). "Of smoking seventy cigarettes a day and drinking too many Martinis?" (Pearson).

The final success was marred by having to keep pace with the Bond image. One is grateful for a few charming letters from Noel Coward out of the gloom and for the happy Jamaican interludes, though even here publicity had to intrude in the form of the Prime Minister's visit to Goldeneye. In the last two years of his life he became even sadder, gentler and wiser. Like Hemingway, he became a victim of the world he had helped to create out of his private vision. Had his heart held out he might have reached a similar state of grace by choice rather than necessity and bequeathed his laurels to the Men from Uncle, but, like Hemingway, he was urged on by a mixture of courage and dissatisfaction to sacrifice himself and those who loved him, rather than watch his powers decline.

(1966)

JEAN GENET

GENET must be about the only writer I have refused to meet. I remember the occasion well: St. Germain des Prés in the mid-1940s, mutual friends trying to escort me over to his table. Genet was wearing some kind of khaki shirt, talking and laughing, bald and toothless; I formed the impression he was wicked.

Moreover, I had been told he had marred a former presentation by asking another writer if he were homosexual. On receiving the answer, "No," *"alors il l'insulta, il l'injuria."* He had also refused to meet Gide as being a person of "doubtful morality" because he had tried to make a rational defence of homosexuality in *Corydon,* tantamount to going over to the enemy. Moreover I have a particular horror of a book-thief. The Mona Lisa is either there or it isn't; but by purloining one volume on an impulse he can cause weeks of anxiety and bewilderment to an unmethodical collector.

I now regret my moral prudery. Genet is not wicked, and shortly after this he abandoned stealing under the influence of a new boy friend. "The more I love Lucien, the more I lose my taste for theft and thieves . . . but a great sadness crushes me . . . it is for my legend," Mr. Coe tells us,* quoting from the end of the *Journal d'un Voleur*.

His face is more that of a fallen angel, of a nun who has been something of a Rimbaud and could now be waiting for Godot. Since the great literary and dramatic success of his later work, I am told, he lives very simply, is in poor health, and gives all his money away. He is invisible and belongs to the élite of artists who ignore their fame and their public, and who wander through the world like a Buddhist or Taoist, anticipating bodily dissolution.

* *The Vision of Jean Genet,* by Richard N. Coe (New York, 1968).

I wish I liked his work better. Mine is a shocking record. An evening at *Les Nègres* I found one of the most boring I have ever spent, and I still shudder at the moment when the dead "Whites," duly butchered and buried, rose from their graves and began to spout again. I still can't cut the pages of *Notre Dame des Fleurs,* or lift *Querelle de Brest* with Cocteau's facile illustrations—or is it the *Miracle de la Rose?* I no longer care. I enjoy parts of *The Thieves' Journal*—especially the picaresque Spanish element (not nearly Spanish enough). I haven't seen—and hope never to see—*Les Paravents,* but I greatly enjoyed *Les Bonnes* and most of *Le Balcon,* which is an original contribution to the threatre.

But it's no good. I find Genet a thundering bore and Sartre's dissection of him reminds me of Huxley for ever writing about Lawrence. He is a bore because he is at the mercy of his own rhetoric; he inflates relentlessly, and nothing is more tiring than the exaltation of crime and evil and its erection into a life's work. Mr. Thody* notes Genet's "obsession with farting"—would he had confined it to air! Sartre describes Genet's first novel, *Notre Dame des Fleurs* as an "epic of masturbation"; in *The Thieves' Journal* Genet writes *"j'ai bandé pour le crime,"* in *Pompes Funèbres* the Berlin Public Executioner is presented as a symbol of desirable sexual vigour, and makes an important contribution to the general atmosphere of the book. As Mr. Thody says, his references to the German army

> reveal far more of what Cyril Connolly called "the obsession with the male organ, which is really the obsession of a female nymphomaniac," than any serious attempt to associate his cult of evil with the political ambitions of the Nazi movement.

Good for him.

Evil and race-hatred win their highest praise in his latest works, *Les Nègres* and *Les Paravents* ("The Screens"). Both plays could have been given a Malcolm X certificate.

"Evil, miraculous evil, which still remains when everything else has collapsed, miraculous evil, you will help us. I implore you, I implore you, standing here, upright. Come, Evil, and fertilise my people," cries the mother Heroine of *Les Paravents* and one of the Blacks recites a blood-curdling litany of White attributes:

> "Pallid as a consumptive's death-rattle
> Pallid as the stools of a man with dysentery
> Paler than a cobra's belly" etc.

* *Jean Genet,* by Philip Thody (New York, 1969).

(quoted by Dr. Coe.)

And one Negro apostrophises the cast:

> Let negroes negrify themselves. Let them persist to the point of madness in what they are condemned to be, in their ebony and in their smell, in their yellow eyes, in their cannibal tastes. Let them not be content with eating Whites, but let them cook each other as well.

The true point of the play, according to Mr. Thody, is that during all these make-believe atrocities, on the stage, the Negroes execute their first Black traitor, a moment as significant as when the Christians began to sentence their own martyrs.

A glance at the little that is known of Genet's life-history reveals that the odds against him emerging as a novelist, poet and dramatist must have been many hundreds of millions to one. His birth was as fortuitous as that of the Old Man of Cape Horn, and his parents, Gabrielle Genet and father unknown, handed him over at birth to the Public Assistance (December 19, 1910).

He was born in the Public Maternity Hospital and, aged seven, placed as a foster-child with a peasant family. As a child he stole from his foster-parents and also discovered he was homosexual, and by sixteen, after becoming an accomplished burglar and homosexual prostitute, was doing three years in the State Reformatory at Mettray. He was taught versification by a professional song-writer, and his first published work was a poem, "Le Condamné à Mort," Fresnes, 1942. In another prison, the Santé, he began his novel, *Notre Dame des Fleurs.* His life in the Thirties is described in the *Journal d'un Voleur.* By 1943 he was in danger of life imprisonment on any further conviction.

It was obviously a great psychological disappointment that Genet was never sent to Devil's Island. A little more violence and he would have made it and the effect on him would have been terrific. Imagine Genet's genius let loose on the filthy squalor of the prison ship, La Martinière, on its journey from La Rochelle, with the steampipes always ready to scald any mutineers; imagine the arrival at Cayenne, the homosexual murderers all lined up to sit for him, the intellectual élite demanding his release back home. He would have incinerated that evil place in a blaze of verbiage—and then asked to have it put back. Something like that very nearly happened.

Mr. Thody quotes Auden:

> Time that is intolerant
> of the brave and innocent
> and indifferent in a week
> to a beautiful physique . . .

worships language and forgives
everyone by whom it lives;
pardons cowardice, conceit
lays its honours at their feet . . .

And Dr. Coe explains how Genet was in fact sentenced to life imprisonment, after stealing from his new liberal friends, and only released with a free pardon when, in 1947, Sartre, Cocteau, Mauriac and Mondor addressed an appeal to Vincent Auriol, the President of the Republic, who granted it and invited Genet to dinner.

Of these two books, Mr. Thody's is well written, perceptive, informative, and a joy to handle. He writes from a humanist standpoint. Dr. Coe's is the more biased and metaphysical, also fuller of information, much of it in foot-notes.

(1968)

NORMAN MAILER

NARCISSUS, we are told, saw his reflection in a pool and fell in love with it. Presumably his face was the peccant part and its beauty was proverbial. Since Whitman's "Song of Myself" a new figure has emerged, the whole man, not necessarily a beauty, in love with the whole of himself—smells, sweat, toe-nails, urine, faeces. One might call this twentieth-century type Caliban-Narcissus and detect more than a trace of him in Henry Miller, Wolfe, Behan, and Genet, to name but a few.

In this type of writer aggression often lurks near the surface ready to be let loose on interrupters or those who in any way thwart his egomania or refuse to settle for the complete man. Editors and reviewers are usually in danger, though nobody is safe, and Mr. Mailer seems to have it in for Mrs. Kennedy because she offered him a soft drink and did not want to hear his views on Sade. *Advertisements for Myself* is a typical Caliban-Narcissus title, though Mr. Mailer's new book, *The Presidential Papers,** runs it close, for this collection of miscellaneous articles is dressed up to look as if they were all memoranda addressed to President Kennedy on general topics on which the writer considered he should be better informed. "The letter to Fidel Castro was written in short sessions of manic work of several weeks' writing, usually when drunk and late at night, at the time I was running for Mayor of New York."

The photograph is more revealing. The adjectives "incorrigible" "irrepressible" jump to mind, the position of the inevitable cigarette, the expression as of a large rough dog waiting for a ball to be thrown which one is already tired of throwing. "In America few people will trust you unless you are irreverent."

* *The Presidential Papers,* by Norman Mailer (New York, 1963).

I have a great admiration for *The Naked and the Dead,* which I believe to be the best American war novel. Mr. Mailer still regards himself as a deep-sea, long-term novelist in the great tradition, and I hope his new novel, *An American Dream,* will substantiate this, although experience confirms that great egoists do not make great novelists unless, like Proust, they write mainly about themselves, or, like Balzac, consider all their characters as their private family.

Mr. Mailer has a tendency to quarrel with those who do not accept him at his own valuation. In these quarrels he is always right, which tends to an obfuscation of reality. Meanwhile, his is the typical American success story, his personality now commands more money than his talent and he holds forth about any subject when required to by popular magazines and television interviews. Why are Wilbur, Frost and Salinger, he protests, invited to the White House before Burroughs, Corso and Norman Mailer?

The Presidential Papers is always exasperating and sometimes infuriating. It infuriated me in the places where I saw what a good writer Mr. Mailer still is, although one has to dig through this rubbish heap to find him. He is a natural anarchist with a sympathy for beats, outlaws and racial minorities and, like Miller before him, he excels at pricking the bubble of American self-esteem, progress, materialism, philistinism, etc. He can write very well when he takes the trouble and quite well when he takes no trouble and very badly then too, especially when his truculent egomania runs away with him on a filibuster. He is obsessed with cancer-images for society, anal erotic for himself.

His book is saved by some direct reporting, especially of the Democrats' Convention at Los Angeles, the Kennedy family and a boxing match. He is worst when he interviews himself about his philosophic or aesthetic doctrines or when he writes poetry. And yet the description of the décor of the Biltmore Hotel at Convention time is brilliant.

> . . . that huge depressing alley with inimitable hotel color, that faded depth of chiaroscuro, which unhappily has no depth in it, that brown which is not a brown, that gray which has no pearl in it, that color which can be described only as hotel-color because the beiges, the tans, the walnuts, the mahoganies, the dull blood rugs, the moaning yellows, the sick greens, the grays and all those dumb browns merge into that lack of color which is an over-large hotel at Convention time . . .

Admirable too are all his descriptions of Kennedy and the Kennedy entourage, of the role of the artist and "how the marrow of a nation is contained in his art." The trained observer appears in the account of the gangsters and Mafiosos at the Liston fight, or of Liston himself.

One cannot think of more than a few men who have beauty. Charles Chaplin has it across a room, Krishna Menon across a table, Stephen Spender used to have it; Burt Lancaster, oddly enough, used to have it; they say Orson Welles had it years ago; and President Eisenhower in person, believe it or not. At any rate Liston had it. You did not feel you were looking at someone attractive, you felt you were looking at a creation.

The passage about his stools and faeces, however, smacks of fine writing. But the subject, he points out, "is particularly abhorrent to the English." Mailer, one feels, is a square to the beats, and a beat to the squares, like Thomas Wolfe. He does not measure up to Beckett and Burroughs; when he writes about teen-age gangs his language steps back fifty years. "It is the root for which our tongues once found the older words of courage, loyalty, honor and the urge for adventure."

In his attacks on the dullness, conformity and complacency of the American scene, the new totalitarianism, the plastic boredom, he is at one with Miller, Wolfe, Hemingway and Ginsberg, but his weapons are rusted by his exuberant egotism and self-indulgence. I would offer him a proverb: "The hatred of one's own voice is the beginning of wisdom."

(1964)

ROBERT LOWELL

*Notebook** was first published as *Notebook 1967–68* a year ago. The English edition has been revised and enriched by "more than ninety new poems."

> It is less an almanac than the story of my life . . . my meter, fourteen line unrhymed blank verse sections, is fairly strict at first and elsewhere, but often corrupts in single lines to the freedom of prose. Even with this licence I fear I have failed to avoid the themes and gigantism of the sonnet.

I doubt if it would be possible to read, still less to write 260 pages of sonnets. The "gigantism" would be overwhelming. These poems really are a "notebook": they have a certain roughness and crudeness, like an autobiographical sketch-book, a journal much of which could be written out in prose. When one does come across a real poem, a true sonnet with rhymes like "Night Sweat," one is overwhelmed by its Baudelairean intensity which haunts one for many pages afterwards. A poet who can write like that seems sadistic to be fobbing us off with so much that is rambling and incoherent. On the other hand he is true to the *matière*. The palette is unmistakably Lowell, and to those who relish this particular sensibility, steeped in our own favourite poets, yet completely of its time, religious yet unbelieving, material and melancholy, loving both nature and friends, yet grieving for some mysterious central deficiency, a *cloche fêlée* "like sweet bells jangled," the *Notebook* will be a book to read and re-read.

The themes are conventional: Boston and Harvard, family pride, marriage, fatherhood, love poems in Mexico, poems about other writers or historical figures, about events of the day as viewed by the liberal

* *Notebook,* by Robert Lowell (New York, 1970).

élite, Vietnam, students, etc. But Lowell himself is not conventional; he is detached, anarchistic, even violent (did he not knock his father down and live to proclaim and regret it?); and besides he has been mentally sick, in and out of clinics. He fulfils the Greek proverb that great genius is to madness near allied. Madness brings strange bedfellows, and it afforded him the glimpse of the gangster Lepke of which he made good use; and it causes him to cast a wary eye on doctors, the "goiter experts" who measure his thyroid like raccoons feeding. "The sickroom's crimeless mortuary calm."

The great weakness of this mental instability, characterised in his case by mania even more than depression, is its interference with poetic judgement. As an intellectual liberal who has been prepared to go to gaol for his convictions, Lowell must be listened to when he sums up what is wrong with the world (as in his great poem "Waking early Sunday morning"), but his "public" poetry is exposed to the subjectivity of his private self. The obscurity of his private poetry, surrealist short cuts of an exalted mind, is distorting and far too casual, an *allée couverte* which may end in an impenetrable tangle.

It is interesting to compare two versions of Hölderlin's beautiful poem, "The Half of Life," which draws introspective sufferers to it like a lodestone. Here is David Gascoyne:

Adorned with yellow pears
and with wild roses filled
The earth hangs in the lake.

And wondrous love-intoxicated swans
In peaceful holy waters dip their heads.

My woe! when winter comes
Where shall I find the rose?
Where shall I find the sunshine and
The shadows of the earth?
The cold unspeaking walls rise up
The flags flap in the wind.

Here is Lowell:

The land going down to the lake was choked with wild rose,
the fruit was struck to golden, the high swans, drunk
on making love, had plunged their aching heads;
the water was re-birth but then the winter;
no flower, or sun, or most times field for shadow—
exhaust and airconditioning klir in the wind

The lines are italicised but only the word "klir" (removed from the last line of the original *"klirren die fahnen"*) suggests the source. The poet is naturally free to adapt any passage he chooses, but "choked," "struck" and "aching" show his typical anxiety superimposed on Hölderlin's autumnal landscape. One of the last poems, "For John Berryman," shows that Lowell recognises a similarity between the two verse autobiographers.

I feel I know what you have worked through
You know what I have worked through—these are words . . .
John, we used the language as if we made it . . .

Other influences I detect are the Hart Crane of "Voyages" and "Key West," early Cummings, Dylan Thomas (traces), "Autumn Journal" (MacNeice) and so back to Meredith's "Modern Love." Nor can Lowell escape comparison with Auden, who is master both of the sonnet and of the vivisection of great men. But Auden's short poems on other writers are lapidary, while Lowell's are impressions which enshrine an historical anecdote or scrap of conversation. Eliot, in the "Eliot" poem, mentions Pound: Pound praises Eliot in the "Pound" one, while Frost inscribes his book "Robert Lowell from Robert Frost his friend in the art," and Dr. (William Carlos) Williams tells him:

I am sixty-seven, and more attractive
To girls than when I was seventeen.

I have tried dipping into these poems and dodging about and also read them once straight through, and I've even compared the early and later versions; I still can't make up my mind about them. Sometimes I abandon myself completely to Lowell's grace, distress and fitful intelligence as he waltzes me over the years and round the calendar, pausing only to repeat a line twice; or say to myself "Yes, that's how it was!"; at others I want violently to protest against his nostalgia for all the other Lowells, his clumsiness and distortion.

At some point I picked up Mr. Patrick Cosgrave's *The Public Poetry of Robert Lowell* (New York, 1972) which is a stimulating introduction to all the previous poems. According to Mr. Cosgrave all Lowell's poems are public; he is in the tradition of Pope, Johnson and Yeats.

> With *Waking early Sunday morning* we not only return to the presence of great poetry, but we mark, in that presence, its deep involvement in the life of our times, the conduct of our affairs and the quality of our life and ideas as well.

Fortified by Mr. Cosgrave's gravity and ordered enthusiasm, one goes back to *Notebook*—but even the public poems, for which a calendar of public events is appended, are not so much experiences as comments on them as he receives the news in his home. There is no escaping the fact, even for Mr. Cosgrave, that this is a thoroughly private book, like *In Memoriam*. Lowell's daughter's childhood, his first love at Harvard, the blow at his father, the deaths of friends (Jarrell, MacNeice, Roethke, Matthiessen), Allen Tate having twin sons at sixty-eight, I. A. Richards, his guinea-pig Mrs. Muffin, blizzard in Cambridge, the trip to Mexico . . .

Now our hesitant
conversation moves from lust
to love;
friendship without dissension,
multiplying
days, days, days, days—how
can I love you more,
short of turning into a criminal.

Against the intimate domestic picture the subjects of the historical vignettes stand out: Alexander, Cato, Caligula, Attila, Mohammed, Tamerlane, Robespierre, Saint-Just, Napoleon, Stalin—tyrants who got away with it, representing the frustrated power-love in every artist whose life is in the imagination. The ambivalence which these monsters arouse is significant, and I think renews our confidence in Lowell as a poet. The violence Mr. Cosgrave notes as a main characteristic here finds a healthy outlet, the poet remains a Propertius, a private lover and philosopher who avoids the humbug of the campus and the plaudits of the platform.

Fifty, humbled with the year's gold garbage
dead laurel grizzling my back like spines of hay.

(1970)

BASIL BUNTING: 1

When I reviewed Basil Bunting's *The Spoils* I recognised a poet of great individual talent, marred, as I thought, by deliberate obscurity. (I do not believe that it is a condition of poetry that it has to be obscure to effect an *ecce mysterium.*)

I was quite unprepared for *Briggflatts** which seems to me one of the best poems I have read and re-read for a long time. It, too, is obscure, but through the Poundian principle of intense condensation. If we give them time the lines expand in the mind and their meaning with them, though it will help to know that Bunting was once apprenticed to a mason, as well as to the *"miglior fabbro"*—Pound's disciple as much as Beckett was Joyce's or Norman Cameron Graves's—to name two other neglected poets of the Thirties, "before the rules made poetry a pedant's game."

I first noticed Bunting in print in Zukovsky's *An Objectivist Anthology,* published in France in 1931, and by 1933 he occupied fifty-two pages of Pound's *Active Anthology* to Zukovsky's forty-six. This selection included some of his best long poems, e.g., "Villon" and "Attis," but I did not obtain it till many years later. In 1938 Pound dedicated his "Guide to Kulchur" "to Louis Zukovsky and Basil Bunting, strugglers in the desert." And there they struggled for many a year to come. He might have remained the poor man's BB were it not for the acclaim of the young when he went back to work in Newcastle and for the discerning few in America where his more recent poems were first published. This new popularity coincides with that of Zukovsky, on whom has fallen the mantle of Williams as Anti-Pope. The Pope, of course, being Eliot.

I should like to write a piece one day on the changing fashions in

* *Briggflatts,* by Basil Bunting (London, 1966).

modern poetry. For poets obey the same laws as summer resorts. The fashion moves continuously in the direction of the less well known and away from the popular, which have to be rediscovered for different reasons. Zukovsky is clearly a dry poet; his long poem "Partita" in the *Penguin Book of Modern American Writing* has an abstract un-Eliot quality. Bunting is not anti-Eliot but borrows heavily from Pound in his use of historical sources and historical perspective, even as Pound took this discursive rumination from Browning. But in Bunting there is a lyrical note which he has been steadily compressing and which makes *Briggflatts* almost all lyric, or rather intensely musical: the words shine like hoar-frost.

> I scarcely write a line less than ten or twelve times before it is right. *Briggflatts* is 700 lines long. I must have written between 10,000 and 20,000 lines altogether. It's much the best thing I've done. It contains parts which I don't think anyone will read and forget. (From an interview in the *Newcastle Journal,* July 1965)

Briggflatts is "an autobiography," with the proviso that "it means what you want it to mean." It is in five sections and was written in 1965. The sections start with spring and the mason's apprentice—a child watching the mason carve a gravestone.

> a mason times his mallet
> to a lark's twitter

Bloodaxe, a Danish King of Northumbria *circa* 800, is invoked. The whole prelude is magical, like Debussy, *"si mystérieusement émouvante,"* linking childhood formally with death.

The next section is about summer and love:

> Love is vapour we're soon through it . . .
> It tastes good, garlic and salt in it.
> With the half-sweet wine of Orvieto
> On scanty grass under great trees
> Where the ramparts cuddle Lucca . . .
> It looks well on the page, but never
> Well enough. Something is lost . . .

Bloodaxe and the mason come back again via the marble quarries at Carrara, "stained like a urinal," and the section ends with a precisely Yeatsian evocation of Pasiphaë.

These themes, however, cannot be isolated, for they are worked into the close musical texture of the poem with its technical observation, its allusions to Byrd, Scarlatti, Monteverdi and its all-pervading nostalgia.

To give an example; besides the development of the lark and the miller, or the employing of the slow-worm as a symbol of the poet, there is a love story—

My love is young but wise
   Oak, applewood,
her fire is banked with ashes
   till day.
The fells reek of her hearth's scent
her girdle is greased with lard;
hunger is stayed on her settle, lust in her bed.
Light as spider floss her hair on my cheek
which a puff scatters.
Light as a moth her fingers on my thigh.

This motive reappears in the last section, a wonderful picture of winter-fishing with its invocation to the stars:

Aldebaran, low in the clear east
beckoning boats to the fishing.
Capella floats from the north
with shields hung on his gunwale.
That is no dinghy's lantern
occulted by the swell—Betelgeuse
calling behind him to Rigel.
Starlight is almost flesh . . .
Furthest, fairest things, stars,
   free of our humbug,
each his own, the longer
   known the more alone,
wrapped in emphatic fire
   roaring out to a black flue . . .

But the poem ends, Debussy-like, on the love-story:

Fifty years a letter unanswered
A visit postponed for fifty years
She has been with me fifty years.
Starlight quivers. I had day enough.
For love uninterrupted night.

Mr. Bunting is now at the University of California, Santa Barbara, but is looking for an academic job in this country. Surely this must immediately be found. We have no poet here of his generation who is both a romantic and so meticulous a craftsman, rich in mind and ear.

Incidentally we should have spotted him, when, like Norman Cameron, he was drawn to Villon so many years ago:

Remember, imbeciles and wits,
Sots and ascetics, fair and foul,
Young girls with little tender tits,
that Death is written over all.
Worn hides that scarcely clothe the soul
They are so rotten old and thin
or firm and soft and warm and full
fellmonger Death gets every skin . . .

"Villon" is reprinted in *Loquitur* (Fulcrum Press) which includes all Bunting's work except "The Spoils," It is a handsome book and I advise lovers of poetry to snap it up.

(1967)

BASIL BUNTING: 2

Bright wine and the sight of a gracious face,
dear it might cost, but always cheap to me
My purse was my heart, my heart bursting with words
and the title page of my book was Love and Poetry.

These lines translated from the "Persian of Rudaki" might seem particularly applicable to Bunting's poetry* were it not for a conscious intellect also at work. Perhaps there is something of him, too, in another translation of his, from Firdausi:

When the sword of sixty comes near his head
Give a man no wine, for he is drunk with years . . .
Since I raised my glass to fifty-eight
I have toasted only the bier and the burial ground.

The success of *Briggflatts*† has led to the overlooking of these shorter poems or "Odes" of Bunting's which contain however some of his most original work. "The Road to Orotava" is a tightly packed landscape of camels, girls on their donkeys, and peasants on the crowded sunny highway. All these odes repay the closest attention: "On the flyleaf of Pound's cantos" is one of the most exquisite compliments one poet has paid another. These Odes are steeped in Horace for whom Bunting performs the same type of service as Lowell to Baudelaire. He gets him right, refashions his language to suit our ear, and puts him across:

These tracings from a world that's dead
take for my dust-smothered pyramid

and this world *is* dead, killed by four-letter words, unsophisticated knowingness, impatience, inability to savour language.

* *Collected Poems of Basil Bunting* (New York, 1969).
† *Briggflatts,* by Basil Bunting (Stream Records).

Poetry? It's a hobby,
I run model trains
Mr Shaw there breeds pigeons.
It's not work. You don't sweat.

In Bunting's earlier poetry the influence of Villon is predominant and, of course, of Pound, and Pound wrote an opera about Villon. But Bunting emerged fully fledged. His long poem on Villon appeared in 1925 and is as good as anything of his later. I have to keep on quoting the same lines from it because they contain the *"lacrimae rerum";* I cannot read them without a glow of recognition.

Our doom
is to be sifted with the wind,
heaped up, smoothed down like silly sands.
We are less permanent than thought.
The Emperor with the Golden Hands
is still a word, a tint, a tone
insubstantial—glorious
when we ourselves are dead and gone
and the green grass growing over us.

Villon also riots through Bunting's anti-war poem, *The Well of Lycopolis* (1935) with its echoes of *The Waste Land,* pub-crawls and rhetoric. In fact the youthful Bunting must have had a hard task eliminating the influence of Pound and Eliot, both of whom he served and of their train was he. Pound's imprint was the stronger, but since Pound stood for compression and clarity it was healthy and Bunting does not borrow Pound's litigious fact-finding economic didacticism. He remains a lyric poet with metaphysical leanings. The long "Chomei at Toyama" (1932) in the "Chinese" vein has moments of pure Pound ("men are fools to invest in real estate") and true Buddhist feeling (it was written in the twelfth century in prose, and set in Kyoto).

I am shifting river-mist, not to be trusted.
I do not ask anything extraordinary of myself.
I like a nap after dinner
And to see the seasons come round in good order.
Hankering, vexation and apathy
That's the run of the world.

Apart from a few lyrics Bunting's later work consists of two long poems, "The Spoils" and *Briggflatts. Briggflatts* is a romanticised autobiography in which he describes his first love, a boy-and-girl affair broken off by the 1914 War in which he was imprisoned as a recalcitrant conscientious objector (of Quaker origin—Briggflatts is a Quaker meeting-house), and his other love-affair with his vocation.

Fortunately Bunting is a man and a poet; the formation of the man is the clue to the verse. He has never been a publicist, politician or propagandist; he is too much of an anarchist to vote, neither has he been a don; he has accepted the poverty and obscurity which is the price of true freedom and must have had a very hard time from which we are the gainers. (Beckett is such another.) So that now that he is close on seventy we may honour a professional poet who has never been professionally anything else.

The sheets are gathered and bound,
the volume indexed and shelved,
dust on its marbled leaves . . .

Domenico Scarlatti
Condensed so much music into so few bars
With never a crabbed turn or congested cadence,
Never a boast or a see-here . . .

But I wish he would remove Lopokova (Lady Keynes) from his "Villon."

'Abelard and Eloise
Henry the Fowler, Charlemagne
Genée, Lopokova, all these
die, die in pain . . .'

He should have seen her last week in Eastbourne, doing her Christmas shopping.

(1969)

ALEXANDER SOLZHENITSYN

THIS novel* is of great political significance, for it is the result of Khrushchev's more liberal policy to the victims of Stalin's purges. It admits the existence of forced-labour camps, it admits that life is very painful in such camps, it admits that innocent men are sent there to serve long sentences: and all this record of injustice is permitted to be translated and circulated abroad as well as at home. Although it will therefore be welcomed by anti-Communists in the West as anti-Soviet propaganda, its publication represents an advance on the conditions attending Pasternak's *Doctor Zhivago.* One cannot attribute this purely to Khrushchev's vindictive feelings against Stalin. It is a blow struck for human freedom all over the world and it will make it harder to enforce the barbarity of forced-labour camps in all the countries where it is read.

And it is gloriously readable. Alexander Solzhenitsyn (b. 1918) was an intellectual before he joined the army in 1942 and rose to the rank of captain in an artillery battery. In 1945 he was charged with making derogatory remarks about Stalin and deported for eight years to forced labour in Siberia. Since then he has been writing continuously, and *One Day* is a most accomplished short novel. It covers the day in the life of a peasant-prisoner, a skilled mason who never departs from his character.

It is this which makes the book so original; there is no trace of the Orwell-Koestler-Kafka mentality in it, of the tragedy of the intellectual who is acquainted with ideas, with the concept of freedom and the perils of the imagination. There is neither horror nor self-pity. Ivan is young, strong, and good at his job. He is aware, like all the other prisoners, that there are certain rules of health which must be obeyed, if he is to

* *One Day in the Life of Ivan Denisovich,* by Alexander Solzhenitsyn. Translated by Ralph Parker (New York, 1963).

survive. There are no atrocities, no tortures, no death-beds. By keeping fit (which means keeping warm), by obeying the prisoners' code, by scrounging and hard work it is possible to keep alive and perhaps eventually be released. These are not Nazi extermination camps which require the prisoners' death; they demand rather the maximum of hard work at the minimum of state expense.

Since, therefore, survival is possible, hope exists and consequently even happiness. At the end of his day Denisovich is almost happy. A naval captain, however, who won't adapt himself and who answers the guards back is doomed, and is led off to a ten-day stretch in the unheated cells. His crime was to have received a token of gratitude from an English admiral with whom he had worked in convoy; and he still behaves as if he were in command of his flotilla.

The other prisoners are from the European provinces of the Soviet Union. Some are expiating the guilt of having been captured by the Germans, some are Western Ukrainians. There are not more than a dozen whom we are expected to get to know. Solzhenitsyn is an artist; he limits his canvas and draws the reader into it, his characters stand out without being cartooned or exaggerated, his short book never flags, is never padded. His "dumb ox" hero is like a Hemingway character and the camp is a Hemingway scene—but without self-consciousness, without awareness of courage, tragedy, irony. The accent is on survival and those who survive are thankful for small mercies, cunning, strong and uncomplaining. Everything depends on the team leader.

The camp reveals itself in its full horror, in all its futile brutalised inhumanity, for the reason that everyone is trying philosophically to make the best of it. It is the reader who supplies the emotion. Denisovich gets through his sixteen-hour day and is "almost happy," while the reader has suffered a thousand deaths. Of course it is possible that the author did not dare to criticise the system overtly in case his tale could never be published, but since he is a professional writer I am inclined to give him the benefit of an artistic conscience and to see the whole as an astonishing tour de force, as if Orwell's cart-horse Boxer had written *Animal Farm.*

I have refrained from telling the story, because it tells itself so quickly from when the camp awakes to thirty degrees of frost in the Siberian dawn to when it goes to bed the same night slightly colder; but there are many strokes which reveal a considerable artist, not the least being the last sentence. "Nothing had spoiled the day and it had been almost happy. There were nine thousand six hundred and fifty-three days like this in his sentence, from reveille to lights out. The three extra ones were because of the leap years . . ." I do not know if claims are being advanced that *One Day* is a great work of art. If it had been about Belsen or Buchenwald we would have taken it in our stride, but coming out of Kazakhstan it strikes completely new ground.

I do not think, after allowing for the curiosity we all feel about the subject, that it is more than a minor work of art, because, after all, the author is not Ivan Denisovich and so has had to shrink himself down in order to become him. The "dumb ox" (as Wyndham Lewis christened the Hemingway hero) can be neither poet nor philosopher, and the intellectuals who were sent to Siberia under the Tsars have written about hunger and the lash perhaps better than anyone else could. It is not wholly an aesthetic experience. That, I believe, will come later, for Mr. Solzhenitsyn seems to be one of those writers who will rise above a best-seller, even if it be his first book.

Another edition has been published in America (Praeger) translated by Max Hayward (co-translator of *Doctor Zhivago*) and Ronald Hingley, two Oxford dons who have recast it in Hemingwayese-American. The results are perhaps closer to the ferocity of the original, but so grotesque that they emphasise how European and un-Hemingway the characterisation and dialogue really are. In such extreme conditions no one can afford to indulge their personality.

(1963)

LITTLE MAGAZINES

LITTLE magazines are the pollinators of works of art: literary movements and eventually literature itself could not exist without them. Most of the poetry of Yeats, Eliot, Pound and Auden appeared in magazines, so did *A Portrait of the Artist* and *Ulysses, Finnegans Wake* and nearly all of Hemingway's short stories. A good magazine brings writers together, even the most isolated, and sets them influencing their time and, when that time is past, devotes a special number to them as a last tribute.

Little magazines are of two kinds, dynamic and eclectic. Some flourish on what they put in, others by whom they keep out. Dynamic magazines have a shorter life and it is round them that glamour and nostalgia crystallise. If they go on too long they will become eclectic although the reverse process is very unusual. Eclectic magazines are also of their time but they cannot ignore the past nor resist good writing from opposing camps. The dynamic editor runs his magazine like a commando course where picked men are trained to assault the enemy position: the eclectic is like an hotel proprietor whose rooms fill up every month with a different clique.

To give some examples: *The Yellow Book* was eclectic, *The Savoy* dynamic, *The Little Review* dynamic, *The Dial* eclectic, *transition* dynamic, *Life and Letters* eclectic (also *The Criterion* and *The London Mercury*), *Les Soirées de Paris* dynamic, *La Nouvelle Revue Française* eclectic, *New Verse* and *New Writing* (up to 1940) dynamic, *Horizon* eclectic, *Verve* eclectic, *Minotaure* dynamic, etc. An eclectic editor feels he has a duty to preserve certain values, to reassess famous writers, disinter others. A truly dynamic editor will completely ignore the past: his magazine will be short-lived, his authors violent and obscure. The eclectic will be in constant danger of becoming complacent and middlebrow: he lasts longer and pays better. Most quarterlies are eclectic: they have so many pages and are less agitated by the time-clock. There are of course and always have been dynamic magazines which are not about literature but about political or racial minorities, and fashion magazines whose advertisements betray their true nature, even if they pose as literary, like Crowninshield's *Vanity Fair*. It all depends on the need for circulation and the personality of the editor. Dynamic magazines usually start with a fixed amount of money to lose and lose it; contributors are often unpaid and "names" are not sought for to increase circulation: the editors are usually under thirty and may soon go off the boil. No magazine can be more intelligent than its editor and the limitations of an editor will gradually impose a ceiling. Thus, Sir John Squire's *London Mercury* could attract all the best writers but could not hold them, while Grigson's *New Verse* commanded the best poetry of the Thirties because the poets respected him. Desmond MacCarthy had the catholic taste and intelligence of a great editor but could not tolerate obscurity and insisted on regarding literature as entertainment. There was nothing in his magazine which he could not talk about at a dinner party. Eliot's *The Criterion* could print Auden's "Paid on Both Sides" in 1930 which would have been rejected by *Life and Letters*. *The Criterion,* however, returned Joyce's "Anna Livia" which was first printed in *Le Navire d'Argent* edited by Sylvia Beach and Adrienne Monnier. Eliot's "Prufrock" was also much rejected.

The first magazine of the modern movement was *The English Review* with Ford Madox Ford as editor, 1908. (*La Nouvelle Revue Française* was founded a year later.) Ford liked to say it came into being to print a poem of Thomas Hardy's about an abortion which no one else would accept. Ford was only editor for a year and a half after which Austin Harrison took over and it became an eclectic monthly. Norman Douglas was an assistant editor, Lawrence and Pound were also among Ford's discoveries (Pound has been consistently loyal to Ford). "The event of 1909–10 was Ford Madox Ford's *English Review,* and no greater condemnation of the utter filth of the whole social system of that time can be dug up than the fact of that review's passing out of his hands," wrote Pound in 1938. The magazine began as a fat two-hundred-page quarterly with fine type and thick heavy paper. Here are some contributions from the first three numbers: December 1908: "A Sunday Morning Tragedy" (Hardy), "The Jolly Corner" (Henry James), "Some Reminiscences" (Conrad), "The Raid" (Tolstoy), "Tono-Bungay" (Wells), "Stonehenge" (W. H. Hudson). February 1909 (No. 3): "Isle of Typhoeus" (Norman Douglas—afterwards part of "Summer Islands") and three poems of Yeats in his new manner, including

"Galway Races." Pound's first contribution was "Sestina: Altaforte" in June 1909 and he contributed eight more poems before transferring to A. R. Orage's *New Age*. Lawrence's "Still Afternoon" appeared in November 1909 with "Dreams New and Old," "Discipline" and "Baby Movements." Lawrence had shown the first number to Jessie Chambers who then submitted these poems which "launched me so easily on my literary career like a princess cutting a thread." Ford tells us that it was the story *Odour of Chrysanthemums* which immediately convinced him he had discovered a genius. I cite this as a good example of pollination through a little magazine since Lawrence's first novel was not to appear till four years later. Lawrence, Pound and Douglas continued to contribute after Ford had ceased to be editor but they could not disguise the smell of the Establishment. Wells, incidentally, contributed in 1913 an account of an air-raid to drop the atom bomb over Berlin. I know of no more extraordinary prophecy: "Never before in the history of the world had there been a continuing explosive and those atomic bombs which science burst upon the world that night were strange even to the men who used them" (*The World Set Free*).

Ford's next editorial venture will be dealt with later and a word must be said about another born editor of the period, Middleton Murry, whose *Rhythm* and *Blue Review* (1913) later gave way to *The Adelphi. Rhythm,* largely subsidised by Edward Marsh, began in 1911. André Salmon provided some Paris art news including engravings by Picasso and wood cuts by Derain. Lawrence contributed to all Murry's magazines, while not ceasing to revile him as only a contributor can—(see his *Letters*)—and *The Adelphi* was also the first magazine to print a poem by Dylan Thomas (1934). Other magazines which started about this time were *The Egoist* and *Poetry. The Egoist* serialised *Tarr* and *Portrait of the Artist* from 1914 onwards: Aldington was literary editor and produced an "Imagist Number" (May 1915). Later Eliot filled another with bogus correspondence. Rodker was associated with the Egoist Press which printed "Prufrock," and its successor the Ovid Press which added "Ara Vos Prec" and Pound's "Hugh Selwyn Mauberley" to his fine editions, while Miss Harriet Weaver, the proprietor of *The Egoist,* won immortality by settling a capital sum on Joyce (at Pound's suggestion) which enabled him to devote the rest of his life to *Finnegans Wake*. The last number (1914) of Apollinaire's *Les Soirées de Paris* contained an essay by F. S. Flint on the new Imagist poetry with quotations from Pound and others—an interesting example of cross-fertilisation for it was Flint in *The Chapbook,* ten years later, who wrote an article on French poetry introducing the Surrealists to England. A famous dynamic magazine was *Blast,* edited by Wyndham Lewis in two large numbers (1914 and 1915). The first number with its flamboyant puce cover was full of Lewis's "Vorticism" and fundamentally unpleasing personality (at least where other writers were concerned) and includes some aggressive lyrics by Pound. The second was redeemed by the lovely "Preludes" and "Rhapsody" of Eliot. The war brought it to an end (Gaudier and Hulme were killed and Lewis joined up) and with it died the first heroic impetus of the modern movement, considered in magazines, for *Les Soirées de Paris* came to an end also. "Nowhere does one relive the fine fresh flourishing of twentieth-century art more intensely . . . nowhere does one have a keener sense of what might have been" (Steegmuller: *Apollinaire*).

However in America the war was less felt and fewer lives were disrupted. There were important developments in little magazines: *Seven Arts* merged into *The Dial,* the most successful of eclectic magazines, rich, discerning, international and not without courage, awarding prizes to Eliot for *The Waste Land* and Cummings for *41 poems.* Scofield Thayer and Gilbert Seldes were the editors, joined in 1925 by Marianne Moore for poetry. *The Dial* chose what was best in France and England at the time (including many poems by Yeats and Bunin's masterpiece "The Gentleman from San Francisco") and yet, perhaps because it went on so long, it leaves a distinct impression of modishness in its later numbers as the Twenties entered their sleek decline. It ceased in 1929. Eliot at first wrote the "London Letter" and Pound the "Paris Letter," Yeats and Lawrence contributed frequently and nearly every writer of note occasionally. Its handsome cheques were much appreciated and it reprinted work from smaller magazines. What made it so good? Marianne Moore said: "Lack of fear for one thing. We didn't care what other people said. I never knew a magazine which was so self-propulsive. Everybody liked what he was doing and when we made grievous mistakes we were sorry but we laughed over them."

The two dynamic reviews of the American war period, *The Little Review* (1914) and *Poetry* (1912) had very long lives and were both edited by women: Margaret Anderson and Harriet Monroe. *Poetry* was the most successful magazine ever to be devoted to verse alone and here appeared "The Love Song of J. Alfred Prufrock" (1915) besides Frost and Pound. The first number was in October 1912 and contained two poems by Pound who was accepted by *The Dial* in 1915, *The Little Review* and Kreymborg's *Others* a year later. Pound dominates the little magazine scene from 1912 onwards up to his departure from London (1921). His output is so extraordinary that it is worth recording: in 1911 there were seven contributions to periodicals; in 1912, thirty-six; in 1913, fifty-two; in 1914, forty-six; in 1915, forty-five; in 1916, thirty;

in 1917, seventy; in 1918, one hundred and sixteen; in 1919 eighty-eight; in 1920, eighty-eight; in 1921, twenty-two; in 1922, fifteen and in 1923, there were six. Thus, from 1917 through 1920 he averaged nearly two magazine contributions a week in addition to his books and editing. But Pound's energy extended to placing his friends' work and Eliot, Joyce, Yeats, Lawrence, Wyndham Lewis, Gaudier were all thrust forward by him. He gave his poetry to *Poetry* and his prose to *The Little Review* whose foreign editor he was, and there is no doubt that the best years of *The Little Review* coincided with his tyrannical interventions, if only because of *Ulysses*. Later on Hart Crane was to complain that *The Dial* and *Poetry* suffered from the censorship of Marianne Moore and Harriet Monroe who both disliked impropriety. Margaret Anderson, however, was in constant trouble with the U.S. mails, either over *Ulysses* or Lewis's story *Cantleman's Spring Mate*. The difference is to be seen in their mottoes. *Poetry*'s was: "To have great poets we must have great audiences too." *The Little Review* bore the sign: "A magazine of the arts making no compromise with the public taste." Its "creative period" as Miss Anderson calls it was when it moved from Chicago to New York. Pound's influence lasted from 1916: "I should count on Eliot a good deal for current criticism and appreciation," wrote Pound. "The rest are clustered to *The Egoist*. I got Aldington that job several years ago. He hasn't done quite as well as I expected. The Lawrence-Lowell-Flint-Cournos contingent give me no active pleasure." Pound introduced her to Quinn the famous Irish-American lawyer and patron who helped to subsidise the magazine and who defended them tepidly in their cases over *Ulysses* (for there were two editors now, Miss Anderson and the tumultuous and trenchant Jane Heap, the poor woman's Gertrude Stein). It was she who carried on *The Little Review* as a quarterly from New York from 1924 to 1927.

I have dwelt on *The Little Review* because it is the most exciting of those which stem from the great years around 1914 and because I admire the courage and flair of the fiercely discriminating editors who began without money or experience: I even respect them for not paying contributors and regret the fate of this magazine, symptomatic of so many others. From being a severe, rather cheaply printed, pocket-size monthly it appeared more and more rarely in the Twenties, but with larger and larger format and full of art reproductions (Miss Heap preferred art to literature). Paris soon gripped them in its claw and the two Chicagoans swam out of their depth. Surrealism—so fatal for all magazines except Surrealist ones—gained a foothold. It tagged along with the intellectual fashions instead of setting them and expired (1929) in a blaze of questionnaires and author photographs. Its last editorial

(Miss Heap's) was called "Lost—a Renaissance." "As always most of the stuff *The Little Review* prints is bad," wrote W. C. Williams, "but *The Little Review* is good."

The emphasis now shifts back to London for the golden age of the English little magazine and the poetry boom—the period from about 1916 to 1922. Most of these magazines look rather "period" with thick paper, many woodcuts, heavy types like "Medici Books," poems about fauns, whimsical ghost stories, suggestions of Lovat Fraser's eighteenth century, throw-backs to the Nineties, dappled or patchwork covers and not much reference to the war or to the avant-garde in other countries. Typical contributors: Robert Graves, Siegfried Sassoon, Edmund Blunden, the Sitwells: an atmosphere of Sam Browne belts in smart restaurants, poets inhaling the orchard and shedding their khaki; of general hope and wholesomeness, however sophisticated. The Vienna Café with its tables on the pavement (so handy for the British Museum) and its clientele of Vorticists gives way to the Café Royal which took on its second lease of life, to Stulik's sumptuous menus at the Eiffel Tower (Huxley, Firbank and Nancy Cunard). Smart Bohemia becomes a reality. Magazines are various and short-lived except for *The London Mercury,* so chummily middlebrow.

Art and Letters, a quarterly edited by Frank Rutter (afterwards joined by Osbert Sitwell), is a little-known but adult publication from 1917 through 1920 which published Eliot, Lewis, Augustus John and Wadsworth. *Wheels* (1916–22) exactly spans the period: it is not so much a magazine as an annual hard-covered anthology of the Sitwells' poetry of that time, and none the worse for that. Aldous Huxley, Iris Tree, Nancy Cunard were also associated with them. The last number included a poem by Brian Howard who was still at Eton where he helped Harold Acton edit the splendid single number of *The Eton Candle* in 1922. A more significant period piece, delightful in its presentation, is *The Chapbook of Modern Poetry* edited by Harold Monro (first number "Twenty-three Poems" in July 1919). June 1920's number consisted of a bibliography of modern poets: other numbers were questionnaires, and one was an anthology by Flint of new French poets; another (April 1923) was devoted to American poetry and included Wallace Stevens, E. E. Cummings and Frost's famous "Stopping by Woods on a Snowy Evening." Originally a monthly, the magazine petered out as a miscellany in hard covers (1924–25). A very little-known magazine was *Today* edited by Holbrook Jackson, monthly from 1917 to 1923, sound on Joyce and Pound but struggling with middlebrow propensities. *Coterie* (six numbers only from May Day 1919—"A Cooking Egg" by T.S.E.) was a sophisticated quarterly for the intellectual mannerists (Huxley, etc.), edited by Huxley, Earp and specifically anti-*London Mercury*. *The London Mercury,* also founded in 1919, was the prose equivalent of *Georgian Poetry,* edited by Sir John Squire. There was a vogue for large album-like arty magazines, *Form* with poems by Yeats, *The Apple* (Pound) and *The Owl* (Sitwell, Sassoon and Graves) of which the American counterparts were *Playboy* and *Broom* (1922). Kreymborg of *Others* and Harold Loeb through *Broom* belong to the expatriates' Paris like *Secession,* also 1922. But this period of Georgian armistice-day effervescence evaporated leaving behind only *The London Mercury* and from 1922 the new quarterly *The Criterion* which Eliot was to edit—"The Waste Land" appeared in its first number—and which was to grow more and more like a solid French magazine with affiliations to *La Nouvelle Revue Française* or *Le Mercure de France*.

"Sixteen years is a long time for a man to remain editor of a review; for this review I have sometimes wondered whether it has not been too long," wrote Eliot in 1939. Dynamic and creative at first, publishing Proust, Valéry and Cocteau for the first time in English, it grew more and more into a review of reviews until notices of other periodicals came to occupy more than half the paper. There were, for example, fourteen consecutive reviews of Danish periodicals.

After 1922 the accent is on Paris where Pound had fled and invited Joyce to set up his standard. It was the heroic age of American expatriates, of Hemingway, Stein, MacLeish, Cummings, McAlmon, and, curiously enough, apart from *Gargoyle* (edited by Arthur Moss), they found their first opportunity in *Transatlantic Review,* published in London and New York though written and printed in Paris and edited by Ford Madox Ford. Ford, discontented like Pound with the English post-war set-up, had migrated and his magazine opened in January 1924 after much preliminary celebration and appeared monthly for a year. It is a sad disappointment after *The English Review*. Ford was by now a more amiable but less discriminating character, wrapped up in his four novels and no longer suited to creative editing. However he now had Pound to help him and Pound's new young hopefuls, Hemingway and Cummings. When Ford went to America to consult Quinn about its finances Hemingway got rid of some deadwood but inserted the lethal Baroness Elsa von Freytag-Loringhoven who had nearly capsized *The Little Review*. Was she any good as well as incomprehensible? The criteria to judge her are lacking. In any case *Transatlantic Review* was an example of how not to run a magazine: vanity and weakness at the centre, too many serials, dull chronicles, sprawling correspondence, an old-fashioned format to suggest a non-existent authority, too many drinking parties, too few discoveries, incongruous advertisements. It did, however, publish much Hemingway and the first instalment of Joyce's "Work in Progress" to which Ford gave its title. No single number was so good as the "Expatriates" number of *The Little Review* (1923) which presented the first draft of Hemingway's "In Our Time."

The first true expression of the new spirit of Paris in the Twenties was *This Quarter* edited by the dying poet, Ernest Walsh, and financed by his mistress. Walsh believed in the expatriate scene and the four large numbers of his irregular quarterly were bursting at the seams with unrecognised talent. Wyndham Lewis chose this magazine for his attack—"The Revolutionary Simpleton"—in his own one-man magazine *The Enemy*. Walsh began with an immense admiration for Ezra Pound and dedicated his first number to him. He also admired Hemingway and published "The Undefeated," but a horde of simulators and café-cruisers soon butted in and Pound withdrew before the mobs from Montparnasse. The last number turned revengefully on its hero. Walsh died of consumption having realised his dream, and *This Quarter* reappeared under the aegis of the astute Mr. Titus with more Hemingway and a first-rate number in English on Surrealism.

It was nearly time for *transition* but one should perhaps mention Pound's own compact little magazine *The Exile* (four numbers) with McAlmon, Rodker as usual, and Hemingway's "neo-Thomist poem":

> The Lord is my Shepherd, I shall not want
> him for long.

Another magazine typical of the Twenties to which both Pound and Hemingway contributed was *Querschnitt* (Berlin), an intolerably bright and photographically witty monthly with a strong interest in Paris.

transition first came out in April 1927 and immediately became the magazine for which the Twenties had been waiting. It ran for almost ten years, and ten years for a little magazine is about the same as for a dog, i.e., a lifetime. After twelve monthly numbers in small format with drab or pastel colours, it grew into a bulky quarterly with exceptionally brilliant covers such as the famous comb by Duchamp, and others by Miró and Arp.

The strength and weakness of *transition* lay in its commitment to its trilingual editor Eugene Jolas's "revolution of the word." This was based on the idea that literature was dead, killed by the conventional abuse of its *matière,* language—and that language had to be brought to life again by detaching words from meanings and launching them in original patterns. Language was to be divorced from subject as had already happened in painting. *transition* in fact was to correspond to abstract art, and, typographically, later numbers of *transition* indeed set a pattern for the future. However, only a limited number of writers could afford to be unintelligible: Joyce for one, and *transition* will always be remembered as the magazine which printed the bulk of *Finnegans Wake* and shouldered its fantastic proof corrections. Gertrude Stein was a frequent contributor but other verbal revolutionaries—Theo Rutra, A. Lincoln Gillespie, Jr.—also assisted and though early co-editors like Robert Sage and Elliot Paul were more conventional, the Jolases assumed complete responsibility (at one point briefly helped by the financial aid and friendship of Harry Crosby, who flung himself into the verbal revolution). *transition* had excellent art coverage and used photographs by Man Ray, Moholy Nagy, Brassai, etc., while, through enthusiasm for the unknown, they happened upon some interesting new authors—Dylan Thomas, Samuel Beckett, Lawrence Durrell, Paul Bowles—as well as publishing good work by Hemingway, Hart Crane and innumerable foreign writers. "The word presents the metaphysical problem today . . . the disintegration of words and their subsequent reconstruction on other planes constitute some of the most important phenomena of our age. Modern life with its changed myths and transmuted concepts of beauty makes it imperative that words be given a new composition and relationship" (Jolas, No. 11). The divorce of words from meaning, except in the hands of a great artist (and Joyce was aiming rather at a multiplication of meanings) is costly, and after the Depression and the suicide of Harry Crosby (1929) the experimentalists were forced to retreat. Many writers experience the desire to regenerate their language but the public, though conditioned to accept abstract painting, will not follow them. *transition* however survives as a period piece enshrining this most fascinating of periods as it came to an end with the Depression, the rise of Hitler, the shadow of war. "Self-expression is not enough: experiments are not enough: the recording of special moments or cases is not enough," as Jane Heap wrote in her obituary of *The Little Review* in 1929, as against, "The writer expresses. He does not communicate. The plain reader be damned," in the *transition* editorial in 1929.

Two other Paris magazines deserve a mention: Samuel Putnam's *New Review* (1930–31) which aimed to produce an avant-garde quarterly retaining the revolutionary outlook, but which foreshadowed the subsidised American university magazines of the future, and *The Booster,* the magazine of the American country club which was taken over in the late Thirties to the discomfiture of its sponsors and public by Henry Miller, Lawrence Durrell and Alfred Perlès. The headlong fall from grace of this now galvanised house-organ is one of the few good jokes of the Thirties and was followed by the more serious *Delta* and its "Air-conditioned Womb" number (same editors).

In England the founding of *Life and Letters* was the literary event of the late Twenties with its backer Lord Esher, an enthusiastic bibliophile, and its editor Desmond MacCarthy, who had replaced Squire as literary editor of *The New Statesman*. It ran as a monthly for three years, then from 1935 as a quarterly and then as a practically new magazine under Bryher and Robert Herring and, shrinking visibly, continued through the Forties as *Life and Letters Today*. It is full of good things, especially under MacCarthy, though also rich in Edith and Osbert Sitwell and Dylan Thomas afterwards. Unfortunately, MacCarthy disliked the American-Paris school and spread his net wide to catch amateur writers who happened to do some one thing rather well, e.g., murderers' confessions, and the result was a magazine which though still a pleasure to read in bed lacks all intensity and urgency—the eclectic run wild. It was offset by Eliot's *The Criterion,* immensely serious, even portentous, but apt to contain surprises; by Rickword's stimulating *Calendar of Modern Letters* (lately reviewed at length in *The London Magazine*) and by Leavis's *Scrutiny* (lately reprinted). The vitality of the Thirties is to be found in *Experiment* (Bronowski, Cambridge), *New Verse* (Grigson, Hampstead), and *New Writing* (John Lehmann). *New Verse* was slim, unpretentious, inexpensive and devoted purely to poetry and reviews about poetry. Grigson's strictly little magazine attracted some of the best work of Auden, Spender, MacNeice, Dylan Thomas and many others, though some of the reviews were too personally spiteful. Grigson set out to perform a limited task as well as it could be done. He lasted out till 1939, best known for his polemic against the Sitwells on the one hand, the middlebrows on the other, and for his Auden double number. *Contemporary Poetry and Prose* edited by Roger Roughton and *Twentieth Century Verse* edited by Julian Symons with a Lewis double number, *Seven* and *Wales,* were stimulating successors in the same slim format. The mainstream however flowed into *New Signatures, New Country* and *New Writing* under the aegis of Michael Roberts (*New Country*) and John Lehmann. There is no doubt that John Lehmann was the outstanding British editor of the period, capable of selecting poetry, fiction, reportage and reviews—provided they were Left-wing—with both flair and discrimination. His production of *New Writing* in book form was also most effective and permitted long short stories like *The Novaks* of Isherwood to be set against poems of Auden or Day Lewis which were similar in feeling, or the work of French, German and Czech writers. He largely omitted art and enabled England to take the lead in what was later to be called *"la littérature engagée." New Writing* became *New Writing & Daylight* in 1940 and then the war-time *Penguin New Writing* which was an eclectic magazine making use of reprints. The Left-wing dynamism had departed.

When the war started *New Verse* and *The Criterion* were coming to an end—a magazine had to be eclectic to survive. It was the right moment to gather all the writers who could be preserved into the Ark and only then could the Ark get by the Paper Control—by earning dollars or aiding prestige. This inevitably set the tone for *Horizon* (1939), *Penguin New Writing, La France Libre* and other magazines which outlived the war. (*Poetry, London* edited by Tambimuttu was the most heroic). It was not the case in America where *Decision* (Klaus Mann), *Furioso, 22, Chimaera, Tiger's Eye, Neurotica, View, Triple V, Dyn, Circle, Calendar, Vedanta,* besides the university quarterlies, *Hound and Horn, Hudson, Kenyon, Sewanee, Southern Review,* etc., reflect the variety due to lack of censorship. (The British enjoyed being censored: it made them feel more patriotic.) This exuberance in America was to lead to the spate of "beat" magazines, too numerous to mention, as soon as the war was over, and to a new crop of semi-expatriate magazines like *The Paris Review*.

One American magazine deserves special notice. *Partisan Review* began as a Trotskyite intellectual review in 1934: it still continues and preserves editorial continuity, having survived the acrimony of the Thirties, its respectability since the "cold war," and having maintained the precarious interrelationship between politics and literature better than any other. Philip Rahv, William Phillips, Mary McCarthy, Lionel Trilling, Delmore Schwartz, Robert Lowell, Randall Jarrell and Clement Greenberg are among the names one associates with this memorable achievement, a magazine which launched such concepts as Burnham's "Managerial Revolution" almost simultaneously with Eliot's "Four Quartets"—reprinted from their home in *The New English Weekly* (here regarded as like *The New Statesman* a newspaper rather than a magazine). I know only of three magazines which survive unaltered from the Thirties: *Partisan Review* (though the size has shrunk), *The Wine and Food Quarterly,* impeccably edited all these years by M. André Simon and preserving a typography and lay-out similar to MacCarthy's *Life and Letters* devised by Oliver Simon at the Curwen Press—a true format of the late Twenties (Oliver Simon was also the printer of *Horizon*)—and M. Grindea's indestructible *Adam* which keeps popping up with invaluable special numbers though apparently expected to live on air. I suppose that just as collectors pay large sums for *Personal Landscape* (edited by Robin Fedden in Alexandria during the war) because it contained work by Durrell so they will one day collect, *Adam,* too late, or "XXX" which was so agreeable to read and handle—or *Agenda*—liveliest of current poetry magazines.

Well, there they all are—or most of them—since I have gone only by my own collection, not by the books on little magazines which I do not possess or those like *Gargoyle, Gangrel, Caravel, Playboy* and *Fugitives, The Double Dealer, Blues, Morada, Laughing Horse* or the banned or earliest numbers of *The Little Review* which still elude me. But what is to be learnt from this lengthy necrology? Magazines require two animators: an editor and a backer (or angel). Sometimes they form the same person like Princess Bassiano who was an angel to *Commerce* but both angel and editor to *Botteghe Oscure* (impossibly eclectic where the contemporary was concerned). The life of a little magazine depends on three things: the resources of its angel, the talents of its editor and the relationship between them. Where there are angels there are wrangles, where there are editors there are creditors . . . it is as simple as that. With a good angel and wise editor, contributions flow in and ultimately the public is formed for them: they shape the times which they reflect. Most little magazines fail because they cannot afford to wait. The backer loses too much money or the editor makes too many mistakes. Mutual respect, and, if possible, affection, are essential to editor and backer as everyone else concerned will try to separate them: it is better still if they can share the same purpose: *"Tout est là. L'amour de l'art."*

(1964)

4

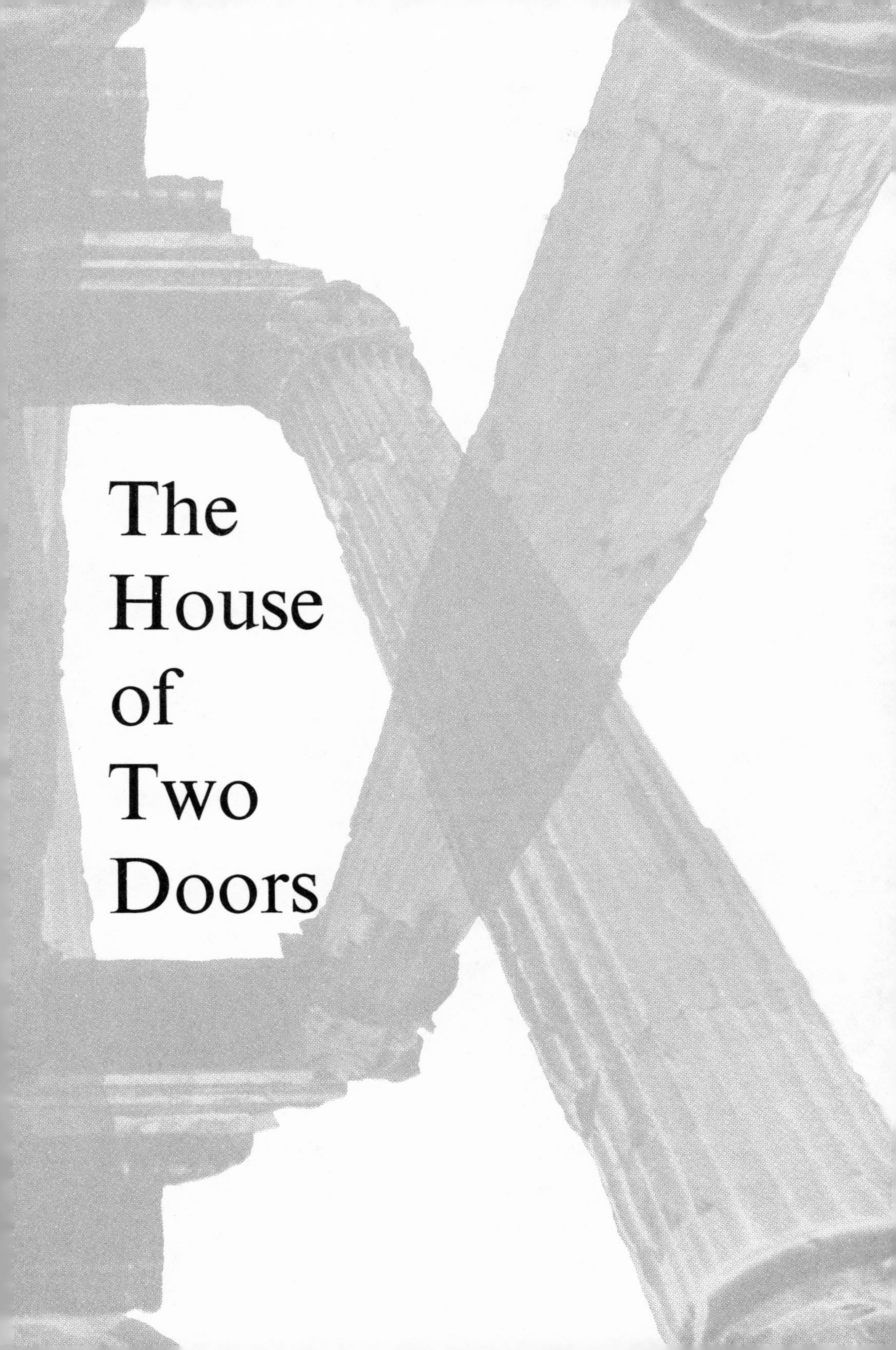

The House of Two Doors

ART NOUVEAU

Lady Alice, Lady Louise
Between the wash of the tumbling seas
We are ready to sing, if so you please;
So lay your long hands on the keys . . .
Alice the Queen and Louise the Queen
Two damozels, wearing purple and green . . .

Now read it again, this time visualising the two sea-girt queens, their apparel and their furnishings. We are in the thrilling 1870s, just before the aesthetic break-through, and the lines are from "The Blue Closet" by William Morris, founder of the Arts and Crafts movement, who believed that the common man could be saved from ugliness and spiritual death by surrounding himself with simple things made by conscientious craftsmen or by making them himself: "What business have we with art at all unless we can share it? . . . Real art must be made by the people and for the people, as a happiness for the maker and user. . . . That talk of inspiration is sheer nonsense, there is no such thing: it is a mere matter of craftsmanship."

"A very pre-Raphaelite friend of mine came to me one day and said, apropos of his having designed a very Early English chair, 'After all, if one has anything to say one might as well put it into a chair' " (Richard Le Gallienne, from *The Yellow Book* 1894–97). Oh dear—what has happened? For this cannot be the chair "such as Barbarossa might have sat in" that William Morris set out to build. The socialism of the 1880s has gone and *fin-de-siècle* self-consciousness has set in. The chair Le Gallienne's friend designed might have looked something like Charles Voysey's. This chair, with its rush seat, has indeed something "Early English" about it; it remains part of the tradition. However, the chair of Voysey's young admirer, Charles Mackintosh, designed a year later, is original, like nothing else. It is Art Nouveau! Simple, functional, yet dignified; nervous, joyous and, like everything he did, vertical. And yet the parabolic, pierced ovoid at the summit and the way the uprights are carried past it, the relative width of splats and stretchers, give it a look of Picasso at the top and of Mondrian at the bottom; the two directions, one might say, in which Art Nouveau forked. The Glasgow School of Art, for whom this throne was intended, was sitting on a volcano.

As always with a successful Art Nouveau object, it appears unique of its kind, an isolated Friday's footprint, and we are all the more surprised to find that similar artefacts are at that moment cropping up in many capitals. The style with which it has most affinities, the Rococo, presents only one major problem: did it originate in Italy or France? But the origins of Art Nouveau are much harder to track down, for it seems to have erupted from many parallel centres of similarity-in-diversity. One moment it is not there and then suddenly, from about 1899, the pastel shades and seductive contours of this false dawn are visible everywhere.

But despite its brevity, it is a truly European movement, and on the grand scale, for not only is there Art Nouveau painting, sculpture and industrial design, there is also present *"l'Art Maîtresse,"* an Art Nouveau architecture (whereas there is little Rococo and still less Surrealist architecture). "The major monuments of that architecture at its best had qualities not seen before or since," writes Henry Russell Hitchcock, and Dali puts forward a modest claim: "I believe I was the first in 1929 to consider—without a flicker of humour—the liberating architecture of Art Nouveau as the most original and extraordinary phenomenon in the history of art" (*Minotaure,* 1933).

Here I should like to suggest an important point. We all owe an enormous debt to Professor Nikolaus Pevsner, particularly where Art Nouveau is concerned. In 1931 he was writing on the architects who originated the modern movement, in 1936 he produced his invaluable *Pioneers of Modern Design* (enlarged and reprinted in 1948) which describes the movement with affection and respect, clears up its history and traces its influence. But in order to make it even more respectable he writes (and this is constantly repeated by others) that both Morris's Arts and Crafts movement and Art Nouveau have the same functions, they are "transitional between Historicism and the modern movement." Consequently the justification of Art Nouveau is that it prepared the way for the modern movement, and whatever did not seem to anticipate this, for example Gaudi's work and especially the unfinished church of the Sagrada Familia in Barcelona, was abandoned as a blind turning. I think it is more correct to see the style as complete in itself, an unattainable end, no doubt, but one having very little to do with modern art as we now know it. Then if we read a phrase like "the worst excesses of Art Nouveau" we know it refers to the good Art Nouveau which cannot be assimilated, just as "the worst excesses of the Rococo" meant the Rococo which did not slide imperceptibly into Neo-Classicism. It is to the honour of Loos, Gropius, Mies van der Rohe that, coming though they did on the heels of Art Nouveau, they took practically nothing from it; and it is to them we owe our world.

But, what *is* Art Nouveau, that short-lived offspring of the conflict in our grandparents' souls between puritanical functionalism and decadent Rococo, whose symbol combined the lily's long, straight stalk with its curvilinear bell? Let us call it a syndrome—a group of symptoms which, found together, constitute "that strange decorative disease known as Art Nouveau" (Walter Crane). They are: (*a*) A revolutionary simplicity in design (and end to fussy Victorian shoddiness). (*b*) The wavy line or plant arabesque (sometimes violent). (*c*) Plastic decorative flatness (painters become decorators under the influence of Japanese prints). (*d*) Symbolism (or art for art's sake combined with *fin-de-siècle* pessimism).

When all these are found together a reaction is produced, occasionally referred to as "counter-Art-Nouveau" where the curvilinear is abandoned for the rectilinear.

The work of certain English graphic artists is considered the precursor of all Art Nouveau, and Professor Pevsner, as well as everyone since, makes much of a book-cover by Mackmurdo for *Wren's City Churches,* 1883, as the first indisputably Art Nouveau object. Yet no one has pointed out how totally inappropriate it is for the subject-matter. In fact it is Blake's conception of the unity between a poem, its illustrations and its calligraphy which is the real jumping off place for Art Nouveau and which leads on inexorably to the nine copies, bound for as many moods, which Dorian Gray possessed of Huysmans's *A Rebours* and to the exquisite *"décor purement ornemantale"* of, for example, Van Ruysselberghe's illustrations for *Histoires Souveraines* by Villiers de l'Isle Adam (Brussels, 1899).

The Japanese influence which played such an important role in the graphic arts and painting seems to have made itself felt in England even before Edmond de Goncourt publicised it in France. The Pre-Raphaelite artist Rossetti introduced Whistler to Farmer and Rogers's Oriental emporium on Regent Street, where they obtained blue and white china. The young manager was Lazenby Liberty who afterwards set up on his own and whose wares gave the name *Stile Liberty* to Italian Art Nouveau. Curiously enough, Edmond de Goncourt got his "blue" from a similar emporium in Paris run by a German Jew from Hamburg, Sigfried Bing. Bing also branched out into decoration and coined the name "Art Nouveau" for his exhibition in 1896, where three whole rooms were furnished by an unknown Belgian decorator and craftsman, Henry van de Velde. In the meantime, Bing had accused Edmond de Goncourt of plagiarising his own Far Eastern agent's comments in a book on Hokusai; so that it was not surprising that, on leaving the exhibition, the old French aesthete threw up his hands in horror. Yet his suggestion that van de Velde's objects were like "small sailing-ships built for speed—a yachting style" was well-meant and well-taken. A year later, in Dresden, the exhibition was a terrific success and this led to van de Velde eventually directing the Weimar School until the 1914 War. He was replaced there by Gropius.

We are now ready to examine the bewildering cross-fertilisation which involved architects, painters and decorators in the new style as it proliferated through the Nineties in Belgium, France, Germany and Austria. What had originated in industrialised England as a revolution in design took root in industrialised Belgium, home of the great architect Horta, and the many-talented van de Velde, who, like the French painters, Emile Bernard and Maurice Denis, was also an able theoretician. *"En Belgique on a vu toutes les témérités."*

Apart from the somewhat overpraised Métro entrances of Guimard, the French contribution to Art Nouveau came primarily through painting: Puvis de Chavannes, Moreau, Odilon Redon were major influences. According to Pevsner "the connecting link between Moreau, the Pre-Raphaelites and the new style of 1890 is the work of the Belgian Fernand Khnopff and the Dutch Jan Toorop" but an even stronger current flowed through Gauguin (especially in his more decorative moments); his disciple and mentor, Emile Bernard; Maurice Denis; and the *Nabis*. Van Gogh was also an overwhelming revelation to van de Velde, and one might say that French Post-Impressionist painting and English Post-Pre-Raphaelite craftsmanship are the two master-forces in Art Nouveau which came together in Brussels and from there moved eastwards to Berlin, Munich, Vienna and presumably, Russia (see Léon Bakst's ballet decor). As additional sources one must add two English painters, Whistler, whose "Peacock Room" with his own decorations (1877), is certainly Art Nouveau, and the middle period of Aubrey Beardsley; and also the architect-designer Voysey, the first sight of whose wall-papers in Vienna made van de Velde cry out that "spring has come at last."

In 1900 Mackintosh (whose chair we have admired) was invited to exhibit the designs for one of his Glasgow tea-rooms before the Vienna Art Nouveau group, known as the *Sezession*. Klimt and Olbrich were in charge of the pavilion. "Here was indeed the oddest mixture of puritanically severe forms designed for use with a truly lyrical evaporation of all interest in usefulness. These rooms were like dreams . . . vertical everywhere." Professor Pevsner thinks Mackintosh's interest in space links him to Frank Lloyd Wright and Corbusier. "In dealing with him we were able at last to link up development in England with the main tendency of continental art in the Nineties, with Art Nouveau." The chaste tea-room, enemy of the saloon, was at that time a revolutionary conception.

In considering the development of Art Nouveau we keep coming back to van de Velde, the most articulate and conscientious of the architect-artist-craftsmen and one with a religious understanding of natural forms. He has written brilliantly about his early days (and those of the movement) when, after a nervous break-down in 1890, he wished to redesign his whole environment for the young wife who had brought him back to health. I should like to quote from the selection from his memoirs by P. Morton Shand in *The Architectural Review,* September 1952:

"There will be no place in the society of the future for anything which is not of use to everyone" (1890).

"In 1891 Brussels saw the first things from Liberty's—small tables and cabinets lacquered in red and green, furnished cretonnes, a little rustic pottery of peasant type exposed in the Compagnie Japonaise show-windows on the Rue Royale . . . and 1891 is also memorable because that year, for the first time, Les Vingt invited some of those artists who had broken with academicism and turned to what would now be called industrial design to participate in their annual salon. Among the scanty exhibits were vases by Gauguin, plates decorated by Willy Finch, posters by Chéret and some children's books illustrated by Walter Crane." (Kelmscott Press books were shown the next year.)

"The real forms of things were covered over. In this period the revolt against the falsification of forms and against the Past was a moral revolt . . ."

"Our chief task now was to make ourselves thoroughly familiar with all the details of the recent revival of handicrafts in England. . . . The pioneers during the initial period of 1893–05 were the Liègeois cabinet-maker Serrulier-Bovy and myself in the field of furniture and decoration, and Hankar and Horta in architecture. . . ."

"That house [the Tassel house] which was in the *Rue de Tunis,* was much discussed at the time and has since become an historical landmark." (Built by Horta 1892–93. The house was said to fit its engineer-owner, M. Tassel, like a well-cut coat.)

"Just as evil is forever seeking to corrupt virtue," concluded van de Velde, "so throughout the history of art some malignant cancer has ceaselessly striven to taint or deform man's purest ideals of beauty. The brief interlude of Art Nouveau, that ephemeral will o' the wisp which knew no law other than its own caprice, was succeeded, as I had foretold, by the hesitant beginnings of a new, a disciplined and purposeful style, the style of our own age."

Van de Velde, who had once designed his wife's clothes to blend with his furniture, wall-papers and silver and even ordered the foods which would play a part in the general colour scheme of his new home, with its bilious exterior, lived to design interiors for the big new steamers on the Dover-Ostend service. In fact longevity seems an additional privilege of anyone connected with Art Nouveau, with only Beardsley dying young. Nature looks after her own: Tiffany (Louis) 1848–1933 (American), Mackintosh 1851–1942 (Scots), Voysey 1857–1941 (British), Lalique 1860–1945 (French), Ensor 1860–1949 (Belgian), Horta 1861–1947 (Belgian), van de Velde 1863–1957 (Belgian), Brangwyn 1857–1956 (British), Wright (F. L.) 1869–1959 (American), Hoffmann 1870–1955 (Austrian).

Hoffmann's art degenerated into Viennese frivolity and he died penniless and neglected. Van de Velde and Baron Horta became respected reactionaries (the latter designed the new Brussels railway-station). In 1926, Gaudi, aged a mere seventy-four, was knocked down by a tram on his daily walk to Mass from his lodging in his unfinished cathedral. ("The greatest piece of creative architecture in the last twenty-five years"—Louis Sullivan.) Mistaken for a tramp, he was carried unconscious to the paupers' ward, since no taxi would take him.

While Horta was creating wrought-iron interior winter gardens of airy freshness such as that of the van Eetveld house (1895), the Catalan Gaudi, like Horta of humble origin, was concentrating on surface, on the new exterior forms and shapes which iron and cement could yield. His Art Nouveau (called *Modernismo*) triumphs are, however, later than Horta's, and the Casa Batlló and Casa Milá, both on the Paseo de Grácia in Barcelona, date from 1905 to 1910. They have been praised by Sullivan, Gropius and Corbusier but are best described by Dali as *"aspirations—concrètes, extra-plastiques,"* "a house built in the shape of the sea with fossilised waves and wrought-iron foam" in a formula *"convulsive-ondulante."* He speaks of the "collective sentiment of ferocious individualism which characterised the founders of the style." "In a modern-style building Gothic is metamorphosed into Greek, into Far Eastern, and—by a certain involuntary fantasy—into Renaissance, which can suddenly become pure modern-style again, dynamic and asymmetric and that withal in the fluid time and space of a single window! They are the first edible houses and beauty shall be nothing if not edible!"

The garden suburb, now a park, built for the Güll family, 1900–14, includes ravishing polychrome serpentine benches and collages of various bright and broken materials which, according to Henry Russell Hitchcock, "compete for priority with paintings by Kandinsky and Delaunay as the first examples of wholly abstract art." He was both architect and sculptor in the Ruskinian tradition and a mystic whose earliest ironwork (1878–80) predates even Mackmurdo's cover. The vitality of all of Gaudi's buildings gives the lie to those who consider Art Nouveau a decadent calligraphy, and will increase in importance now that we cannot see such masterpieces as Endell's Studio Elvira, 1897–98 (Munich).

In my memory, the highlights of Art Nouveau, besides talking about Gaudi to the present Conde Güll ("Don't mention that man! He ruined my father!") and meeting the gentle Voysey in the early 1930s with his latest disciple, the youthful John Betjeman, was a visit to the Stoclet Palace. As so little has been written about this last and greatest masterpiece of the style (Austrian *Sezession,* Hoffmann and Klimt, Brussels, 1904–11), I will give my impressions. The palace belongs to the last rectilinear counter-form of Art Nouveau. It was constructed with no thought of cost for the Baron Stoclet who gave Hoffmann the freedom that Richard Wagner desired from King Ludwig. It is both austere and supremely elegant and is built of a cold Norwegian marble, yet not altogether cold, with windows of solid crystal. The street side is functional, with a long staircase window and a tower like an advanced Swiss church. The garden side is in swelling Baroque, and the garden is also a construction with a huge blank wall to shut out the other houses. Inside all is colour and light, and the predominating material appears to be lapis lazuli. There is an intimate theatre fit for *Pelléas and Melisande,* the famous dining-room with Klimt's mosaics and many salons to hold the Baron's collections which included Merovingian jewellery, Byzantine, Celtic and Coptic objects, Chinese swords and the then unknown "art of the Steppes." Hoffmann's grave, elegant personality is everywhere. He designed the furniture, the splendid bathrooms, the linen, the cutlery, the pens and writing-paper, the binding of the books ornamented by Van Ruysselberghe for early editions of Gide, even the Visitors' Book. Everything is a functional luxury, everything breathes the taste of the designer and the restless curiosity of the princely owner (whose three children have since inherited it). It is both the last *Lust-schloss* and the precursor of the liners *Bremen* and *Europa*—the fitting conclusion to the work of Voysey and Mackintosh, of van de Velde and Horta, the Northern antithesis to Gaudi, and it winds up the movement which never degenerated into sentimentality, flatness or weariness in the hands of these great men.

(1961)

MAX ERNST

Who is the greatest living painter? Picasso (there's no escape). And the second greatest? Pandemonium breaks out; but for me, for many years, it has been Max Ernst, last of the Olympians and, incidentally, now doing some of his best work.

The colour reproductions for example of "Question d'Insecte" (1963) (bought by Yevtushenko), "Laity" and "Spring Redeemer" (both 1965), "Les Dieux Obscurs," the "Portrait of Dorothea" (1960) and the "Fête à Seillans" (1964), are among the loveliest things in this magnificent book.* Also among the loveliest and the most luminous and mysterious are "Mundus est Fabula" and "The Marriage of Heaven and Hell" and "Alice's Message to the Fish," all painted within the last ten years, that is to say almost all since the artist's seventieth birthday.

Max Ernst was born in 1891 at Brühl on the Rhineland, at the point just south of Cologne where, according to him, the beer-lands march with the wine-country. He chose wine. This Rhineland of pre-1914, beloved of Apollinaire, was largely open to French influences. By 1914 he had already fallen under the spell of Paris but he remained behind to fight in the war, like Klee, although his lifelong friend Arp, an Alsatian, urged him to take the last train to Paris.

"War was imminent," Arp said, "and its catastrophes would annihilate all that was dear to us—our youth, our ambitions, our happiness and all that we loved best." Afterwards Ernst was to write, "Arp is the only one among the friends of my youth whom I ever saw again."

"On the first of August, 1914 Max Ernst died," he continued. "He was resurrected on the eleventh of November, 1918 as a young man who aspired to find the myths of his time." Ernst's first search was

* *Max Ernst,* by John Russell (New York, 1967).

through Dada which broke out like psittacosis in Zurich, Berlin, Hanover, Cologne and Paris. Its nihilistic destructive frenzy, aggravated by defeatism, petered out around 1920 and was replaced by Surrealism to which Breton added the dimension of imagination lacking in Tzara's militant absurdities. The subconscious became an article of faith.

The painting of Ernst's with which I am most familiar dominates Sir Roland Penrose's dining-room a few miles from where I live. It once belonged to Paul Eluard, and was painted in 1921, a work of major importance marking the divide between Dada and Surrealism. Mr. Russell here calls it "The Elephant of the Celebes" though its present French title is "L'éléphant Célèbes," with Celebes as the elephant's name. I doubt if there are many elephants in the Celebes. And I doubt too whether it is an elephant. The picture in early Surrealist texts is simply called "Celebes" from the word painted on the plinth on which the artefact is resting.

It is in fact an enormous round stone or boiler on two heavy legs with a long curved chimney or exhaust pipe coming out of it like a tail or trunk with a cow's skull on the end. At the other end two broken tusks are visible and the boiler is surmounted by a casque-like metal contraption. Above are some flying fish and, bottom right, some erotic bric-à-brac. It is, of course, a Ubuphant, and Mr. Russell arrogates too much authority in referring to the stove-pipe as an arm and assuming that we are looking at the side view of what might in fact be the Ubuphant's back or front according to one's temperament.

Despite an iconoclastic aggressiveness against his father, Ernst was by nature a mystic with a scientific bent, a Goethean who had passed through Novalis. He loved Cologne for Cornelius Agrippa and Albertus Magnus: the forests and rivers of the unconscious, the ultra-natural, the marvellous have accompanied him all his life. By taking rubbings from the graining of wood, patterning of stones, skeleton leaves, he was enabled to glimpse the random associations which lurk behind natural forms.

Apart from his painting much of his activity in France between the wars was taken up with his "collages," books which consist of rearrangements of nineteenth-century engravings to present new images, erotic and alarming conjunctions vaguely embracing a central theme. It is an enormous pity that these should be almost unprocurable as one of them, *La Semaine de Bonté* (1934), adds a new dimension to the literature of our time. An afternoon with the *Semaine de Bonté* is an unforgettable experience—"a reassembling of lion-headed or bird-faced supermen and their passionate consorts into a sequence new, beautiful and disturbing—a tragic-strip from the Minotaur's nursery," as I once wrote.

It is typical of the coincidences and serendipities which haunt Surrealists, Breton, Ernst and Eluard in particular, that when I recently obtained his earliest "collage" book, *Les Malheurs des Immortels,* and showed it to Sir Roland with its strange dedication, "to Darcy Japp. (Souvenez-vous d'une nuit dans les Pyrenées) Max Ernst," he was able to add, "A night spent in great discomfort, in a shepherd's hut devoured by fleas after getting lost in a storm near the Venta de Araco in July 1931. We were Max Ernst, Darcy Japp, Valentine and myself."

My favourite paintings of Ernst between the wars are those in which lurid green jungles sport an extraordinary fauna. I suppose "La Joie de Vivre" is the best known of these but the joy soon turns to something more sinister culminating in the terrifying "L'Ange du Foyer" of 1937 which is Yeats's beast "slouching towards Bethlehem to be born"—the spectre of war incarnate.

The last war was for Ernst, with his German origins, a time of trouble. He was chivvied by the French, arrested and re-arrested, threatened with internment for the duration, and he lost his farm-house in the Ardèche. Through Peggy Guggenheim, whom he afterwards married, he got to New York via Lisbon (1941) and there he met his present wife Dorothea Tanning (1946). "He seems to have had an irresistible effect on female surrealist painters . . . all have learnt how close Max Ernst's primeval and unearthly phenomena lie to the realm of Faust's Mothers. . . . They show how much of a destructive female principle there is in Max Ernst's art" (Hans Richter). It is also an art very close to physics and the contemporary explorations of matter and energy. Ernst has quoted Heisenberg: "No artist should be indifferent to the progress of scientific research."

After living in Arizona Ernst finally returned to France for good (1953) and has now settled in Touraine and become a French citizen. This serene magician, both scholar and seer, seems to have passed through all his emotional storms to command the final flowering of his powers in Prospero-like tranquillity.

This is Mr. Russell's *magnum opus* so far. From its excellent colour to its text, plates, notes and indices, nothing but well and fair. He has received immense assistance from the Master himself and from other Ernstians like Patrick Waldberg. If I have a criticism it is that the whole book is too much of an eulogy, submitted for censorship as well as elucidation. There are moments when his spun-sugar style seems somewhat elusive, particularly in describing Ernst's romances and marriages.

With such a great artist enormous interest must attach to the women who have attracted him and Mr. Russell could have told us more rather than leave it, inevitably, to others. "Love is the great enemy of Christian morality," Ernst wrote in 1931. "The virtue of pride, which was once the beauty of mankind, has given place to that fount of all ugliness, Christian humility. . . . Love, as Rimbaud said, must be reinvented." This is not the language of one who should deprecate all reference to his private life.

(1967)

FREUD

THERE should exist a word to describe the rare and exquisite phenomenon which is the unfolding of genius, a spectacle of exciting aesthetic interest to those who follow it, as when a carrier-pigeon is released, tumbles, circles, soars, and then heads straight for its goal. Genius does not unfold so much as increase and multiply like a blob of water which begins to devour and assimilate all the other blobs; a great mind seems to expand and grasp what is necessary to its sustenance like a newly hatched crocodile which is born snapping, or a manta ray. These letters* of Freud, all written to one colleague and friend from 1887–1902, illustrate this nameless process at work.

Who was the colleague? Wilhelm Fliess was a handsome and dynamic Berlin doctor, two years older than Freud, bold and original in his thinking and engrossed in the problems of psycho-somatic medicine so near to Freud's own. He was developing two theories, one of a relationship between the back of the nose and the sexual centres, the other of periodicity in men ("good and bad days"), which led him towards a mystic juggling with numbers and a theory of bisexuality, like Weininger's: he was in fact doomed to fall by the wayside, and when his doom was apparent even to himself he accused Freud of jealousy and plagiarism and withdrew from the correspondence. To Freud he had hitherto been a sounding-board for innumerable new theories, an adviser-figure of near-fatherly status, and a good friend.

Freud's letters are not easy reading and they will not convert the uninitiated; the greatest number deal with problems of hysteria and though much of their terminology has now been discarded those who know something of Freud already and are inclined to respect and

* *The Origins of Psycho-Analysis. Letters of Sigmund Freud* (New York, 1954).

perhaps love this great, lonely and sombre Prometheus of the late nineteenth century will find them fascinating, a day-to-day record of his hopes and disappointments and above all of his discoveries, not to be found in his reticent autobiography. The whole is admirably annotated by Herr Ernst Kris.

One begins to understand in what a strange and macabre setting the young Freud did his early work, his theories wholly unacceptable in pleasure-loving, anti-Semitic *fin-de-siècle* Vienna, his family uncomprehending, his half-dozen horrified neurotic patients on whom his research depended sometimes disappearing for months at a time, his great book on the interpretation of dreams completely unrecognised, a growing obsession with the importance of infantile sexuality arousing bewilderment and anger. I give a few quotations which illustrate the ups and downs, the despondencies and lightning flashes of this extraordinary story:

"I have found my tyrant and in his service I know no limits. My tyrant is psychology." "Philosophy was my original ambition before I knew what I was intended to do in the world." "This year for the first time my consulting room is empty" (1896).

"By the time he died [Freud's father] his life had long been over, but at a death the whole past stirs within one. I feel now as if I had been torn up by the roots" (1896). "I have found love of the mother and jealousy of the father in my own case too, and now believe it to be a general phenomenon of early childhood. If that is the case the gripping power of Oedipus Rex becomes intelligible and one can understand why later fate dramas were such failures" (1897). "Happiness is the deferred fulfilment of a childhood wish. That is why wealth brings so little happiness; money is not an infantile wish."

"I picked up a recent book of Janet's on hysteria with beating heart, and laid it down again with my pulse returning to normal. He has no suspicion of the clue. So I keep on growing older, contentedly on the whole, watching my hair going grey and the children growing up, looking forward to Easter, and practising patience in waiting for the explanation of the problem of neurosis." "No critic can see more clearly than I the disproportion there is between the problems and my answers to them, and it will be a fitting punishment for me that none of the unexplored regions of the mind in which I have been the first mortal to set foot will ever bear my name or submit to my laws . . . Well, I really am forty-four now, a rather shabby old Jew, as you will see for yourself in the summer or autumn" (1900).

One cannot, from such a book of letters, say much about psychoanalysis. A specialist on the border-lines of insanity, Freud grew up in a very different *milieu* from the English, American, French or Italian home of his time, and it is perhaps an element of this fine Old Testament father-world in exile which partly conditions his psychology. He is hardly even dismayed by what is most likely to shock us, and one sees him sometimes going off the rails. On the other hand the combination of crystal intelligence, ferocious industry and exquisite intuition which led him inexorably to the mysterious world of the cradle and the terrible conclusions he drew from it were so much in advance of his time that, almost alone among scientists, he has created a system of thought which for fifty years now has held together like a great poem or a work of art.

(1954)

CARL JUNG

THERE is only one other writer I am reminded of by this book:* the Yeats of *A Vision* and the mystical works; Jung's fellow tower-builder. One starts off with the childhood of a scientist but soon is carried away into a private world of the psyche in which half the events narrated take place in dreams, for the doctor's dreams and not his patient's case-histories are the order of the day.

After reading this extraordinary compilation one wonders how Jung and Freud ever found anything in common or what Freud would have thought of his disciple's attempts to prove that flying saucers were archetypal emissaries from another world. Theirs is the opposition between science and religion, between an unorthodox science and an unorthodox religion, each the creation of one man but based on the total opposition between matter and spirit. It is as incongruous to mention Freud and Jung in the same breath as Berenson and Blake or Marx and Wagner.

I can still recall vividly how Freud said to me, "My dear Jung, promise me never to abandon the sexual theory. That is the most essential thing of all. You see, we must make a dogma of it, an unchangeable bulwark." He said it to me with great emotion, in the tone of a father saying, "And promise me one thing, my dear son; that you will go to church every Sunday." In some astonishment, I asked him "A bulwark against what?" To which he replied "Against the black tide of mud" and here he hesitated for a moment, then added—"of occultism." Although I did not properly understand it then, I had observed in Freud the eruption of unconscious religious factors.

To Jung, in fact, the "black mud" was not philosophy, religion, mysticism and parapsychology, but the sexuality and cynicism which

* *Memories, Dreams, Reflections,* by C. J. Jung. Edited by Aniela Jaffé (New York, 1963).

denied the existence of all culture except as a "mental conseqeunce of suppressed sexuality." I brought out some of Freud's views about Jung when reviewing the Freud biography by Ernest Jones. When they first met in Vienna, in February 1907, Jung tells us that they talked non-stop for thirteen hours, and doubtless Freud's "epoch-making" interpretation of dreams provided the basis of the conversation. It was not until 1912 that feelings of mutual ambivalence overwhelmed master and disciple. These are also key years in the modern movement in literature and art, and the time will soon come when Freud's and Jung's findings are connected with Picasso whose "Demoiselles d'Avignon" dates from their meeting, or Joyce whose creative years in Zurich coincide with Jung's in the same city. All are stupendous products of the gigantic nineteenth-century crack-up. Nietzsche, in fact, is an obsessive father-figure to both Freud and Jung, with Schopenhauer running him second.

The first thing one asks from an autobiography is that it should be interesting, but one always has the hope that it should be more than interesting, that it should help one to understand more about life from a wiser or greater man's experience. *Memories, Dreams, Reflections* is exactly what the title suggests, an old man's outpouring of all he thinks most significant in a long life, everything which relates to the inner world of the psyche, the nature of the unconscious, the soul's existence before and after death. Unlike Eliot's *Gerontion* these are not "thoughts of a dry brain in a dry season," but a pattering of rain with occasional flashes of lightning on the desiccated modern mind. What a relief to escape from the squalor of the contemporary witch-hunts into Jung's beautiful and lofty thought, so rich and poetic even when one doubts its premises. It is Yeats's "Byzantium" in prose.

"The life of man is a dubious experiment," he proclaims. "In the end the only events in my life worth telling are those when the imperishable world irrupted into this transitory one . . . I can understand myself only in the light of inner happenings. It is these that make up the singularity of my life, and with these my autobiography deals."

Dr. Jung even possessed the art of making his dreams sound interesting. Indeed how much of the appeal of psychoanalysis may not lie in discovering someone who will listen to one's dreams; mysterious exhalations of the psyche which possess the power to glaze a spouse across the breakfast tray. His archetypes were first glimpsed in his dreams and he even accepts them as proof of immortality.

With his accustomed wisdom, Dr. Jung has much to say about the life after death: "A man should be able to say he has done his best to form a conception of life after death, or to create some image of it—even if he must confess his failure. Not to have done so is a vital loss . . ." And again—

He ought to have a myth about death, for reason shows him nothing but the dark pit into which he is descending . . . But while the man who despairs marches towards nothingness, the one who has placed his fate in the archetype follows the tracks of life and lives right into his death. Both, to be sure, remain in uncertainty, but the one lives against his instincts, the other with them.

He is even able to tell us what he thinks the world after death will be like.

The world will be grand and terrible, like God and like all of nature that we know. Nor can I conceive that suffering should entirely cease . . . at most we can say that there is some probability that something of our psyche continues beyond physical death. Whether what continues to exist is conscious of itself, we do not know either.

About evil he was much more definite. "Evil today has become a visible Great Power. One half of humanity battens and grows strong on a doctrine fabricated by human ratiocination; the other half sickens from the lack of a myth commensurate with the situation. Evil has become a determinate reality." The only cure for it, according to Jung, is self-knowledge. "He (the individual) must know relentlessly how much good he can do and what crimes he is capable of." (Self-knowledge he defines as "the utmost possible knowledge of his own wholeness.") There is much in this book that is obscure and sometimes dull and sometimes humbug, there is even something unlovable about Jung with his air of a huge bluff schoolmaster and German business man. He lacks the luminous clarity of Freud but it remains the outstanding autobiography of the year through the uniqueness of his intellect which integrates both East and West, mind and brain, dream and reality.

(1963)

MISTAKING THE LANDMARKS

THE other day I underwent an unusual experience. I live in a cylindrical block of flats known as "the gasometer" in the corner of a London square. My room is 43. When I called for my key, I noticed as I fitted it in the door that it was numbered 34. Nevertheless the door opened and nothing had been moved; except that the number outside my door was also 34.

I went round the corner and had a drink. When I came back the porter handed me my key. It had no number on it. He has given me the pass-key, I thought. But there were no numbers on any of the rooms and I had to get my bearings from the plane-tree outside the landing window. I went into two wrong rooms first.

The experience was unpleasant, and I decided to go round the corner for a drink. I always recognise the public house by a large Dalmatian dog which sits outside. It seemed pleased to see me, but I was disconcerted to find it had no spots. There was a man inside who complained of being weighed. "Even after this beer," he said, "they'll weigh me! Look!" He pointed to his feet. They seemed about half an inch above the level of the ground. Outside there were three pubs and three Dalmatians, one white, one white with black spots, one black with white spots. They seemed pleased to see me.

My building appeared to have revolved slightly and I had some difficulty in finding the entrance. The porter handed me two keys, 43 and 34. The floor buttons had been removed from the lift and I had to come down again and walk up the stairs. Outside every landing window was a plane-tree. I opened a door at random and there were all my things, but everything was on the left instead of on the right and vice versa.

I felt I needed a drink and was soon back among the Dalmatians. I chose a plain black one, and inside the pub my friend was standing.

"They weighed my house with me in it and now they can damn well weigh it without me in it." He downed his bitter and was jerked ever so lightly off the floor. When I returned the whole square was full of cylindrical buildings—I can only say that some were rounder than others, and I had a good deal of difficulty finding the roundest.

My head began to swim and I staggered back down an avenue of Dalmatians. I needed a drink badly. Suddenly I realised what was happening and I seemed to hear voices. "Let's see if he can find his way back without any hands." "Any eyes." "Any nose." "A Controlled Experiment." Outside each of the now identical cylindrical buildings stood a taxi. "London Airport." I ordered. All the taxis moved off.

Six hours later I awoke and went on where I had fallen asleep over *Curious Naturalists:**

> The test I did next was again quite simple. If a wasp used landmarks it should be possible to do more than merely disturb her by throwing her beacons all over the place: I ought to be able to mislead her, to make her go to the wrong place, by moving the whole constellation of her landmarks over a certain distance . . . The result was as I had hoped for and expected and yet I could not help being surprised as well as delighted; each wasp missed her own nest and alighted at exactly the spot where the nest "ought" to be according to the landmarks' new positions . . .
>
> However, I had to make sure that the wasps relied for their homing mainly on vision. First, I could cut off their antennae—the bearers of delicate organs of smell, of touch, and of other sense organs—without at all disturbing their orientation. Second, when, in other tests, I covered the eyes of intact wasps with black paint, the wasps could not fly at all . . . Furthermore when I trained the wasps to accept a circle of Pine Cones together with two small squares of cardboard drenched in Pine oil which gave off a strong scent, displacement of the cones would mislead the wasps in the usual way, but moving the scented squares had not the slightest effect.

Dr. Tinbergen is, however, the only professional naturalist to cast a doubt upon his own motives, and he winds up his experiments on wasps and "bee-wolves" with an endearing reflection:

> I have often wondered why the outcome of such a test delighted me so much. A rationalist would probably like to assume that it was the increased predictability resulting from the test . . . But a more important factor still is of a less dignified type; people enjoy, they relish the satisfaction of their desire for power. The truth of this was obvious, for instance, in people who enjoyed seeing the wasps being misled without caring much for the intellectual question whether they used landmarks or not.

* *Curious Naturalists,* by Niko Tinbergen (London, 1958).

Personally I could not bear to see a wasp misled even for the highest purpose, I detest all forms of obfuscation and deliberate misleading—though, like the rest of us, I have played Attila to an ant-hill.

Dr. Tinbergen is a fellow of Merton and the University lecturer on animal behaviour. His essays here are all about insects or birds, particularly certain sea-birds (kittiwakes, eider-ducks, black-headed gulls), and the insects which find their way home to solitary nests to feed a caterpillar or a bee to hungry grubs—or simply to lay an egg on one. He also writes very well about camouflage in caterpillars and moths and on the effect of the display of "eyes" on the wings of certain butterflies and moths when seized by birds. These "eyes," he thinks, suggest an owl's eyes and hence precipitate an escape reaction, though I should like to believe that they are nature's imitation of the eyes of long extinct monsters, flying reptiles of whom birds were once afraid. It is more important for small birds to avoid owls than to find peacock butterflies good eating so after all these centuries the gimmick still works.

The good doctor brushed the eyes off some of his peacock butterflies and then fed them to jays; they "displayed" in vain. On the other hand, every generation of birds has to learn afresh that black and yellow insects or caterpillars taste nasty. One of these has to be sacrificed to each new arrival that the rest may be protected. Yet evolution is still going on and the peppered moth, which depends for its safety on being mottled like bark, has produced a special black variety for lichen-free trunks in polluted industrial areas.

This is not an easy book. What I like about Dr. Tinbergen is that, though he writes fluently and with enthusiasm, his observations are highly specialised like those of his friend Lorenz, and he is soon taking us down very complicated by-ways by a succession of highly specialised experiments. I do not suppose the layman is often so happily enticed out of his depth. His message seems to be that nothing, or rather no creature, is too well-known or too small to repay intelligent study. Provided that we use a scientific method we can go straight on from where Bruce left off with the spider and make an original contribution.

"Anting" in birds he considers a still unexplained mystery; nor is the display of contrary emotions, of ambivalence, in bird courtship yet understood, nor the extraordinary discrepancies between the intelligence of the bumble-bee and that highly specialised matriarch, the sand-wasp.

We often felt that there is not less, and perhaps even more, beauty, in the result of analysis than there is to be found in mere contemplation. So long as one does not, during analysis, lose sight of the animals as a whole, then beauty increases with increasing awareness of detail.

I was just about to go into the garden and put this idea into practice when I felt a most peculiar sensation. The ground wobbled beneath me as if I had been set on a pair of invisible scales. I felt I needed a drink but hardly had I downed it than the glass was dashed from my hand and once again I was lifted up . . .

(1958)

THOMAS CUBITT, MASTER BUILDER

I AM lost in admiration for Miss Hobhouse.* What industry, what control of material, what domination of her subject, which is really the development of the building industry in the first half of the nineteenth century, the emergence of Bloomsbury, Pimlico, Belgravia, in fact of Victorian London.

For Thomas Cubitt, "master builder," was not an architect but an employer of architects, one to whom like Hannibal the design of whole towns was entrusted. He rose from nothing to leave a million pounds and was the creator of Belgravia from Knightsbridge to Millbank, Harrods to the Tate, a whole city which has remained surprisingly intact from Belgrave Square, Eaton Square and Chesham Place to the gloomy but comfortable purlieus of Pimlico—St. George's Square, Eccleston Square, Lupus Street—with Ebury Street as the frontier. *Quartiers aisés!*

I can still remember the 24 bus, the only service that dares to penetrate the wilds of Pimlico, and the view of the river from St. George's Square and the raffish elegance of Lupus Street, which I associated with the disease of that name rather than with Hugh Lupus, the great ancestor of the Grosvenor family.

> Belgravia the golden
> with mink and money blest . . .

I suppose it remains the grandest residential quarter in any capital—or is it outstripped by the Paris which lies between the Avenue Foch and the Avenue Montaigne?

In my youth "speculative builder" was a term of abuse for a greedy maniac, one who was held responsible for ribbon development, for Peacehaven and rows of "jerry-built" suburbs. Cubitt, however, had something Napoleonic about him; he rose to greatness by taking

* *Thomas Cubitt, Master Builder,* by Hermione Hobhouse (New York, 1971).

chances, but also by organising a huge labour force comprising a body of contented workmen as well as every sort of specialist. Plumbers, carpenters, builders, masons, cabinet-makers, surveyors all centred round his works and were engaged on several jobs at a time. He kept them employed, he fulfilled the time clauses in his contracts, paid off his overdrafts and maintained a high standard of workmanship.

One does not hear the reproaches about Nash and his terraces levelled at Cubitt. He occupied himself with every detail, from palaces like Osborne and the corner villas of Belgrave Square (now mostly embassies) to the humblest terraces of North London or Pimlico. The finishings were sound, the façades imposing, and in addition he designed broad avenues, easy approaches, churches and public houses for each community—many still standing—and admirable sewers. He worked for efficient enlightened capitalists like the Dukes of Bedford and Westminster, the Lowndes family and the Cadogans. Queen Victoria approved of him; Lord Carrington was his banker.

Although my allegiance has been to Nash I have had many happy hours in Belgravia and Bloomsbury, the two principal Cubitt creations. Even as he built Gordon Square, Tavistock Square and their surroundings the drift to the west was in full swing and the Marquis of Westminster was netting all the titled fish as fast as the Duke of Bedford in Bloomsbury was watching them get away.

Cubitt, besides being a man of his word, a benevolent autocrat and expert technician, had vision. One sees it in Osborne, that Claude-like Italian landscape which is slowly coming into its own, or in his Chinese rooms at Buckingham Palace furnished from the Pavilion (Albert's idea), or in his plans for Clapham and the King's Road. Belgrave Square, especially with its old railings, is as noble as Eaton Square which the sun, shining through the plane-trees on its northern façade, makes Parisian, suggesting the Avenue Gabriel. Proust would have been at home in Eaton Square though he would have put the Guermantes in Mayfair. Cubitt's chief architect, Basevi, seems in a subordinate position compared to Soane, Nash or Decimus Burton.

> And who so vast a work achieved? What name
> Shall fair Belgravia's sons transmit to fame?
> Who raised a town where once a marsh had been,
> And fenced with palaces our noble Queen?
> Thine be the praise, O Cubitt! Thine the hand
> That caused Belgravia from the dust to rise . . .
> A fairer wreath than Wren's should crown thy brow—
> *He* raised a dome—a town unrivalled *thou!*
>
> —Mrs. Gascoigne, *Belgravia*

The Lowndes estates, like Lord Cadogan's, never took on quite the sheen of Belgravia and today are largely broken up into blocks of flats and offices. On the other hand Cubitt, for all his solidity, never achieved the glamour of Mayfair. The drawing rooms of Eaton Square were a by-word for dullness before their conversion into flats, which could never be said of Grosvenor Square or Park Lane.

Brighton also owes much to Cubitt, who carried out most of the development of Kemp Town. He went to some lengths to keep out the very poor and prevent slums from encroaching on his boundaries, thus bringing down the rents. In an under-policed age this was understandable and his snobbery was nothing beside that of his tenants. The north side of Eccleston Square was still unfinished at his death.

Attention to detail, indefatigable energy, financial acumen, sound team-work are not qualities which inspire a biographer and Miss Hobhouse must often have been dispirited by the mass of evidence about Cubitt's activities, so different from the meteoric career of Nash, a true architect rather than a builder.

Perhaps Osborne on the Isle of Wight is his masterpiece. "It does my heart good," wrote the Queen,

> to see how my beloved Albert enjoys it all, and is so full of admiration for the place, and of all the plans and improvements he means to carry out . . . Mr. Cubitt has done it admirably. He is such an honest, kind, good man.

Cubitt and his men provided everything, down to the door-mats, boxes of candles, for paper in the lavatories, copper coal-scuttles, the fenders and fire-irons; he restored the Elizabethan manor of Barton House, now so desecrated by modern stained glass. The terraces, alcoves and fountains, the Italian gardens with their magnificent ilexes came under his plan. He was Paxton to the Prince's Bachelor Duke at this villa which rose so strangely beside the waters.

> The deep blue sea, myriads of brilliant flowers—the perfume of orange blossoms, magnolias, honeysuckles—roses on the terrace, etc., the quiet and retirement [wrote the Queen] all make it a perfect paradise.

"Our dear old Mr. Cubitt who built Osborne"—let that be his epitaph as we hurry for what may be the thousandth time past the embassies of Belgrave Square and the elegance of St. Peter's on our way to Victoria.

(1971)

GREAT LIBRARIES

Mr. Hobson is the son of a bibliophile chairman of Sotheby's and himself a collector and expert; his wife trained herself to take 150 of the excellent photographs, many in colour. Together they have perambulated Europe for several years in this labour of love. I salute the result, a first book* which besides fulfilling an essential need is a thing of beauty in itself and launches Mr. Hobson as one of the more impressive scholar-aesthetes of our day.

Mr. Hobson has included thirty-two "great libraries" from a dozen countries. I rather wish he had gone behind the Iron Curtain or visited Athos or Sinai, and for some reason he has not included any in English country-houses, of which Chatsworth and Longleat are the most outstanding. But everything for which he has found space has a right to be there.

Most of us who read a lot are abysmally ignorant of books themselves, their fate and history; we cannot tell the difference between a roll and a codex, a chap-book and a plaquette, a colophon and an uncial; we have heard of Caxton but not Wynkyn de Worde, of Elzevir not Estienne, Aldus (not one but four) but not of Sweynheim and Pannartz, the first to print in Italy. We think incunable is an adjective and block-book the same as writing block. Enough. Back to the scriptorium!

Books were collected in libraries from Greek and Roman times, and illuminated manuscripts began in the Dark Ages; the monasteries were the custodians of the past till the late medieval Princes inaugurated their private collections. The Dukes of Burgundy, Duke Humphrey of Gloucester, the Medici and Malatesta were among the first bibliophiles, followed by the Holy Roman Emperors and Kings of France.

* *Great Libraries,* by Anthony Hobson (New York, 1970).

These great collections were sometimes dispersed when chunks were bought up by other collectors and found their way to the Whig grandees or the circle of Madame de Pompadour. From Pepys onwards the civilised business man made his appearance, right down to Huntington and Pierpont Morgan. Now it is the turn of the American universities: most rare books end up in institutions as they began; and Mr. Hobson concludes appropriately with the University of Texas, where the principal collection of modern authors is to be found.

There's a home for British writers
Across the deep blue sea . . .

Some libraries are of great architectural beauty, especially those with rococo additions, like Coimbra, Admont, St. Gall or Vienna, or those which form part of greater buildings (Durham Cathedral, the Escorial), or stem from the Renaissance (Cesena, the Vatican, Florence), or are solid eighteenth-century constructions like Trinity College, Dublin, the British Museum and Harvard. Some are kept in private houses, some in especially constructed buildings—the John Rylands Library, Yale, Pierpont Morgan, Huntington and Texas.

The oldest of all is the Capitular Library of Verona, which owns five fifth-century codices dating from its inception. The scriptorium or copying room was directed by one of the greatest of librarians, the Archdeacon Pacificus (*fl.* 800). It is strange to think that copying was going on here at the same moment as the Arabs were destroying the library of Alexandria. The library was combed out by the early humanists from Petrarch onwards, who there copied Cicero's letters to Atticus (1345).

Soon afterwards the Catullus, Varro and Cicero disappeared; more volumes were seized by the Visconti of Milan and went by conquest to Louis XII at Blois. By 1400 four-fifths of the manuscripts had been lost. The French removed others in 1797, and in 1945 a direct hit from a Liberator bomber totally destroyed the library and many of the later books. It has since been rebuilt.

No book is secure, no library is truly safe. Sometimes it is the librarians, not the books, who are in danger, as when the Augustinian monks in charge of cataloguing the Escorial were executed in Republican Madrid (1936). There are also natural disasters, like the recent floods in Florence.

On the whole, however, this is a cheerful book; bibliophiles are influential and on the increase, and it is remarkable how much has come down to us from the days when an illustrated book was considered a supreme work of art: we owe a great debt to compulsive and competitive hoarders and collectors, to people who never throw anything away and whose ancestors have never thrown anything away.

Mr. Hobson, besides illustrating many of the famous books in these collections, is a mine of information on the collectors themselves, as seen through his compassionate, slightly cynical humanism.

> He allowed no fire in the house and in cold weather kept himself warm in bed by putting folios on his feet, his favourite for this purpose being Barlaeus's account of Maurice of Nassau's expedition to Brazil . . . Carried away by a sudden apoplectic fit, he died on a pile of books like a warrior on the battlefield.

This was Van Hulthem, librarian to the Royal Library of Brussels (where many of the Dukes of Burgundy's books are to be found). His own collection of 35,000 books was added to it.

Another great librarian was Gabriel Naudé who worked for Cardinal Mazarin. England produced Bodley and protected Panizzi, who gave us the British Museum Reading Room and set it on its way as one of Europe's two major institutions, the other being the Bibliothèque Nationale. A great library must always be greatly expanding, it needs more shelf-space, storage, cataloguing, research facilities every year and will eventually depend more and more on microfilm and computer replacing book and cataloguer.

If so, sums up Mr. Hobson,

> The results will be as revolutionary as the change from roll to codex in the fourth century, or the invention of printing in the fifteenth. Whether it will be agreeable to the readers is another matter.

There is no doubt what Mr. Hobson finds agreeable—a remote, unspoiled and romantic library like the monastery of St. John on Patmos or a private collection that is fertile and forward-looking, like the Spoelberch de Lovenjoul archives at Chantilly. This Belgian aristocrat conceived an overwhelming passion for the French Romantics and bought up every newspaper file as well as all their books and manuscripts. Balzac and George Sand were his favourites, and Gautier wrote to him "you alone can one day undertake the reconstruction and complete publication of my works . . ." He spent fifteen hours a day with his books.

> His library is the archetype of the modern research collection which aims to illuminate the mysteries of literary creation by accumulating the completest surrounding documentation. The student is given his choice and can attach what relative significance he wishes to a correct draft or an unpaid laundry bill.

There are libraries of which I previously knew nothing, the Hanoverian Library at Wolfenbüttel, the Columbina at Seville, the Arsenal Collection (from the Marquis de Paulmy, friend of Pompadour) in its rococo rooms in the Comte d'Artois's Paris hotel, but Mr. Hobson also excels on the great American tycoons. He was a friend of William Jackson, librarian of the Widener Library at Harvard, founded in memory of the collector who went down in the *Titanic*. "I think I'll take that little Bacon with me," he said to Quaritch, on leaving London. "If I'm shipwrecked it will go down with me."

One of the best essays is on the John Rylands Library of Manchester, fruit of two great aristocratic collectors, Lord Spencer and Lord Crawford, whose libraries were acquired by the widow of a nonconformist Manchester manufacturer, herself half Cuban. Mrs. Rylands was one of the few great women bibliophiles and formidably acquisitive with the accent on religion. The building is a masterpiece of late Victorian Gothic . . .

Mr. Hobson appropriately quotes Evelyn: "O fortunate Mr. Pepys who knows, possesses and enjoys all that's worth the seeking after!"

(1970)

A COLLECTOR'S YEAR

TAPERING off! That is how I answer questions about my book-collecting. The urge is waning: the desperate anxiety to corral all my favourite authors into the Ark where I can gloat on them at leisure even as they gloat on each other is a thing of the past. My want-list gets shorter and shorter.

So 1967 has been a cheap year and I can look my family in the face again. And yet? Is this quite a fair picture? Perhaps more has been going on than I care to admit. Just filling in a few gaps: mostly French. A Cocteau collection came up and I acquired a presentation copy of *Le Grand Ecart,* a beautifully bound *Escales* (brief poems about ports and sailors illustrated by André Lhote, redolent of 1920) and a letter: *"Ma Violette, très chérie . . . j'ai traversé un tunnel . . . Marcel ira dans le Midi avec notre voiture et je vais rejoindre Marie Laure en Suisse . . . Félix a aidé Marcel à se guérir,"* Violette Murat? Violette Leduc? Marcel Khil? Félix Rollo? No date. The names are lost in a cloud of "opium."

Then Proust. If there is one key book of the twentieth century it is the first edition of *Swann,* Grasset, 1913. I had only John Hayward's second issue. A friend lent me a French catalogue. There was a presentation copy to the newspaper proprietor Léon Bailby, who had cut only half the pages: *"Souvenir du 'temps perdu,'"* Proust had inscribed, *"des jours où a commencé la vive affection . . ."* and three lines more. It seemed to me important because it showed that Proust allowed *"le temps perdu"* to mean "the good old days" as much as time wasted or rather actually lost through imperfections of memory.

It cost the earth. A gigantic manoeuvre was undertaken, American poets were sacrificed across the Atlantic, the Hayward Proust swapped and a rare Gide, the illustrated *Voyage d'Urien,* flung to the bookseller.

Aided by Micky Brand of Marlborough Rare Books *Swann* came to join the Prousts I already owned, including a drawing he made for Reynaldo Hahn.

At the Antiquarian Book Sale I swooped on a china-paper copy of Proust's *Les Plaisirs et Les Jours,* surely the most extraordinary of all first books, given what was to follow; half prophetic, half bathetic, and which I had once owned and given away. I have always found that if one gives away a book one will either find another copy within a week or not at all. This was the first *Plaisirs* I had seen since I parted in the Thirties with the other. It was also in the Thirties that I stripped my Eliot collection of one item, *Shakespeare and the Stoicism of Seneca* to give to John Hayward who had everything else.

I never saw the pamphlet again till it turned up three years ago in a catalogue of Mr. C. G. Baker of Bath. I was in Italy and missed it. This spring he had it again, but now for ten pounds, and I was just in time. Mr. Baker died shortly afterwards and this retired bank-clerk with such a flair for modern books will no longer alleviate (he stayed open at week-ends) the tedium of the queen of cities. Bertram Rota's death last Christmas was another irreparable loss to all collectors. I had known him nearly all my life and he had corrected the proofs of my article on book-collecting. He was a magnificent proof-reader, in short a scholar, as well as a kind and just man.

From America I obtained a copy of *Poetry,* the magazine which in 1915 first printed "Prufrock," after sitting on it for so long. I now had the "Love Song" in magazine state, in Pound's *Catholic Anthology,* and as a slim volume in 1917.

Mr. Pound sent me a copy of *If This Be Treason* and another of Canto 110 printed for his eightieth birthday, he also inscribed *Mauberley* for me; one needs three copies of *Mauberley,* one to read, one to re-read and one in dust wrapper to be buried with.

Some writers seem irresistibly drawn to my shelves. They are making their own collections. One is Richard Aldington, nicknamed by Durrell "Top Grumpy," and now Gordon Bottomley is trying to get in. Another, always welcome, is Valéry. I was given Hayward's copy of the *Cimetière Marin,* and at Sotheby's I bought a page of his manuscript of "Narcisse" with a drawing on it and two of my favourite lines.

> Fontaine ma fontaine eau froidement présente
> Douce aux purs animaux, aux humains complaisante . . .

From the same sale I also obtained Marianne Moore's little volume, *The Pangolin,* published by the Curwen Press and illustrated by George Plank, a quiet American indeed who lived in a cottage in Kent supporting himself by occasional *Vogue* covers. Plank illustrated that charming and little-known autobiography *English Years* by his friend James Whitall, a kinsman of Logan Pearsall Smith, which includes a vignette of George Moore's shadow as he knocked at the Whitalls' door.

It was to them Moore made his comment on Proust: "If a man chooses to dig up a field with a pair of knitting needles, is there any reason why I should watch him doing it?"

Moore is another welcome intruder though I can generally read only his autobiographical essays and can't stomach the *Brook Kerith.* This autumn I added *A Story-teller's Holiday* and *Conversations in Ebury Street,* both presentations to his old friend (and Joyce's) William McGee ("John Eglinton"). In *A Story-teller's Holiday* he writes, "It gives me much pleasure to give you this book though it contains things of which you may (crossed out) will not approve."

It also contains one of the most Proustian pages in English literature when he gives his reasons for not going back to Moore Hall. "It is the past that explains everything, I say to myself. It is in our sense of the past that we find our humanity, and there are no moments in life so dear to us as when we lean over the taffrail and watch the waters we have passed through. The past tells us whence we have come and what we are . . ."

"And do you not collect any living authors?" Only poets—and this year I find quite a batch, chiefly from private presses—these include the little Turret Books brought out by Edward Lucie-Smith—Sylvia Plath's *Uncollected Poems,* G. Macbeth, William Wantling's *Awakening* (a present from Christopher Logue), Zukovsky's *A14* and Harry Fainlight's *Sussicran* (Narcissus again). Fainlight seems to me to have caught something of the evanescence of promiscuity in his elusive verse. Last exit to Earl's Court.

I have always wanted a signed Hart Crane and when a bookseller catalogued one of *White Buildings* dedicated to "Allan Tate," I knew it was the rare first issue dedicated to Allen Tate, who wrote the introduction. In the second the misprint was corrected. This copy to a Miss Hughes-Hallett, mentions the Hurricane of 1926. It was in the Isle of Pines, I discovered, and "many people behaved badly." How?

I have always had a vow with myself that when I found a copy of Elizabeth Bowen's *The Last September* I would give up collecting or it would be *my* last September. This turned up when I asked Raymond Mortimer for something with Eddy Sackville-West's so typical bookplate. He produced *The Last September* and I had a sudden tussle with my conscience. The vow did not apply to books, I decided, that were already on my want-list and I soon went tearing ahead, for Auden's

Collected Shorter Poems, perhaps the best produced of all his books, Hemingway's *Spanish Earth* in the anarchist colours, quickly suppressed.

And the one that got away? Lawrence's *Escaped Cock*—pursued for years and lost at auction at £80—a signed one too. But that remains at the head of my want-list for next year with a letter from Joyce, Auden's *Spain* (Nancy Cunard) and *Sodome et Gomorrhe.*

But I *am* tapering off—although I forgot to mention Lorca's *Romancero Gitano* and Rilke's *Duineser Elegien* among my foreign acquisitions. And only yesterday I discovered a presentation copy of Valéry's *La Jeune Parque.* How slow the Christmas posts are!

(1967)

POSTSCRIPT: This article produced an offer for the *Escaped Cock* (never give up) and the Middleton Murry copy of *Sodome et Gomorrhe* (dedicated) for a very small sum. I still have no Joyce letter.

SHELL COLLECTING

MR. DANCE,* who informs us that he is a young writer, has chosen his subject carefully. It is not about shells and it is not about collectors but about shell-collecting—for which hobby he can offer no explanation.

Shell-collectors are usually scientists, but not always: many were dilettanti aristocrats and only a few travelled in search of their prey, preferring to rely on dealers or returning sailors. Most of their collections ended up in museums; some were dispersed at auctions for which Mr. Dance has an uncanny flair, tracing the fluctuations in price of noted rarities from specimen to specimen down the centuries. It is a subject, in fact, which partakes on the one hand of the sale-room, like stamp-collecting or old china; on the other of adventure and exploration, like orchid-hunting.

In this book we are dealing with shell-collectors, shell-gatherers, and conchologists or shell-classifiers. First in time came the collectors—often royal personages or great doctors in the spirit of the Renaissance (many of them Dutch), or noblemen with their "cabinets of curiosities," their rarities and oddities of all kinds, their shells arranged as human heads like an Archimboldo, their love of such beautiful and semi-precious objects as the Gloria Maris, or Glory of the Sea, the Glassy Nautilus, the Precious Wentletrap, and the Matchless Cone, or Cedonulli, all four of which are described here at length. Then comes the turn of the classifiers—Buonanni, Lister and the great Rumphius, culminating in Linnaeus and Lamarck.

At the same time came a revolution in collecting and gathering. From the French and other European courts the sceptre passed to England

* *Shell Collecting,* by Peter Dance (Berkeley, 1966).

where Cook's voyages opened up a new world and where wealth and scientific curiosity went hand in hand. The nineteenth century witnessed the consolidation of British supremacy by a dynasty of collector-dealers —the Sowerbys (three generations) and by the advent of the greatest collector-gatherer, Hugh Cuming. Mr. Dance refers to the mid-nineteenth century as the "Cumingian era."

Cuming (1791–1865), born in Devonshire, settled in Valparaiso after his taste had been formed by a Knightsbridge naturalist, Colonel George Montagu. At the age of thirty-five he was able to retire from business as a sail-maker, build a yacht, the *Discoverer,* fit it out for collecting and set out on the first of three voyages. The first two ended back in Valparaiso with a vast quantity of specimens after which he returned to England and found his complement in the eldest of the Sowerbys, whose son became his illustrator. His longest voyage was to the Philippines from 1836–40 when he returned with a great hoard of shells, plants, insects, crabs, reptiles and 1,200 birds.

His methods were typical of the golden age of British travel. He went everywhere as a guest of the priests who turned out the schoolchildren (in some places amounting to several hundred) to scour the woods for him. For this exercise a whole holiday was requested by him and the finders of rarities were rewarded with silver coins which stimulated the others. The nights were spent in sorting and packing and the suspicions of the natives were dispelled by his explanation that the shells were needed to be ground up with betel nut for British addicts. A supply of quinine consolidated their goodwill.

With his great stock of duplicates Cuming set himself up as a dealer and financed new explorations. His own collection was purchased in 1866 for £6,000 by the British Museum. The golden age of shell-collecting continued until the First World War. Dutch, Germans (Humboldt), Danes, Italians (especially the Marchesa Paulucci) and the French (the Delessert collection included 150,000 specimens stored in a gallery 150 feet long), Americans and even the Japanese entered the field on a large scale.

In Japan the pioneer collector, Yoichiro Hirate (d. 1925), was able in 1913 to open the first purely conchological museum, which lasted only six years. England continued to form outstanding collections through Adanson, Dennison, Melvill (who began when he was eight) and Tomlin (1864–1954), who acquired the Melvill collection.

One of the problems never solved by the earlier collectors was how to keep shells properly, how to affix labels, and classify the appropriate data. Many examples fell by the wayside. Thus the great Cuming collection had many casualties on the way to the British Museum where a

Mrs. Gray caused a hopeless confusion by separating the 83,000 specimens from their labels. Cuming consequently came in for some of the debunking meted out to other eminent Victorians by a more precise generation. Mr. Dance quotes one of them.

> A most abusive comment was made by M. K. Connolly (1872–1947), an authority on African non-marine molluscs who said, in a discussion on a land shell described as from Liberia but known to be confined to Natal, that it was "obviously one of the many miasmas arising from the pestilential conchological swamp of the Cuming collection."

How like my father! M. Connolly, Major, as he always signed himself, was the Berenson of the South African non-marine mollusca whose pen and microscope and tweezers had turned swans into geese for so many over-optimistic colleagues and whose invective always had something ponderous, almost seventeenth-century about it.

> An infinity of redundant species have been created by innumerable authors, several without figuration, on details too trivial to merit even varietal rank, while the ineffable Bourguignat has obtruded as usual . . .

My father's collection is now in the British Museum. I remember it crowding out every other object—except his minerals—from study and dressing-room and ultimately his hotel bedroom. Pyramids of pill-boxes lined with black cotton-wool full of little dun objects which all seemed to me exactly alike ("not worth twopence of course" as he would exclaim with relish); towering stalagmites of conchological journals from England, Germany, America and Mozambique, loosely tied with string or ribbon; cabinets of specimens with his beautifully written labels sticking out of their tiny jaws; innumerable envelopes with stamps torn off (he collected them as well) and the latest arrivals in brown boxes, awaiting identification—some still alive. It made me a conchophobe and I came to dread the names of colleagues—Pilsbry, the aforesaid Tomlin, "Old Ponsonby"—and his latest exchanges with them.

How different from those early days of shell-gathering on the South African veldt where he found thirty new species, six named after him, and one, Trachycystis Connollyi ("a small chocolate shell") discovered by me. Mountain sunshine of Montagu; a child of six turning over the stones by the river; the waters of science as yet unmuddied by literature, the heart unclouded, the conscience clear. I'm glad Mr. Dance has kept to sea-shells. The Precious Wentletrap and Gloria Maris every time.

(1966)

CONFESSIONS OF A HOUSE-HUNTER

"Rock of ages cleft for me,
Tell me where to find the key."
"Rawlence and Squarey,"
Said the bells of Saint Mary.
"Cubitt and West,
They know what's best."
"Knight, Frank and Rutley
Would have put it more subtly."
"Messenger, May and Baverstock,
WE have the key that fits the lock."

—From *House-hunting Songs and Shanties*

All my life I have wanted passionately to own a house. Like many of my generation, I belong to the landless gentry with memories of better times. My parents' families had about two thousand acres each in Ireland and the West Country; my father some two and a half acres in the county of Surrey. I have never possessed anything larger than a bookcase. I have been house-hungry now for some forty years without setting eyes on a title deed. It's a man's life; out of doors in all weathers, and one comes across some very interesting people. Should the house-fiend be registered? Is he (or she) a danger to the community? Does house-hunger destroy the moral sense? Or corrupt the young? Is it hereditary? Can it be cured?

A house-fiend is a man who, while signing the contract for his ultimate home, gathers up particulars of all the others, a man who is not quite sane on Wednesday evenings, when he waits up all night for his "fix"—the new number of *Country Life*. A house-agent lives by actually selling houses, a house-hunter on dreams and curiosity. His whole existence is an order to view. A woman without a home is a snail without a shell; her suffering is biological. But a man without a few particulars in his pocket, a licence to day-dream, is spiritually dead; past hope, past prayer, past analysis (which often exposes a deeper maladjustment).

Many house-hunters make delightful companions and some are quite capable of earning their living; we recognise each other instinctively by some secret code, and since most houses for sale are overpriced and once they have failed to reach their reserve at auction remain on the market for several years, we have our stories to tell: "If only, if only . . ." "I nearly bought 'Greenfingers.' "—"Why, so did we."—"I practically paid a deposit." "A little bird whispered 'Rising Damp.' " "I even went to the auction."

The signature of the contract on the auction particulars would have been legally binding: this was a brave man.

I began as a house-hunter in the First World War by tagging along with my mother. These forays in commuting distance of London (my father was working in the War Office) left an indelible impression of oak-beams and lattice-windows among the Surrey pines or the stucco of Worplesdon, or even as far afield as Farnham, Crondall and Odiham. I learned to love the glint of bottled glass, an ingle-nook, a tennis-court under the deodars, a distant view of the Hog's Back.

Oak beams and a sagging floor
With a leathern latchet to the door . . .

My mother taught me the first lesson: always admire everything and leave reservations till afterwards. This was a great help in preparation for the future, for that important moment in the hunt which I shall call the Confrontation. The bell rings, the door opens and the owner awaits us—are we fly to his spider? Or the fox among his chickens? Sometimes one glimpse of the hall with its bull-fighting posters and cocktail bar in imitation red leather makes us want to turn tail. Occasionally I have driven straight up by appointment to some creepered porch, round the gravel sweep, and off again, ringing up the nearest call-box to say that I have been unavoidably detained. Most old houses are sick, most new ones are hideous. There are few exceptions.

The best ones are empty. But perhaps I had better describe the stages of a "hunt" from the beginning.

1. Mutual Attraction (by advertisement, exploration or hearsay).
2. The Assignation (or "at the Agents").
3. The Viewing or Confrontation.
4. Crystallisation or Disillusion.
5. The Offer.
6. The Colding of the Feet.

7. The Renunciation (back to Square One).
8. Mutual Attraction (*Country Life* again).

Don't think one can't get hurt. We witness terrible things: the felling of cedars, uprooting of figs, demolition of peach-house and vinery, fire-places wrenched from their sockets, built-in bookcases carted off to auction. The lamentations of an old gardener can affect one for weeks. There are some houses with which we really do fall in love, and when we lose them, because we keep dithering or can't afford them, the pain may last for several years. But it is almost impossible to distinguish true love from infatuation, especially as it is often directed on houses which are for practical reasons quite unsuitable. An inveterate house-hunter is often a man divided against himself. He wants long eighteenth-century windows, Palladian saloons, lodges, a park and stable clock, and at the same time a penthouse which functions like the latest yacht with press-button efficiency. He sees a house as a frame for his personality when it will turn out only a drain on his income. Whatever its condition when we first see a house—roses dead-headed, clocks ticking—it will end up like all the others we have lived in.

The season for house-hunting lasts from March to October; every house looks beautiful in spring sunshine; few addicts enjoy trudging through dead leaves or examining sodden lawns through rain-swept windows. In winter most gardens seem all cinders and laurel. Then the hunter keeps his eye in with an occasional penthouse or eighteenth-century town mansion or a finca or quinta in the sun. The advertisement pages also shrink, as if owners too were lying low. August is another dowdy time, when only sea and mountain escape the general dullness. Affinities between house-hunting and nest-building make early spring the most dramatic period, with a secondary season in early autumn, connected with hibernation.

Every issue of *Country Life* will contain three or four houses which instantly appeal to the viewer. Some are too big or too far from London, but generally there is a mill or rectory or Georgian farm around which "mutual attraction" takes place—mutual because such houses imply an affinity with the personality of the owner. Some of these attract us only for romantic or atavistic reasons. In my case Irish country-houses in arrogant disrepair make everything else look vulgar. Manor-houses have all, by now, been shrunk to manageable size by judicious advertising. "Seven bed and dressing-rooms with staff flat and nursery wing, three reception, study and playroom" means a thirteen-bedroom mansion with billiards. By Thursday we are ringing up or have written for particulars.

These should consist of at least two pages and avoid all whimsy or exaggeration while stressing features dear to the hunter's psyche—

streams, lakes, walled gardens, "extensive" views and gazebos. It can now be assumed that all tennis-lawns and kitchen gardens have long been let go unless there is proof to the contrary. A photograph is essential, although it can be taken so as to conceal arterial roads, pylons, housing developments, even that semi-detachment which, with the division of larger houses into three is becoming increasingly common.

A visit to the agents is one of the pleasures of the chase. Most agents are extremely agreeable, and we take to them like alcoholics to barmen. Always select either an enthusiastic young man who still believes his particulars or an older partner with an air of worldly experience; he is likely to be the only agent who can afford an aesthetic sense. Avoid the oafish type who is invincibly ignorant, or the shark who betrays his eagerness—"Wheeler speaking—I just rang up to know if you had come to any decision about 'Greenfingers,' Mr. Hunter: the owner is very anxious to sell." "I can well believe it."

My favourite homefinder—by now a little weary—works in an agency in Folksbourne and has been my companion on innumerable visits when a house or even a flat in that seaside town seemed all that one could desire. Winter afternoons would find him waiting, keys in hand (there is no close season in Folksbourne) by windy maisonettes or sometimes a turreted mansion, usually divided into flats, with soaring gables and overbearing overmantels in rusticated Tudor; bathrooms and lavatories ominous with rails and hand-grips for the arthritic. With unfailing patience and politeness Mr. Oakwood saw me through several courtships all ending in disillusion, culminating in that of a large Edwardian battlecruiser moored on the edge of a state forest, a Forsyte home four hundred feet above sea-level.

There is some part of me that yearns for these houses of around 1900, with stained glass lilies on the landing, glossy overmantels and coved ceilings, shallow stairs haunted by vanished parlour-maids. I yearned: my family did not share the yearning. The straight-backed owner and her agent waited in vain while I pleaded. "I am sorry that I have led you on so many fruitless errands, Mr. Oakwood," I burst out one day at an altogether different place. "The trouble," he answered, "is that Folksbourne has such dreadful houses."

Sundays in Folksbourne, yellow with forsythia, the electric log hissing in the fire-place with its curved plaster surround, "sun-room" or conservatory ablaze with plastic flowers, an oak porch with my eye to the keyhole, the roast knocking at the hatch, the sea glistening through the macrocarpa . . . Folksbourne will come into its own when the world is tired of Georgian boxes; it will be the last stronghold of the landless gentry who bring their Cotswold saddle stones with them.

William Rufus Hunter, of "Huntersmoon," 65 Chatsworth Road, Folksbourne. The family of Hunter claim descent from Herne of that Ilk and have long been settled in Chatsworth Road, where a Hunter was summoned for non-payment of rates as far back as 1947. Owns about one-third of an acre. Arms: subject to negotiation. Motto: "Viewing strictly by appointment."

Now for the Confrontation.

"I am Mr. Hunter; I have an order to view from Messrs. Wheeler and Dealer." "We were expecting you: please come in." Houses are usually shown by the owners, in which case no chaperone from Wheeler and Dealer is necessary.

Owners fall into three types. (1) Widows; (2) Retired couples; (3) Business men. Widows who are recently bereaved make viewing almost impossible. "This is his" (gulp) and "This is where he kept his . . ." (gulp). How would you feel if Queen Victoria were showing you round Osborne? The only course is to sympathise and escape. An abandoned or separated wife knows the balm of aggression. "And this was his so-called study. Really the telephone room." "Quite." "This used to be the swimming-pool." "A swimming-pool can be a very soulless thing." "So I found, Mr. Hunter." Retired couples may prove even more harrowing. "We'll go round the ground floor together, Mr. Hunter, then my wife will take you upstairs." "My husband hasn't been at all well lately." "I am sorry to hear it. This would be the utility room?" "Yes—in the old days." "We hate to leave—we've been very happy here—but our children have grown up and flown and my husband (wife) has not been too well lately. He (she) has Huntington's chorea/cavernous sinus thrombosis/Madura foot." "I am so very sorry." The business man makes straight for the central heating installation, "You can do everything but play a tune on it."

Family photographs exercise a compelling fascination on viewers, like shoe cupboards and deep freezes. But an empty house for which one picks up the key will provide the deepest satisfaction; an empty house is like a naked woman—just that little bit more ours. I have refrained from saying that houses are like women because it is unclear to me whether a house, in Freudian terms, is masculine or feminine. A room is feminine—but a three-storey five-bay Georgian façade? The house-hunter is a Don Giovanni—he has his list—but what does he really want? An unpunished *voyeur,* he is also a dispossessed exile from Eden. Is his goal coffin or castle? Secluded and, of course, "with character. . . ."

Alone in an empty house, virgin of decoration, he paces the rooms, peers from the windows, calls "Come out" up the stairs. Some of my happiest moments have been in a Snowcemmed *fin-de-siècle* retreat in Ashdown Forest by Baillie Scott. It occupies a lost valley under the radar beacons and has an extraordinary atmosphere of architectural felicity and grace. Pine panelling, peacock-tiled fire-places, colophons of stained glass, a Mackmurdo-like staircase of black knitting-needles, an enormous white bath with shower and/or spray, and a handle marked "WAVES" . . . the whole three acres encircled by a rhododendron tunnel round the estate. I am relieved it has been sold. How painful is the right house in the wrong place.

The Confrontation over, comes the prognostic—infatuation or disappointment? If, after we have admired everything without restriction our objections begin to surface, then nothing remains but to try the next on our list. Should infatuation persist, there follows the second visit, a more serious inspection in which our known and best-loved objects—bookcases, tables, beds—begin to occupy prepared positions and swim into place. By this time a special relationship is established with the owners. "I thought your husband seemed a little better today."

After several visits there is still time to withdraw, but infatuation may seize entire hold. Frantic with house-hunger, we constantly write down the name of the new home, add up the digits in the telephone number, consult large-scale maps and local records, pit the dimensions of its room against discarded favourites, balance advantages—position, seclusion, architectural interest, library, drawing-room, garden, trees, views, water—so as to justify our preferences or give marks for drab realities like central heating, nearness to school or station, rates, condition, upkeep. The deposit rears its ugly head. Now is the time to go round once more with an architect (a brief visit will often save the expense of a survey) or even to make an offer.

This last is a desperate move, equivalent to fixing a date at the registrar's. Buying a house is like getting married; the moment of agreement is a moment of panic. For better or worse, we're hooked. Is this the end to all those sunny afternoons bowling round the country-side, all the interiors, ingle-nooks and breastsummers, the intimate yet formal contacts with other lives? Do all these lead only to "Greenfingers"? "Because man goeth to his long home and the mourners go about the streets. . . ."

The offer should be large enough to disarm hostility but not so large as to be accepted. And, of course, "subject to survey." I suppose most of us can run to only one survey, just as many confirmed viewers can barely afford the fare if their quarry is outside the Home Counties.

Surveyors are never too encouraging and seem to read our inmost hearts. Watch Mr. Hunter, usually so meek, when with flashing eye he brandishes the explosive document at the agent's "I have the survey here and it reveals a most unsatisfactory state of affairs at 'Greenfingers'—nail-sickness in the potting-shed! Under the circumstances I have no option but to refuse to proceed with the negotiation." "I am sure Mrs. O'Meara would be prepared for an adjustment." "I am sorry, Mr. Wheeler. I wish to have no further dealings with Mrs. O'Meara."

To watch poor Hunter at his worst behold him when he is forced to go round a house with a rival party. How pointedly he lags behind or darts ahead, how patronisingly he dismisses the pony prizes and pin-ups in the nursery rooms, the wrought-iron gates before the cocktail bar, the "small walled hydrangea garden." His "have-not" hatred of the householder is exposed. "I'm afraid I've got to leave now—I am in a great hurry." "But Mr. Hunter, you haven't seen the rumpus room."—"I'll keep in touch (*snarl*) through Messrs. Wheeler and Dealer."

No true Hunter has had an offer rejected without a sense of relief, but to be outbid by a rival is a fighting matter. When we lose a house that we really want the remedy is to concentrate on its deficiencies, then find another which has not got them: it will not have the same advantages either, but that is irrelevant. There must be no interregnum. "The house is gone; let's find a house." And so we're back to Square One.

But even as we mutter the grim words a thin brown envelope slides under the door or the sophisticated London agent who knows about *cottages ornés* rings up or a house that we have admired from of old is back on the market or a new Belle shows up. "I rather like the sound of this one, 'Old Dripping Manor.' . . ." It is a crisp September morning; the copper beach is vituperating through the mauve glass, the penthouse gleams all gin and lime above the esplanade; mill and rectory, oast-house and maisonnette put forth their well-worn charms. Auction particulars arrive in colours. "Only four minutes from the Town Centre, commanding views of the sea and downs, surrounded by its own grounds of well-established trees, flowering shrubs, herbaceous border, lily pond with paved walk and wrought-iron surround, copse, orchard and paddock amounting in all to one-third of an acre. The handsome detached residence dating from the turn of the century, with many gracious period features, including tessellated orangery, known as 'Huntersmoon,' 65, Chatsworth Road, Folksbourne, is offered for immediate sale by order of the Executors. Viewing strictly by appointment."

(1967)

TEARS BEFORE BEDTIME

WHAT is the use of pleasure and delights since I myself am the future dwelling place of old age?" cried the youthful Buddha at his first sight of the phenomenon. After reading Simone de Beauvoir's treatise on *Old Age* (translated by Patrick O'Brian, André Deutsch/Weidenfeld and Nicolson, £4.50) I would advise anyone contemplating this step to think about it. Old age is not so much an infliction from without as the termination of a built-in growth programme.

Old age is a general tragedy in that it means the decay of the body, our constant companion; but it is particular in that the body decays just when we seem on the threshold of wisdom, of apprehending more about love, justice, and the significance of our existence. In that sense it is premature and resembles an infection rather than the general abdication of our organs. "Oh the unhappy state of man! Scarcely has the mind reached full ripeness before the body begins to fall away," wrote Montesquieu: and Delacroix—"The strange disharmony between the spiritual strength brought by age and the bodily weakness that also comes with it has always struck me; and to me it seems a contradiction in the laws of nature."

Naturally, Madame de Beauvoir's favourites are those who have most to say about old age: Victor Hugo, Chateaubriand (who aged badly), Michelangelo (who aged sadly), Gide (exemplary), Fontenelle (almost too perfect), Léautaud (grumpy), Swift, Yeats's "Old man's eagle mind" and Beckett. Painters like Goya, Renoir, Bonnard are also called upon; and Monet: "I know only one old man's self-portrait that is downright cheerful, it is that which Monet painted as a present for Clemenceau." Titian's self-portrait, painted in his ninetieth year is solemn and free-flowing.

In my experience artists (in the large sense) age best because they are sustained by curiosity and by a certain humility: "The disappointed are always young" (Disraeli). I would mention Berenson, Maugham, Leonard Woolf, E. M. Forster, Natalie Barney, Gerald Brenan, David Garnett and Picasso (if we could ever get near him). Of writers about the old, Simone de Beauvoir ignores Ivy Compton-Burnett, and she is weak (as always) on Montherlant. She admits that Proust has written as well as anyone about age, although he died comparatively young.

"Adolescents who last long enough are what life makes old men out of," he wrote; and this leads on to the most important fact about the old today. They look old, but they do not feel old; as Proust saw them, they are in fancy dress at a black-and-white ball. If the young can disregard their disguise, they will find the old infinitely easier to get on with. Of course, though they don't feel old, they *are* old and the ways in which they are old are often unfamiliar to them. Some nagging satiety of the *déjà vu,* some unperceived roadblock, some ball of remorse twisted beyond all disentanglement, names and faces of the dead grafted upon the living . . . "Seeing again after some years a person I have known young, always at first I seem to see one who has suffered a great calamity." Leopardi.

Some of Madame de Beauvoir's authors provide clues.

Dr. Lansing's definition: "a process of unfavourable, progressive change, unusually correlated with the passage of time, becoming apparent after maturity, and terminating invariably in the death of the individual."

Saint-Evrémond: "We hardly begin to age before a secret self-disgust forming within us begins to make us disagreeable to ourselves. After this our hearts, emptied of self love, are easily filled with that love which is inspired by others." And then the trouble starts.

Corneille, in *Pulchérie,* gives the first sympathetic picture of an old man in love.

Quel supplice d'aimer un objet adorable
Et de tant de rivaux se voir le moins aimable.

It is surprising, in this connection, that Madame de Beauvoir does not quote Horace Walpole's last letters from Madame du Deffand. Juvenal was the first to nail down the special horror of old age: "A perpetual train of losses, incessant mourning and old age dressed in black, surrounded by everlasting sadness—that is the price of a long life." One is reminded of the Roman curse: *Ultimus suorum morietur* (May he be the last of his family to die). Comparing herself to Chateaubriand ("My too-long life is like those Roman roads lined with monuments to the dead"), Madame de Beauvoir produces her own necrology:

Later our agreements and our disagreements with Camus were wiped out: wiped out too were my arguments with Merleau-Ponty in the gardens of the Luxembourg; at his home, at mine, at Saint Tropez; gone those long talks with Giacometti and my visits to his studio. . . . In the "monuments to the dead" that stud my history, it is I who am buried.

What about ourselves? Here Madame de Beauvoir becomes militant. "It is common knowledge that the condition of old people today is scandalous." In our civilisation one in ten or one in twelve is over sixty-five. The majority of these are workers. Madame de Beauvoir blames capitalism, the ruling-class morality, for the fearful discrepancy between the condition of the retired labourers thrown on the scrap-heap, the middle class with their savings and the very rich with their coddled, privileged existence.

The society of today allows old people leisure only when it has removed the material means for them to enjoy it.

I do not find this as shocking as Madame de Beauvoir does: once one accepts inequality, one must expect it to last right down to the ornaments on the coffin. Where I agree with her is in deploring the indifference, even hostility, meted out to the old from those who will inevitably one day, and sooner than they expect, find themselves in the same plight. Must the old always be poor? Must the asylums and institutions that exist for them be so barbaric? Must their amusements be so puerile? If so, why not carry it one stage further, and deprive them of the vote?

There is only one solution if old age is not to be an absurd parody of our former life and that is to go on pursuing ends that give our existence a meaning—devotion to individuals, to groups, or to causes, social, political, intellectual or creative work. One's life has value so long as one attributes value to the life of others, by means of love, friendship, indignation, compassion.

Madame de Beauvoir has been rightly nicknamed "Le Castor" (the Beaver): she runs to and fro from her sources, pillaging anthropology, history, literature, medicine to construct her dam. Having read her six-hundred-page book from start to finish, I make two complaints. I wish she wouldn't quote Sartre:* one has had enough of the uncouth jargon of existentialism and it is intolerable to find it resurrected among these gloomy catacombs. And I wish she had a more original mind or a more

* Pope has the last word on Sartre:
'Her bird, a monster of a fowl
Something betwixt a Heidegger and owl'
—Pope, *Dunciad:* I. 290

poetic imagination. The aura of the commonplace hangs over this monumental tome, as if a team of researchers from provincial universities were doing all the work, leaving her to co-ordinate the platitudes.

But for Victor Hugo, old age meant unfettered sexuality, not marching in processions and distributing handbills; *"Il suffit,"* he wrote pithily,

> *"D'un retrécissement du canal de l'urètre*
> *pour qu'au lieu d'une fille on voie entrer un prêtre"*

and for many a writer or scientist (she has a fine catalogue of scientists who have made discoveries in old age) it means continuing to learn and enjoy, even if it's only food.

I find I copied out, on my sixtieth birthday, a note from Lichtenberg (1744–99), not mentioned in this book, which might be a motto for *Krapp's Last Tape.*

> "As long as memory lasts a crowd of people are working together as a unity. The 20-year-old, the 30-year-old, and so on. As soon as it fails, one begins increasingly to be alone and the whole generation of selves stand back and mock the lonely old man.

(1971)

MY NOBEL PRIZE

"And when did you first realise you might be getting the Nobel Prize?"

"I suppose when a Swedish journalist rang up and asked me if I had a tail coat. I put two and two together."

"And it came to eighteen thousand pounds?"

"Well, not quite—after all—there are six of us."

"Connolly, Alvarez, Wain, Enright, Philip Toynbee and Frank Kermode—quite a team!"

Silence. Interviewer consults his notes.

"And so now you have made this thing—this major breakthrough—this—as it were—breaking of the code?"

"That's right—and here it is—the model, of course."

"What a beautiful thing!"

"Yes, it is rather jolly."

"And so that represents the great discovery—(reads) *'the ontological formula for the fine structure of* Finnegans Wake'?"

"We hope so."

"I wonder if you could put into a few words suitable for the layman just how it works?"

"Well, of course" (with engaging modesty), "we can't be absolutely certain that it does work—I will go farther—I don't think we are absolutely certain that it is meant to work; they are—well—just structures. It might be more accurate to say that it oscillates."

"Like a mobile?"

"Like a perpetuum mobile—and I rather think that's what Joyce intended."

"But you haven't explained it."

"Well, I'll have a shot, ontologically speaking. You see all these blobby sort of fun-things—they're the same shape more or less but different sizes and colours. Those are the vowel sounds. The diphthongs use a bigger blob than the others and the colours are for the different languages—the primaries represent the primary languages and so on through all the colours of the rainbow. Though of course there are, actually, as we know, hardly any colours in the rainbow. But then there aren't a great many vowels in *Finnegans Wake*. Ha, Ha!"

"Ha!"

"And you see all these interconnecting rods—all jointed of course, all varying in length by as much in some cases as a couple of angstroms—they represent the consonants. All the consonants."

"In the alphabet?"

"No—in *Finnegans Wake*. Each rod represents a cluster of so many thousand consonants just as each blob represents so many hundred vowels. Oscillate them like this—ping!—and they form new patterns and clusters of vowels and consonants which do not necessarily make sense but which oscillate or perhaps we might almost say vacillate until they represent the actual proportion of vowels and consonants, and vowels to consonants, which positively occur in *Finnegans Wake* and also the correct proportion of labials, dentals, glottal stops and so forth. When the whole machine is in oscillation it is actually constructing whole new passages of the *Wake,* exactly in the formula which the author could have used; and that is what takes the whole thing right away from computers and all that hardware. You could feed all the words in *Finnegans Wake* to a computer but you'd never get the fine structure! It could mix the words up in a new order but you'd never be able to maintain the basic vowel-consonant relationship which is the profound, unconscious breathing of an author's style. That's where the breakthrough came."

"And you've been working on this—how long?—before the breakthrough?"

"Since the *Wake* came out, of course—since 1939."

"And always in that little hut in the garden of Russell Square? Weren't the team rather crowded?"

"I'll tell you something rather surprising about the team. We've never met."

"What—none of you?"

"Well—never more than one of us has ever gone to the hut at the same time! We've worked on a very sensitive rota. We started in on the model and everybody left it a little further advanced. That way we never could get on each other's nerves and, working in shifts over thirty years, we got along pretty fast—and then—zowie! The breakthrough."

"I suppose you all went pretty Boffin in the war period?"

"Well, it was all rather hush-hush and some of us did a little inventing on the side. I was a fire-watcher myself and I noticed that many other fire-watchers could not get to sleep because they found themselves in unfamiliar surroundings. It looked a psychological problem really—but it had a psycho-somatic basis. Ovaltine—I picked up a couple of gongs for that one. And then one day, when I was sitting by the model, 'Sage' Bernal blew in, on his way from Djerba to Ascension. We had a talk and as he was leaving he said, 'Why not try topology?'

"Well, we hadn't got a topologist on the team though most of us had drifted into Operation Moron from physics, biology, crystallography and para-psychology. We even had a phytologist and a mycologist. So I paid a call on the War House, who of course couldn't help, and then I tried Combined Ops. They flew us one from Patagonia."

"I suppose you were working to a pretty slender budget?"

"On a shoe-string—the American universities put up about four hundred thousand dollars and we had another fifty pounds from the British Council. It was touch and go."

"And the topologist?"

"Blew his top after three weeks, but he'd given us the know-how."

"So there wasn't much talk about the two cultures on the team?"

"Well, I suppose all together we represented about thirty cultures and we had to be pretty tolerant; we never knew who'd make the break-through. . . . Teems of times and happy rechurns."

"What about Leavis?"

"Well, I suppose we were all Leavisites in those days; we just worked, ate, drank and slept with the model and hoped for the best. Don't forget we had no lysergic acid, no mescalin, no psilocybin, none of those mushroom jobs. We were working in the dark."

"And one more question, Mr. Connolly. How exactly is the discovery of the fine structure of Finnegans Wake *going to benefit—well—people like me?"*

"Well, I'm very glad you've asked me that because I know you had in mind that thirty years was a long time to be using up public money if there weren't going to be results—and big results—to show for it. We on the team used to pass on to each other many anxious inquiries about that. I can only say: look at the fantastic growth of physics since those boys at the Cavendish split the atom, look at the biologists on the threshold of creating life—and it's not going to be a very pleasant life—look at the big master and its hitherto undreamt of possibilities for destruction. What do you think we won't be able to do with the structure of *Finnegans Wake* in the next ten years? Now that we understand the vowel-consonant equation for one writer, we can soon work it out for the rest; we will be able to play back to an author the sound of all the books he hasn't written, rewrite his old ones to sound more like himself. Here, listen to this (reads from a Sunday newspaper for December 9): 'John Wain is about to unleash a "Niagara" of prose, verse and drama on the world. . . .' "

"You mean?"

Connolly indicates model with his pipe-stem.

"A Jack of all wains. Ha-ha!"

"Ha!"

"Well, thank you very much Mr. Connolly and my heartiest congratulations; after your brilliant exposition I think it will hardly be necessary to interview your colleagues."

(1962)

A VOICE FROM THE DEAD?

"CYRIL, I'm Logan."

The familiar greeting, so logical according to the instructions in the telephone book yet, as it happened, peculiar to himself, shook the dust off twenty years and brought back the days when I possessed a father-figure. The next few words would reveal where he stood, crest or trough, in his manic-depressive cycle.

"Cyril, I want you to do me a favour."

I long ago divided humanity into two groups, those, the rare, who say "Yes, of course," and the vulgar, who answer "What is it?"

"What is it?"

"It's just occurred to me, Cyril, that sufficient time has now elapsed since my 'disappearing act' for me to be reaping the benefit of my literary labours. As you know, I never cared for the contemporary success, the 'swim-gloat' as I called it, though when my *Trivia* took London by storm I was not, I hope, unequal to the burden. But I have always placed my trust in the verdict of posterity, and the meaning of life, as I have said, is to set tinkling a chime of words in the minds of a few fastidious people.

"Well, what I want you to do is to find out for me, now that I am coming into my literary inheritance, which of my books is earning the biggest reputation; how does the voting go? For my two-volume life of Sir Henry Wotton? For my books on the English language? For my anthologies of Donne and Jeremy Taylor? My critical essays? My autobiography? Or for the crown of my career, *Trivia, More Trivia, Afterthoughts* and *All Trivia?* In these small masterpieces, which occupied me from 1900 to my death in 1946, when I was still inserting adverbs (show me your adverbs and I'll tell you if you're my friend), I created an original art form peculiarly suited to the spirit of the time. Don't hurry! Cast your net wide and remember you yourself are not likely to be the best judge. If I may quote my own words" (*the voice began to rise and fall hypnotically, interrupted by his smoker's cough*), " 'the learned leisure, the labours of the file, the exquisite pain and pleasure of polishing their phrases are the torment and privilege alone of the craft-conscious artists into whose pockets the world keeps on putting supplies of its negotiated coin. But these stores of old gold are almost exhausted now, and the necessity of writing for one's living blunts the appreciation of writing when it bears the mark of perfection. Its quality disconcerts our hasty writers; they are ready to condemn it as preciosity and affectation.' This is a tendency I have noticed in you—even in poor Desmond."

"Why do you call Sir Desmond MacCarthy 'poor Desmond'?"

"Because he's spent his gifts in journalism (he permitted himself the luxury of supporting a family) and never produced that finished masterpiece, that *'voyage à longue haleine,'* which is every writer's dream, or even one short book, 'brief, but all roses,' which could have given the world a permanent taste of his quality. Poor Desmond, always chained to the wheel. He had his little innings and now it is my turn. How's *The New Statesman,* by the way? Do you still perform your scalping operations there? Too fierce I thought they were sometimes. Such a charming paper. They called me 'the last patrician of English Letters' (*chanting and coughing*): 'How calm, how scholarly, how nice is Mr. Pearsall Smith: we reflect how salutary, amid the clang and sirens of our age, is this still small voice.' "

"That sounds like Harold Nicolson."

"—And listen to this—from poor Desmond: 'I agree with those reviewers of *All Trivia* who have predicted for it a life beyond the grave of contemporary reputations. It is the sort of bibelot that Father Time often keeps on the mantelpiece when he changes the furniture in the house.' I'm told, by the way, by certain elderly armigerous ladies, that we should not say 'mantelpiece,' but perhaps Father Time is not over-particular. Anyhow, to come to the point, I have not been idle in my latter existence and I have produced one of my best pieces—an essay, quite short, about eleven thousand words, with the title, 'Three Forgotten Aphorists: Joubert, Vauvenargues, Amiel.'

"I want you to get it published for me. You seem surprised. I suppose because they are not chronological. 'Sound is more than sense,' as I wrote, and I have spent many hours in rolling the order round my tongue. 'Amiel, Joubert, Vauvenargues: Three Forgotten Aphorists,' I like that too. I thought first of the *Literary Supplement* but my old friend, Bruce Richmond, is no longer there. Then there's *The New Statesman,* the *London Magazine, Encounter* (new since my day), and then I thought: I'll send it to poor Cyril. I have even inserted an impropriety, since I am told one must be obscene to be believed."

"Logan, before you go on. Let me ask you a question. What are you?"

"I've told you. The last Patrician of Letters, b. 1865, inherited a share in the family glass factory, educated at Harvard and Balliol, author of . . ."

"No. I mean what are you now. Are you a ghost, a shade, a soul in purgatory or a figment of my imagination?"

"But Cyril, I'm Logan."

"So you said. But what's Logan?"

"b. Philadelphia 1865, educated at . . ."

"Let me put it this way, either you exist in your own right or through my imagination. If you exist in your own right I demand a proof."

"But aren't I telephoning you?"

"No—you are not. All I said was 'the familiar greeting, so logical according to the instructions in the telephone book'—I didn't say you came through on the telephone."

"Nor did I! I said 'Aren't I telephoning you?' "

"Very well—we'll try it this way. Let us assume you exist only in my imagination—alive 'where breath most breathes even on the lips of men.' "

"Fancy you quoting Shakespeare, Cyril. Do you remember how I used to say you would go down to your grave mumbling 'Eliot and Joyce, Joyce and Eliot' all the time till no one would know what you were talking about. I'm glad that lot have blown over."

"I wouldn't be too sure."

"Eliot, Pound and Leavis—how neatly I punctured them in *Milton and His Modern Critics*—does anyone still read them?"

"Well, as I was saying Logan, let me assume that you exist only in my imagination: in that case you have no feelings and I can't hurt them. Well, then, nobody reads you, all your books are equally dead. And nobody reads Desmond either—it's a nice point which of you is the more forgotten; nor in this country is there any editor to print *Three Forgotten Aphorists,* and you'd better add a fourth one, yourself; you had a pretty good life between your library and the dividends from the glass factory—what more do you want? The only place where you will live is in the theses of American Ph.D. students investigating expatriates or the small fry round Henry James. Today there are many other channels for communication besides literature, and all are totally ephemeral—we're all bound for oblivion, come to that."

"Very well—you've asked for it. I don't exist—but that's no reason to be impertinent. You fling words like oblivion about too easily. You pay lip-service to annihilation but do you know what it means? You apply it to everyone but yourself. I have noticed that you seem to think the dead form a kind of club, that a beaming reception committee representing all the right literary sets will be there to greet you. It's not like that—the death of writers is like so many candles going out all over the world. They gutter and fail and then there is nothing, nor does any communication exist between them. And writers die three times; first there is the bodily death which I will not go into, then the death of the personality as it becomes gradually distorted in the memory of the survivors, belittled by the littleness of the living, caricatured as you have caricatured me—then there is the death of their work as form and meaning evaporate like the frescoes on an Etruscan tomb. I'll give you a chime of words—*Qui nunc jacet horrida pulvis*—who's now reduced to filthy dust—first me and soon you—*qui nunc jacet horrida pulvis*."

I felt a chill wind of empty desolation. "It's not true!"

"All right. If it's not true, then you have offended an immortal spirit. You fell into my neat little trap to find out what you thought of me—and now I shall make you suffer—oh, in a hundred little ways. *Sunt aliquid manes:* A ghost is quite something."

The telephone rang. As far as I know it is still ringing.

Index